The Origins of the First World War

Great Power Rivalry and German War Aims

The Origins of the First World War

Great Power Rivalry and German War Aims

EDITED BY
H. W. KOCH
SECOND EDITION

MACMILLAN

First published 1972 by
MACMILLAN EDUCATION LTD
Houndmills, Basingstoke, Hampshire RG21 2XS
and London
Companies and representatives
throughout the world

ISBN 0–333–37298–0

British Library Cataloguing in Publication Data
The Origins of the First World War.—2nd ed
1. World War, 1914–1918—Causes
I. Koch, H. W.
940.3'11   D511

Printed in Hong Kong

First edition reprinted 1977, 1979, 1982
Second edition 1984
Reprinted 1985, 1988, 1990, 1991

Available in the United States from St. Martin's Press
175 Fifth Avenue, New York, NY 10010

U.S. ISBN: 0–312–05576–5

Contents

Preface

The purpose of this revised edition is, as was the case in the first edition, to introduce readers who cannot easily read German to some of the main strands of the renewed argument over the origins of the First World War and Germany's war aims. Instead of the editor selecting excerpts from articles or books, with one exception all articles have been reprinted in their entirety. The exception is the article by Fritz Fischer, the first part of which has been omitted since it discusses in great detail the objections of some of his German critics, a discussion so technical as well as polemical in nature that it would have required the complete reprinting of their articles as well.

Inevitably, a volume such as this can never take the place of reading Fritz Fischer's, Egmont Zechlin's, Erwin Hölzle's or Gerhard Ritter's work, or for that matter the diaries of Kurt Riezler edited by K. D. Erdmann. Fischer's two main works have been made available in a translated but unfortunately heavily abbreviated version. Gerhard Ritter's main work, *The Swords and the Sceptre*, has been available in an excellent translation since 1974, though it runs into four volumes. A translation of two of Egmont Zechlin's major articles is offered in this volume. Regrettably, footnotes had to be omitted for one major reason: in the case of both Fischer's and Zechlin's contributions the text of the notes amounts to more than the actual articles. Including the notes would in fact have meant doubling the number of pages of the present volume. Hence the harsh decision had to be made to omit footnotes from all the articles reprinted. However, personalities with which the reader may not be familiar are adequately identified in the index.

Apart from those articles which have previously been published in English, most of the German originals have been translated by the editor with considerable assistance from Dr Derek McKay of the London School of Economics, for whose help I am greatly indebted. The exception is Egmont Zechlin's contributions, which were translated by the late Heinz Norden and Brian Follett respectively. However, any mistakes which occur are my responsibility, as is the selection of the articles, which like all selections represents an uneasy compromise between what is desirable and what can actually be done, especially in view of the length of the two major contributions. It is a pity that there has been no room to include some of the work of East European historians, but this shortcoming is partly counter-balanced by the fact that Fritz Fischer, for instance, appears to have drawn heavily on their research as well as sharing some of the lines of their argument.

H. W. KOCH

Acknowledgments

I am grateful to Fritz Fischer, Imanuel Geiss, Egmont Zechlin, James Joll, Karl Dietrich Erdmann, Paul W. Schroeder and Joachim Remak for their permission to include their essays in this collection. I wish to thank the following for permitting the use here of material originally published by them: *Past and Present*; Batsford Ltd., London; *Historische Zeitschrift*; *Journal of Modern History*; and *Zeitschrift für Politik*, Munich.

H.W.K.

Introduction

Since the publication of the first edition of this volume the debate about the origins of the First World War and Germany's war aims has, until very recently, calmed down. The temper and the tone in which the debate was conducted, so it seemed, were back to normal again. This, however, does not mean that a generally accepted consensus has been established. Optimistic historians like Joachim Remak concluded that: 'Fritz Fischer's decade has ended. It began, neatly enough, in 1961 with *Griff nach der Weltmacht*, and drew to a close, in 1969, with *Krieg der Illusionen*. In between, there has been more discussion, scholarly and otherwise, than has been caused by any other single historian in our lifetime.' That this conclusion was somewhat premature, the publications between 1970 and 1983 have shown. Hence in the light of these publications it has been considered necessary to revise this volume in order to include new material, unfortunately at the expense of some of the earlier contributions which, though intrinsically important, have had to be omitted.

But first we have to pose the question why Fritz Fischer's theses should have caused the furore they did? Any answer to this question is bound to be complex. For one thing we have to look at the roots of modern German historiography and here we are immediately confronted by the massive and impressive work of Leopold von Ranke whom Lord Acton once described as 'the Columbus of modern history'. He taught history to be critical and applied to the best of his ability the regulative idea of objectivity, for which he was seriously criticised even by his contemporaries such as Droysen. But his primary concern was *the state, the power of the state* and the relations between the states. To avoid any misunderstanding at the outset, Ranke's concept of power was contained by moral restraints and was never an end in itself – as it was to become to his successors in an environment strongly influenced by Social Darwinian notions.

He would have rejected outright the claim 'all power to the state, and to one state all the power!'

The main emphasis of his work lay on 'the state' and on the primacy of foreign policy. Some members of the present generation of German historians, such as Hans-Ulrich Wehler, claim to write, in contrast to Ranke, 'problem-orientated structural analyses'. Methodologically the contrast is purely artificial but for Ranke the problem was 'the state', and the structure of international relations. But why should this be so? Given that Germany was in the front rank in the development of modern 'scientific' historical scholarship nourished by the rich traditions of classical humanism, one is bound to ask how that scholarship could focus itself so narrowly. Any answer is bound to include the simple fact that during the nineteenth century and before, Britons and Frenchmen, for instance, could take their state for granted while Germans could not. It was hardly comfortable for them to be a loose federation surrounded by strongly centralised nation states, for whom the fragmentation of Central Europe ensured 'the balance of power' in Europe. Moreover, and this is often forgotten these days, throughout most of modern history Germans were more often the victims than the aggressors. Hence the necessity for a reunited strong German national state. Hence also der Primat der Aussenpolitik, the primacy of foreign policy, or to quote Ranke: 'It is the degree of independence which determines the position and status of a state in this world. It imposes upon it the obligation to arrange domestic conditions in such a manner that it can maintain itself.' Germany's national unity was achieved belatedly and only partially. Germany was and remained on the international scene as Helmuth Plessner put it, 'die verspätete Nation', the belated nation. The re-establishment of a strong and consolidated nation state in the heartland of Europe was bound to inconvenience those powers already saturated or deeply involved in further aggrandisement because with the German Empire a new competitor had emerged: the balance of power in Europe, as it had existed since the Treaties of Westphalia in 1648, was completely destroyed. But from the very outset of unification it was, as Bismarck rightly felt, fragile within and without. Hence, as is argued by the historian K.-D. Bracher and the sociologist Ralf Dahrendorf, the maintenance of an archaic but apparently stable social order, harnessed to modern industrial techniques. Therefore, also, the readiness of all sectors of German society, ultimately including even the Social Democrats, to subject their interests to those of 'the state' and to allow it to become both the preserver of the social and political *status quo*, and the initiator of all change. Thus began allegedly 'der deutsche Sonderweg', Germany's own peculiar path that was to lead into catastrophe not only in 1918 but also in 1945. This thesis has now come under strong challenge, notably from two British historians, Geoff Eley and David Blackbourn, as well as from the American historian David Calleo, who reject the *Sonderweg*, pointing to the truism that each nation developed in its own peculiar way. Calleo, for instance, argues that the German Problem is too often treated as an isolated case, 'a country with broad characteristics presumed not to exist elsewhere'. He indicts present-day German historians of taking 'a certain perverse relish in claiming for their society a unique wickedness among humankind'. After all, every national society is many respects unique. But Germany was and it is not the only society with closely knit families, authoritarian traditions and an emphasis on private rather than public virtues. Neither was Germany the only nation that has ever hoped to play a major role in bringing the world to order or to take great pride in military prowess. 'Nor indeed have such traits and ambitions been conspicuously absent from the international arena since Germany's defeat in 1945.' Lenin for once was right with his observation that Imperial Germany's international problems sprang less from its peculiar domestic characteristics than from the timing of its development, which brings us back to the belated nation.

All this is by way of explaining why German historical scholarship was so preoccupied with 'the state', foreign policy, rather than for instance with social history, though there are quite a number of notable exceptions, such as Otto Hintze, to mention but one, who made a major contribution to German social history during the Wilhelmine period as well as during the Weimar Republic. However, it was the cataclysm of the First World War, the end of the Hohenzollern Empire and the birth of the Weimar Republic that seemed to bring forth a new beginning. One of the first pathbreakers of a 'new school' was the brilliant young historian Eckhart Kehr, but he killed the impact of his work with his own polemical and extreme formulations. It was Kehr who, in opposition to traditional German historiography, formulated the primacy of domestic policy, meaning that in the German Empire domestic policy determined the course of Germany's foreign policy, blind to what should have been obvious even then, and certainly had been obvious to Ranke, that no such primacy exists, that domestic policy and foreign policy are interdependent, though there may be short periods in which either one or the other dominates. The endemic instability of the Weimar Republic and the advent of Hitler made sure that, at least within Germany, the works of Kehr, Veit Valentin, Alfred Vagts, Hans Rosenberg and others remained short-lived ventures. Hitler's rise put an end to them and after 1945 it took almost a decade and a half for new methodological approaches to emerge.

Inevitably, the emergence of a new school of historiography implies the revision of the traditional historical picture. Perhaps any such revision would have stirred few minds other than those of the specialists had the subject-matter been something more remote than the origins of the First World War. Indeed, if we are looking for the causes of the failure of a new German historiography to establish itself after the First World War, we should have to add to the reasons Article 231 of the Versailles Treaty which in effect saddled Germany with the 'sole guilt' for the outbreak of the First World War. This article was sufficient to ensure the continuance of the 'primacy of foreign policy' in German historiography and it incensed the German nation from Left to Right. After all, millions had fought in the war in the conviction of facing 'a world of enemies' who had 'encircled the Fatherland'. Since then, however, not only British and French but also German historians have dismissed 'encirclement' as a myth. Yet if 'encirclement' was really a myth how come that the British Ambassador in Berlin on 4 April 1935 wrote that Britain's choice was one between disinterest in Europe 'and a *renewed* policy of isolation and encirclement of Germany'. Through the eyes of the British

Foreign Office and its representative past 'encirclement' seems not to have been a myth after all.

Already during the first month of the war the German Foreign Office had indicated the 'guiding principles' of any future publication of official documents: German reaction towards the Allied policy of encirclement; grandiose German war aims were to be denied. After the collapse of the German Empire, the Weimar Republic found itself faced by two tasks. Firstly, it had to discredit the policies of the Imperial government as much as it could; secondly, it had to prove the Allied indictment of the German government and the German nation wrong. That this policy, if consistently pursued, amounted to squaring the circle appears not to have occurred to the Weimar politicians. But be that as it may, this essentially was the twofold objective of the first German official post-war publication, *Die deutschen Dokumente zum Kriegsausbruch*, edited by Count Max Montgelas and Walter Schücking.

However, the apologetic tone towards the victors which marks those five volumes soon disappeared in other official publications after the signature of the Versailles Treaty. The signature of Germany's plenipotentiaries was only the first dribble of ink of a veritable flood that was to be spent on the 'war guilt' question. Convinced of the righteousness of its own cause, the German Foreign Office financed a vast campaign against the 'war-guilt clause' by supporting various bodies who publicly tried to repudiate Article 231. The most prominent and prolific member of some of these was Alfred von Wegerer, himself – unknown to the German public – an employee of the German Foreign Office. In his vast number of publications Wegerer primarily indicted Russia and France for unleashing the war, maintaining a somewhat more reserved and 'benevolent' attitude towards Great Britain. Much of his supporting evidence came from Russian archives which the Bolsheviks, for a time at least, lavishly published and which were immediately translated into German. But the greatest documentary support for the vindication of German policy was derived from the publication, between 1922 and 1927, of large parts of the German diplomatic archives in *Die Grosse Politik der europäischen Kabinette 1871–1914*, edited by J. Lepsius, A. Mendelsohn-

Batholdy and F. Thimme. Some 15,889 documents were published in 40 volumes, arranged in 300 chapters. Like *Die deutschen Dokumente* the material published in this vast collection was almost exclusively diplomatic in nature, in the main ignoring military and economic aspects. Moreover, as in the case of similar publications by countries which emulated the German example, such as for instance Great Britain, France (which to this date keeps documents on its policy during the 1914 July Crisis under lock and key, inaccessible to the historian) and Austria, ample grounds exist for suspecting a tendentious procedure in the selection of the documents published.

The German attempt to revise Versailles historiographically also received considerable support from historians outside Germany, notably in the United States where S. B. Fay's *Origins of the World War* proved a bestseller, and although in many respects dated, this work has withstood the test of time, and to this day remains one of the most readable and balanced accounts. By comparison the conclusions of Bernadotte E. Schmitt (a compatriot of Fay's) were hardly noticed, at least not in Germany. The last man to analyse the origins of the First World War in the inter-war years in considerable detail was the Italian journalist and politician, the former editor of the Milan *Corriere della Sera*, Senator Luigi Albertini. At first Albertini's massive three volumes had little influence upon German historiography in particular and the historiography of other countries in general. To begin with, the work was not completed until 1942, by which time the world had other worries than the First World War. The first complete English translation was not available before 1957. Furthermore, however detailed and meticulous Albertini's work may be, it is not free from case-pleading. He himself had been a leading advocate of Italy's intervention on the Allied side and inevitably his work is marked by his political preferences. Still, whether 'revisionist' or 'anti-revisionist', most of the historiography is marked not only by its partisan nature (the exception is Fay) but also by its purely political frame of reference in which social, economic and institutional questions are hardly posed, let alone answered. By and large, within and without Germany, the 'consensus' was established, aptly summarised by none other than Lloyd George himself (and he should know!), that all the nations of Europe had 'slithered over the brink into the boiling cauldron of war'. This meant that Germany was no longer the party carrying the sole guilt for the war, and that it had not unleashed the war premeditatedly. This 'consensus' even survived the Second World War and a Franco-German historians' conference in the 1950s concluded that the 'documents do not allow one to ascribe in 1914 to any one government or people the conscious desire for a European war', a conclusion endorsed in the late 1960s by the historian Jacques Droz. But carefully phrased as it is, the statement allows one to read it any way one wants.

By comparison with the 'war-guilt question' the question of German war aims appears to have been a secondary one, though it was discussed by historians during the Weimar Republic and found entry into pacifist novels of that time, such as Arnold Zweig's *Education before Verdun* and Theodor Plivier's *Der Kaiser ging, die Generäle blieben*. At any rate, for the more extreme demands the Pan-Germans, whose vociferousness had always been in inverse proportion to their membership, could be indicted, though it would be difficult to dispel the impression that in print this question was evaded by historians such as Hans Delbrück and Victor Bredt, whose conclusions culminated in charging wholesale the Third OHL, notably Ludendorff, with the responsibility for such traces of official annexationism as could be found. Historians seemed to have settled all the issues, so much so that one of them could conclude that 'the history of the period 1914 to 1918 has been researched as thoroughly as hardly any other epoch'.

Four years after this statement had been made, in 1959, the Hamburg historian Fritz Fischer published an article in the *Historische Zeitschrift* whose thesis was that German expansionist aims were pursued during the First World War not simply by fringe movements like the Pan-Germans or militarists like the army High Command under Ludendorff, but by sectors and personalities who had previously been classified as moderates, such as the Chancellor, Theobald von Bethmann-Hollweg. Already at this stage the implicit thesis of Fischer's argument existed – influenced perhaps by the more polemical writings of E. Vermeil, A. J. P. Taylor and Sir Lewis Namier –

namely, that there was a continuity of Germany's political and economic aims from Wilhelm II to Adolf Hitler, a thesis which more than a decade later led to the absurd and irresponsible assertion by H.-U. Wehler that Bismarckian and Wilhelmine Germany were no more than the antechamber of the Third Reich. At that early stage though, few but the initiated were aware of the potential challenge which this argument in Germany presented to established historiographical orthodoxy.

Fischer's article concerned itself with Germany's war aims in Eastern Europe, and his views corresponded closely to those of Hans W. Gatzke who in 1950 had published a brief study, *Germany's Drive to the West*, a study based mainly on printed materials, but new in the sense that it analysed the role of economic interest groups in the formulation of German war aims in the West. Gatzke's work was little noticed until Fritz Fischer's *Griff nach der Weltmacht*, published in 1961, drew attention to it.

Surprisingly enough, at first it was not the main body of Fischer's book, an exhaustive and exhausting study of German war aims, which caused havoc among the historical profession inside and outside Germany, but his assertion that Germany had accepted the risk of general European war during the July crisis. This was sufficient to upset current orthodoxy, and under the pressure of public controversy, instead of mellowing, Fischer's attitude hardened further, as we shall see, moving to somewhat extreme positions.

Fischer's views and those of his pupils, the most notable being Imanuel Geiss, were bound to be highly explosive in an atmosphere in which the problem of responsibility for the First World War was considered settled once and for all and in which the divided German nation to a greater or lesser extent was concerned in coming to terms with and explaining the recent phenomenon of National Socialism. Therefore much fuss was caused, especially outside Germany, when the Bonn Foreign Office refused to finance a lecture tour by Fischer in the United States, which was to have taken place under the auspices of the Goethe-Institute. Those American historians who publicly protested against the attitude adopted in Bonn all came from well-endowed institutions and could very well have financed the invitation themselves. The Goethe-Institute, on the other hand, is a German public institution financed by the German taxpayer. And what interest could the German taxpayer have in financing a highly expensive lecture tour by a historian whose views were not only controversial but subject to considerable valid challenge, from historians whose reputations and integrity were beyond any doubt?

If in fact it was part of Fischer's intention to challenge his colleagues, the challenge was taken up. Although the late Gerhard Ritter, then the *Nestor* of the German historical profession, had long preached as well as practised a more critical approach to the history of Bismarckian and Wilhelmine Germany than had hitherto been customary, particularly in his four-volume main work, *The Sword and the Sceptre*, Fischer's assertions were too much for him. He was able to point out serious methodological and factual errors in Fischer's study of German war aims, such as the quotation of documents of which one page had been read but not the other, a criticism which this editor can support on the basis of his own research on German policy in the Baltic countries. Although as the author of the work Fischer must bear the responsibility for any error, the fault may not be entirely his own but inherent in the German university system where it is quite customary for a professor to send his assistants and/or PhD candidates into the archives to carry out the basic research for 'their professor's work'. This certainly is one way in which it is feasible that error slip in. Fischer would not be the first victim of this procedure – his opponent, Gerhard Ritter, suffered also.

Ritter died in 1967, but opinions are still sharply divided, not simply for and against Fischer but over a wide spectrum. Even East German historians, who felt themselves compelled to side with Fischer and his pupils generally, also point out that theirs is blinkered history because it not only ignores the fundamental readiness of the other European Powers to go to war but also their excessive war aims which made any form of negotiated peace impossible. What is missing is the comparative yardstick and method.

As far as Germany's war aims in the First World War were concerned it can be categorically stated that at all times they were negotiable, but Bethmann-Hollweg, his successors, and the army always insisted that the representatives of the warring powers should come to the negotiating table first, a demand which the Allies adamantly rejected. Neither was the German OHL, then still under Falkenhayn, intractable. Thus the American ambassador in Berlin, James W. Gerard, on 6 March 1915 wrote to President Wilson's close adviser Colonel House that 'the people who were in favour of accepting reasonable peace proposals were, strange to say, the military general staff'.

One factor often forgotten when discussing German war aims, or for that matter German military strategy at the outbreak of war, is the factor of geography. It would be well to remember at all times G. P. Gooch's dictum that: 'Geography is the mother of history'. Germany's geographic position was, to say the least, highly vulnerable. And the historical memories of nations are not short. Most of the Germans who in 1914 marched to war were aware that in the centuries of Germany's weakness and fragmentation she had been the battleground of Europe. France's consolidation into a centralised nation state to a large extent had taken place at Germany's expense. Convinced that the country was encircled, that in the light of the massive Russian arms build-up and France's desire for revenge for 1871 war would come sooner or later, the craving for almost absolute security was, economic aspects apart, a major constituent force in the formulation of war aims. Both east and west should provide 'glacis' areas which would serve for the protection of the homeland, to ensure that no attack could be unexpectedly launched against Germany. And after two world wars which produced the self-emasculation of Europe, what is Europe today other than a divided 'glacis' for a potential confrontation between the United States and Soviet Russia? The factor of geography is one that not only Fischer but also his critics miss.

But irrespective of this, Fischer's study of German war aims has opened new methodological avenues for German historiography by abandoning the well-trodden paths of purely political history in favour of analysing sectional, economic and class interest and their bearing upon the formulation of German policy – whether one is prepared to accept his conclusions *in toto* is another matter. But German historians in the Federal Republic have discovered Karl Marx at last – with a vengeance perhaps – and allowed him to enter, if only through the back door, very much in the same way as the American historian Charles Beard who had disguised his basically Marxist approach to American history by labelling it an 'Economic Interpretation'.

Ritter's death did not mean the end of the debate. Fischer had and still has to face the challenge of his former Hamburg colleague Egmont Zechlin and the Kiel historian Karl Dietrich Erdmann. In a number of brochures published by Fischer and his pupils they moved into increasingly extreme positions, sustained in their efforts rather less by a new consensus among their compatriots than by historians of other nations with whose image of German history, determined largely by the experience of Hitler's Germany and the Second World War, Fischer's interpretation ideally corresponded. His work was quickly translated into English, although both Great Britain and the United States are notorious for their disinclination to publish important historical monographs in any language, though it must be added that the French in this respect are even more insular than the British. It took five years to find a publisher for Ritter's main work in the United States and only via that country did Ritter's work reach the shores of Britain.

Fischer's successive volume *Krieg der Illusionen* (*War of Illusions*) was translated equally fast. In it he distanced himself from his previous assertion that Germany had accepted the risk of a general European war during the July crisis, an assertion which had in the meantime been accepted by his opponents, and went one step further by claiming that the German government wanted this great war and prepared for it and provoked it accordingly.

The lynch-pin of his argument is the 'War Council' of 8 December 1912. In fact there was no War Council at all in Berlin. It was a sarcastic description by Bethmann-Hollweg when he heard that the Kaiser on that date had called together his closest military advisers, against the background of the Balkan crisis, and in response to a despatch by the German ambassador in London, Lichnowsky, according to which Haldane had declared to him that Great Britain's interest lay in the maintenance of the balance of power in Europe and that it would under no circumstances tolerate an overthrow of France.

In other words, in any war involving France and Germany, Great Britain would march with France. That Poincaré earlier in the year had given Russia what amounted to a blank cheque by promising French support under *any* circumstances, thus transforming the Franco-Russian alliance of 1894 from a defensive into an offensive one, which made at least the first Balkan War possible, is a fact which Fischer ignores. The first Balkan war was a Russian war which Russia fought by proxy. The Kaiser was incensed by the contents of Lichnowsky's despatch and rallied his military advisers around him. They included Tirpitz, the Chief of the General Staff von Moltke, the chief of the naval cabinet Admiral von Müller and Vice-Admiral von Heeringen. Conspicuous by their absence were the politicians. Bethmann-Hollweg did not know what was going on. The Kaiser developed his view that in order to remain a great power Austria would have to act as one. Since Russia was supporting the Serbs, war for Germany was inevitable. Austria should direct all its strength against the East while Germany would turn to the West and naturally the German navy would have to be prepared for war against England. Moltke supported the Kaiser but first the war against Russia would have to be popularised in Germany. The navy was more reluctant. Tirpitz argued in favour of postponing any action for another eighteen months at least, though Moltke argued that the longer Germany waited, the more unfavourable would be the conditions for her successfully fighting a war. Irrespective of what was said at that meeting, once he heard of it Bethmann-Hollweg cancelled all the decisions made. The Balkan crisis which had been the cause of this gathering produced neither the propaganda campaign demanded by Moltke nor any economic mobilisation, and even the German army bill of 1913, resulting from a demand by the general staff for an increase of 300,000 men, demanded only less than half of that and was nothing more than an attempt to catch up with Russian and French armaments and manpower, for numerically the German as well as the Austrian armies were inferior to the combined total of the Russian and French armies.

Admiral von Müller kept a diary, which was published in 1965. In 1969 the Anglo-German historian J. C. Röhl published an article in which he mentioned that the editor of the diaries had omitted two important paragraphs relating to the 'War Council', namely that the Chief of the General Staff had said the sooner there was war the better but had failed to carry out the natural consequence of this demand, which would be to confront Russia or France or both with an ultimatum: 'that right is on our side when war is unleashed'. But Röhl himself fails to quote the final summing up by Müller of the practical results of this so-called 'War Council': 'The result was rather Zero'. And so it was. But for Fischer this is the key document, explaining all subsequent events. 'The war in the summer of 1914 was spiritually, militarily, politically, diplomatically and economically well prepared. It needed only to be unleashed' (Fischer).

What Fischer means by the term *Weltmacht* remains as vague and nebulous as in his work on German war aims. In the minds of contemporaries, at home and abroad, Germany was a world power. Bethmann-Hollweg's biographer E. v. Vietsch describes an episode in which Tirpitz demanded that the Chancellor should direct the German people towards a great aim; 'What aim?' replied the Chancellor with a shrug. And against the background of the second Moroccan Crisis in 1911, when national passions ran high, Bethmann-Hollweg wrote to a friend that one could not conduct a war because no war aim existed. Bethmann-Hollweg's own aim was quietly and with patience to consolidate Germany's position in the world, a policy, so he hoped, which would bring Germany a few additional colonies here and a few trading advantages there. Fischer himself, apparently unaware that he was contradicting his own thesis, quotes a letter from Bethmann-Hollweg written as late as 1913: 'Hopefully the raising of the question of Asia Minor can still be postponed. But raised it will be, and probably earlier than we would like. It can be solved in a manner acceptable to us only with England.' This means nothing other than a solution *without* war.

Fischer's description of the second Moroccan Crisis is one-sided and distorted and an excellent corrective to this is Geoffrey Barraclough's recent study *From Agadir to Armageddon*, propounding that the power which escalated the crisis to the threshold of war was Great Britain. Among the powers involved it was only in Great Britain where Grey alarmed the fleet for fear of a German naval pre-emptive strike.

The question why Bethmann-Hollweg accepted the risk of a general European war in July 1914 Fischer answers rather unconvincingly since his key document is the so-called 'War Council' of December 1912, already discussed. Why in 1914 and not at a time which would have been much more favourable to Germany, such as during the first Moroccan Crisis in 1905 when France was internally divided in the wake of the consequences of the Dreyfus affair and her ally Russia neutralised because of the defeat suffered at the hands of the Japanese? By early 1914 the Chancellor as well as the German general staff had become highly alarmed at the Russian arms build-up and the massive extension on Russia's western frontier of her strategic railway net, in the financing of which German banks were heavily involved, just as German heavy industry was in Russia's arms build-up. At the height of the Balkan crisis in 1913 Krupps still supplied heavy artillery to the Russians. Not only the Germans perceived this danger. As late as March 1914 Great Britain's ambassador to St Petersburg, Sir George Buchanan, summarised Germany's military dilemma with the words: 'Can Germany still afford to wait till Russia becomes the dominant factor in Europe or will she strike while victory is still within her grasp?' General Sir Henry Wilson, the director of military operations, after examining the Russian arms programme also commented that, 'it's easy to understand now why Germany is anxious about the future and why she may think that it is a case of now or never'.

As far as Bethmann-Hollweg was concerned the last link that convinced him of Germany's encirclement was the news that Great Britain and Russia were about to conclude a naval convention analagous to that concluded between Great Britain and France in 1912. It envisaged joint Anglo-Russian naval operations in the North Sea, and British naval support for a Russian landing on the coast of Pomerania. From 1909 until 1914 the German Foreign Office received documents relating to Anglo-Russian negotiations directly from the Russian embassy in London whose second secretary, Benno von Siebert, a Baltic-German by origin, leaked them steadily. The matter was treated with such secrecy that besides the Chancellor only three members of the Foreign Office knew of it, not even the Kaiser was party to it. Bethmann-Hollweg felt a deep sense of betrayal by Grey, since after all his main endeavour was to bring about an Anglo-German rapprochement and both he, and even more so Lichnowsky, seemed to have been taken in by Grey's smooth tongue. In order not to provoke Great Britain Bethmann-Hollweg had the *Berliner Tageblatt* publish an article which referred to the envisaged Anglo-Russian naval convention 'as the next stage on the way to an alliance'. London took notice, the Foreign Office suspected a leak in Paris, 'a deplorable indiscretion' as Eyre Crowe put it. But officially it kept silent. Then the German press became more explicit, spelling out what the German Foreign Office knew. This led to questions being raised in the House of Commons. Grey replied that in the event of a European war no unpublished agreements existed which would deprive the government and parliament of the liberty to decide whether or not to participate in such a war – the only direct lie Grey ever told parliament, according to G. P. Gooch. Grey equally denied such plans to Lichnowsky, who actually believed him.

British historians have made light of this episode since, after all, such a convention was never concluded. The fact is that the Russians pressed for a speedy conclusion and signature of the convention while the British, partly in response to the German reaction, wanted to combine signing with a trip by the First Sea Lord, Prince Louis Alexander Battenberg, who was married to a Russian princess, to St Petersburg in August 1914 when the signature could take place without causing undue attention.

However one weighs these negotiations what cannot be ignored is that Grey's dishonesty broke Bethmann-Hollweg's confidence in him completely. Among German politicians he was still one of the very few left who had trusted Grey's assurances. Confronted by the stream of Russian documents about the Anglo-Russian negotiations and Grey's barefaced denial of them, that trust was shattered and this was to determine his attitude during the July crisis. Erwin Hölzle and Egmont Zechlin, two of Fischer's most trenchant critics, place great emphasis upon this episode.

When Fischer wrote his last work he had only very limited

access to the diaries kept by Bethmann-Hollweg's closest confidant and adviser, his *alter ego* Kurt Riezler, a Bavarian. And from this diary, or at least those parts they knew, Fischer and his students quoted very selectively, to substantiate their thesis. When in 1972 the complete diary was published, edited by the Kiel historian Karl Dietrich Erdmann, quite a different Chancellor emerged from it than Fischer and his school would have us believe in; a man not bellicose and set upon imperialist expansion at any price, but a man increasingly pessimistic, almost a fatalist, who viewed Germany's internal intellectual decline with deep sorrow and Germany's deteriorating external position with alarm. After Sarajevo, on 7 July 1914, Riezler noted:

> The secret news of which he informs me, provide a shattering picture. He [Bethmann-Hollweg] considers the Anglo-Russian negotiations for a naval convention, landing in Pomerania, as very serious, the last link of the chain. . . . Our old dilemma as in any Austrian Balkan action. If we encourage them, then they say we had pushed them into it; if we advise against it, then it is said we have left them in the lurch. Then they approach the western powers whose arms are wide open, and we lose our last ally. This time it is worse than in 1912; because this time Austria stands in defence against the Serbo-Russian machinations. An action against Serbia can lead to a world war. The chancellor expects of the war, irrespective of the way it will end, the overthrow of all that exists. What exists has become obsolete, devoid of ideas 'everything has aged very much'.

Bethmann-Hollweg, according to Riezler, saw three alternatives in July 1914. Firstly a localised Austro-Serbian war, which practically would blast the entente but a pre-condition would be quick Austrian action. One ought to add here that, as Sir Herbert Butterfield has demonstrated, Sir Edward Grey's hopes initially went in the same direction. Secondly, a continental war with Russia and France but a pre-condition for that would be that Russia for the time being would remain neutral. Thirdly, a world war with England. The Chancellor preferred the first solution but Austria wasted time to an extent which allowed other issues to crystallise compared with which Serbia became a minor item. Initially he put some hope on British co-operation as had been the case during the first Balkan war, but British neutrality in the event of conflict he ruled out. His hopes lay in being able by means of a threat of war to intimidate the other powers, while Austria would achieve a *fait accompli* in Serbia. If it were to come to war then it would be a preventive defensive war. Fischer argues it could not have been a preventive war because no-one wanted to attack Germany; this may have been the case as far as Great Britain was concerned, but certainly not, as the Russian documents conclusively prove, in Russia's case and it was Russian mobilisation which ensured German action. Moreover, if one were to accept Fischer's argument then one would also have to ignore the fears of the German politicians and the military, which as we have shown were certainly appreciated in Great Britain's diplomatic and military circles. They felt sure that from 1916 onwards a policy of calculated risk could no longer be pursued, that therefore they would be compelled to watch the disintegration of Austria-Hungary without being able to do anything about it, and as a consequence see German power rapidly decline. The fear of encirclement was genuine enough, and the last piece of evidence to substantiate it was the Anglo-Russian naval conversations.

German military planning was determined by this fear, as well as by Germany's geographic position, which allowed only a preventive defensive stroke. The Schlieffen plan was its ultimate expression. Gerhard Ritter, years ago, had subjected this to scathing criticism both from the military and the political point of view. It has been taken as evidence of the primacy of the military over the politicians, an untenable contention because both Bülow and Bethmann-Hollweg were completely informed about it. Neither was Ritter in a position to point to an alternative way of reacting to a war on two fronts. Obviously generals plan in order to win a conflict, not to lose it. Theoretically it could be argued that instead of fighting an offensive war of annihilation, the Germans should have fought a defensive war of attrition. Certainly Germany's advantage of having interior lines of communications would have favoured such a strategy, but that was about the only advantage

Germany enjoyed. The major pre-condition for fighting a war of attrition successfully is self-sufficiency of foodstuffs and vital raw materials. Contrary to Paul Kennedy's assertion, as far as foodstuffs were concerned, Germany by the outbreak of war imported almost a third of its requirements from overseas, in 1913 almost 3,000 million Marks worth. What effect the Allied blockade had upon German food supplies during the war is too well known to need any further elaboration. The only raw material which Germany possessed in abundance was coal, but it possessed hardly any iron ore, no oil or any of the other more precious raw materials. Such a situation did not allow a war of attrition. Hence the answer was a quick and decisive stroke against the opponent one thought could be defeated quickest, before turning to what was taken to be a long-drawn-out contest in the East, with the awareness that Russia's major ally was its geography. That this plan miscarried and why is a question the answer to which is beyond the scope of this volume.

With one exception, as yet no comparative study exists analogous to those which appeared in the inter-war years which examines the origins of the First World War and the question of war aims on a comparative basis using Fischer's approach. Zara S. Steiner's volume, *Britain and the Origins of the First World War*, claims, or at least does so on the cover, 'that, in the British case, the Fritz Fischer thesis does not hold'. This claim, in an otherwise highly perceptive and immensely readable study, is simply misleading because the author does not proceed from methodological and theoretical premises identical with those of Fischer. Economic, social and institutional analysis receive only very marginal attention whereas in Fischer's work they represent its very core. What remains is in essence traditional diplomatic history which does not reach the high level achieved in her other book, *The Foreign Office and Foreign Policy 1898–1914*. In that study Steiner, among other things, demonstrates the impact made upon the Foreign Office and British foreign policy by the change of a generation of personnel, when level-headed diplomats such as Thomas Sanderson, who still bore the imprint of Salisbury's conduct of foreign policy, had to make way to a younger generation of diplomats some of whom were almost paranoid and certainly aggressive, like Eyre Crowe, himself half-German and married to a German, compensating his origins with an excessive Germanophobia, or Sir Arthur Nicolson who, during the Coronation festivities of 1911, at a dinner party loudly and emphatically declared that as long as *he* was at the head of the Foreign Office, 'England should never, never be friends with Germany!'

The exception referred to above is the late Erwin Hölzle and his work *Die Selbstentmachtung Europas*. Whereas most of Fischer's critics have expressed their detailed criticism in articles or in the footnotes of their work, Hölzle takes issue with him directly in the 593 pages of his work and manages to build up what amounts to a very substantial counter-argument to Fischer. Although of a rather higher literary quality than Fischer's tomes, Hölzle's work received only scant notices, one British literary journal refusing to have it reviewed on the advice of a historian who thought it was of little public interest. Hölzle also raises the question why it was not possible to come to a negotiated peace during the First World War. The answer to this question he sees in the agreement made between Great Britain, France and Russia on 5 September 1914 not to conclude a separate peace and not to discuss peace conditions without prior mutual consultations. Now at this point Hölzle may well be straining his evidence beyond the permissible limit, but Sir Edward Grey, more than once, was recorded as saying that there could be no peace until 'Prussianism', whatever that may mean, had been completely eradicated. War it was to be, to the bitter end. But when actually discussing peace feelers Hölzle's work finds considerable support from the former pupil of Gerhard Ritter, the historian Wolfgang Steglich, who in two monographs has examined the peace feelers. Needless to say, neither Hölzle's work nor that of Steglich is available in an English translation. This editor has met British and American experts on German history who can neither read nor speak a word of German. As one such expert put it in 1983 in a well-known historical 'affair', 'life is too short to learn a language like German'.

But the question of the responsibility for the outbreak of the First World War is still on the table. Neither Fischer's answer nor that of his critics is fully satisfactory. Perhaps because it may be the wrong question. Why were the politicians in 1914 not prepared to pay the price which the preservation of peace may have cost? This question, excluding moral concepts, may provide an answer which while evading 'guilt' still would provide us with an insight into why decisions were taken the way they were. As far as *Austria–Hungary* is concerned the murder of Archduke Francis-Ferdinand was only the straw that broke the camel's back. Ever since the bloody massacre of the Obrenović dynasty in 1903 by Serbian army officers led by Captain Dragutin Dimitrijević – the very officer who instigated the murder of Francis-Ferdinand eleven years later – and the advent of the aged Peter Karageorgević, Austro-Serbian relations had been rapidly deteriorating. Serbia, the vanguard of Russia and Pan-Slavism in the Balkans, was likely further to inflame the nationalist fervour within the multinational empire and thus bring about its destruction. Within that context the *de jure* annexation of Bosnia-Herzegovina was only of minor significance since *de facto*, with the agreement of the powers represented at the Congress of Berlin in 1878, it was already in their possession. In the Balkan wars of 1912 and 1913 Serbia more than doubled its territory. The Serbian danger could not be ignored. In 1914, viewed from the perspective of the Vienna *Hofburg*, it was not a question of prestige, but one of survival. To evade the Serbian challenge, so it seemed, would have been a further step towards the inevitable disintegration of the Hapsburg Empire.

For *Germany*, as already indicated, not to back Austria-Hungary would have implied the loss of her one remaining reliable ally and facing a potential conflagration with Russia, and therefore also with France, on her own, once the Russian arms build-up and her railway network had been completed, which was expected to be the case by 1916/17. And, as the Anglo-Russian naval conversation seemed to suggest, Great Britain was likely to side with France and Russia. Therefore if conflict there were to be, then 'rather sooner than later' while there was still a chance of victory. If Austria by a quick pre-emptive strike could localise and solve the conflict then there was no problem, but if it meant general war then Germany was also ready. Anything else would have led to isolation and her decline.

For *Russia* not to support Serbia would have meant a serious loss of prestige, with repercussions inside Russia of incalculable extent. It would also have meant renouncing her ambition to restore the Cross of the Orthodox Church over Constantinople, an aim which circumscribed Russia's ambition for her Black Sea Fleet to enter the eastern Mediterranean and establish bases at the Dardanelles. The throne of the Czar was shaky, the energies of the Pan-Slavist movement could direct themselves with equal fervour against the throne as they directed themselves against Austro-Hungary and Germany.

France was not directly involved in the dispute, but she had done her best to reinvigorate the Franco-Russian alliance and, as we have noted, converted it to an alliance of an offensive character, thus further stoking the fires that were to erupt in the Balkan wars. Even if Germany, in order to keep to the military timetable, had not declared war on her first, it is highly improbable that she would have stood aside and broken her alliance obligations. To do so would also have meant the renunciation of 'the lost territories' of Alsace-Lorraine. In addition, in the event of a German victory over Russia she would have confronted an enemy stronger than ever before.

Of all the powers involved *Great Britain*, besides Russia, had on the surface the widest range of options. Though not formally committed, the extent of her informal commitment was such that, as Grey readily admitted, for Great Britain not to join Russia and France would have meant, to say the least, Grey's own moral bankruptcy. In spite of attempts at mediation, Grey did not go far enough, to the extent of exerting serious pressure on Russia not to mobilise. This would have jeopardised the Anglo-Russian entente and would have been the end of friendship with Russia. As Buchanan wrote to Grey in April 1914, Russia was becoming powerful so fast 'that we must maintain her friendship at almost any price'. Great Britain had concluded her ententes with France and Russia primarily for imperial considerations. She had overextended herself beyond the limits of her resources. The Anglo-Russian entente in particular was to ensure security for India and Asia Minor. The fact that in spite of the entente the Russians still proved troublesome, especially in Persia, was uncomfortable, but therefore all the more reason to accommodate them even further. The end of the ententes, their blasting by Germany, would have made the Empire, especially Britain's position in India and other parts of Asia, highly vulnerable again. War in Europe was preferable to imperial insecurity which might well lead to the collapse of the Empire altogether. Grey played a highly dangerous game, from which only Germany's invasion of Belgium saved him. 'Poor little Belgium' became the rallying cry, if one was needed, although the treaty guaranteeing Belgium's neutrality contained no provision calling for armed intervention in the event of violation, only a consultative clause. Three decades before, when the question of Belgian neutrality and of Britain's intervention was raised in the House of Commons, Salisbury had firmly declined such an obligation. But in the 1880s and 1890s there did not exist that which threatened in 1914. the German High Seas Fleet. Its potential domination of the Belgian coast put a different light on Britain's obligations. But 'poor little Belgium' was as much a good propaganda ploy as was Bethmann-Hollweg's alleged reference to the treaty guaranteeing Belgian neutrality as 'a scrap of paper', another propaganda move, as the recently published diaries of Great Britain's ambassador in Berlin, Sir William Edward Goschen, show.

There would be much to add and to enlarge upon, but the events of 1914 viewed along these lines take on a different and more varied picture from that provided by Fritz Fischer. In the past few years the Fischer debate had showed signs of simmering down until, in 1983, it once again burst forth into full flame. It was reignited by Fritz Fischer, who in 1983 published a thin paperback volume, *Juli 1914: Wir sind nicht hineingeschlittert. Das Staatsgemeinis um die Riezler-Tagebücher (July 1914: We have not stumbled into it. The State Secret of the Riezler Diaries)*. Fischer believes that the debate has now returned to the point where it began over twenty years ago. His aim runs in two directions, primarily against his critics such as Zechlin, Erdmann and Andreas Hillgruber, the other target being the Riezler diaries themselves. When Erdmann published the diary in 1972 in his introduction he described in great detail the chequered history of the diary. Fischer repeats this history, spiced by critical and polemical comments which offer no insights except to raise doubts on the authenticity of the diary,

doubts based on letters written to him by a German émigré who
in order to substantiate his charges refers to conversations
conducted by him with a German historian now deceased and a
third party whose name he does not reveal. Other historians
have raised doubts, especially over the passages written during
the July crisis, alleging that they have been manipulated,
possibly by Riezler himself, or after his death in Munich in 1955
by his brother. Only hearsay evidence has it that originally
Riezler had testified to Bethmann-Hollweg's willingness to go
to war. Even the subtitle of Fischer's book is misleading. At no
time were the diaries ever a 'state secret', they were not even in
the hands of the state but in the possession of the Riezler family.
Bethmann-Hollweg's willingness or readiness to go to war is an
assertion that can neither be proved nor disproved.

However, doubts at any time are legitimate, but the creation
of theories of conspiracy is quite another matter, as when
Fischer writes 'important representatives of the historical
profession had in accordance with the tradition of the German
conservatives manipulated a historical document in order that
the historical truth would remain hidden, in favour of an
outdated morality of the "clean nest" '.

Fischer indeed contradicts himself, dismissing the diaries on
the one hand as a doubtful and dubious source, but using them
all the same when the entries correspond with his own frame of
reference. His own thesis that German policy in July 1914 was
calculated from the very beginning for a great war he tries to
substantiate with a diary entry of 8 July 1914: '. . . if the war
comes from the east so that we go to war for Austria-Hungary
and not Austria-Hungary for us, then we have a chance of
winning it. If war does not come, if the Czar does not want it or
a startled France counsels peace, then we would still have the
prospect of manoeuvring the entente apart over this action'. To
use this entry as Fischer does in support of his thesis is, to put it
mildly, stretching the evidence to the point of excess. At the
same time he ignores Riezler's entries where they do not fit in
with his picture.

However, Fischer's main motive is to have a final reckoning
with his critics, for fear that the discussion and debate will
return to the point where they had started. Back in 1965, at a
historian's conference in Dijon, Fischer vainly pressed his

French colleagues, Pierre Renouvin, Jacques Droz and others, to dissociate themselves from the joint declaration by the Franco-German historians of the 1950s mentioned above. Far from complying, Erdmann and Renouvin agreed that war aims in France and in Germany were the product of war, not its cause, and Jacques Droz then stated that no document existed which would prove the thesis that the German statesmen had acted 'with a conscious and well thought out will to aggression'. The assertion that Bethmann-Hollweg and his advisers had reckoned at least with Great Britain's neutrality has been completely contradicted. After all, Fischer's key document, the so-called 'War Council' of December 1912, clearly shows that the gathering was caused by Haldane's blunt statement that if there were to be a war between France and Germany, Great Britain would have to side with France.

German calculation, however mistaken, had many levels ignored in Fischer's virtually monocausal explanation of a hegemonial war prepared long before and staged according to plan. Zechlin and Hillgruber especially, have provided subtle analyses in many of their articles which provide an insight into and an understanding of the peculiar mixture of defensive and aggressive elements which characterised Germany's risky policy, or as Kurt Riezler was to call it, 'the leap into the dark'.

In his criticism of the Riezler diaries in 1983 Fischer appeared to receive major support from the young historian Bernd Sösemann in an article published in the *Historische Zeitschrift*. The arguments are too intricate, above all too technical to allow recapitulation here but in essence they culminate in three points: (i) Walter Riezler (Kurt Riezler's brother) who transcribed the diary entries of the July crisis has distorted and falsified what Kurt Riezler had actually written; (ii) Kurt Riezler himself, for personal as well as political reasons, rewrote his original diary after the war; and (iii) 'The shadow of the editor' (Erdmann) has obscured and blurred these facts. Sösemann in the course of his argument changes both language and tone. What begins with 'editing', moves on to 'distorting' and ends up with 'falsifying'. In the same issue of the *Historische Zeitschrift*, Erdmann was given space to reply, and without much polemic refutes Sösemann's artifice point by point, again an argument highly intricate and technical but fully convincing, except of course for those who simply do not want to be convinced even by a highly objective and incisive analysis.

However, historical debate and controversy are fruitful and helpful, they shake the consensus and put an end to the stagnation which unfortunately characterises so much of the historiography for the period 1933–45. Fritz Fischer in his work has thrown out a challenge both in his approach and in his conclusions. Irrespective of whether one shares these conclusions, no-one will look at the origins of the First World War again in the same light as they were before 1961. No mean achievement for Fritz Fischer – or for his critics.

In the essays selected for this volume James Joll, who basically shares Fischer's viewpoint, outlines the debate as he saw it in the late 1960s. The first edition of the book contained a contribution by P. H. S. Hatton, which unfortunately now for reasons of space has to be omitted, showing just how closely Great Britain and Germany were collaborating on the colonial level shortly before the outbreak of war.

Imanuel Geiss adds his own interpretation to the origin of the First World War which, as has been rightly pointed out, because of his own pre-conceived and strongly held notions does not clarify the motivations of the other Great Powers and their readiness to accept war as an alternative to the political process. Geiss has frequently accused a previous generation of historians of selectivity and omission. True as this charge may be, L. C. F. Turner, in an article published in the *Journal of Contemporary History* entitled 'Russian mobilisation in 1914', supplies evidence that this charge holds true of Geiss as well, as he appears particularly blind towards Russian and French policy during the crisis. Moreover, Geiss has argued elsewhere that to ask Russia in 1914 to cease supporting Serb nationalism and France to cease supporting Russia in such action would have been tantamount to asking the 'impossible of the two Great Powers', given the historical situation. Quite apart from the questionability of the argument as such, there is nothing which could not make it fit Austria-Hungary or Germany. Nor does it occur to Geiss that had Russia taken no action, Austro-Hungary, indecisive as it was in the conduct of its policy during the July crisis, would have been likely to have

done nothing against the Serbs for lack of German support –
unless, of course, Germany was prepared to unleash a war one
way or the other and thus accept the onus of being the power to
make the first move. However, this is a step which
Bethmann-Hollweg was unlikely to have taken because of his
need of the support of Germany's Social Democrats, since 1912
the largest party in the Reichstag. That support was only sure
once Russia was fully mobilising. Recent evidence also shows
that the Kaiser would not believe the news of Russian
mobilisation until German military intelligence provided him
with a Russian poster announcing mobilisation from Russia's
western provinces. That German military intelligence had not
been put on a war footing prior to the outbreak of war, and was
caught by it completely off guard, thus putting another nail in
the coffin of the thesis of German premeditated war, is
demonstrated in Ulrich Trumpener's article, 'War Premeditated? German Intelligence Operations in July 1914', published in *Central European History*, 1976, an article which
unfortunately for lack of space could not be included in this
selection.

Geiss's reinterpretation of the background to the July Crisis
is strongly supported by Fritz Fischer's contribution, 'World
Policy, World Power and German War Aims'. Fischer interprets German policy during the July crisis as a product of its
failure to expand politically and economically in south-eastern
Europe during the preceding four years. He then goes on to
argue his case of establishing a continuity between Germany's
war aims and the pre-war aims of *Weltpolitik*, a continuity
existing – within the frame of reference of the article – in the
main in Germany's engagement in Austro-Hungary, the
Balkans and Turkey.

Unfortunately, Gerhard Ritter has never criticised Fischer's
work in its entirety but only isolated aspects of it, such as
German pre-war policy, its policy during the war, or Fischer's
treatment of the Chancellor, Bethmann-Hollweg. Ritter postulated a fundamental difference in aims between Bethmann-
Hollweg and Ludendorf, between civil power and the army.
Fischer has argued that such a difference is a purely artificial
one which never existed. Both politicians and army were
agreed on the ends, they only differed over the means. To

reprint Ritter's own interpretation would have required the reprinting of not only one but a whole series of them. This was clearly impossible; hence one of Ritter's ablest pupils, Karl-Heinz Janssen, provides a fair but also critical assessment of Ritter's position. Egmont Zechlin's contribution illustrates the point that one cannot simply speak of a for and against Fischer school in Germany. It would be an unwarranted over-simplification to place Zechlin halfway between Ritter and Fischer. After all in the final analysis, in spite of the bitter feud between them Ritter had found it necessary to adapt his own position as a result of Fischer's work. Zechlin, however, appears to agree in several respects with Fischer and attributes to German policy during the July crisis a more active role than German historians had been ready to allow before. He emphasises Germany's readiness to accept the risk of general war, but makes the very important distinction between readi-ness to accept what appears to be inevitable and desire to provoke war to further expansionist aims. The picture he presents is considerably more complex and varied than Fischer's and devoid of over-simplification. Unlike Fischer as well as Ritter, Zechlin, like Hölzele mentioned above, sees the documents as bearing out the impression on German policy-makers of being subjected to an encirclement policy by the Powers of the Entente. This policy Germany countered with a limited defensive offensive war. But once the traditional nineteenth-century pattern of limited Cabinet warfare had been replaced by total war, Germany, in Zechlin's view, had only one alternative, of wresting its allies on the European mainland from Great Britain by speedily defeating them and fusing them into an economic as well as a political unit. *Mitteleuropa* was the product of the breakdown of a Cabinet warfare with limited aims, and its degeneration into hegemo-nial warfare was conducted both by the Central and by the Entente Powers.

Joachim Remak's contribution looks at the First World War through the perspective of the 'Third Balkan War' and analyses the policies and the shortcomings of each of the belligerent countries while his American colleague, Paul W. Schroeder, in a reply to Remak affirms the former's criticism of an overtly determinist interpretation such as Fischer's. He rejects any monocausal approach but analyses the multiplicity of factors that led to war. He looks for their interaction. One cause, one force operating in one direction would logically produce a non-event, it is the interaction of a variety of factors which causes an event. He does not ask 'Why World War I?' but in the light of the preceding crises, 'Why not?' He analyses the wide spectrum of European foreign affairs since the turn of the century, in order to focus sharply upon Austria-Hungary and to what extent it was affected by the ententes concluded by Great Britain, effects which in practice had a more serious effect upon the stability and security of the Hapsburg empire than upon Imperial Germany.

Karl-Dietrich Erdmann provides a summing up of the balance of new research on the question of 'war guilt', making extensive use of the Riezler diaries, while Egmont Zechlin provides a reply to Fritz Fischer's latest book discussed above, in which it is not so much the question of 'guilt' which stands to the fore, but rather the discussion of the configuration of forces that brought about war in 1914.

'Can we be certain that Bethmann-Hollweg and his colleagues were so different from other European statesmen in their almost unconscious assumption of the Darwinian necessity and empirical morality of war?' a reviewer once asked in the Times Literary Supplement, and goes on: 'The mood suggests . . . that the German attitude was not wholly isolated from a general European fever'. Actually, Imanuel Geiss has argued that a specifically German ideology of the permanent struggle of the peoples lay at the base of German Weltpolitik which tried to justify 'philosophically' Germany's bid for world power status. Indeed, not only Bethmann-Hollweg himself but also Kurt Riezler provide sufficient evidence to demonstrate the existence and general currency of Social Darwinian premises which caused Fritz Fischer implicitly to treat this phenomenon as though it were a German invention.

The editor's own contribution, from which since publication of the first edition of this volume a monograph has emerged, albeit in German, Der Sozialdarwinismus: Seine Genese und Einfluss auf das imperialistische Denken, questions the postulation of a specifically German ideology and looks at what James Joll has aptly called 'The Unspoken Assumptions' of the period in a wider context, suggesting that Social Darwinism was part of the intellectual fabric of western and Central Europe as well as North America and pointing to the ultimate result of this ideology once both men and circumstances existed to carry it to its ultimate logical conclusion thirty years later.

1. The 1914 Debate Continues: Fritz Fischer and his Critics

JAMES JOLL

Two recent academic controversies, one in England and one in Germany, have aroused interest and repercussions far outside the university world in which they originated. Mr A. J. P. Taylor got into trouble for suggesting that Hitler did not plan the war that broke out in September 1939; Professor Fritz Fischer, of Hamburg University, has got into even worse trouble for saying that the German government did plan the war of 1914. While Mr Taylor's *Origins of the Second World War* has been subject to endless discussions in England and, as often with controversial works, has been, in part at least, accepted by many as a new orthodoxy, the stir provoked by Professor Fischer's *Griff nach der Weltmacht*, although it has been noted by British scholars such as Professor F. L. Carsten, has not yet been closely examined in this country. However, it is perhaps worth studying, not only because of the important new evidence which Professor Fischer has discovered about the origins and nature of the First World War but also because of the light which the reception of the book in Germany throws on certain fundamental attitudes and problems. Moreover, the book provokes reflections about historical method and even, it may be, about the way wars in general may start in a tense

From *Past and Present*, no. 34 (July 1966).

international situation dominated by an unrestricted arms race.

Professor Fischer's book was first published in 1961. It is a large detailed work, some 900 pages long, and is based on a vast collection of German government archives hitherto not available for study. While one might sometimes criticise the style and the construction of the work – it is perhaps over-long and, if anything, over-documented – no-one can deny that it is an important major work of scholarship which contains a mass of new evidence about Germany's methods and goals in the First World War, and that it will oblige other scholars of all nationalities to look again at accepted versions of the policies and aims of their own countries. Why, then, has a scholarly monograph with no great obvious appeal to the general public and little stylistic attraction caused such an outcry? It so scandalised some German historians that one of the most respected of them (Gerhard Ritter) wrote, 'I could not put the book down without feeling deep melancholy: melancholy, and anxiety with regard to the coming generation. . . .'

To answer this, it is necessary to look at Professor Fischer's main thesis and then to examine some of the criticisms, both general and detailed, which have been made against him. But even before doing this, it is important for English readers to remind themselves just how dominant a role the 'war-guilt question' played in the study of contemporary history in Germany between the wars and how sensitive a point it still is. Article 231 of the Treaty of Versailles laid down that Germany accepted responsibility for the war imposed 'by the aggression of Germany and her allies'. This, quite apart from its political effects, was to impose on German historians – and later on some foreign historians too – the duty of assembling the evidence to refute the view that Germany was responsible for the war. One of the most notable acts in this connection was the German government's decision in the summer of 1919 to publish a long series of volumes of documents from the German Foreign Ministry archives, *Die Grosse Politik der europäischen Kabinette*, an example which was followed by other major belligerent Powers, and which was again adopted as a precedent after the Second World War, thus providing historians with a wealth of material, though at the same time provoking in some of them a suspicion that there were still in the archives hidden secrets which the publication of selected documents only served to conceal.

It might have been thought that, after the Second World War, the issue would have died, since even the Germans agreed that it was Hitler and the Nazi leaders who were responsible for the war and that the Nuremberg trials, whatever may be thought of them from a legal or political point of view, had at least served to clear up the question of war guilt for the Second World War once and for all. For the Germans this was extremely important: if the blame was put squarely on to Hitler, then the rest of his countrymen were absolved. Hitler and the Nazis, instead of being regarded, as they are by some historians, as a product of German society and German ideologies, could be treated as a unique phenomenon, a sort of inexplicable scourge inflicted on the German people from outside, and alone responsible for the disasters and horrors of the Third Reich. It is for this reason that many Germans resent any suggestion, such as that made by Mr Taylor in his *Origins of the Second World War*, that what Hitler was doing (at any rate up to 1939, which is when Taylor's book ends) was no different from what other German statesmen had wanted to do.

This brings one back to Professor Fischer, for, as he expressly states in his Introduction,

> The book points beyond its own limits, in that it demonstrates certain ways of thought and formulation of aims for German policy in the First World War, which have continued to remain active. From this point of view it may also be a contribution to the problem of continuity in German history from the First to the Second World War.

It is this suggestion – and it is no more than that – which has particularly aroused many Germans to criticise Fischer, and started a controversy in which even the German government apparently intervened by trying to stop Professor Fischer from undertaking a lecture tour in the United States, while the President of the Bundestag accused him and his students of being intellectual flagellants, and the editor of a respected newspaper denounced him for 'national masochism' and suggested that he should resign from his university chair.

Fischer's main thesis – perhaps over emphasised by the title 'Grasping at World Power' – is that Germany was ready to resort to war in order to establish herself as a *Weltmacht*, a Great Power, that is, which could take its place along with the other World Powers, who had established their position in the world before Germany had achieved national unity. This idea of achieving true Great Power status in a world balance of power – a concept which Professor Ludwig Dehio, although he has criticised some of Fischer's conclusions, had previously examined and developed in some interesting essays – was easily turned into a plan for organising the world, or part of it, in such a way that it should be dominated by Germany and serve German economic, cultural or strategic interests. Professor Fischer demonstrates, by a detailed examination of the documents, first, that the German government, if they did not actually want war in 1914, were at any rate prepared to face the risk of it in pursuit of their general aims, and that they systematically encouraged their Austrian allies to provoke war with Serbia even when they saw that it could not be localised; and secondly, that, as soon as the war had started, they developed plans, which they had already previously discussed, for large-scale territorial annexations and for the establishment of a German-controlled new order in Europe.

This is a very crude summary of an argument that is built up with great subtlety and detail in the early chapters of the book, and it is these that have aroused the most interest and provoked the most controversy. Later chapters deal with the development of German war aims as the circumstances of the war changed – with the attempts to start subversive movements in Russia and in the British Empire, with the proposals for restoring a semblance of Polish independence or for establishing a Flemish State in Belgium. The main purpose of the later chapters is to show how, in spite of the varying fortunes of the war and in spite of the growing anxiety by 1917 about the nature and purpose of the war, the aims for which Germany continued to fight remained essentially those which had already been set out in September 1914, in a memorandum by the Chancellor, Theobald von Bethmann-Hollweg – a document the discovery of which forces us to reconsider the nature of German policy in general and the position of Bethmann-Hollweg in particular. All this is easy for non-Germans to find plausible and convincing; and, indeed, some of it is already familiar through the work of Professor Hans Gatzke, for example, who has shown the extent of Germany's ambitions in western Europe in his book *Germany's Drive to the West*, while in the East, the Bolshevik Revolution and the military collapse of Russia enabled the German government by the Treaty of Brest-Litovsk to put their war aims into practice, so that, instead of being recorded in secret archives, Germany's aims were there on the ground for all to see – though even here Professor Fischer shows that the vast territorial and political gains of March 1918 were considered by many Germans in authority as only the beginning of even more extensive conquests to serve German hegemony on the European continent. But for the Germans this apparent reopening of the war-guilt question is extremely painful.

The most striking section of Fischer's book – and it has led many of his critics to overlook the interesting elaboration of his themes in later chapters – is the early part in which he deals with the crisis of 1914 and with the formulation of German aims in the first weeks of the war, when it still looked as if a speedy victory over the French, as foreseen by the German military planners, might be possible. In the discussion of this section of the book, some of Professor Fischer's original intentions have perhaps been forgotten and misunderstood. He is anxious to show that Germany's plans for war and her aims once the war had begun were the product of the social and economic situation in Germany, so that the presuppositions of Germany's leaders and the pressures to which they were subjected were such that, in a sense, the personalities and decisions of individuals were of little importance and their choices in fact strictly limited by the political, social, economic and ideological climate within which they were operating. The critics of Fischer's views, however, have tended to concentrate on the personalities of the men whose actions were crucial to German policy in the months of July and August 1914 – the Kaiser, Bethmann-Hollweg (the Imperial Chancellor), Gottlieb von Jagow (the State Secretary in the Foreign Ministry) and Helmuth von Moltke (the Chief of the General Staff). In particular, it is the new view of Bethmann-Hollweg's character and purposes as it emerges from the documents Professor Fischer has discovered that has upset people most. Indeed, it has, in spite of Professor Fischer's expressed intentions, turned the discussion largely into one about personalities. Once this is so, then the interpretation of documents necessarily depends on the interpretation of character; for the way in which one reads the documents is determined by one's general view of the nature and motives of the writer of the document, and divergent views of a man's character will result in differing interpretations of what he writes.

In Professor Fischer's view, Bethmann-Hollweg's policy had been based on the assumption that British neutrality in the war – a war which, on this view, he regarded as inevitable – could best be secured by making sure that the outbreak of war appeared to have been provoked deliberately by Russia or by France. Thus when, at the end of 1912, the German government was collaborating with the British to keep the Balkan War localised but when, at the same time, they were preparing for new military and naval increases, Bethmann-Hollweg wrote that a war with Russia in the Balkans would certainly involve France, but that it was 'from many indications at least doubtful whether England would actively intervene if Russia and France appear directly as provoking the war'. For Professor Fischer this is evidence of the continuity of Bethmann-Hollweg's policies, and he suggests that the Chancellor in 1912, as in 1914, was less concerned with pursuing peace than with dividing Britain from France and Russia and with keeping Britain neutral by making sure that France and Russia appeared to be in the wrong. This is one of several points at which Professor Gerhard Ritter, the most formidable of Fischer's critics, to whom we shall return later, challenges Fischer's interpretation and accuses him of misreading the documents. He says that Bethmann-Hollweg in this particular report was making a purely tactical point intended to calm down the Kaiser, who was always ready to fly into a rage with the British, and to try and make him resist the proposed naval increases, which to the British appeared as German provocation. If one reads the report in question dispassionately, it can, it seems to me, be taken either way, and one's interpretation is not conditioned by the document itself, or even entirely by the circumstances in which it was drafted, but rather by one's view of Bethmann-Hollweg's character and policies as a whole. A historian's view of a man's aims and motives is formed to a large extent by the documents, but it necessarily also influences the way he reads them; and it is unrealistic to expect Professor Fischer, who, on his reading of the evidence, has formed one opinion of Bethmann-Hollweg's political personality, to agree with Professor Ritter, who, from the same evidence, has come to a radically different conclusion. Each, when interpreting a particular document, is looking for support for a view already formed through reading many other pieces of evidence.

Let us look, however, at Fischer's general view of Bethmann-Hollweg and his policy. For Fischer, Bethmann-Hollweg is a typical product of the forces which dominated German life at the beginning of the century, a period in which Fischer (following Ludwig Dehio) sees the Germans convinced of their own strength – politically, militarily and industrially – and wanting desperately to be a World Power, to have a vaguely defined and obscurely conceived world mission which would, in the world balance of power, make up for the disadvantage under which Germany suffered because of coming too late as a united nation on to the world scene. Bethmann-Hollweg was, Fischer shows convincingly, already before the war in touch with people who were specifically thinking in terms of a German-dominated *Mitteleuropa*, and to a large extent shared their thinking. Although he hoped for the possibility of achieving *Weltmacht ohne Krieg*, he was ready to accept the idea of war and to base his policy on the necessity of ensuring, if it came, that it was under conditions as favourable to Germany as possible. According to Fischer, Bethmann-Hollweg over-estimated Germany's strength and, above all, maintained up to the final crisis an unfounded belief in the probability of Britain's neutrality. It is in the light of these general assumptions about Bethmann-Hollweg that Fischer interprets his conduct of affairs in the crisis of July 1914 and in the early weeks of the war.

It is here that the importance of Bethmann-Hollweg's Memorandum of 9 September 1914 lies, and it certainly forces

us to reconsider the conventional picture of Bethmann-Hollweg as the liberal statesman (who reminded Lord Haldane of
Abraham Lincoln), striving in vain to maintain peace against
the machinations of the militarists. The Memorandum was
sent by Bethmann-Hollweg from GHQ in Koblenz to his
deputy, Clemens Delbrück, the State Secretary of the Interior,
in Berlin, just at the moment when the French counter-attack
on the Marne was going to transform the course of the war, but
before the outcome of the battle was known, so that the
Germans still seemed to be faced with the problems that would
confront them on achieving victory in the West. Bethmann-
Hollweg laid down that the aim of the forthcoming peace
settlement must be

> the security of the German Empire in the West and in the
> East for the foreseeable future. To this end, France must be
> so weakened that she cannot rise again as a Great Power,
> Russia must be pushed as far as possible from the German
> frontier, and her rule over non-Russian subject peoples must
> be broken.

Professor Fischer makes two important points about this
document. Firstly, he shows in the subsequent chapters of his
book that it in fact contains the minimum aims which some
German leaders consistently attempted to pursue throughout
the war: the reduction of France to a second-class Power by
territorial annexations, the establishment of some form of
long-term control over Belgium, the spread of German power
eastwards, either by direct annexation or by the creation of a
German satellite State in Poland, and the weakening of Russia
by the encouragement of subversive movements of all kinds,
while at the same time Germany would lay the basis of a new
colonial empire by the acquisition of large areas of Central
Africa. Secondly, Professor Fischer shows that this programme
has strong similarities both with the ideas of a number of
leading German industrialists for establishing a German-
dominated, economically unified *Mitteleuropa*, and even with
the more outspokenly annexationist demands of the Pan-
German League, which had been drafted shortly before.
Fischer shows convincingly that in fact Bethmann-Hollweg

was in close contact with Walther Rathenau (the head of the great German electrical combine, the A.E.G., and one of the directors of the Berliner Handelsgesellschaft) – a neighbour and frequent visitor at Bethmann-Hollweg's country-house – and with Arthur von Gwinner of the Deutsche Bank, and there can, I think, be no doubt that their ideas directly influenced the formulation of war aims by Bethmann-Hollweg at a moment when he had every reason to expect an early peace.

For the Anglo-Saxon reader, there is perhaps nothing very surprising in all this: and some of it is already known – the paper on war aims which Rathenau sent to Bethmann-Hollweg on 7 September, for example, which expresses the necessity for controlling France in order to defeat England, and reiterates the importance of German supremacy in central Europe. But Fischer's exposition does suggest a consistency and continuity in German planning; in combination with his insistence that in July 1914 it was the Germans who were egging on the Austrians to war, it makes the comfortable thesis difficult to maintain, that – to use the phrase coined by Lloyd George – 'the nations slithered over the brink into the boiling cauldron of war'.

Since it is Fischer's account of the period July–September 1914 on which his critics have largely concentrated, it is worth looking at what they say on this point. One of the most widespread grounds for attacking Fischer is that he has dealt exclusively with German war aims and worked exclusively on German documents. This seems to me a silly line of attack: Fischer was writing a monograph on German war aims and not a history of the war; he has shown enormous industry in reading a vast quantity of documents and, apart from anything else, it just would not be physically possible for one man to cope with the material that would be involved in making an analysis on a similar scale of the policies of all the belligerent Powers. It is true that there were annexationist and expansionist ideas to be found in the Allied camp as well as on the German side; and this has in fact been well known, at least since 1918 when the Russians published the details of the secret negotiations in which the Tsarist government had been engaged with Britain and France. Moreover, victorious Powers use their victory to put their war aims into practice (as Germany did at Brest-Litovsk), and we all know what the Allies did with their victory, for better or for worse. This does not mean that now that the British archives are opened there will not be an interesting study to be made of the development of British war aims on the lines pioneered by Professor Fischer, and it is to be hoped that this will soon be undertaken.

Some of the criticisms of Professor Fischer are more serious. The most respected and the most formidable of the older generation of German historians, Professor Gerhard Ritter, has not only suggested that Fischer misinterprets documents but has also implied that he has a political purpose in doing this. One German newspaper, reporting the Congress of the German Historical Association in Berlin in September 1964, at which the Fischer controversy was the main attraction, wrote of Professor Ritter's 'short lesson on exact work with historical sources and the citation of false or incomplete quotations from the sources which made not only Fischer but many other historians blush'. My own reading of Ritter's published criticisms of Fischer suggests that Fischer has no need to blush, but it is true that Ritter has a view of the origins of the First World War which is entirely different from Fischer's. Professor Ritter is seventy-five years old, and he himself tells us that he still has the manuscript of a speech which he made in September 1914, when he was a teacher in a secondary school, in which he warned his pupils against premature rejoicing and against misuse of power if Germany won the war. He is, that is to say, a member of the generation which was directly involved in the First World War and the great surge of patriotic emotion of August 1914, whereas Professor Fischer is a generation younger and was still a child when the war began. Moreover, Professor Ritter is himself at present engaged on a major work, *Staatskunst und Kriegshandwerk*, in which he analyses with great learning and with a stylistic brilliance which most German historians (or, indeed, historians of any nationality) lack, the problem of civil–military relations and the concept of militarism, with particular reference, of course, to Germany. A large section of the second volume is devoted to the immediate origins of the First World War, and the third volume to the development of Bethmann-Hollweg's policies after the war began.

It is worth comparing the general picture which emerges

from Ritter's book with that which is to be found in Fischer's *Griff nach der Weltmacht*, as this illustrates the difference of interpretation which underlies the current controversy. Owing to the publicity given to the argument – the fact that it was prominently featured in the popular weekly *Der Spiegel*, for example – and the personal bitterness which some of Fischer's critics injected into it, it is hard not to feel obliged to take sides with one or the other party. But perhaps this would be a mistake, and it may be that each book illuminates one aspect of German behaviour in 1914, and that it is because German society and German ideology in the twentieth century were so ambivalent that they are hard to understand and lend themselves to different interpretations, not one of which is wholly adequate to explain the facts. For Professor Ritter, the German leaders, and especially Bethmann-Hollweg and Moltke, are the helpless and often anguished victims of circumstances, carried into war against their will by the inexorable unfolding of military plans which they did not devise and whose political consequences had never been properly foreseen. This view has been reinforced in the case of Bethmann-Hollweg by the extracts which Professor K. D. Erdmann, of the University of Kiel, has published from the diary of Kurt Riezler, Bethmann-Hollweg's personal assistant and a close friend.

'The Chancellor', Riezler noted on 27 July 1914, 'sees a doom greater than the power of man hanging over the situation in Europe and over our people'.

And Bethmann-Hollweg's son told Professor Egmont Zechlin (Fischer's colleague at Hamburg and one of his severest critics) that not long before the war the Chancellor said that there was no point in planting trees in the park of his country-house as the Russians would be there in a few years.

There is no doubt that Bethmann-Hollweg was wracked by doubts, hesitations and fears. There is equally no doubt that Helmuth von Moltke, the *Feldherr wider Willen*, was so haunted by his own inadequacy and so broken by his physical and neurotic weaknesses that he virtually collapsed as soon as the war started. Even the Kaiser, although I think Fischer is right in taking his violent racist outbursts seriously, had his moments of lucidity, responsibility and anxiety. It is quite true, as Professor Ritter emphasises both in *Staatskunst und Kriegshandwerk* and in his study of the Schlieffen Plan, that the military plans had irrevocable political consequences with which their authors had not been very much concerned and which their successors, and especially those responsible for foreign relations in 1914 – principally Bethmann-Hollweg and Jagow – had to face. And yet, in the light of the new evidence produced by Fischer, it is hard to accept the picture of Germany's leaders as helpless victims of a fate they were trying to avoid.

Professor Fischer's critics have, if they take this view of the characters and motives of the rulers of Germany, still to explain away that September Memorandum and the speed with which the government produced a statement of aims – a statement which is certainly more understandable if it is taken as revealing the assumptions which underlay their actions when they took the risk of war. One view that has been suggested is that Bethmann-Hollweg, instead (as Fischer says) of gambling unsuccessfully on Britain's neutrality, expected England to enter the war but was confident that the war would be a limited one or that Britain could swiftly be persuaded by diplomatic means to withdraw again. On this view, put forward by Professor Zechlin, the September Memorandum is not so much a statement of the ends for which Germany entered the war but a proposal of the means – the economic organisation of Europe and the occupation of strategic points on the Channel coast – by which Britain might be defeated. In the discussions about Germany's position in the world before 1914, Britain did perhaps occupy the largest place as being the World Power with whom Germany would have to reckon if she was to emerge as an Imperial nation with wide overseas interests, and the Kaiser's almost paranoiac outbursts against English encirclement are characteristic of one strand of German thinking. Moreover, in September 1914, Rathenau was pointing out that, whatever the outcome of the battle in France, Britain would remain Germany's principal enemy. Nevertheless, it is hard to see the September Memorandum just as a tactical statement of means rather than a strategic programme of ends, just as it is hard to believe that the war was purely a defensive reflex on Germany's part, and an attempt to break the circle of hostile Powers which she felt to be closing in on her.

Professor Hans Herzfeld, the most generous as well as the

wisest of the historians who have commented at length on
Fischer's book, reproaches him for not doing justice to the
shifting political scene in German internal politics during the
war – and for not giving enough importance to those elements
in Germany which were trying to resist the more extreme
annexationist aims of the military leaders and Pan-German
propagandists. There were undoubtedly some Germans who
stood out against the prevailing mood, just as there were some
Germans who resisted the Nazis, but in neither case did they
have any influence on the course of events, and their main
historical importance has been to give the Germans some slight
comfort in retrospect. Just how strong was the current against
which they were struggling is shown by an example which
Fischer quotes in an article in the *Historische Zeitschrift* where he
effectively answers some of his critics and produces further
evidence in support of his views.

At the time of the sinking of the *Lusitania* in 1915, Admiral
von Truppel, a former Governor of Kiaochow, who was at the
time working for the Hamburg–America shipping line, predicted that the adoption of unrestricted submarine warfare
could lead to the United States entering the war and to
Germany's downfall. Thereupon the Hamburg Chamber of
Commerce protested to the Hamburg–America company
against the Admiral's views, and its President (Albert Ballin,
often regarded as a moderate in such matters) assured the
President of the Norddeutsche Bank that the Admiral would be
dismissed.

It is this climate of opinion that has to be taken into account
to understand how even high-minded civil servants like
Bethmann-Hollweg could go a long way with their more
extreme colleagues, and how *Griff nach der Weltmacht* is not an
unfair summary of Germany's aims and motives in 1914.

History can be written in many different ways. Some of those
who have discussed Fischer's book have quoted a dictum of the
historian Hermann Oncken that 'nuance is the soul of politics',
and have suggested that Fischer, by singling out one theme and
following it throughout his long work, has oversimplified the
nature and evolution of German politics in the First World
War. Fischer has answered this with the assertion that in

certain circumstances 'nuance' is less important than *Wesen* – the essence or core of a political development.

Certainly, one of the effects of the salutary opening-up of the whole subject which Fischer's book has achieved has been to concentrate attention on the true nature of German policy of the First World War and to get away from the self-justifications and evasions into which, ever since 1919, the discussion has very easily slipped. Moreover, just as history can be written either as a history of nuances or as a history of main themes, so too government archives can be used in two different ways. Some historians – a good example is Gallagher and Robinson's *Africa and the Victorians* – when confronted with ministerial records are impressed by the confusion and the apparently accidental way in which vital decisions are taken. As a result, actions which have been thought of as acts of deliberate policy or part of a long-term plan can be shown to be the result of *ad hoc* administrative decisions or of some obscure precedent unearthed in the files. Officials, however, seldom make plain the underlying premises on which their decisions are based, and it is only by understanding these and the framework of ideas within which they are operating and the social and other pressures to which they are subject that the true grounds for their actions can be comprehended. This, it seems to me, is the justification of Fischer's method. By concentrating on a single theme and by following it through the enormous mass of archival material which he has used, he has contributed to our understanding not only of the actual causes and course of the First World War, but of the presuppositions, the *Weltans-chauung*, and the intellectual, social and political limitations within which the leaders of Wilhelmine Germany were working.

It is this aspect of Fischer's work that accounts in part for the extreme hostility it has aroused in Germany. For the older generation of his critics, such as Professor Ritter, Fischer must seem to be attacking many of the values on which their lives have been based. (It is significant that Professor Ritter is the biographer of Carl Goerdeler, whose upright old-fashioned Prussian conservative principles led him into active opposition to Hitler and who embodied many of the ideals of pre-1914

Germany.) If men like Bethmann-Hollweg were carried so far in the same direction as the extreme militarists like Ludendorff and were powerless to resist them because they shared some at least of their aims, then the presuppositions of the whole generation of 1914 are called in question, and there is more continuity between 1914 and 1933 or 1941 than many Germans would like to admit. The reopening of the war-guilt controversy and the suggestion common to both Professor Fischer and Mr Taylor that Hitler's aims were foreshadowed by the German leaders of 1914 is bound to be disturbing, since it suggests that many other questions in German history are still not settled. Germans have assumed, perhaps too readily, that the truth about 1914 was known, that the verdict of history had been passed and the Germans acquitted. They have sometimes ignored those historians, such as Luigi Albertini, who have shown how much blame the German government had to bear for the First World War, and they have forgotten that there is by no means uniformity among non-Germans in absolving the Kaiser and his generals and ministers. And if 1914 has to be thought of as an open question, then the examination of the German past cannot stop there, and the whole achievement of Bismarck must be reassessed, and where, it might be thought, will this process end?

It is understandable if Germans of the older generation, shaken by what they have experienced in their own lifetime, are reluctant to see the apparent certainties of the past overthrown or at least challenged. What is encouraging is that the younger generation seem to have responded to Fischer's lead and to be ready to look at the evidence in an unemotional and dispassionate way. It seems that both at the Historical Congress in Berlin in September 1964, as well as at the International Historical Congress in Vienna in 1965, some of the personal heat and animosity in the controversy was dying down, and it must be hoped that the participants will see that, in Professor Hans Herzfeld's words,

> Only one thing is certain: that the value of German research – even at the cost of from time to time calling in question apparently firm conclusions – can only increase in

the eyes of foreigners, if it avoids giving the impression of being based on unthinking reaction from political motives.

What will remain is a lesson in historical method which will influence historians outside Germany and which doubtless some English historians will be ready to apply now that the British archives for the First World War are available for research.

2. Origins of the First World War

IMANUEL GEISS

BISMARCK'S LEGACY

The events of July and early August 1914 cannot be properly understood without a knowledge of the historical background provided by the preceding decades of Imperialism. On the other hand, that background alone is not sufficient to explain the outbreak of the First World War. Two general historical factors proved to be decisive, and both were fused by a third to produce the explosion known as the First World War. Imperialism, with Wilhelmine *Weltpolitik* as its specifically German version, provided the general framework and the basic tensions: the principle of national self-determination constituted, with its revolutionary potential, a permanent but latent threat to the old dynastic empires and built-up tensions in south-east Europe. The determination of the German Empire – then the most powerful conservative force in the world after Tsarist Russia – to uphold the conservative and monarchic principles by any means against the rising flood of democracy, plus its *Weltpolitik*, made war inevitable.

Although the forces of national and revolutionary democracy were most active in south-east Europe just before the war, their roots go back to the French Revolution of 1789. Before 1914 the principle of national self-determination directly threatened the Ottoman Empire and caused the First Balkan War against Turkey, as a kind of war of national liberation. After the new Balkan nations had practically pushed Turkey out of Europe, the next target was inevitably Austria-Hungary, which, how-

Introductory chapter to the author's own selection of documents published in English by Batsford Ltd, London, under the title *July 1914* (1967).

ever, was closely allied to Germany. Although the German Empire was a nation-state, it in fact included compact national minorities on its borders constituting about 10 per cent of its population: Frenchmen in Alsace and Lorraine; Walloons in Eupen-Malmédy; Danes in Schleswig; Poles in West Prussia, Posen and Upper Silesia. They led the more or less marginal existence of second-class citizens; they resented the arbitrary separation from their compatriots and their enforced inclusion in the German Reich. Thus, at least indirectly, even the German Empire was implicated in the rise of national self-determination.

The third factor which made the First World War inevitable in the form and at the time it did occur was the German Empire itself. It was important for two main reasons: firstly, its ambition to attain the status of 'a World Power beside other World Powers' (Erdmann), but without seeking an agreement with at least one of the World Powers already firmly established; and secondly, its self-proclaimed role as the great bulwark against revolution and democracy. It is significant that both factors, even if in a rather confused way, had played a dominant role in the revolution of 1848–9. While we shall probably never know whether a victory of liberal and democratic forces in Germany at that time would really have meant large-scale expansion of a newly founded empire, it is certain that Bismarck started his career by fighting both liberalism and democracy on the one hand, and expansion to at least a Greater German Empire, including Austria (with or without the non-German provinces), on the other. His Lesser German Empire founded in 1871 was a modest affair compared with the day-dreams of many a liberal Greater-German patriot. But it established Prussian predominance and was accomplished only by three wars in rapid succession. The victories of the Prussian armies – in 1870 over Bonapartist France, about to liberalise herself, and after Sedan over post-Bonapartist, democratic France who resisted German demands for annexations – in themselves introduced a new, disquieting element into the European scene. It was partly Bismarck's cunning diplomacy and Moltke's strategy of *Blitzkrieg* (to use a fitting expression of a later period) that made it possible for Bismarck to unite the Germans in the face of misgivings in Europe.

The immediate effect of the re-establishment of the Reich was to change profoundly the balance of power in Europe. Since the late Middle Ages Europe had been accustomed to weakness in its centre, in one form or another. Either there existed a confused political vacuum, created by the old Reich in its perennial agony, or two great German Powers largely neutralised each other by their rivalries. The unification of a majority of Germans in the 'Lesser' German Reich under the leadership of Prussia helped to make the new Germany 'into the greatest concentration of power on the mainland in Europe'. Unification, rapid industrialisation, military power and bureaucratic efficiency were sufficient to raise even Bismarck's 'Lesser' Germany almost automatically into a position of 'latent hegemony' over the Continent. Since then, the future of Europe and the Reich depended on the wisdom of Germany's political leaders, whether or not they successfully resisted the temptation to convert this latent hegemony into an open one.

Just as Frederick II of Prussia lay low after his conquest of Silesia, so did Bismarck after his successful *coups*. He wanted to accustom Europe to the new balance of power and to the emergence of Germany as the potential leading Power in the centre of Europe. Bismarck's 'peaceful' policy after 1871 thus finds a very simple explanation. On the other hand, his new caution, after nearly a decade of gambling, recklessness and limited wars, probably also appealed to his conservative instincts. He had been successful beyond reasonable expectations, he did not want to run the risk of losing everything by aiming at even higher prizes. Bismarck's watchword that Germany was 'satiated' had two aims: to reassure Europe about the danger of German hegemony, and to restrain elements in Germany which were not satisfied with his achievements. In the short run, Bismarck seemed to have succeeded again, at least as long as he was Chancellor. After 1871 he figures as the statesman of moderation and peace. Yet, in the long run, he and his work became the victim of those elements with which he had co-operated and which he afterwards tried to moderate or channel. And after his fall we see him allying himself with those very elements which dreamt of expansionist schemes.

The real roots of Bismarck's triumph and of Germany's emergence as the leading Power on the Continent in 1871 had been Prussia's industrial preponderance over her more agrarian Austrian and French rivals. Soon after the foundation of the Second Reich heavy industry was developed beyond the immediate needs of an expanding economy. From the early 1890s onwards industrialists, in particular Krupp, pressed for fuller use to be made of the inflated capacity for steel production. The demands were translated into political agitation by the Navy League, which was one of the first modern pressure groups in Germany and inspired and largely financed by Krupp.

Similarly, the German economy expanded overseas and entered into conscious rivalry with British industry and finance, even though this was mitigated by short-term cooperation on such schemes as the Baghdad Railway. Soon after 1871 the pressure of foreign trade and increasing participation in world markets created the demand for a German share in world domination, or *Weltpolitik* as it was called. At least that was the explanation given, not by a Marxist but by Kurt Riezler, writing under a pseudonym shortly before the outbreak of the First World War. Bismarck, mainly for domestic reasons, had tried to give these expansionist elements a limited outlet by inaugurating German colonial policy in the early 1880s. Anti-British and anti-Russian economic policy (in order to satisfy agrarian interests) made Germany drift into a hopeless dilemma.

In spite of his sound insights into the dangers of open German hegemony, even Bismarck was unable to hold down for good the new demands for greater German power. After his fall, which was widely welcomed over practically the whole of Germany, Caprivi's cautious policy of consolidation stood on the shoulders of Bismarck's peaceful policy of the post-1871 period. Caprivi cared little for colonial and less for naval ambitions, but concentrated his efforts rather on strengthening Germany's position on the Continent, especially vis-à-vis Russia – to the chagrin of many German conservatives and patriots. In particular, the Zanzibar–Heligoland deal of 1890 provoked the anger of the new forces in Germany, and Bismarck, now in enforced retirement, viciously denounced the very policy of restraint that he himself had pursued for almost two decades. Out of this agitation against the 'soft' Caprivi arose the Pan-German League. For the period of Caprivi's Chancellorship, and again mainly for domestic reasons, Bismarck now openly allied himself with the incipient Pan-German movement. Yet the old Bismarck apparently did not realise in his anger that he was supporting a cause which, in the long run, would endanger his own work. Consequently, especially after his death in 1898, Bismarck became the patron of a new wave of German chauvinism, embracing all champions of German *Weltpolitik*.

GERMAN *WELTPOLITIK*

The new feeling was articulated for the first time in a powerful and persuasive way by Max Weber. In his famous Inaugural Lecture at Freiburg University in 1895, he pleaded for a new policy of striving for world power:

> We must understand that the unification of Germany was a youthful folly, which the nation committed in its declining days and which would have been better dispensed with because of its expense, if it should be the conclusion and not the starting-point for a German *Weltmachtpolitik*.

Max Weber's eloquent plea was immediately taken up by Friedrich Naumann and by a vociferous group of Liberal Imperialists, in constant rivalry with the more conservative Pan-Germans in whose ranks Max Weber had played a role as one of the founder-members. Between them they provided the climate of public opinion and the ideology for the actual change of German foreign policy.

The emergence of the Pan-Germans and Liberal Imperialists was one of the results of the new movement in German public opinion that clamoured for Germany to play a bigger role in the world. It is not surprising that the young Kaiser Wilhelm II, flamboyant and constantly torn between cutting a figure as a great Prince of Peace (*Friedenskaiser*) and a great Warlord (*Oberster Kriegsherr*), should have been among the first to voice the new sentiment, even if only in the strictest privacy.

As early as the summer of 1892 he revealed to his intimate friend and adviser Count Eulenburg the 'fundamental principle' of his policy: 'a sort of Napoleonic supremacy . . . in the peaceful sense'. In the Kaiser's versatile mind 'Napoleonic supremacy', albeit 'in the peaceful sense', seemed perfectly compatible with his extraordinary illusion that the Poles were craving to be 'liberated from the Russian yoke' by the Germans: 'In the event of a war with Russia the whole of Poland would revolt and come over to my side with the express intention of being annexed by me.'

Perhaps even more significant is a private memorandum composed in 1896 by Georg Alexander von Müller, later Chief of the Imperial Naval Cabinet, under the title *Zukunftspolitik*. Müller proceeded from the assumption that world history was at present characterised by a violent economic struggle, especially in Europe. While *Mitteleuropa* was becoming too narrow, the 'free expansion of the nations living there was limited by the existing distribution of the inhabitable parts of the globe, in particular by England's world domination'. Out of the tensions 'war can and, as many maintain, must arise'. According to Müller there was common agreement in Germany that the aim of such a war must be 'the destruction of English world domination in order to acquire the necessary colonies for the mid-European states in need of expansion'. Apart from Germany, Austria-Hungary and Italy were rated as such States 'in need of expansion', while Müller also considered the candidacy of Scandinavia and Switzerland. But, 'In the necessity and justification of expansion . . . Germany excels by far.'

However, Müller, who had some liberal inclinations (liberal, that is, by German standards), did not entirely agree with that common view, since Germany would gain little from the destruction of the British Empire. Instead he preferred an alliance with Britain against Russia. As Britain for reasons of racial comity would be Germany's 'natural ally', such an alliance would also give the 'economic struggle an ideological trait, the preservation of the Germanic race against Slavs and Romans'. While the final result might be a clash between the two powerful 'Germanic empires', he preferred permanent co-operation between them in the interest 'of the future struggle for the hegemony of the Germanic race'. Müller clearly saw the two alternatives for Germany: 'Either to commit all the power of the nation, recklessly, not even shirking a great war, or else to limit ourselves to a continental Power.' He was against both a feeble compromise and the attempt to forge ahead against Britain.

The most interesting aspects of Müller's analysis and recommendations are his testimony of how general the German desire in 1896 must have been for expansion of the Reich – the realisation that the desired breakthrough to the status of World Power would be possible only by war was, it seems, equally widespread – and the emergence of a crude racism, even in one of 'liberal' repute. The implication of the new *Weltpolitik* – the Great War – was thus clearly seen in Wilhelmine Germany, even before it was launched. Although it would be of interest to assemble all the evidence showing that Germany's political élite understood this implication – before and after the crucial decision to plunge into the breakneck adventure of *Weltpolitik* – one more example must here suffice. Again, we quote not an extremist but a well-known moderate, the liberal-conservative historian and publicist Hans Delbrück, who, as one of the few German 'critics of the Wilhelmine era', was certainly not prone to extravagant pronouncements. As early as 26 November 1899 he proclaimed in his *Preussiche Jahrbücher*:

> We want to be a World Power and pursue colonial policy in the grand manner. That is certain. Here there can be no step backward. The entire future of our people among the great nations depends on it. We can pursue this policy with England or without England. With England means in peace; against England means – through war.

Like Müller, Delbrück would have preferred the former solution, but the government's *Weltpolitik* was conducted not only without Britain, but even against Britain. Müller and Delbrück differed from the mainstream of political thought, as represented by the Kaiser, the court and the navy, in their caution vis-à-vis Britain. But all were agreed on the need for a powerful German fleet as the most important instrument of *Weltpolitik*. Even before 1897 the navy pressed for a more powerful battle fleet. After the Kaiser had revealed to his intimate friend Eulenburg his Napoleonic dream in 1892, Eulenburg persistently pushed Bülow's candidacy as Foreign Secretary and Chancellor, while Bülow was only too willing to translate his Kaiser's ideas into action. Both were convinced that only a spectacular success in foreign policy could restore and enhance the popularity of the monarchy and establish the Kaiser's personal rule. Out of all those dreams, sentiments, ambitions, cross-currents and pressures emerged German *Weltpolitik*. It was apparently advocated for the first time at government level in July 1897 by the National Liberal Prussian Minister of Finance, Johannes von Miquel, as an indispensable part of his new policy of 'Collection' (*Sammlungspolitik*) – of rallying the well-to-do classes around the throne against Social Democracy. At the same time, the emphasis on foreign policy was to help overcome serious differences between the industrial and agrarian wings of Germany's wealthier classes and to create a united front of the whole nation against the world. Thus German *Weltpolitik* was partly created by a domestic policy, which aimed at diverting the attention of the masses from social and political problems at home by a dynamic expansion abroad. In this the essentially demagogic slogan of *Weltpolitik* proved only too successful. Through its 'national' appeal it soon acquired a momentum of its own, and finally domesticated the Catholic Centre Party, the left-wing Liberals, and even the SPD. It gave rise to a distinct political tradition that prevented even the most sensible and strong-willed German statesman from avoiding the collision course on which Germany was set. If there is anything tragic about Bethmann-Hollweg, as is nowadays often claimed, it lay in the situation he inherited and was unable to affect, even if this had been his genuine desire. By 1914 the Reich had become victim of its own most valued slogan.

Bülow's arrival at the Foreign Ministry, the launching of Tirpitz's crash programme of naval armament and Germany's seizure of Kiaochow in 1897 all point to the effective inauguration of German *Weltpolitik*. The German navy, built not only 'for our commerce, our security, our future', but also 'especially for the person of our dear Kaiser', was understood by Britain as a 'challenge to her naval supremacy'. Both Tirpitz's concept of the *Risikoflotte*, designed to frighten Britain at least into neutrality, and the Battle of Jutland in 1916 prove that British fears were not unfounded. As late as February 1914 Jagow, the Secretary of State at the Foreign Ministry, wrote to Lichnowsky, the German Ambassador in London, on the question of British neutrality in a future conflict:

> We have not built our fleet in vain, and in my opinion, people in England will seriously ask themselves whether it will be just that simple and without danger to play the role of France's guardian angel against us.

German *Weltpolitik* pursued the tactics of claiming equality with the established World Powers and demanded 'compensations' for any territorial or other changes of the *status quo* anywhere on the globe. The character of Germany's new course was thus one of irritating vagueness, but it was clearly based on the consciousness of growing power. German uncertainty about the present status of Germany in the world and her future role only increased confusion at home and suspicion abroad. Whereas Max Weber in 1895 still demanded a new *Weltmachtpolitik*, the Kaiser proclaimed that Germany had already become a 'World Empire' (*Weltreich*) as early as 18 January 1896. Nobody doubted or disputed Germany's status as a great continental Power. But it was increasingly hard to define her position in world politics.

THE EFFECT OF *WELTPOLITIK* ON THE BALANCE OF POWER

Germany's *Weltpolitik* had far-reaching effects. A less obvious one was the change in the character of the Triple Alliance. The Dual Alliance between Germany and Austria had originally been concluded in 1879 as a purely defensive treaty. The inclusion of Italy in 1882 did not alter that basic fact, although complications were introduced on account of Austro-Italian rivalry. The new *Weltpolitik*, however, gradually transformed the Triple Alliance into the basis for German ambitions as a fledgeling World Power. When Italy tried to do the same on a limited scale with her Libyan war against Turkey in 1911 (a power open to German influence), and when Austria tried to use the Triple Alliance 'to support her own policy in the Balkans, the Triple Alliance lost much of its defensive character and its superficially imposing unity and power.

Even more startling was the effect on the other Powers. In 1871 there was no system of alliance in existence; in 1885, when the 'scramble for Africa' began, there existed only one alliance – the Triple Alliance; by 1907, however, the Triple Entente had emerged. Among the first symptoms of the new development had been the Franco-Russian Alliance of 1892–4, which put an end to the isolation of France, created by Bismarck's diplomacy after 1871. It also ended for good the co-operation between the great conservative Powers of the East, Russia, Germany and Austria. Partly as a reaction to Germany's *Weltpolitik*, her naval armament and her refusal to enter into a loose arrangement with Britain, and partly as a counter-move to the completion of the Trans-Siberian Railway in 1902, Britain's foreign policy after the Boer War was designed to end her erstwhile 'splendid isolation'. The alliance with Japan in 1902 was followed in 1904 by the Entente Cordiale with France. Although it was primarily an arrangement over colonial questions, political co-operation between the two Western Powers soon followed. In 1907, after the Russo-Japanese War of 1904–5, Britain and Russia concluded an even looser arrangement. The so-called 'Triple Entente' was, therefore, no solid alliance. There was no formal treaty of alliance between all three partners; there was only the treaty between Russia and France. There were no formal and binding agreements for military co-operation between Britain and the other partners. The tensions between Britain and Russia over Persia were a constant source of friction between the two countries, even in early July 1914. Neither the Triple Alliance nor the Triple Entente were the monolithic power blocs they seemed to be. But most contemporaries and participants in the diplomatic negotiations at the time felt strongly about the differences between the two groups. At least Jagow, on 1 August 1914, attributed the deeper reasons for the outbreak of war to 'this d—d system of alliances', as he remarked in a conversation with Sir Edward Goschen, the British Ambassador in Berlin.

Contrary to traditional German belief, the Triple Entente

was not conceived as an offensive alliance. None of the three Powers pursued expansionist aims, over which they would or could have gone to war: British 'envy of the Germany economy' (*Handelsneid*), French 'revanchism' and Russian 'Pan-Slavism' were, and still are, grossly exaggerated in Germany. Alsace-Lorraine was of course in the minds of many Frenchmen, but France would never have gone to war in order to reconquer the two provinces, if only because public opinion was on the whole pacific, as the German Ambassador in Paris stressed in detailed reports from France. On the other hand, the French, in their *nouvel esprit*, were no longer prepared to swallow such a humiliation as having to sack Delcassé merely to avert threats from Germany, as happened during the first Moroccan crisis of 1905–6.

Russian 'Pan-Slavism' amounted to a vague feeling of solidarity among all Slavs, and active, chauvinistic Pan-Slavs in Russia were limited to small circles as, again, the Kaiser and the Chancellor could have learned from their top expert on the question, the German Ambassador in St Petersburg. Tsarist Russia, it is true, had her traditional ambitions for Constantinople. Yet there she encountered not only German interest, but also British and French suspicions, which by themselves would have been enough to neutralise any Russian aggression against Turkey. The Russians, furthermore, faced a serious dilemma: 'a struggle for Constantinople was not possible without a general European war', as was pointed out in the famous secret conference of 21 February–6 March 1914 in St Petersburg, but in a general war military action against Constantinople would be impossible, as all forces would be needed on other fronts. Nor would an isolated *coup* against Constantinople succeed because it was bound to provoke a general war which the Russians knew they were too weak to wage on their own; neither France nor Britain would come to their help in a provoked war, let alone one provoked by the seizure of Constantinople. This dilemma proved to be insoluble, and in fact during the crisis of July 1914 Constantinople figured only in the back of the minds of a few statesmen: Sazonov apparently wanted to prevent the Germans from taking over in Constantinople once Serbia was crushed by Austria, while the Austrians and Germans apparently feared

Russia's expansion through the alliance with the south Slavs, whose success would isolate the Central Powers from Turkey. Constantinople was not a direct cause of war in 1914.

The two most highly industrialised countries of Europe – Britain and Germany – were each other's best trading partners, and in Britain there was a strong pro-German current, from the monarchy down to a rather sentimental feeling of 'kith and kin' on the part of the Left, who were most outspoken in their opposition to entering the war on the side of Tsarist Russia. Britain was also opposed to any offensive war against Germany provoked by Russia or France and would effectively have vetoed it.

There were, however, circles in Britain who were disturbed and even frightened by the menace of the German fleet, of Germany's vague, ill-defined demands, her pretensions and the ostentatious display of her military and naval power. This group became strong in the navy, the army and the Foreign Office. The most detailed articulation of their misgivings is to be found in Sir Eyre Crowe's famous memorandum of 1 January 1907. His memorandum is, it seems, more denounced as anti-German than actually read (at least in Germany), perhaps on account of its length. In the light of subsequent events and of our present knowledge, it proves to have been the most intelligent and precise analysis of German *Weltpolitik* for a very long time to come. Far from being crudely anti-German, it was a balanced judgement of German intentions and sought to find a rational explanation for the apparently irrational and bewildering manifestations of German *Weltpolitik*. Crowe set it in historical perspective, in the same sort of way as many German historians, then and later, have traced the rise of little Brandenburg into the mighty German Empire, via Prussia. A close look at Crowe's memorandum is, therefore, highly relevant in the present context, if only because it was long considered in Germany as a major factor contributing to war.

Crowe saw the rational core of German *Weltpolitik* in the drive for equality of Germany overseas:

> Germany had won her place as one of the leading, if not, in fact, the foremost Power on the European continent. But over and beyond the European Great Powers there seemed to

stand the 'World Powers'. It was at once clear that Germany must become a 'World Power'.

The result was the inauguration of German colonial policy. Crowe's way of summing up political sentiment in Germany is worth quoting. In answering the question why Germans thought they must have colonies, a powerful fleet and coaling stations, he answers for the German mind:

> A healthy and powerful State like Germany, with its 60 million inhabitants, must expand, it cannot stand still, it must have territories to which its overflowing population can emigrate without giving up its nationality. . . . When it is objected that the world is now actually parcelled out among independent States, and that territory for colonization cannot be had except by taking it from the rightful possessor, the reply again is: 'We cannot enter into such considerations. Necessity has no law. The world belongs to the strong. A vigorous nation cannot allow its growth to be hampered by blind adherence to the *status quo* . . .'

After quoting some of the most revealing remarks of the Kaiser ('The trident must be in our hand', 'No question of world politics may be settled without the consent of the German Emperor', etc.), Crowe reached a provisional conclusion, which is more moderate than extreme:

> The significance of these individual utterances may easily be exaggerated. Taken together, their cumulative effect is to confirm the impression that Germany distinctly aims at playing on the world's political stage a much larger and much more dominant part than she finds allotted to herself under the present distribution of material power.

Crowe warned that it was not a matter of moralising, as examples of history showed. Again he revealed how well he knew the German mind:

> No modern German would plead guilty to a mere lust of conquest for the sake of conquest. But the vague and

undefined schemes of Teutonic expansion (*die Ausbreitung des deutschen Volkstums*) are but the expression of the deeply rooted feeling that Germany has established for herself . . . the right to assert the primacy of German national ideas. And as it is an axiom of her political faith that right, in order that it may prevail, must be backed by force, the transition is easy to the belief that the 'good German sword', which plays so large a part in patriotic speeches, is there to solve any difficulties that may be in the way of establishing the reign of those ideas in a Germanized world.

Turning to the analysis of German *Weltpolitik* proper, Crowe made it clear that he was no anti-German, for he did not question 'that the mere existence and healthy activity of a powerful Germany is an undoubted blessing to the world'.

In spite of all English 'sympathy and appreciation of what is best in the German mind', created by 'intellectual and moral kinship', Crowe attached one condition to his welcoming an increase of Germany's influence and power in the world:

> There must be respect for the individualities of other nations, equally valuable coadjutors, in their way, in the work of human progress, equally entitled to full elbow-room in which to contribute, in freedom, to the evolution of a higher civilization.

On the following page Crowe put the same argument in a different form:

> So long, then, as Germany competes for an intellectual and moral leadership of the world in reliance on her own national advantages and energies England cannot but admire, applaud, and join in the race. If, on the other hand, Germany believes that greater relative preponderance of material power, wider extent of territory, inviolable frontiers, and supremacy at sea are necessary and preliminary possessions without which any aspirations to such leadership must end in failure, then England must expect that Germany will surely seek to diminish the power of any rivals, to enhance her own by extending her dominion, to hinder the

co-operation of other States, and ultimately to break up and supplant the British Empire.

Crowe noted that, of course, German statesmen denied any such intentions. He pointed out that, even if such assurances were sincere, they might be 'incapable of fulfilment'. Furthermore, 'ambitious designs against one's neighbours are not as a rule openly proclaimed'. Crowe cautiously introduced the idea of what is now called 'continuity' in German policy, by suggesting 'that a further development [of German policy] on the same general lines would not constitute a break with former traditions, and must be considered at least as possible'. And he asked:

> Whether it would be right, or even prudent, for England to incur any sacrifice or see other, friendly, nations sacrificed merely in order to assist Germany in building up step by step the fabric of a universal preponderance, in the blind confidence that in the exercise of such preponderance Germany will confer unmixed benefits on the world at large, and promote the welfare and happiness of all other peoples without doing injury to any one.

Crowe had his doubts. Again he stressed 'that a recognition of the dangers of the situation need not and does not imply any hostility to Germany'; he was ready to mete out to Germany the same as he expected for England: 'Not to be wantonly hampered by factitious opposition' when pursuing schemes which are not harmful to third nations.

After a lengthy and detailed survey of the many frictions between Germany and Britain, which Crowe blamed on Germany's *Weltpolitik*, he returned to the question of what German intentions could be. He saw two possible explanations:

> Either Germany is definitely aiming at a general political hegemony and maritime ascendancy, threatening the independence of her neighbours and ultimately the existence of England; or Germany, free from any such clear-cut ambition, and thinking for the present merely of using her legitimate position and influence as one of the leading

Powers in the council of nations, is seeking to promote her foreign commerce, spread the benefits of German culture, extend the scope of her national energies, and create fresh German interests all over the world wherever and whenever a peaceful opportunity offers, leaving it to an uncertain future to decide whether the occurrence of great changes in the world may not some day assign to Germany a large share of direct political action over regions not now a part of her dominions, without that violation of the established rights of other countries which would be involved in any such action under existing political conditions.

And he added: 'In either case Germany would clearly be wise to build as powerful a navy as she can afford.' One might add today: the overall result would have been the same – the Great War. To meet either possibility Crowe recommended falling back on the traditional policy of the balance of power. This would not mean that Germany need be reduced to the rank of a weak Power, for

> So long as Germany's action does not overstep the line of legitimate protection of existing rights she can always count upon the sympathy and good-will, and even the moral support, of England. Further, it would be neither just nor politic to ignore the claims to a healthy expansion which a vigorous and growing country like Germany has a natural right to assert in the field of legitimate endeavour. . . . It cannot be good policy for England to thwart such a process of development where it does not directly conflict either with British interests or with those of other nations to which England is bound by solemn treaty obligations. If Germany, within the limits imposed by these two conditions, finds the means peacefully and honourably to increase her trade and shipping, to gain coaling stations or other harbours, to acquire landing rights for cables, or to secure concessions for the employment of German capital or industries, she could never find England in her way. Nor is it for British Governments to oppose Germany's building as large a fleet as she may consider necessary or desirable for the defence of her national interests. . . .

Crowe summed up his policy, which could be called one of 'containment', in a remarkable passage:

> It would be of real advantage if the determination not to bar Germany's legitimate and peaceful expansion, nor her schemes of naval development, were made as patent and pronounced as authoritatively as possible, provided care was taken at the same time to make it quite clear that this benevolent attitude will give way to determined opposition at the first sign of British or allied interest being adversely affected. This alone would probably do more to bring about lasting satisfactory relations with Germany than any other course.

But he warned of one road which would be disastrous:

> That is the road paved with graceful British concessions – concessions made without any conviction either of their justice or of their being set off by equivalent counter-services. The vain hopes that in this manner Germany can be 'conciliated' and made more friendly must be definitely given up.

Crowe's memorandum can be regarded as the key document of British policy before 1914, which amounted to accepting the expansion of German influence and power in the world, as long as it was peaceful; provided, that is, that it did not violate vital British interests either directly or indirectly, nor tried to upset the then existing balance of power in Europe and in the world. Crowe was against a policy of concessions, merely to 'conciliate' (we would now say 'appease') Germany on her road to more power. British policy of containing Germany could only lead to collision if Germany were to bear out the worst suspicions and fears of Crowe and his group.

No one who knows the course of German history since Bismarck or the attitude of pre-1914 Germany (as reflected both in the writings of the time and in the minds of the present older generation) can doubt that Crowe's assessment, on the whole, was to the point, was just and fair. Even if Crowe had not read Max Weber's Inaugural Lecture of 1895 and had not known Müller's ideas on Germany's *Zukunftspolitik*, even if one were to dismiss the Pan-Germans as representing the 'lunatic fringe' in German society (which they certainly were not), he could not have known the revealing German counterpart of his own analysis of the situation and of the German mind, since it was published only some years later.

Kurt Riezler is not a figure whose historical relevance can easily be ignored or belittled; he came from a respectable, well-educated family, was the young but influential adviser of the Chancellor, Bethmann-Hollweg, and had written two important books, couched in the traditional (and often unreadable) jargon of German philosophical idealism. His second book, published under a pseudonym, appeared just before the outbreak of the First World War and reflects the position of the most liberal and peaceful wing of German patriotism. Nevertheless, in it Riezler gave expression to the widespread Social Darwinism of the time and he seems certainly to have been influenced by Max Weber, the greatest intellect of German Liberal Imperialists. It is not surprising that for the same reason Riezler, in spite of his criticism of the Pan-Germans over details of policy, betrayed many affinities with them over basic questions of German *Weltanschauung*. In many respects Riezler confirmed Crowe's analysis of the German mind before 1914, as did Müller's almost twenty years earlier.

For Riezler there was no question of a rational principle which would allow or make desirable the peaceful co-existence of nations, small and large. He not only fell back on a Hobbesian philosophy of war of all against all, but even proclaimed the theory that the eternal struggle – not for survival, but for obtaining world domination – was the supreme aim of all nations. If this was true of all nations, then it applied to the Germans:

> Ideally, every nation wants to grow, to expand, to rule and to subject [others] without end, wants to coalesce and to incorporate ever more [nations], wants to become an even more powerful unit, until the Universe has, under its own rule, become one organic unit.

In his next book, Riezler went as far as to use the precise term

for this circumlocution – 'world domination' – as the supreme
prize in the political struggle. It is logical that for Riezler
enmity was the underlying principle governing the relations
between nations, a principle which could only be temporarily
modified by tactics and expediency. In his more popular book,
he pleaded for the supremacy of German *Kultur* in the world by
endorsing the Kaiser's view that the world should one day be
healed by German ideas and methods. Like Max Weber,
Riezler saw in Germany's economic expansion the impulse
towards German *Weltpolitik*; he also saw in the foundation of the
Reich by Bismarck in 1871 the basis for further political
expansion:

> The young German Empire pushed out into the world. Its
> population grows annually by 800,000–900,000 people, and
> for these new masses food must be found, or, what amounts
> to the same, work. . . . The economic interest had to be
> followed by the political. The enormous potential and
> achievement of the rising nation pushed the young Empire
> into its *Weltpolitik* . . . Germany's unification was, on the one
> hand, a culmination of the national development, a fulfilment
> of national aspirations. On the other hand, it was the
> beginning of a new development, the germ for new, more
> far-reaching aspirations. Just as in the strivings of the
> individual, so in the aspirations of the nations there is neither
> culmination nor end. Parallel to the increasing interest in
> *Weltpolitik*, German nationalism orientated itself towards
> *Weltpolitik*. The demands of the German nation for power
> and prestige, not only in Europe, but throughout the world,
> have increased rapidly.

But Riezler feared that Germany's territorial basis in Europe
for pursuing her *Weltpolitik* was too narrow. He wanted to free
the Reich from Bismarck's *cauchemar des coalitions* by making
Germany so powerful that, in the interest of her *Weltpolitik*, she
would have the chance of victory in 'any possible constellation',
thus deterring any possible combination of adversaries or rivals
throughout the world. And Riezler concluded his analysis of
German *Weltpolitik*, which he took for granted:

Hemmed in by unfavourable frontiers, it [the German nation] needs to display great power, so long as it is obstructed in many ways from freely pursuing its *Weltpolitik*. For the sake of freedom in its world policy it must be guarded against any eventuality. It cannot allow those spheres of activity to be blocked which are still open for its world policy. The attempt to contain this policy might be temporarily successful, but in the long run it will fail because of the nation's effective power and its tremendous *élan vital*.

Riezler's philosophy amounted to a thinly disguised claim to German world domination to be attained in successive stages. His views, which were still the more 'moderate', 'soft' version of the prevalent German *Weltanschauung* of the time, were bound to produce war, once translated into practical policy. For on the one hand, it was unlikely that the other Powers would passively allow Germany to advance towards world domination; on the other hand, Riezler apparently saw even a policy of containment as hostile obstruction, which would be brushed aside by Germany's 'effective power and its tremendous *élan vital*'.

THE GROWING CRISIS

German *Weltpolitik*, the containment policy of the Entente and Germany's refusal to be contained made war inevitable. The elements of containment became apparent from the time of the Entente Cordiale of 1904. Germany's first political reaction of significance was the move against France over Morocco in 1905–6. It would have been a success but for German insistence on a fully fledged international conference to underscore the German diplomatic triumph, after Delcassé's fall under German pressure. The Bosnian crisis of 1908–9 brought another temporary victory for Germany, when Serbia was dropped by Russia under the veiled threat of German mobilisation against Russia. But Russian humiliation was such that a repetition of the same manoeuvre was unlikely to be successful – as Prince Bülow, then German Chancellor, claims to have warned his Sovereign while taking his farewell after his dismissal in 1909.

The second crisis over Morocco in 1911 was in many ways a repetition of the first, but this time without the initial German success. The dispatch of the German gunboat *Panther* to Agadir produced anxieties in Britain, and British warnings, expressed by Lloyd George in his famous Guildhall speech, were prompter and clearer this time than ever before or after. When Italy and Austria refused to support Germany on her course of collision, Germany backed down with the help of a face-saving compromise, which gave her some additional territory in the Cameroons. The net effect of German endeavours was to weld together the Triple Entente, and to raise a new spirit of national defiance in France. Sir Edward Grey, the British Foreign Secretary, and Paul Cambon, the French Ambassador in London, exchanged their famous letters in which they promised to co-ordinate the foreign policy of their countries in future periods of crisis, while arrangements for naval and military co-operation between Britain and France were made in the event of a German attack against France. The possibility of Germany's trying to breach Belgian neutrality was seriously considered and co-operation with the Belgian General Staff sought for that contingency.

The effect of the German diplomatic defeat in the second Moroccan crisis was even more dramatic in Germany: German propaganda, from now on, loudly proclaimed that the Reich was 'encircled' by the Entente Powers, by a coalition of envious and mischievous Powers, who were only waiting for their chance to overwhelm the Central Powers. Probably the first, at any rate the best-known, expression of the new 'encirclement' complex had come a few years before from Field-Marshal Count Schlieffen, the prolific ex-Chief of the Prussian General Staff. In his famous article 'Der Krieg in der Gegenwart', written as early as January 1909, we find most of the relevant clichés gathered together: Britain envious of Germany's economic and industrial progress, France thirsting for revenge, Russia full of Slav resentment against the Teuton, treacherous Italy lined up against Austria. They had all built up powerful fortresses around unprotected Germany and Austria-Hungary.

An endeavour is afoot to bring all these Powers together for a concentrated attack on the Central Powers. At the given moment, the drawbridges are to be let down, the doors are to be opened and the million-strong armies let loose, ravaging and destroying, across the Vosges, the Meuse, the Niemen, the Bug and even the Isonzo and the Tyrolean Alps. The danger seems gigantic.

These were not just the wild rantings of a frustrated retired general, who had never had the chance of conducting a great battle in actual warfare, but views shared by many of the Wilhelmine Establishment. Schlieffen's successor, General Moltke, to whom Schlieffen had sent the manuscript of his article before publication, warmly praised it. The Minister of War, General Einem, had nothing against publication and merely suggested that Schlieffen should discuss his article before publication with the Foreign Ministry (which he did not do). The Kaiser read the article aloud to his commanding generals on 2 January 1909 and commented with a succinct 'Bravo'.

The naval equivalent of Schlieffen's hair-raising nightmare has recently been well described by Jonathan Steinberg as the 'Copenhagen complex', the almost obsessive fear of many Germans that the British fleet might attack the German fleet any day without warning, in order to cripple the unwelcome commercial and naval rival. Those fears arose even before *Weltpolitik*, at a time when there was virtually no German fleet in existence. The German fear of 'encirclement', as outlined above, was mistaken – and there are reasons to doubt whether the German leaders themselves believed in the 'fairy tale of encirclement' (H. Kantorowicz). In any case, at least some of them seem to have realised that the Entente Powers, with their sometimes conflicting aims (Persia, Constantinople), had no aggressive intentions. In the comparatively quiet pre-*Weltpolitik* and pre-Entente days, in early December 1894, Holstein had countered the argument that a successful war might help to establish the Kaiser's personal rule by pointing out to Eulenburg that there was 'little prospect just now of a defensive war, for no one wants to do us any harm'. The exact wording recurs just over one decade later: one of the most capable and level-headed German diplomats, Count Metternich, wrote to his government in 1905 during the first crisis over Morocco: 'If we eliminate the problem of Morocco, our position in the world will be completely unchallenged, for no one wants to do us any harm.' In 1910 Alfred von Kiderlen-Wächter, rated as one of the most brilliant German Foreign Secretaries, went even further: 'If we do not provoke the war, others will hardly do so.'

Schlieffen concluded his alarmist article of 1909 on a more sober note, admitting that war might be delayed or, indeed, might not break out at all, as the 'enemies' were still hesitating. The Pan-Germans seem to have shared the sentiment, even after the second crisis over Morocco. In November 1913 one of their leaders, the retired General Gebsattel, wrote in a memorandum for the Kaiser and the Chancellor that the Entente Powers were unlikely to take the initiative in starting a war (which Gebsattel fervently hoped for in order to improve the domestic situation in the Reich), since they would not dare to attack Germany. In the early days of July 1914 there was no talk in Berlin of an immediate danger of attack from the other Powers. On the contrary, their present peaceful intentions were given by the government as arguments for the policy of localisation.

Those Germans who sincerely believed in the threat constituted by 'encirclement' – and this was the overwhelming majority – clearly misunderstood the intentions of the Entente. But German public opinion by now understood well enough that to become a World Power within a short time, and in opposition to the established Powers, could not be achieved without conflict. The answer, however, was not drastically to revise or forgo *Weltpolitik*, pursued now for half a generation; rather the widespread German desire to achieve the breakthrough must be intensified. In the years before 1914 public opinion was characterised by a strange mixture of pride in Germany's growing power and gloom about the future, of the obsessive will to push ahead with *Weltpolitik* and of Germany's *weltpolitishe Angst*.

THE GERMAN CONCEPT OF A PREVENTIVE WAR

The only major modification of German foreign policy was that introduced by Bethmann-Hollweg. While armaments were increased in both the military and naval sectors, German efforts were concentrated on the Continent itself. At the same time, Berlin sought to improve relations with London, hoping to bring about by means of peripheral agreements not involving concessions on German naval armaments – such as the Baghdad Railway and the future of Portuguese colonies – an understanding with Britain that would keep the latter neutral in a continental war. Such a war was thought to be inevitable and imminent by many circles within Germany. Leading German geographers, especially Friedrich Ratzel, had taught that growing populations needed growing territories, that industrialised countries needed *Ergänzungsräume*, i.e. colonial or quasi-colonial territories of lower population density. Eminent German historians had helped to implant the idea that Germany in a changing world had either to stagnate and be relegated to the status of a minor Power, or to promote herself to the status of a firmly established World Power. They saw Germany as a fortress besieged by enemies, and as they felt the ring around Germany drawing closer and closer the idea of a sudden desperate charge out of the fortress become respectable.

The logical consequence was the concept of preventive war. Objectively, German fears were unfounded. But the more Russia recovered her former military strength after her defeat at the hands of Japan and the revolution of 1904–5, the more urgently the idea of preventive war was formulated in Germany. The agitation of the Pan-Germans more or less openly accused the Imperial government of cowardice for not taking the plunge. General Bernhardi's widely read book, which appeared in several impressions before 1914, spoke openly of the next war. It is true that the group round Richard von Kühlmann, Secretary of State in the Foreign Ministry in 1917–18, did plead meekly for a *Weltpolitik* without war. But the Chancellor, Bethmann-Hollweg, although after 1945 credited with having subscribed to such a programme, apparently could not and did not dare to come out in the open with what was, by German standards, a near-pacifist line: he was afraid of a new outburst of Pan-German agitation which might have endangered his position. Ruedorffer's (Riezler's) book, which, until recently, also belonged to those books that are more often quoted than read, was equally far from advocating a peaceful German policy, as he was accused of before 1945 and praised for since then in Germany. He only warned of Pan-German impatience and pleaded for a more temperate pursuit of *Weltpolitik*.

Traditional German historians have always angrily denied the existence of the concept of preventive war in Germany before 1914. There is, however, sufficient evidence to support the view that it not only existed but also exercised a strong influence on German policy. It is natural that preventive war should have found its keenest champions among the military, whereas the government, following the post-1871 tradition of Bismarck, was reluctant. It is also significant that the concept of preventive war very soon included an attack through neutral Belgium. At the beginning of German *Weltpolitik*, in 1897, there existed a plan – initiated by the Kaiser and seriously discussed by the navy – to seize Antwerp by sea in a sudden commando raid, without any declaration of war, and to hold it until troops were marched through Belgium. For Antwerp was thought to be important for mounting an invasion of Britain. The idea was quietly dropped, not on moral grounds or because international law would have been violated, but for technical reasons. In the event, the seizure of Liège in the first days of the First World War took the place of a *coup* against Antwerp.

During the Russo-Japanese War at least part of the German General Staff were for seizing the chance of a preventive war against Russia, weakened by war and revolution. Even if Count Schlieffen, Chief of the General Staff, had not been a member of the war party, at least junior officers on the General Staff were vaguely for war, and Groener after 1919 proudly confessed that even after 1919 he supported the concept of preventive war. General Einem, Prussian Minister of War, boasts in his memoirs that he had supported the Chancellor, Bülow, in his struggle against Delcassé, hoping fervently then that the matter would be decided by the sword: 'Militarily, the situation then was more favourable for us than at any other moment.' Schlieffen's successor, Count Moltke, was of even softer metal than Schlieffen. But as 1914 approached he became more and more outspoken about the need for a war. Just before the peaceful settlement of the second Moroccan crisis he deplored the fact that the chance had been lost to seek a showdown with Britain:

If we again slink out of this affair with our tail between our legs, if we cannot pull ourselves together to present demands which we are prepared to enforce by the sword, then I despair of the future of the German Reich. Then I shall resign. But first I shall ask that we abolish the army and put ourselves under the protectorate of Japan.

In the summer of 1911 Kiderlen-Wächter, Secretary of State in the Foreign Ministry, pursued a policy which his formal superior, the Chancellor, Bethmann-Hollweg, was not sure aimed at war or not. He could only find out by making Kiderlen-Wächter drink heavily one night. The Secretary, according to Riezler's diary, did not aim at war under all circumstances (and in fact did avoid war on that occasion), but even the comparatively mild Bethmann-Hollweg was then convinced that a war was necessary for the German nation. Apart from the Social Democrats and the left-wing Liberals, the parliamentary spokesmen of the German nation apparently were of the same opinion. For, in the great Reichstag debate after the settlement of the crisis, the Conservative and National Liberal parties were furious at the Chancellor because he had disappointed a nation which had been ready for war. It was on this occasion, on 9 November 1911, that August Bebel, the veteran leader of the SPD, gave his impressive warning of a general war and its revolutionising effects. But his warning was laughed at and went unheeded. One heckler in Parliament is recorded to have interrupted him with the words: 'After every war things are better!' Only a few months later, on 2 February 1912, Spahn, the leader of the Catholic Centre Party, construed in the Reichstag the precise situation which was to lead to war in August 1914: Austria would attack Serbia, Russia would support Serbia. Spahn interpreted Russian assistance as aggression against Germany, so that the *casus foederis* would arise for Germany as well.

After the second Moroccan crisis the disposition towards war in Germany only increased. The pre-war diaries of Admiral Müller give the impression that leading circles in Germany were obsessed with the inevitability of a great war, without admitting that they themselves, by their own *Weltpolitik*, created the essential conditions for it. During the crisis the

Kaiser had told Müller in an argument on whether the German navy was prepared for war or not:

> Its unpreparedness has always been objected to me in a moment of crisis. Now, in any case, is the moment for action. The people demand it. If the Chancellor and Kiderlen and Wermuth [Secretary of State for Finance] do not want to comply, they will be sacked. The Chancellor should inform himself better of the mood of the people.

Admiral Müller himself was convinced that war with Britain could not be avoided in the long run. One of his reasons for preferring to see the showdown postponed for the time being was that the Kiel Canal, which would have allowed the free passage of German capital ships from the Baltic to the North Sea, was still under construction. The Canal was finished in June 1914.

During the First Balkan War the Kaiser suddenly recognised Serbian aspirations and was for holding back Austria against Serbia. But on 8 December 1912, the Kaiser, Müller, Tirpitz and the Chiefs of the General and the Naval Staffs held a kind of war council. Prince Lichnowsky, the new German Ambassador in London, had reported a warning of Haldane's that, if Germany were to attack France, Britain would have to come to the aid of France. The Kaiser welcomed this declaration, because it clarified the situation, and went on to outline the shape of things to come:

> Austria had to act vigorously against the foreign Slavs [Serbs], because she would otherwise lose her power over the Serbs in the Austro-Hungarian Monarchy. If Russia were to support the Serbs [Sazonov's declaration: Russia would immediately invade Galicia, if Austria were to invade Serbia], war would be inevitable for us. . . . The Fleet, of course, would have to face the war against Britain.

The Kaiser's analysis, it should be noted, is the same as that made by Spahn only ten months before. Moltke's reaction to his Sovereign's expectations is typical: 'In my opinion war is inevitable, and the sooner the better.' But he advised that 'the popularity of a war against Russia as outlined by the Kaiser, should be better prepared' in the Press. The Kaiser agreed and gave instructions accordingly. Admiral Müller himself passed on the Imperial injunction to the Chancellor, who had not even attended that important policy-making meeting: 'to enlighten the people through the Press of the great national interest, which would be at stake also for Germany, if a war were to break out over the Austro-Serbian conflict'. The reason is simple:

> The people must not be in the position of asking them-selves only at the outbreak of a great European war, what are the interests that Germany would be fighting for. The people ought rather to be accustomed to the idea of such a war beforehand.

One week later the Chancellor too had apparently 'accus-tomed' himself 'to the idea of such a war', as the Kaiser told Admiral Müller. He expressed his surprise because Bethmann-Hollweg had said one year earlier that he could never advise a war.

Again two weeks later the Kaiser related his conversation with the Belgian King Albert to Moltke and Bethmann-Hollweg. When Wilhelm II and Albert had met in Munich on 19 December 1912, Albert had expressed anxieties over a possible threat to Belgian neutrality, but the Kaiser assured him that 'his desire was only to have the right flank safeguarded in the case of war'. By now the Chancellor must have learned of the German intention to march through Belgium at the beginning of the war. For Moltke replied to the Kaiser's account:

> He has to consider the situation. Our plan of deployment against France is based, as is well known (*bekanntlich*), on our advance through Belgium. Nothing could be changed in regard to the deployment.

The following year gave ample opportunity to 'accustom people to the idea of such a war'. The centenary of the war of 1813 and the twenty-fifth anniversary of the Kaiser's reign occasioned military and academic ceremonies all over Germany during 1913, and was perhaps the emotional climax of Wilhelmine Germany before 1914. But in early 1913 the German government did not yet want to risk a great war. On 10 February, both Moltke and Bethmann-Hollweg warned their respective Austrian counterparts in separate letters of the danger of making war with Serbia at the present moment over the Albanian question. Moltke expressed his conviction 'that a European war is bound to come sooner or later, in which the issue will be one of a struggle between Germandom and Slavdom', and he proclaimed: 'To prepare themselves for that contingency is the duty of all States which are the champions of Germanic ideas and culture (*Geisteskultur*).' But he warned Conrad von Hötzendorf, the Austrian Chief of Staff, that the great war 'necessitates the readiness of the people to make sacrifices, and popular enthusiasm', and therefore he was against provoking war with Serbia, especially after Serbia had gone back on her Albanian demands. Now, Moltke wrote, it would be difficult for Germany to 'find an effective slogan' for a great war. At the same time, he told the Austrian Military Attaché in Berlin: 'When starting a world war one has to think very carefully.'

In his letter to Berchtold, the Austrian Minister of Foreign Affairs, the Chancellor raised two other points which became relevant in the crisis of July 1914: Russian intervention in the case of Austria attacking Serbia, and British neutrality:

After analysing the situation objectively, one has to conclude that, considering her traditional relations with the Balkan States, it will be nearly impossible for Russia passively to watch military action by Austria against Serbia without a tremendous loss of face. The exponents of a pacific orientation, whom we can see no doubt in Messrs Kokovzov and Sazonov, would be simply swept away by the indignation of public opinion, if they were to try to resist it. The consequences of Russian intervention, however, are obvious. They would result in a warlike conflict of the Triple Alliance – probably without enthusiastic support by Italy – against the Triple Entente, and Germany would have to bear the full brunt of the French and British attack.

Bethmann-Hollweg hoped instead for a 'reorientation of British policy' – in other words, for a drifting apart or even disintegration of the Triple Entente, which would automatically improve prospects for the Triple Alliance:

The British attitude [in the Balkan crisis] is only one of several symptoms which suggest that the Entente has passed its climax and that we may look forward to a reorientation of British policy if we succeed in emerging from this crisis without conflicts. These are, of course, developments which are just beginning and which will take some time to bear fruit. But to precipitate a violent solution – even if some interests of the Austrian–Hungarian Monarchy were to demand one – at the very moment when we seem to have the chance, if only a remote one, to have the conflict under conditions much more favourable for us, would be, in my opinion, a mistake of incalculable consequences.

Only seventeen months later the 'much more favourable conditions' for the showdown seemed to have arrived: the treaties over the Baghdad Railway and over the future of the Portuguese colonies as a further step towards the creation of a German *Mittelafrika*, and the visit of a British naval squadron to Kiel in June 1914, seemed to inaugurate a new phase of Anglo-German co-operation and to offer the chance of eventual British neutrality in a continental war. If neutrality were not to be had, at least the Kiel Canal had been completed by now.

Meanwhile, the diplomatic crisis over the Second Balkan War provoked new outbursts of warlike sentiment behind the scenes in Germany. During the spectacular ceremony at Leipzig, when the great monument in memory of the Battle of Leipzig in 1813 was unveiled, the Kaiser told the Austrian Chief of Staff, Baron Conrad, that he supported Austria against the Serbs:

I am with you there. The other [i.e. the other Powers] are not prepared, they will not do anything against it. Within a few days you must be in Belgrade. I was always a partisan of peace; but this has its limits. I have read much about war and know what it means. But finally a situation arises in which a Great Power can no longer just look on, but must draw the sword.

About the same time, the Kaiser commented on Berchtold's appreciation of German support for an Austrian *démarche* in Belgrade and the hope expressed that the Serbs would give in forthwith, so that extreme measures would be unnecessary, with the words: 'This would be very regrettable! Now or never! For once things down there have to be put right and calm restored!' The Kaiser's patience was apparently wearing thin, and he voiced some sentiments which were to reappear in July 1914 – even the magic formula of 'Now or never!' While the government did not dare openly to embrace the course of '*Weltpolitik* and no war', in late 1913 they came under pressure from the Pan-Germans, this time mainly for reasons of domestic policy. The elections of 1912 had made the SPD the strongest party in the Reichstag; the policy of *Weltpolitik* for diverting the attention of the masses from the Socialists had apparently failed. (In fact it had only superficially failed because the SPD in the process had become largely nationalist in their turn, as not only the war in 1914 was to show.) This is why some circles now returned to the old idea of a *coup* against Reichstag and Constitution. After legislation for a massive expansion of the army had been passed by the Reichstag in the summer of 1913, the Pan-Germans stepped up their campaign against the Chancellor.

In October 1913 their leaders sent an important memorandum to the Crown Prince, whose Pan-German sympathies were notorious; he passed it on to the Kaiser in mid-November at the peak of the crisis over the Zabern incident. The memorandum suggested the abolition of the Constitution, the suppression of freedom of the Press and discriminatory legislation aimed at the Jews; and it accused the government of wanting to preserve peace at any price. Even an unsuccessful war would be preferable to a 'long and cowardly peace'. Since the other Powers would hardly attack Germany, the Reich had to take the initiative. While Bethmann-Hollweg, in a long letter to the Kaiser, rejected all the concrete proposals of the Pan-Germans, he revealed that he did not differ basically from them on some points, but differed rather on tactics and emphasis. He merely maintained that what counted was to be successful: a *coup* against the Reichstag would fail, because it would start a civil war which in its turn would lead to war with foreign Powers. The Chancellor also rejected the charge of wanting to preserve peace at any price. He could envisage only two cases in which he would advocate war: if the 'honour and dignity of Germany were to be affected by another nation', which had not happened so far, according to Bethmann-Hollweg, and if he could 'envisage vital aims for the nation' which 'could not be accomplished without war'. As examples he quoted Bismarck's wars: 'In order to accomplish such tasks and aims Bismarck wanted, and made, the wars of 1864, 1866 and 1870.'

One such 'vital aim' for Germany was to achieve the status of a World Power on an equal footing with the others. It was Riezler who formulated this in 1914, a few weeks before the outbreak of war. Although the geographical basis was apparently too narrow for such a course, he insisted that

> *Weltpolitik* must nevertheless be pursued . . . German policy must escape the *circulus vitiosus*. It cannot opt for a purely continental policy. The task which arises out of the situation is the essential problem of the foreign policy of the German Reich. Everything that happens can be interpreted as an attempt at its solution.

And what was the supreme task of German policy? To make the Reich stronger than any combination of possible enemies. Such a *Lebensaufgabe*, to quote Bethmann-Hollweg, was, of course, impossible without war: of this others besides Riezler were well aware. Again, the final logic points to preventive action, before the potential enemies were strong enough to prevent German expansion, which would sweep away the barriers of containment.

The tensions with Russia over the mission of the German General Liman von Sanders to Turkey had hardly abated when Moltke was pressing more urgently than ever before for an early war. He was especially worried about the military recovery of Russia. On 12 May 1914 he spoke to Conrad at

Carlsbad about the possibility of war. According to Conrad he said that 'any delay meant a lessening of our chances; we could not compete with Russia in masses'. The same obsession with Russian armaments was revealed a few days later by a conversation between Jagow and Moltke, on either 20 May or 3 June 1914, when both travelled in Moltke's car from Potsdam to Berlin. Moltke feared that Russia would have built up maximum armaments in two or three years and thought no other way was left but to 'wage a preventive war in order to beat the enemy while we still have some chance of winning'. Moltke, therefore, advised Jagow 'to orientate our policy at the early provocation of a war'. Jagow refused, pointing to the steady improvement of Germany's economic situation, but after the war he admitted that he himself 'never condemned in principle and *a limine* the idea of the preventive war'. In his view even Bismarck's wars had been preventive. It is perhaps as a consequence of this conversation between Moltke and Jagow that Bethmann-Hollweg spoke with the Bavarian Minister in Berlin, Count Lerchenfeld, early in June 1914, about 'the preventive war demanded by many generals'. When Lerchenfeld objected that the right moment had passed already, the Chancellor agreed, but added:

> There are circles in the Reich who expect of a war an improvement in the domestic situation in Germany – in a conservative direction. He, the Chancellor, however, thought that on the contrary a world war with its incalculable consequences would strengthen tremendously the power of Social Democracy, because they preached peace, and would topple many a throne.

In spite of his correct insight into the consequences of a world war, Bethmann-Hollweg was either too weak or too inconsistent to translate his theoretically sound judgement into practical politics. Apparently he was the prisoner of the tradition of *Weltpolitik*, now nearly two decades old, of some of his own ideas and of his surroundings: he himself was no longer in principle against a war, and he was ready to fight one to accomplish the great, vitally important aims of the nation. Riezler had pointed to one such vital aim – the need to broaden the basis for pursuing the *Weltpolitik*. Moltke pressed for an early preventive war, and Jagow was not against it in principle. The Pan-Germans and most political parties accused him of cowardice, while the Kaiser oscillated.

The Kaiser's person was an additional reason for Jagow's hesitation to risk a preventive war, because he thought Wilhelm II would not have the strength to see a great war right through. A similar view had been expressed by Tschirschky, the German Ambassador in Vienna, a few months earlier. When, on 16 March 1914, Conrad suggested an early war against Russia, Tschirschky objected: 'Two important people are against it, your Archduke Franz Ferdinand and my Kaiser.' Tschirschky added that only under compulsion of a *fait accompli* would they resolve to go to war.

On 28 June 1914, one of the two obstacles to war had been removed – Archduke Franz Ferdinand. His murder provided Berlin with the chance to 'find an effective slogan' in Germany for a great war, for which the German nation had been psychologically and materially prepared since at least December 1912. The showdown came at a time when the German 'chance . . . to have the conflict under conditions much more favourable' than in February 1913 seemed to be brighter than ever before.

AUSTRIA-HUNGARY AND SERBIA: THE ASSASSINATION OF ARCHDUKE FRANZ FERDINAND

The spark which set off the First World War sprang from the apparently only secondary field of tension between Serbia and Austria-Hungary. In reality there lay concealed beneath this the secular conflict between the dynastic, supranational, conservative idea of State and the modern national revolutionary and national democratic principle of self-government, which in its many different forms has determined the course of world history from the French Revolution down to the present day – a conflict which opens up perspectives of a universal historical nature far beyond and above the mere consideration of the question of 'war guilt'.

The Danube Monarchy had had to contend with the problem of the emergent nations, in one form or another, throughout the nineteenth century. As the successor to the Holy Roman Empire of the German nation on southern European soil, the Habsburg Monarchy had never been able to come to terms with a modern world of heterogeneous nationalities all agitating for emancipation. As far back as 1859, in circumstances strikingly similar to those which led to the First World War in 1914, she had been defeated by a national revolutionary movement allied with a European Great Power – the then emergent Italy, which could count upon active support from France under Napoleon III. Then, to be sure, Austria had only lost the greater part of her Italian possessions, but the loss left behind an incurable resentment against the liberal, national revolutionary Italy of the Risorgimento. At least as important as this was the Austrian quest for a substitute for Venetia and Lombardy. Almost two decades later the Danube Monarchy found itself in occupation of Bosnia-Hercegovina, which only intensified the underlying problem. With the occupation and annexation respectively of these two south Slav provinces (in 1878 and 1908), the Danube Monarchy incorporated the political explosive which was to cause its destruction in 1918. Yet it was the south Slav nationalists, above all, who were struck by the example of Piedmont and the need to win the support of a Great Power in the struggle against Austria. The same combination as in 1859 – a national revolutionary movement inside Austria and its support by an already existing national State, receiving help in turn from a Great Power – led in 1914–18 to the collapse of the Danube Monarchy.

Since the almost total elimination of the Italian element after the war of 1859, the Danube Monarchy found itself confronted with the nationalist movements of the Slavs, mainly south Slavs and Czechs. After the defeat in 1866 in the internal war for German hegemony, the Habsburgs could only prevent the secession of the Magyars by allowing them to share power with the Germans who had, in effect, had a monopoly of power up till then. For the Hungarians, and more especially the powerful and self-assertive Magyar aristocracy, it was in the interest of survival to keep down the south Slavs. The reorganisation of the Imperial State into the Dual Monarchy by means of the Compromise of 1867 (which had to be endorsed and modified every ten years in laborious negotiations) gave the Magyar aristocracy a kind of veto over Vienna. Even the threat of withdrawal from the Imperial Alliance would have been enough to block any kind of federal or democratic reform which could have undermined the dualism of Austrians and Magyars or even granted to the Slav nationalities complete equality of rights.

For decades Austria-Hungary had been content with a system of 'muddling through' which had led to a state of complete political paralysis. As a result of her anachronistic construction and concomitant stagnation, she had from the turn of the century drifted helplessly into the maelstrom of the Slav nationalist movement. After the overthrow of the Obrenović dynasty in 1903 the Serbs constituted the most dynamic element in the Balkans and, as such, the greatest threat to the Danube Monarchy; for the immediate aims of unification of the Serbs with Montenegro, parts of Macedonia and ultimately the south Slav provinces of the Danube Monarchy, Bosnia and Hercegovina, would inevitably result in the addition of Dalmatia, Croatia and Slovenia to an enlarged south Slav national State. The realisation of the national right of self-determination for south Slavs (whether of the Greater Serbian, Centralist or south Slav Federalist variety) thus constituted a threat to the Dual Monarchy if she failed to remodel herself in time into a federalist and democratic structure. The leading Austro-Hungarian statesmen were fully aware of the basic problem; thus Conrad von Hötzendorf wrote to the heir apparent, Archduke Franz Ferdinand, on 14 December 1912:

The unification of the south Slav race is one of the powerful national movements which can neither be ignored nor kept down. The question can only be, whether that unification will take place within the boundaries of the Monarchy – that is at the expense of Serbia's independence – or under Serbia's leadership at the expense of the Monarchy. The cost to the Monarchy would be the loss of its south Slav provinces and thus of almost its entire coastline. The loss of territory and prestige would relegate the Monarchy to the status of a small Power.

With his realistic analysis Conrad unwittingly anticipated the end of the Danube Monarchy, for it proved incapable of creating the necessary basis for a constructive solution; and the development of Serbia from 1903 onwards had already progressed too far for it still to be possible to compel a unification of the south Slavs with the increasingly self-assertive Serbs within the framework of the Danube Monarchy. The ruling class of Austria-Hungary, notoriously unable to adapt their conservative, dynastic régime to the exigencies of modern times, abandoned themselves to a chivalrous mood of decline: if their traditional positions of power could no longer be assured by political means, there was a wish at least to 'go down with honour'. For the ruling class, still adhering to their feudal modes of thought, this was only conceivable in a war, which it was hoped – against all reason – would somehow succeed in prolonging an existence which had long since become questionable.

The most influential exponent of this fatalistic conception of war was Conrad. He hoped to save the Danube Monarchy by a preventive war, at one moment against Italy, which although officially a member of the Triple Alliance sympathised with the south Slavs, and at the next against national democratic and national revolutionary Serbia herself.

Austria-Hungary had already on two occasions demonstrated her hostility to the expansion of Serbia and had even partially mobilised her army in the annexation crisis of 1908–9 and the Balkan wars of 1912–13. The tense atmosphere was shattered by the shots at Sarajevo on 28 June 1914. Several factors combined to make the outrage possible.

Franz Ferdinand, the heir apparent, had the reputation of wanting to reconstruct the Dual Monarchy into a Triadism, with the south Slav nationalities as the third pillar, thereby saving the situation and taking the wind out of the sails of south Slav nationalism. In the light of this the choice of the heir apparent as the victim of the assassination was certainly no coincidence, the less so since Franz Ferdinand made his entry into Sarajevo at the close of the manoeuvres in Bosnia on 28 June, the anniversary of the Battle of Kosovo in 1389.

The second factor was the south Slav movement emanating from Serbia. Earlier German and Austrian interpretations which take the guilt or complicity of the Serbian government as their point of departure do not stand up to examination. Still less tenable, if only because the murder was the most extreme and violent expression of south Slav nationalism, is the monstrous theory of collective guilt which attempts to pin the responsibility for the outrage of Sarajevo on to the Serbian people as a whole. Rather it would seem necessary to show careful discrimination: the outrage of Sarajevo was by no means the work of the Serbian government; in any case, the latter did not have enough knowledge of the plans to take preventive measures in time. On the contrary, Sarajevo was planned and organised by the extreme wing of Serbian nationalism, the secret society 'Death or Unification', better known under the name of the 'Black Hand'. This consisted of an association of nationalist officers, officials and intellectuals. In the summer of 1914 the 'Black Hand' was locked in a struggle with the Serbian government, which may have led to the fall of the head of the society, Colonel Dimitriević-Apix, Chief of the Military Secret Service.

In this tense situation the outrage resembled an attempt to plunge the more prudent government of the Old Radicals, under Nikola Pišić, headlong into the alternative of either submitting to the Austrians, with the subsequent risk of an armed revolution such as was frequently feared in the July crisis, or postponing its more cautious programme for the liberation of the south Slav provinces and taking on a war with Austria-Hungary instead.

Recent research has shown that Pašić had certainly heard rumours of arms smuggling over the frontier into Bosnia and that he consequently demanded an inquiry. Dimitriević-Apix, however, while conceding in a long written report to Pašić that the pistols emanated from army stores, claimed that they were only employed for the protection of his Secret Service agents in Bosnia. Despite this deliberate deception by Apix, Pašić did not allow matters to rest there and issued an order to the frontier authorities to prevent arms smuggling and the illicit entry of young men. In view of this, Apix attempted to call off the whole undertaking. Like the Norodna Odbrana, whose agent heard of the planned attempt, Apix tried at the last moment to put a stop to the outrage through his contact man with the group of conspirators in Sarajevo. The conspirators, however, with Gavrilo Princip at their head, refused to abandon their plan for assassinating the Archduke.

At this point a third factor comes into play: the perpetrators all came from Bosnia itself and were thus Austro-Hungarian subjects. They were much less blind and willing tools of the 'Black Hand' than has up till now generally been accepted in Germany and Austria. Princip and his circle of friends belonged to the national revolutionary movement among young intellectuals, students and schoolchildren, commonly known as 'Young Bosnia'. In contrast to the more exclusively Pan-Serbian ideas of the 'Black Hand', they stood for a south Slav, federal solution on the basis of equality for all south Slav groups. The idea of an attempt on the life of Franz Ferdinand in Sarajevo originated in 'Young Bosnian' circles, and merely happened to fit in with similar, but as yet uncrystallised ideas of the 'Black Hand' which finally took over the practical preparations for the attempt (such as procuring the weapons and equipment, training the accomplices, and helping them over the frontier). At the decisive point in the crisis, when Apix tried hard to prevent the outrage, it was Princip's firm determination to carry out the attempt at all costs that prevailed. In the last analysis, the murder at Sarajevo was thus primarily the deed of Princip himself and can only indirectly be charged to the 'Black Hand', and virtually not at all to the Serbian government (let alone the Serbian people).

In a deeper sense the ultimate responsibility falls on the ruling class in Austria-Hungary, less because it sent Franz Ferdinand into an 'alley of bomb-throwers' than on account of its inability to satisfy the legitimate struggle of their various nationalities for freedom, equality and social justice (a motive which is generally overlooked in the wholesale condemnation by Germany and Austria of the conspirators of Sarajevo). By their rigid adherence to outdated political and social conceptions, the traditional Powers left no room for the political agitations of the young south Slav intelligentsia who, in their desperation, were finally driven to the crime of political murder. No historical account seeking to do justice to the complicated events of July and August 1914 can any longer afford to ignore this important aspect, neglected for so long in

Germany and Austria. It becomes clear that the Austrian and German governments were in fact mistaken in their assumptions about the background to the outrage.

Sarajevo was the dramatic culmination of the conflict between the Danube Monarchy and the south Slav national movement which had been smouldering for so long. Everything now depended on how Austria-Hungary would react. The manner of her reaction could give rise to a confrontation with Russia, and create the constellation which would make world war inevitable, a constellation so accurately predicted by Spahn in February 1912, by Bethmann-Hollweg in February 1913 and by the Kaiser in October 1913.

3. 1914 – The Third Balkan War: Origins Reconsidered

JOACHIM REMAK

> Everything the statesman creates is perishable, and in the long run, every decision is wrong. If it were otherwise, we would have no 'history.'　　　　　　　　　　(Golo Mann)

Fritz Fischer's decade has ended. It began, neatly enough, in 1961 with *Der Griff nach der Weltmacht*, and drew to a close, in 1969, with *Krieg der Illusionen*. In between, there has been more discussion, scholarly and otherwise, than has been caused by any other single historian in our lifetime. Some of it has been stimulating. But the debate has just about run its course. Brecht's lines come to mind. I always hear Caesar did, Caesar conquered. Was not there at least a cook along?

> Phillipp von Spanien weinte, als seine Flotte Untergegangen war. Weinte sonst niemand?
> (Philip of Spain cried when his fleet had perished. Did no-one else cry?)

Were not there some Frenchmen, too, in 1914, or some Serbians, who wept or laughed? A book that contains forty-five references in the index to Matthias Erzberger, and eighty to Karl Helfferich, and none to Sir Mark Sykes and none to

From *Journal of Modern History*, 1971.

Georges Picot, makes an interesting discussion guide but not a complete one. (This quite aside from the fact that the war's aims and origins were not always precisely identical.)

Where, though, if we cannot make Fischer's convictions or those of his partisans our own, does the responsibility for the First World War lie? What have the sixties taught us? Which statesmen, which nations, must bear the blame for war? To answer these questions, let us consider, in ascending order – and in the grand historical perspective which the drying of the blood and the passage of well over half of a century should provide – the responsibility of each of the belligerents.

This direct, national approach will be an old-fashioned one, but the exclusion of supranational, long-range causes is deliberate. The reason is that the arguments and counter-arguments that can be made in connection with the latter too often cancel each other out. The alliance system, for instance, did contain a major danger of escalation; large nations, as has often been pointed out, were likely to be drawn into the quarrels of their lesser allies. Yet, to this one can reply that in the first place, alliances were not that binding in 1914; the Italians certainly did not think so. And one might add that if only the alliances had been firmer, if only, let us say, the Austrians had been totally certain that an attack on Serbia meant an attack on Russia, war might never have come that year.

Or there is the problem of imperialism. It is easy enough to show that it contributed to national antagonisms and to the atmosphere of violence in Europe and overseas. Yet when 1914 came, some of the fiercest colonial antagonists of former years found themselves fighting on the same side, as in the case of Britain and France, or of Britain and Russia. As for economic rivalries, these greatly added to the ill humour of Europe, but divergent national interests in the field of commerce did not make for armed conflict; in times of crisis, 1914 included, business-men on all sides were among the strongest advocates of peace.

As far as the roles of the press, of the arms race, or of militarism are concerned, the arguments and counter-arguments may not balance each other quite so neatly. But what is worth saying here is that problem-free ages are a myth, and that all these long-range factors were part and parcel of the mood and the realities of early twentieth-century Europe. This was the world in which the nations and their leaders had to operate, and the truly significant question is how well they did so – in the non-mythical, non-ideal continent they jointly inhabited.

On the other hand, history, in Pieter Geyl's fine phrase, is an 'argument without end', and another decade, or another year, may well see the rediscovery of the importance of the forces and trends so easily dismissed here.

FRANCE AND BRITAIN

The nation that, all these many decades later, can still be held least responsible for the outbreak of the war is France. This is so even if we bear in mind all the revisions of historical judgements, and all the revisions of these revisions, to which we have now been treated. And it is so even if we use Fischer's approach and ask ourselves just what the aims of France were in the years that preceded the war and after. Now it is true that some of the things that some of the French were making a bid for entailed the risk of war. More than a generation after Frankfurt, a majority of Frenchmen still had not reconciled themselves to the loss of Alsace and Lorraine. Poincaré and his friends were still pursuing what Boulanger had, except that they were doing so with greater intelligence, patience, tact and skill, and hence with greater effectiveness. The desire to undo the decision of Frankfurt was as powerful a motive force in France's system of alliances as any. Germany, to put the matter differently, did not wish for any territorial change in Europe between 1871 and 1914; France did. It was equally true that during the July crisis, France failed to urge restraint on St Petersburg. One cannot very well indict the Germans for their blank cheque to Austria without noting that the Russians held a similar piece of paper from France.

Yet how tentative and cautious the bid to recover the lost provinces was! When we consider the restraints that the French were imposing upon themselves in the pursuit of their aims, how minor the responsibility of France must appear. The French might mourn Strasbourg, but they were plotting no war to retake it. Even the most irreconcilable groups of Frenchmen were organising no Pan-Gallic movements; there was nothing in France to compare, for ambition and folly, with either the Pan-Slavs or the Pan-Germans. Also, all speculations about France's ultimate objectives have about them a certain irrelevancy. Perhaps France would, some day, have fought to avenge Sedan, perhaps France would not. We will never know. The fact is that the French, in August 1914, did not go to war for Alsace, but because the Germans, lacking the political imagination and the diplomatic skill to keep France neutral, first presented an unacceptable ultimatum and then began to march on Paris.

The French, in 1914, entered the war because they had no alternative. The Germans had attacked them. History can be very simple at times.

But if the French had no choice once the Schlieffen Plan had gone into effect, the British did. (The British public certainly thought so, and so did several members of the government.) What, then, was Britain bidding for in 1914? That question seems to matter more today than the point, discussed at such length in the twenties and thirties, of whether the British had given to the Germans sufficient notice of their intent to protect Belgium. That whole argument – and it includes the implication that if only the British *caveat* had been stronger, the Germans might have acted with greater restraint – strikes us as fairly unreal today. For no matter what Grey's precise words, or what his silences, any responsible German statesman must have known that it was a matter of vital interest to Great Britain whether France survived as a power, and who would control the channel ports of Belgium and France. The implications of the Entente Cordiale, and the very plain provisions of the Treaty of 1839, were quite sufficient warning here.

No, let us consider the British bid instead. What was involved here was no sudden, novel move, but something quite long range. There had taken place, in the half-century or so before the war, a tremendous expansion of British power, accompanied by a pronounced lack of sympathy for any similar ambitions on the part of other nations. If any nation was compensation-conscious, it was Great Britain; if the Austrians wished to occupy Bosnia, for instance, then the British must have Cyprus. Even without this particular diplomatic gambit, the British, between the 1870s and the turn of the century, were adding, adding, adding to their empire: Burma, Egypt, Uganda, Somililand, Kenya, Zanzibar, Rhodesia, the Boer Republic, all were flying the Union Jack. If any nation had truly made a bid for world power, it was Great Britain. In fact, it had more than bid for it. It had achieved it. The Germans were merely talking about building a railway to Baghdad. The Queen of England *was* Empress of India. If any nation had upset the world's balance of power, it was Great Britain.

The usually more modest appetites of others, however, were a different matter. That the French in Morocco or the Germans in South West Africa were doing quite as well as colonisers as were the British in Uganda was something that seemed very difficult to perceive through the London fog. British territorial acquisitions were a part of the progress of mankind; those of others were a menace to world peace and civilisation. Russia's desire for access to the Mediterranean was a provocation; 'Britannia Rule the Waves' reflected a noble and natural sentiment.

After the turn of the century, this attitude was directed with special force at Germany, although it was seldom made clear just what the Germans were to do with all *their* excess energy. Some of the British documents of the period convey an impression of near-hysteria in the face of a rising Germany, reaching from a British admiral's simple suggestion to sink the German fleet without warning to the more erudite memoranda of some of the senior officials of the Foreign Office decrying the German menace. Unfortunately, if one nation imagines for long enough that another is a menace – 'the natural enemy' was Sir Eyre Crowe's phrase – the likelihood is strong that the other nation will some day have to play the role it has been assigned.

Such a judgement does not exculpate the Germans, who had been willing to endorse a Balkan war that clearly contained the risk of a war in the West. As far as Great Britain's direct responsibility for the final crisis and the outbreak of hostilities is concerned, it is indisputably less than Germany's. It was units of the German army, not of the British navy, who were sending shells into Belgium. Before the guns had been moved into position, however, it can scarcely be said that the British did much better in restraining the Eastern member of the Triple

Entente than they would accuse the Germans of doing vis-à-vis Vienna. 'Will to war' is too grand and at the same time too elusive a term to use with any degree of comfort, but what do we do about the memory of what would happen a quarter of a century later? In 1938, when the British definitely did not wish war, their prime minister would hurry to Germany three times within the space of two weeks and negotiate peace under terms far worse than those of 1914 with a leader infinitely more dangerous than the Kaiser in his most Wagnerian moods. The lamps were not 'going out' (Lord Grey's celebrated figure of speech) in 1914. Many people, the author of the phrase included, were helping to put them out.

RUSSIA AND GERMANY

What, though, of Russia's will to war, or rather of the willingness to accept war as a possible means of policy? Here, too, our emphasis today may profitably be shifted away from some earlier assumptions. The Russian response to the Austrian threat against Serbia, as we know, consisted not only of mobilisation against Austria, but against Germany as well. Here, the argument went, was Russia's major responsibility for the war. She was the first great power to mobilise. Not only that, but the manner of her mobilisation frustrated all hopes for localising the conflict; what could the Germans do but react with military means. And above all, the Russian decision came at a time when mobilisation was understood to equal war.

Today, the argument seems only partly valid. For mobilisation did not automatically have to mean war – except to the Germans, that is, for whom each minute counted lest the Schlieffen Plan was to fail. For every other nation, peaceful alternatives existed even after the men had been called to arms.

Not that the old argument was wholly irrelevant. For the Tsar and his advisers, by their behaviour at the end of July, indicated very plainly that they were perfectly well aware that mobilisation, while not war, was more than a symbolic show of strength and was bound to be interpreted as an act of war by Germany. Then why did they go ahead with it? Because, and here again we owe much to Fischer and his approach of looking

at a nation's boldest dreams, it was a question of the whole
thrust of Russia's foreign policy over the decades that preceded
Sarajevo. The year 1914 was not the first time that Russia
refused to rule out the possibility of war in the pursuit of certain
long-range aims. Since the middle of the nineteenth century
Russia had been involved directly in two wars – the Crimean
War and the War of 1877–78 – indirectly in two more – the
Balkan Wars of 1912 and 1913 – and, directly or indirectly, in
crises too numerous to list, all with the intent of weakening the
empire of the Sultan to the benefit of that of the Tsar. It was a
policy that acted as an irritant to Austro-Russian relations;
threats to one's survival tend to annoy. Yet the Russians
persisted. It was Russia rather than Austria who was the
expansionist power in south-eastern Europe. The Annexation
Crisis was the exception, not the rule. Under ordinary circumstances, Austria had considerably more to fear from Russia's
Balkan ambitions than Russia had from Austria's, even if we
add the reservation that, customarily, Russian official policy
was more restrained and rational than some of the truly
extravagant Pan-Slav spokesmen would have liked. Customarily, for in July 1914, as it had on some previous occasions, the
borderline between Pan-Slavism and government policy once
more became blurred. If Serbia chose to resist Austria's
demands, then Russia would support its Slavic brethren. The
story of Germany's 'blank cheque' to Austria is well known, but
the Russians were doing no better at counselling caution on
Belgrade. On the contrary, St Petersburg was giving Serbia as
much reason to rely on Russian support as Berlin was giving
Austria to rely on that of Germany.

Perhaps the Russians had no real choice. Caution would
have equalled surrender, and 1908 was too recent a memory.
This time, the alternative to active military aid might indeed
have been a grave diminution of Russian influence, not only in
Serbia but throughout the Balkans. Certainly the Austrians
had had no reason to assume that Russia would merely look on,
let alone look the other way, while they were shooting their way
into Belgrade. Though if we say that, must we not in fairness
add that the Russians had no more right to expect the Germans
to acquiesce in a Habsburg fiasco?

Here it is, the question of German guilt. How do we deal with it, after Fischer? We deal with it in large part as non-revisionist historians have before – by simply saying that German responsibility for 1914 goes back at least to the 1890s, to the whole conduct of German diplomacy after Bismarck. The master's touch was shown by moderation, the touch of his successors by what Bismarck had accused post-Cavour Italy of: a large appetite and poor teeth. And to what did Germany's appetite really run after 1890? To 'world power', to rivalry with Britain, to a German Central Africa, to security against France? None of these policies had been thought through. Activity there was aplenty; what was lacking was a sense of purpose.

By 1914, as a result of all this ill-directed energy, a new spectre had come to haunt Europe, the spectre of *furor teutonicus*. German behaviour in the final crisis certainly did little to banish it. The list of German blunders is an all too familiar one: the blank cheque to Austria; the failure, once it had become plain that an Austro-Serbian war was likely to become European in scope, to search for a compromise with every last ounce of energy; the final triumph of the military over the political rationale with the invasion of Belgium and France. 'During the whole crisis prior to August 4, 1914,' writes a historian whose sympathies are anything but anti-German, 'not a single constructive move was made by Germany to stave off the impending disaster.'

The list is familiar, so familiar that we need to pause and see if there is not another side to it. Just what were Germany's motives in 1914? Was it really a bid for world power that impelled the Germans to court catastrophe?

Actually, Germany's motives were far less sinister than this, though that makes them no more wise. Motives, of course, are seldom unambiguous or simple, but two great desires seem to dominate Germany's actions. One was to maintain the Austrian alliance. The other was to use the Sarajevo crisis to register a spectacular diplomatic victory, to break what Berlin considered the noose of Allied encirclement. As for the defence of Austria, it was not only that the Germans were afraid, as has been said often enough, of losing their last ally. It was also that they feared that if Austria failed to cope with the crisis posed by Franz Ferdinand's assassination, the country would be finished as a great power. 'We must maintain Austria *proper*', was the way Bethmann-Hollweg put it in the summer of 1914. 'Were Russia to unleash the South Slavs, we would be lost.' As for the concurrent diplomatic coup, the Germans felt, and rightly so, that their luck was running out, that their prestige had seldom been lower, and that they faced an overwhelmingly hostile Europe. A show of strength – and on an issue where moral right appeared to be on their side, as it did after Sarajevo – might radically alter the situation. Bethmann's response to Sarajevo 'was determined by what he had long thought was Germany's precarious position, not by the immediate effects of the assassination itself. Sarajevo unrequited would worsen Germany's situation; Sarajevo properly exploited might lead to a dramatic escape from that situation.' Or, to quote the German Chancellor himself: if the gamble should succeed, 'if war does not break out, if the Tsar is unwilling or France, alarmed, counsels peace, we have the prospect of splitting the Entente.'

Too many ifs, we know. And besides, the German gamble was based on two major miscalculations. One was that Austria would act quickly, would 'move immediately in the wake of the murder'. There would thus be 'a rapid *fait accompli*, and afterwards friendship towards the Entente'. The other was that the worst risk the Germans were able to imagine was that of a limited, local war.

It was these two miscalculations that account for Germany's fearful part of the responsibility. These and the Schlieffen Plan, of course, which inevitably spread the war once the Austrians had made their leisurely move against Serbia, and the Russians would not be deterred from coming to that country's aid. And as the gamble started to go wrong, the diplomats found that there was no way to withdraw their stakes. What had begun as a diplomatic move (admittedly a risky one) had passed, in the nature of things, into the hands of the generals. 'We have lost control and the landslide has begun.'

It is here that Germany's guilt lies, not in dreams of world domination. It lies, to repeat, in risks taken that were immeasurably too high; in allowing military planners to dictate policy; and beyond that, in the general amateurishness that marked the nation's diplomatic behaviour in the quarter-century before Sarajevo. These things were quite bad enough. There is no need to add imaginary sins to real ones.

AUSTRIA, SOME BOSNIANS, AND SERBIA

But how had the Germans become involved in the first place? Through a minor and obscure Balkan quarrel? Yes, if by obscure we mean that it was insufficiently understood by outsiders, and by minor that no vital interests of the great powers were involved. To the two nations directly affected, however, to Austria and Serbia, few crises could have mattered more, or been clearer in their implications, than Sarajevo. And both nations behaved with great recklessness in 1914.

We have stood stooped over for too long now, searching for the underlying causes of the war. We have become so involved in subtleties that the obvious has sometimes escaped us; we have not seen the forest for the roots. The obvious fact is that the issue that led to Verdun and Versailles not only was Austro-Serb in origin, but that in the immediate crisis that followed, some of the most basic decisions affecting peace or war were made by Berchtold rather than Bethmann, and by Pašić rather than Sazonov.

It is a moot question which nation practised the worse sort of brinkmanship. Let us evade it by dealing with them in alphabetical order. As for Austria, then, it was the whole general direction of the Ballplatz's policy after Sarajevo, and the ultimatum of July 23 in particular, that invited war with Serbia, and the wider war as well. What an appalling document it was – tardy, incompetent, deceptive, designed to be rejected. Austria was setting the course, and neither friend nor foe had been allowed an honest look at its direction.

It is entirely possible, of course, to present a case for the defence. Sarajevo was no pretence; the Habsburg monarchy had some perfectly legitimate interests to defend – Serbia was a good deal closer to Austria than southeast Asia is to the United States. Surely, self-preservation is as sensible and honourable a motive as any, and the state one wished to maintain had a great deal to be said in its favour. 'All my libido is given to

Austria-Hungary', wrote Dr Freud the day after Serbia's reply had been received. Austria's decision meant 'liberation through a bold deed'.

What alternative did the Habsburg monarchy have? Its vital interests were involved, in a way those of no other European state were in 1914; not Russia's and not Germany's, not those of France nor of Great Britain. Of all of Europe's crises and conflicts, the Austro-Serbian issue was unique in that it seemed to allow no leeway between either surrender or war. None of the others had 'led to actions that produced war. They were either negotiable or repressible. The one problem that was neither negotiable nor repressible was that raised by threats to the integrity of Austria-Hungary.'

Still, to understand all is *not* to forgive all. It is true enough that, as a committee of distinguished French and German historians put it in 1952, 'the documents do not permit attributing, to any government or nation, a premeditated desire for European war in 1914'. But Berchtold and Conrad had very much of a premeditated desire for a simple Balkan war to recover some of the monarchy's lost prestige. Did they want that war to spread? No, but the truth was that the reckless and inadequate people who were deciding policy in Vienna did not really care. This was Austria's war; perhaps only the fact that the countrymen of Johann Strauss and Sigmund Freud ordinarily made such poor villains (there would be some fairly obvious exceptions such as Adolf Hitler) allowed that simple fact to be forgotten so thoroughly.

Austria's war, and Serbia's. Two Austrian victims, seven Bosnian assassins, and no-one can say to this day how many Serbian helpers. Sarajevo was more than an excuse for war. It was one of its major causes.

The assassins, in a sense, were innocents. Had he known that his deed might mean war, one of them said during his trial, he would have preferred his own death to that of his victims. But he was speaking for himself, not for Colonel Dimitrijević. Apis was a man who considered the consequences of his actions.

But to what extent did the involvement of Serbia's chief of military intelligence reflect on his government? The assassination, after all, had been planned by the Black Hand during the colonel's off-duty hours, and not by Pašić or any of his ministers. In fact, was not the crime largely a local affair, and is not the question whether any of the assassins even belonged to the Black Hand still unresolved?

Yes and no. Of course the act had its local roots. It involved Young Bosnia as much as Union or Death. Social ferment played its part along with national enthusiasm. The two great trends of nineteenth-century Europe – nationalism and the desire for reforms affecting the land – had not halted at the borders of Bosnia-Herzegovina. 'I am from the village', said Princip at his trial. 'Nine-tenths of our people are farmers who suffer', said Čabrinović, 'who live in misery, who have no schools, who are deprived of any culture. We sympathized with them in their distress . . . we loved our people.'

Yes and no. We have complicated things too much. The roots were in Sarajevo, and they were in Belgrade. Each side was using the other. Each could do so without guilt feelings, for each loved their common nation.

Of the seven assassins, two survive to this day. One is the director of a historical institute in Belgrade, the other the curator of the ethnographic department of the Sarajevo museum. In the late sixties this author talked to both, and two questions and answers above all others remain in his mind. Who, if any, were the Black Hand members in the group? Come now, was the answer. Perhaps some, perhaps none. What did it matter? 'We have many Black Hands in this part of the world.' And the question of motive? He had read all the theories, and they were all of them right, and all of them wrong. 'Look, we were seventeen.'

We have complicated things too much. Just what, scholars have asked for years now, did Pašić know about the preparations for Sarajevo: to what extent was the Serbian government involved? Can we trust a disgruntled minister's recollections; can we put any credence in some fragmentary document intercepted by an Austrian border guard? The details are complex; the experts have never been able to agree on them entirely. Yet certain basic truths really are not very complex at all. And among them is the fact that Dimitrijević's action did incriminate the Serbian government, for reasons both long-range and immediate. That government had for too many years been tolerating or even encouraging a movement for a Greater

Serbia whose aims were bound to be offensive to Austria-Hungary and whose methods were bound to be offensive to anyone. Very specifically speaking, the government in 1914 had taken no effective action to prevent the assassination of Franz Ferdinand, of which it very probably had some foreknowledge, nor had it managed to end the influence of the Black Hand, of which it assuredly had knowledge.

Not that there was anything in the least ignoble about either Pašić's or Dimitrijević's aims. The concept of a Greater South Slav State was fully as defensible as was Austria-Hungary's right to survival. Tragedy, in the Hegelian definition, consists not of the conflict of right with wrong but of right with right. But the Serbians set about achieving their purposes with a truly frightening disregard of the consequences. Here, then, was Serbia's vast share in the responsibility for the First World War, one that was matched only by Austria's; Belgrade surely knew that it was set on a collision course, yet it would not alter direction. There is, in the British files, a report from the ambassador to Vienna, Sir Fairfax Cartwright, written in January 1913 in the wake of the First Balkan War, which sums up the entire matter better than any later historian can:

> Servia will some day set Europe by the ears, and bring about a universal war on the Continent. . . . I cannot tell you how exasperated people are getting here at the continual worry which that little country causes to Austria under encouragement from Russia. It may be compared to a certain extent to the trouble we had to suffer through the hostile attitude formerly assumed against us by the Transvaal Republic under the guiding hand of Germany. It will be lucky if Europe succeeds in avoiding war as a result of the present crisis. The next time a Servian crisis arises. . . . I feel sure that Austria-Hungary will refuse to admit of any Russian interference in the dispute and that she will proceed to settle her differences with her little neighbour by herself 'coûte que coûte'.

Had Belgrade not been bidding for a Greater Serbia, there could have been a way out even after the Austrian ultimatum. Pašić, in that case, could have upset all of Austria's plans by accepting the ultimatum *in toto*. 'Such an acceptance would have made it impossible for the Austrians, in the eyes of world opinion, to start a war, and the few Austrian officials dispatched to Serbia to investigate the assassination would have provided a perfect spectacle of helplessness. The claim that such a mission could not be reconciled with the Serbian constitution cannot be taken very seriously. Worse things had happened in Serbia that were not in accord with the constitution.'

No, the reason some Serbians were willing to play the game the way the Austrians wished them to was that they thought the prize justified the stakes, and that with Russia's aid chances were good that the prize might be won. Nor did they play the game at all badly. Their reply to the ultimatum was a triumph — but it was a triumph in public relations rather than in settling the crisis. Which was what Belgrade had in mind. The pursuit of Serbia's aims was worth a war with Austria. And if that war should activate Europe's alliances and bring about an Austro-German-Serbian-Russian-French war, so be it. No fear of international complications, after all, had been capable of forestalling two earlier Balkan wars. Turkey was dying and now Austria was; 1914–18 was the longest but by no means the only war of the Turkish succession. It was the Third Balkan War.

Overlooking Belgrade stands the great Yugoslav World War I memorial, the tomb of the unknown soldier. A vast flight of steps leads up to a sort of temple where eight female figures in black marble represent the nations of Yugoslavia: Serbia, Coatia, Dalmatia, Bosnia, and the rest. On the floor, there is a single inscription, which reads:

1912–1918

Seen that way, Serbia was wholly right in the decision of 25 July, and the question of 'war guilt' becomes unreal and irrelevant. Of course, so was everybody right, and one wishes that Versailles had never introduced the concept of guilt. Serbia was right in wanting to expand. Austria in wanting to survive. Germany was right in fearing isolation. Great Britain in fearing German power. Everyone was right. And everyone was wrong, for no one foresaw what war would mean, either in terms of costs or of consequences. All were sinners, all were sinned against.

But then, discussions of causes, like so many other things in history, are constructions after the event. How many people, in 1914, were really that aware of all the origins of the conflict, immediate and long range, that we abstract in leisure from the documents later? How many had thought through every move of the diplomatic game, from Princip's opening to checkmate? Not even Berchtold or Pašić. What most of them did feel – and act on – was that here was another crisis, one that contained great risks, obviously, but that might reasonably be expected to end as non-cataclysmically as the diplomatic crises of the past decades had. That it did not, that this time the rhetoric of war would be followed by the reality, none of them foresaw, let alone planned. Only prophets after the event would be able to see the inevitability of arriving, step by step, stage by stage, by a series of moves and counter-moves that all seemed logical, reasonable, and containable at the time, at a road which had no turns left. And perhaps, all one can truly say in the end is that World War I was a modern diplomatic crisis gone wrong, the one gamble, or rather series of gambles, that did not work out, the one deterrent that did not deter. It happens.

4. World War I as Galloping Gertie: A Reply to Joachim Remak

PAUL W. SCHROEDER

In a recent article, Joachim Remak argues that modern research on the origins of the First World War, led by Fritz Fischer and his students, has distorted our view while expanding our knowledge. The search for more profound causes of the war has tended, in Remak's phrase, to make us miss the forest for the roots. World War I was really the Third Balkan War. It arose from the last of a long series of local Austro-Serbian quarrels, none of which had led to war before; it involved a series of political manoeuvres and gambles typical of the great power politics of that time, manoeuvres which previously had not issued in general conflict. Only the particular events of 1914 caused this particular quarrel and this diplomatic gamble to end in world war.

There is much truth in this familiar view, and considerable point to Remak's criticism of an overly determinist interpretation of 1914. Yet his version appears to me as unsatisfactory as those he criticises. This essay, without claiming to exhaust the literature or to say anything brand new, will suggest another way to look at the origins of the war, and propose a view different from Remak's, Fischer's, Arno Mayer's, and others now current.

To start with Fischer: most of what he says about Germany

From *Journal of Modern History*, 1972.

and her bid for world power is true. Many of his formulations and emphases are open to challenge. He is too hard on Bethmann-Hollweg and misinterprets the motives of his crucial decision in 1914. He often underestimates the importance and persistence of concerns other than *Weltpolitik* in German policy, and he tends to blur the difference between Germany's pre-war and wartime goals in emphasising their continuity. But these points do not destroy his main argument. From 1890 on, Germany did pursue world power. This bid arose from deep roots within Germany's economic, political, and social structures. Once the war broke out, world power became Germany's essential goal. Fischer and his students have made the old apologias for German policy impossible.

The difficulty arises in accepting the notion, implicit in all of Fischer's work and explicitly drawn by many historians as the chief lesson of it, that Germany's bid for world power was the *causa causans*, the central driving force behind the war. Fischer never demonstrates this convincingly. His case is far more informative, compelling, and reliable on Germany's policy and national character than on the origins of the war. He may be able to tell us what Germany was like without worrying much about the policies of other powers (although even here the comparative dimension is lacking). But he cannot assume, as he constantly does, that German policy was decisive for other powers without a great deal more investigation than he has done. Moreover, Fischer's own principle of *der Primat der Innenpolitik* should have led him to assume that other powers would, like Germany, act mainly from their own indigenous drives, rather than mainly react to what Germany did, as he depicts them doing.

More important, the whole attempt to find a *causa causans* behind the multiplicity of contributing factors is misconceived. It is like looking for *the* driving force behind the French or Russian Revolutions, or the Reformation, or the American Civil War. Immediately, one encounters a plethora of 'causes' far more than sufficient to account for the phenomenon one wishes to explain, clearly connected with it, and yet not 'sufficient' in the sense that any set of them logically implies what occurred. The fact that so many plausible explanations for the outbreak of the war have been advanced over the years indicates on the one hand that it was massively overdetermined, and on the other that no effort to analyse the causal factors involved can ever fully succeed. When on top of earlier valid arguments Fischer and his disciples insist that Germany's bid for world power was really behind it all, when Marxist historians insist that the war was the inevitable outcome of monopolistic capitalist imperialism, when Arno Mayer proposes domestic political and social unrest and the dynamics of counter-revolution as decisive, and when Peter Loewenberg argues in reply that this role belongs to the fundamental drives revealed by psychodynamic theory, one begins to suspect that all these approaches, however much valuable information and insight they may provide, cannot deliver what they promise. Not only is an attempt to reduce or subordinate the various contributing factors to some fundamental cause methodologically very dubious, but also, even if it worked – even if one managed to fit all the contributing factors into a scheme of causal priority through factor analysis – this would still not give the *causa causans*. For in the breakdown of a system of relations such as occurred in 1914 as a result of various intertwined and interacting forces, the system itself enters into the work of destruction. In the process wittily described by Hexter as 'Galloping Gertie', the very devices built into a system to keep it stable and operative under stress, subjected to intolerable pressures, generate forces of their own which cause the system to destroy itself. (Hexter, *The History Primer*, pp. 118–35. 'Galloping Gertie' was the popular name for the Tacoma Narrows Bridge in Washington, which collapsed in 1940 when winds induced pressures on supporting members sufficient in turn to cause the supports to generate destructive forces within the bridge.)

World War I seems to me clearly a case of 'Galloping Gertie'. Witness how statesmen and military leaders everywhere in 1914, especially in the Central Powers, felt themselves to be in the grip of uncontrollable forces. They sensed that their calculations were all futile and that what their actions would finally produce lay beyond all calculation. Remak, appreciating this fact and rejecting the search for a *causa causans*, rightly insists that the answer must lie in the narrative and in analysis within it. But his particular answer to the question, Why World

War I? is similarly misleading. True, it required certain
contingent events to start a war in 1914; but this does not mean
the whole development was purely contingent, with nothing
inevitable about it. Europe's frequent escapes from crises before
1914 do not indicate the possibility that she could have
continued to avoid war indefinitely; they rather indicate a
general systemic crisis, an approaching breakdown. Remak's
view of July 1914 as the one gamble that did not succeed
overlooks the fact that those who gambled in Germany and
Austria did not expect to succeed in avoiding general war.

Thus the search for the fundamental cause of World War I is
futile, while the argument that the war simply happened is
unhelpful. Is there no exit from the cul-de-sac? A different
question may help: not Why World War I? but Why not? War
was still the *ultima ratio regum*. World War I was a normal
development in international relations; events had been building toward it for a long time. There is no need to explain it as a
deviation from the norm. In this sense, the question Why not?
answers the question Why?

More important, it points to what is unexpected about the
war and needs explanation: its long postponement. Why not
until 1914? This question clearly needs answering in regard to
Austria. Historians continue to exercise themselves over why
the Austrian Monarchy risked its own destruction by insisting
on punishing Serbia. The favourite (and very unsatisfactory)
answer is that this was the kind of futile, absurd action to be
expected from so decrepit an empire with so inept a ruling class.
In fact, the problem is non-existent. Preventive wars, even risky
preventive wars, are not extreme anomalies in politics, the sign
of the bankruptcy of policy. They are a normal, even common,
tool of statecraft, right down to our own day. British history, for
example, is full of them; the British Empire was founded and
sustained in great part by a series of preventive and pre-
emptive wars and conquests. As for the particular decision of
June 1914, the evidence is plain that Berchtold, although often
wavering, resisted the idea of a punitive war on Serbia until the
assassination. With the death of Francis Ferdinand, leader of
the peace party, Berchtold simultaneously ran out of alternatives, arguments, and support for any other policy, and gave in.
The real problem is to explain why Austria waited so long and

tried so many other futile devices to stop the steady deterioration of her Balkan and great-power position before resorting to force. The idea of eliminating Serbia as a political factor by conquest, occupation, or preventive war was at least sixty years old, and constantly advanced. For over two centuries Austria had lived under the brooding threat of Russian encirclement in the south. 'Why did she act only in the desperate situation of 1914, with all alternatives exhausted?

A similar question arises with Germany. Why, with her powerful impulse toward *Weltpolitik*, did she fail to resort to war under favourable circumstances in 1905, or 1908–9, or even 1911, and try it only in 1914, when military and political leaders alike recognised the gambling nature of the enterprise? The same question, What held her back? applies to Europe in general. Fischer, Mayer, and the Marxists insist that the war did not just happen, but was caused. This is true, but so is the converse. Until 1914 peace did not just happen, but was caused. The wars that did not occur seem to me harder to explain than the one that did. Arno Mayer contends that we know all we need to about the European system; we lack an adequate analysis of the domestic sources of the violence that destroyed it. I disagree. We know more than we need to (although more knowledge of course is always possible and valuable) to understand in general what was impelling Europe to destruction. We neither fully understand nor appreciate the restraints holding her back, and why these gave way only in 1914.

This essay therefore deals with the question, Why not until 1914? It proposes to account for the critical difference between the system's surviving the challenges facing it and its failing to do so, by pointing to a vital element of stability within the system which in 1914 finally became destructive and generated the collapse of the system. That element, it will surprise no one to hear, was Austria-Hungary. The essay will also, briefly and sketchily, make a case for a point less trite and obvious: that a chief source of the pressures turning Austria from a stabilising into a destructive member of the system, besides her own internal debility and Germany's policy for becoming a world power, was Britain's policy for remaining one.

The most important change in European politics after 1890,

as everyone knows, was that Germany lost control of the system. Who gained the initiative she lost? For a short time, Britain seemed to; but the long-range gainers were France and Russia. Their alliance, giving them greater security in Europe, freed them to pursue world policy. Manchuria, China, Indochina and Siam, Persia, Central Asia, the Mediterranean, the Senegal, the Niger, the Congo, and the Upper Nile were the areas where Russian and French pressures were brought to bear. In every case, Britain was made to feel it.

The challenge to Britain's world leadership, coinciding with Germany's loss of control of the European system, helped conceal the latter phenomenon from the Germans themselves and contributed to their persistent belief that they could play the game of two irons in the fire and that eventually Britain would have to seek German help. Part of the challenge to Britain came from German and American industrial and commercial competition, but there was not much to be done about this. Counter-measures like imperial tariffs and economic union were likely to hurt Britain and anger the dominions rather than hamper her rivals. Besides, the main threat was to the security of the Empire, not to trade, and this danger stemmed from France and Russia. Far from threatening the British Empire in the 1890s, Germany hovered about Britain like an opportunistic moneylender, ready to offer her services at exorbitant rates and hoping for a favourable chance to buy into the firm. France and Russia competed directly with Britain and tried to drive her out of key positions. Isolated and foolish challenges like Fashoda could be faced down, but the fundamental vulnerability of Britain's position in Egypt, South Africa, the Straits, Persia, the Persian Gulf, the Far East, India, and India's Northwest Frontier oppressed the British daily. Added to this was the rise of the United States to world power and the danger of native unrest and risings in Egypt, South Africa, Ireland, and above all India. The challenges could doubtless be met, but not by the old policy, and also not by great new expenditures or tests of strength. The empire had always been acquired and maintained on the cheap, and Parliament required that it be kept so, especially now that new demands for welfare measures were being added to the old Liberal and Radical calls for cuts in military spending. As for tests of strength, the Boer War convinced most Englishmen of the dangers of isolation and the severe limits to British resources for overseas ventures.

It was therefore inevitable that Britain would meet her new problems mainly by trying to devolve some of her imperial burdens on others (the dominions or other friendly powers), and by trying to come to terms with her opponents. Bowing out gracefully in favour of the United States in the Western Hemisphere was easy and relatively painless; equally natural was the limited alliance with Japan. But the main answer to Britain's difficulties would have to be a deal with her chief opponents, France and Russia. Far from representing a great break in British tradition, such a rapprochement was the obvious step for Britain, a move for which there was ample precedent and tradition throughout the nineteenth century. What held it up was not British reluctance to break with splendid isolation – Salisbury, the great defender of this tradition, had been looking for chances to come to terms with France and Russia all through the 1890s. It was the refusal of France and Russia to make a deal on terms acceptable to Britain, counting as they did on British vulnerability to make her ultimately come to them. It took more than a year after Fashoda fully to convince Delcassé that there was no way to get Britain out of Egypt, and five years to be ready to admit it openly. Even then the British made concessions to France over Morocco which her business community there did not like at all. As for Russia, only military defeat and revolution in 1904–5, plus an expanded Anglo-Japanese alliance, finally convinced her that she must forget about putting pressure on Britain in Afghanistan. Even then, the Russians proved difficult to deal with in Persia before and after 1907.

This suggests that there is no need to bring in the German menace to explain Britain's rapprochement with France and Russia. The Triple Entente was a natural development explicable purely in terms of the needs and aims of the three powers – especially Britain. Her friendships with France and Russia were ends in themselves, vital for her imperial interests, and not means of checking Germany, and remained so. Rather than seeking friendly agreements with France and Russia because of the German threat, Britain tended to see Germany as a threat because of the agreements she sought and obtained from France and Russia. Repeatedly, before the war British spokesmen's main complaint against Germany was that she resented British agreements with other powers and tried to break them up. The great British fear was that Germany might lure France and Russia into her camp, leaving Britain isolated.

'But you forget three things,' one might reply. 'Britain did not approach France and Russia until she had first attempted an alliance with Germany and failed. The agreements with France and Russia were strictly extra-European and colonial in nature, and not directed against Germany; only Germany's dangerous conduct made them into a coalition against Germany. Above all, it was Germany's direct, overt, and formidable naval challenge which forced Britain to draw close to France and co-operate with Russia in Europe.'

The first point errs on the facts. The story of a missed opportunity for an Anglo-German alliance in 1898–1901 is a myth, as Gerhard Ritter argued long ago. Britain never really tried for it or wanted it. Naturally she would have liked to get Germany to defend British interests for nothing, but a mutual tie was never seriously in question. There was no basis for an alliance. Lord Curzon pointed out in 1901 that the German navy was too weak to be of much help to Britain and the army was not available where Britain needed it. Frances Bertie put the general political case against an alliance: it would be useful only in the extreme case of a losing British war against France and Russia, but such a war would compel Germany in her own interests to help Britain, alliance or no. Tied to Germany, Britain would lose her freedom to conduct world policy and to hold and exploit the balance between rival continental powers. Even Lansdowne quickly saw that a German alliance would draw French and Russian antagonism on to Britain, costing her the desired rapprochement with the Dual Alliance.

As for British co-operation with Germany, the only possible basis for this was the one laboriously erected by Bismarck and grudgingly accepted by Salisbury in the Near Eastern Triplice of 1887: British co-operation with Austria and Italy to uphold the Near Eastern *status quo*. This was undermined in 1893 by the Admiralty's conclusion that the fleet could no longer defend Constantinople against Russia while a French fleet operated from Toulon in Britain's rear. Once the British government accepted this conclusion, it eliminated any possibility of serious support for Austria in the Balkans, and thus of co-operation between Germany and Britain on the Continent. The only way now open for Britain in the long run to defend her Near Eastern interests, and the only one seriously pursued, was a deal with Russia. It took somewhat longer for Britain to conclude that Italy was no real help in the contest with France over East Africa, but after 1898 she also became largely superfluous.

What happened in China, where Britain and Germany supposedly came closest to real partnership only to have Germany back out, again illustrates the impossibility of an alliance. Salisbury never designed or intended the Anglo-German Agreement of October 1900 to stop Russia in China. He wanted it to hold Germany back, keeping her out of the British sphere in the Yangtze which she hoped to penetrate, while Salisbury negotiated what he really desired, an agreement over spheres of influence with Russia. When Prince Bülow told the *Reichstag* in March 1901 that Germany was not obliged to oppose Russia in Manchuria and would not do so, he merely expressed bluntly the letter and spirit of the 1900 agreement. Naturally and typically, when Lansdowne's and Chamberlain's illusions were pricked, Lansdowne promptly turned to Japan, while Chamberlain became not long after the most strident Germanophobe in the Cabinet.

The second point, that Britain's colonial agreements were not directed against Germany, but only became so because of Germany's conduct, is true in the sense that Britain did not want to encircle Germany but to protect her empire; this is precisely my contention. It also touches on an important truth, that Germany was not in fact the prime target of Entente diplomacy – of which more later. But what about France's and Russia's purposes in these colonial agreements? Whether Delcassé's policy of trying to encircle and isolate Germany was mainly a reaction to German moves or the product of his own ambitions for France (undoubtedly it was both), his whole programme, especially as it reached a climax in Morocco, was so overtly and rashly anti-German that most of his colleagues, including some ardent colonialists, warned him against it. The British knew quite well about this aspect of French policy. They chose to accept the agreement with France for their own reasons and to let Germany worry about the European consequences. As for the Anglo-Russian Convention of 1907, its fundamental presumption was that Britain would pay Russia for co-operation in Central Asia by helping the Russians improve their position in Europe, especially in the Balkans and the Straits – directly at Turkey's and Austria's expense, indirectly at Germany's. The British knew that Russia had been exerting pressure on India in great part in order to make Britain subservient to Russian policy in Europe, and they had long been contemplating using the Balkans and the Straits as lures for Russia.

It becomes even more disingenuous to claim that Britain's ententes were not intended to apply to Europe or to hurt Germany when one sees how they were used. From 1904 on, the British understood perfectly that the price of their friendships with France and Russia was diplomatic and moral support for these powers in their disputes with Germany and Austria. They gave that support even when, as often happened, they strongly disapproved of French or Russian policy. Germany and Austria, and France and Russia, respectively, being tied by firm alliances, could afford sometimes to restrain their partners and deny them diplomatic support. Britain, refusing all military commitments, had to give her friends moral support more unstintingly or risk seeing them go into the other camp.

Furthermore, even if Germany's encirclement was not a British aim, the 'circling out' of Germany, her exclusion from world politics and empire, *was* Britain's goal in good measure. Grey and others made it clear time and again that the purpose of Britain's ententes, next to keeping France and Russia friendly, was to deter Germany from 'interfering' and 'bullying' in Asia or Africa, to keep her out of areas like Persia where she had no real business, to stop the Baghdad Railway, to neutralise the *baton égyptien*, and to teach Germany that she had to settle all imperial questions *à quatre*, before a united front of Entente powers. The *Auskreisung*, which Fischer portrays as the result of German aggressiveness and blunders, was precisely the outcome British diplomacy was bent on achieving.

As to Germany's naval challenge, all the facts, old and new, can be freely acknowledged. There was a great German naval programme aimed directly at Britain and designed to promote *Weltpolitik*. It undoubtedly became ultimately Britain's greatest naval danger (after the Franco-Russian danger faded away) and the foremost element in Anglo-German rivalry. No improvement could come in Anglo-German relations without some naval settlement. But it is one thing to see the naval challenge as a real, serious issue, sufficient to itself to compel Britain to be on guard against Germany. It is quite another to argue that it primarily shaped British policy toward Germany, or that an end to the naval race would have significantly changed British policy. The latter assumptions remain unproved. The German naval challenge did not cause the revolution in Britain's political alignments, and an end to the naval race would not overturn them. The German navy was not really taken seriously by either the government or the Admiralty until 1906–7, by which time the Entente Cordiale was a fixture in British policy and the search for an agreement with Russia had long been under way. Nor will the naval challenge do to explain the rise of Germanophobia in Britain. The anti-Germans were clearly gaining control of the Foreign Office by 1901; popular hatred of Germany was ripe with the Kruger Telegram and the Boer War. Anti-German spokesmen in the government and the press did not need the German navy for their propaganda, though they exploited it fully. They centred their fire on the general danger of German power, the evil of Prussian militarism, and the German bullying and blackmail of Britain since the 1880s.

Nor should one ignore the fact that Germany's naval challenge was the only one among the many threats facing Britain which the British always knew they could beat. The realignment of British foreign policy came at a time when she enjoyed almost unprecedented naval superiority. The recognition in 1906–7 that Germany was now the only possible naval foe greatly improved, not worsened, Britain's strategic position; it facilitated the concentration of the fleet in home waters more than it forced it. Even the Tories, always alert for any sign of naval unpreparedness, agreed in 1905–6 that naval spending could be reduced. British publicists and a hysterical public might dream of a German invasion; Sir John Fisher dreamed of Copenhagening the German fleet and, like his successor, wanted to land 100,000 men on Germany's Baltic coast in case of war. Contrast the British confidence that they would be able to drive Germany from the high seas, destroy her commerce, and conquer her colonies with relative ease, with British pessimism on other scores – the knowledge that they could not hope to match American naval strength in the western Atlantic or Japanese in the Far East, and that the only long-range answers to the problems of Egypt and India were deals with France and Russia. Of course the British were angered by Germany's naval challenge; it was expensive, gratuitous, and worrisome. But they never doubted they could meet it; it had its domestic and foreign policy uses; it was much easier to get money voted for ships than for men and supplies to defend the Northwest Frontier. All in all, it was a price Britain was willing to pay for the friendship of Russia and France, although she would have preferred not to pay at all.

Above all, no naval agreement would have ended Anglo-German rivalry or caused Britain to abandon the anti-German coalition. To be sure, Germany demanded an unacceptable price for a naval agreement, Britain's promise of neutrality in continental war. But then Britain was never willing to pay for a naval agreement, except possibly with the poisoned fruit of a colonial agreement at Portugal's or Belgium's expense. If a naval agreement were concluded, the British would say, the improved atmosphere and friendly feelings it would produce would facilitate future amicable agreements on subjects of mutual interest – which is diplomatic language for 'No concessions'. In fact, Nicolson, Hardinge, Crowe, and other influential foreign-policy leaders were deathly afraid of a naval agreement. As Hardinge argued, the Russians 'must not think for a moment that we want to improve our relations with Germany at their expense. We have no pending questions with Germany, except that of naval construction, while our whole future in Asia is bound up with the necessity of maintaining the best and most friendly relations with Russia. We cannot afford to sacrifice in any way our entente with Russia – even for the sake of a reduced naval programme.' Grey constantly reassured France and Russia that no agreement with Germany, naval or other, would disturb Britain's existing friendships, and he meant it.

If one needs further evidence that an end to the naval threat would not change Britain's basic policy toward Germany, the secret Anglo-Russian naval talks of June 1914 over co-operation in the Baltic and the Mediterranean supply it. Perhaps Egmont Zechlin makes too much of the impact of these talks on German policy in 1914, but the point here is what they show of British policy. Britain agreed to these talks, it must be remembered, after the naval race had ended on terms favourable to her, after Germany had co-operated with her during the Balkan Wars, and while agreements with Germany over the Portuguese colonies and the Baghdad Railway were in their final stages. British writers argue that the talks meant nothing to Britain. Since her naval authorities had recently concluded that the Royal Navy would not be able to penetrate into the Baltic in case of war anyway, the conversations would lead to nothing, and were merely a political sop to Russia. But that is precisely the point. At a moment when better relations with Germany seemed uniquely possible, and when Grey believed such relations would be vital to prevent war over the Balkans, Britain was willing to destroy this hope (for these talks, like the similar ones with France, had little chance to remain secret and did not), to risk creating a grave new strain with Germany, to promote Russo-French hopes and German fears of a full Anglo-French-Russian alliance, and to deliver the best possible propaganda to navalists in Germany for resuming the naval race – all in order to avoid disappointing the Russians. This marks a high point in the British appeasement of Russia that had been going on for fifteen years, and proves further that the *raison d'être* of British policy was her ententes with France and Russia, regardless of what Germany did, just as Germany was determined to try for world power regardless of what Britain did, and that rivalry with Germany was a price Britain was willing to pay for the sake of these ententes.

'Very well,' someone will say, 'what of it? Britain was simply playing the game by the normal rules. Was she supposed to have appeased Germany instead? What possible concession would have done any good?' In any case the anti-German coalition Britain joined was a loose, defensive one which never would have caused war unless Germany tried to break it by force, which she did. Far from refuting the Fischer thesis, you have made it more plausible. Faced with the impossibility of achieving world power and standing by peaceful means, Germany chose war. Rather than condemning British policy, you vindicate it. For whatever her motives (and what power ever acts for motives other than self-interest?), Britain was preserving the European balance of power against the unmistakable threat of German domination. That this defence was desperately needed, two world wars would seem to give adequate proof.'

The argument is tenable, provided its basic premises are accepted. If Germany's main activity was her pursuit of world power; if, further, the greater problem for Europe was how to cope with Germany's growing power; if the main aim of British policy, whatever its ulterior motives, was to preserve a balance of power in Europe, and the chief effect of British policy was to restrain German ambitions, then British policy was justified regardless of its motives and even of its outcome. In pursuing her own interests. Britain was also upholding the best interests of Europe as a whole, and of peace.

But in fact the premises are unsound. Of course Germany played world policy; so did every other power that could, and some that could not. The point is how Germany played it. Somehow Fischer never quite succeeds in explaining the contrast between the remarkable growth of Germany's power and wealth and her uniform failure to translate that power into corresponding diplomatic, political, and territorial gains. Even a small power like Belgium, or a would-be great power like Italy, could emerge from the imperialist scramble with impressive gains; Portugal and Holland could consolidate their possessions while hungry great powers looked on. But Germany ended up with little more than Bismarck had already gained in 1884–5, and this at the cost of weakened alliances and a ruined European position. It will not do to explain this failure simply by German aggressiveness and blunders. Who could be more aggressive and commit more blunders than Imperial Russia? Yet she survived a disastrous war, revolution, and bankruptcy and emerged by 1914 with her alliances stronger than ever and her expansion once again under way. Nor will it do to cite Germany's inconsistency, her repeated failure to know what she really wanted. For the point is that no matter what Germany tried, she lost. She lost ground in Morocco when she remained passive and waited for France to come to her; she lost ground when she tried standing up for the principle of the open door; and she lost further ground when she tried to pound her fist on the table and demand compensations. Whether she tried to challenge Britain or France or Russia, or (as she did repeatedly) tried to win their friendship, she always finally succeeded in tightening the Entente against her.

The main reason for Germany's failure is not ineptness and aggressiveness, or her late start in *Weltpolitik*, or even unfavourable geography, although these are involved. It is that Germany could not pursue *Weltpolitik* all out. Each of the Entente powers could carry on a world policy without directly overthrowing the European system (although their imperialism indirectly undermined it). They could even, as the British did, indulge in the flattering belief that *their* world policy sustained the European system and made it work. But an unrestrained *Weltpolitik* by Germany, as the Germans were forced to recognise, was bound to isolate her and destroy the system upon which she had to rely for security as much as upon her army. Thus the exigencies of continental policy repeatedly imposed themselves upon Germany and restrained her.

This explains what most needs explaining about pre-war German policy. The problem is not, as is often imagined, one of accounting for her reckless conduct in terms of her aggressive, imperialist character and aims. It is one of accounting for the surprising moderation of German policy until 1914, in view of her aggressive character and aims. It is clear that the Entente powers were counting upon Germany's desire for peace and exploiting it; even Germanophobes like Eyre Crowe insisted that she would back down before a firm front. The restraints lay, of course, not in Germany's policy or character or the supposed peace party at Berlin, but in the position and role the system forced upon her – which made it all the more important for the Entente not to overstrain the system holding her back.

The contradiction between what Germany wanted to do and what she dared do and was obliged to do accounts in turn for the erratic, unco-ordinated character of German world policy, its inability to settle on clear goals and carry them through, the constant initiatives leading nowhere, the frequent changes in mid-course. It is commonly said that after 1890 Germany played the game of international politics like a plunger on the stock market, always looking for quick short-term gains. The truth is worse than this. Germany played it like a plunger looking for quick gains without making any investments, a gambler trying to win without betting. The Germans were always hoping to be paid for doing nothing, merely for being where they were; expecting to be feared and to have their interests respected because of the power they possessed but dared not exert. They wanted Britain to pay them in Africa for the trouble Germany refrained from causing Britain with the Boers. They wanted Russia to pay for benevolent German neutrality during the Russo-Japanese war, and Britain and Japan to pay for plain German neutrality during the same war. Russia and Britain were supposed to do something for Germany on account of her not penetrating Persia, and France likewise if Germany did not cause more difficulty over Morocco. The British ought to concede Germany something if she stopped building more ships. Disappointed, the Germans wondered with querulous self-pity why everyone was against them – the same mood they had often expressed before unification, and which would become the national disease after 1918.

Of course German restraint was not worthless to other powers; often it was invaluable. Russia was extremely lucky to have Germany and Austria-Hungary covering her rear in 1904–5, and the Russians knew it. But no one pays for such services when they can be had for nothing, especially since it was not too hard to see that the real reason why Germany refrained from causing more trouble was that she dared not do so. Like it or not, she was bound to her alliances and to her central European position. Even Italy had more freedom for *Weltpolitik* than she, and used it. For the Entente powers and Italy, alliances were primarily associations for profit; for Germany and Austria, they were of necessity associations for security.

Nor can one agree without serious reservations even to the universal assumption that British policy was directed toward maintaining a European balance of power. Of course it was in one sense: Britain wanted to keep Germany from dominating the Continent by either overpowering France and Russia or luring them into her camp. This was entirely legitimate and necessary, but it alone is not enough to make Britain's a real balance-of-power policy. For, quite apart from some general reservations one may have about the whole character of British equilibrist thought, the important point is that the British neither recognised nor did anything about the most critical threat to the European balance after 1900, but helped make it much worse. The immediate threat to the balance in 1914 was not German power. That danger existed, but it was under control, so far as it could be by peaceful means. The impression everywhere in Europe was that the Entente powers, especially Russia, were gaining the upper hand. The greater danger stemmed not from German or Russian power but from Austrian weakness. One of the few incontestable points in balance-of-power theory is that preserving the system means preserving all the essential actors in it. Equally obvious, nothing is more likely to occasion a major war than a threat to the existence or great-power status of an essential actor. Whatever the underlying causes of the nineteenth-century European wars may have been, they were all touched off by a violent reaction from some declining or threatened essential actor to a menace to its existence, essential interests, or prestige. This was true of Turkey in 1853, Austria in 1859 and 1866, France in 1870, and Austria in 1914. Long before 1914 it was obvious that Austria's existence was threatened. Everyone saw her as the next sick man of Europe after Turkey. The British virtually wrote off Austria as a great power by the mid-1890s. In 1899 Delcassé tried to reach agreements with Russia and Italy in the expectation of her impending demise. From 1908 on almost everyone anticipated that the long-awaited general war would probably arise over a Russo-Austrian quarrel involving Serbia. From 1912 on the Russians and Serbs repeatedly told their Western friends that Austria's collapse was imminent, and that they intended to have the lion's share of the remains.

Yet Britain's 'balance-of-power' policy entirely ignored this immediate danger, and served actually to increase the threat from Germany as well. Germany ultimately might well have gone to war for world power (although she passed up chances earlier); but she was virtually bound to accept war, even provoke it, rather than let Austria go under and thus lose her last reliable ally. This was not a matter of Germany's ambitions, but of her vital interests, as the British well knew.

Once again, even if this trite contention is true, what of it? Was Britain to blame if Austria in 1914 decided to commit suicide out of fear of death, and Germany decided to join her, or rather pushed her into it? Were the Entente powers supposed to sacrifice their interests to save a rival power from succumbing to its own internal weaknesses?

As it happens, the theoretical answer to both these rhetorical questions is yes. A real balance-of-power policy would have required from the Entente precisely such a policy of restraint for themselves and controlled support for Austria, just as maintaining the Near Eastern balance had always required the powers to support Turkey, not exploiting her weaknesses or seeking individual gains. It indicates the inherent contradictions of balance-of-power politics that the actions it promotes, which its proponents consider normal and natural, actually serve to undermine the balance rather than maintain it. But there is a practical answer more important than the theoretical one. The threat to Austria's existence, which I would argue was primarily international rather than internal in character, was a product in great part of Entente policy. As a result of the preoccupation of diplomatic historians with motives and aims instead of effects, both German and Entente policies have always been discussed almost exclusively in terms of the German problem, when in fact their effects were far greater on the Austrian problem. The best answer to the German encirclement myth is not that Entente policy was really moderate and unprovocative; there has been too much whitewashing of British, French, and especially Russian policy in this whole debate. The answer is rather that the Entente really encircled Austria rather than Germany. Of course Germany was hemmed in and constrained. But she still had allies she controlled or strongly influenced, neutral states still leaned her way (Denmark, Sweden, Holland, Switzerland, Turkey), and she was still inherently so strong that no one wished to challenge her directly. If her bid for world power was frustrated, the more modest aim of eventually loosening the rival coalition and insinuating herself into Britain's favour was not foreclosed. Grey resisted all pressures from France, Russia, and the Foreign Office to turn the ententes into alliances, and may even have entertained the hope ultimately of bringing a chastened and more moderate Germany into the Triple Entente, as the Radicals urged.

Austria, in contrast, was hopelessly encircled by 1914 and knew it. Russia, supported by France, was forming a new Balkan League around Russia's protégé and Austria's worst enemy, Serbia. Rumania was defecting, Bulgaria was exhausted and wavering under strong Russo-French pressure, Turkey was leaning toward Russia, Italy was co-operating with Russia in the Balkans; even Germany was a wholly unreliable support politically, and Austria's chief competitor economically in the Balkans.

This isolation and encirclement resulted, moreover, principally from Entente moves and policies, always discussed as if they had nothing to do with Austria. Delcassé's policy, for example, was obviously aimed against Germany (and for a good while against Britain). But is there no significance to the fact that virtually his first move in strengthening and transforming the Dual Alliance was to seek an agreement with Russia over the spoils of the Austrian Empire, and that even after his fears of a German seizure of Austrian Adriatic ports proved groundless, he still hoped Austria's demise might give France the chance to recover Alsace-Lorraine? Who was menaced by French efforts to lure Italy out of the Triple Alliance and to get her to concentrate her attention on the Balkans and *Italia irredenta*? Not Germany; Austria. Whose vital interests and security were ultimately threatened by France's move to take over Morocco? Not Germany's; only the Pan-Germans and some ardent colonialists claimed Morocco as a question of vital interest. The Kaiser, the Foreign Office, and the bulk of Germany's military, naval, and business leaders saw it as a question primarily of prestige and honour. What the French protectorate in Morocco actually did was to pave the way for Italy to attack Turkey over Tripoli and to spread the war into the eastern Mediterranean, to encourage Russia to advance her plans for the Straits, and to promote the assault of the Balkan states upon Turkey, thus raising life-and-death questions for Austria. This was not merely what happened in the event; it was what sensible leaders foresaw and planned for, what was in good part provided for in written agreements.

It is true that Austria did not oppose either France's move on Morocco or Italy's ambitions for Tripoli. This was because, knowing that she could not stop them, she pursued the forlorn hope that, distracted by these gains, they might lessen the pressure on her, or that by supporting them she might persuade France and Italy to keep these Mediterranean moves from having dangerous repercussions for Austria in the Balkans, and to recognise her vital interests there. This policy, which had never worked for Austria throughout the nineteenth century, suffered absolute shipwreck in 1912–14, when it became apparent that all the powers, grateful though they were for Austria's restraint, intended to make her pay for everyone else's gains, and pay precisely in the only area where she had vital interests, the Balkans.

Whom (besides Persia) did the Anglo-Russian Convention of 1907 endanger? Not Germany, whose role and interests in Persia were secondary. The agreement, as intended and promoted by Britain, served to turn Russia's attention toward the Straits, the Macedonian question, and her Balkan rivalry with Austria. France's and Britain's loans to Russia, French economic penetration of the Balkans, France's arms deliveries to Serbia and Greece, and her closing her money markets to Vienna while opening them to Austria's enemies were all intended to hit Germany, in so far as they had a political purpose; but Austria was much more directly hurt. The same is true of Russia's policy, fully backed by France, of uniting the Balkan states into a league under her direction, pulling Rumania and Turkey also into her camp. Intended supposedly to protect the Straits and Turkey from German influence, it served above all to destroy Austria's position. Even the Anglo-French and Anglo-Russian naval talks were directed as much against Austria in the Mediterranean as against Germany in the North and Baltic Seas. From 1912 on France was determined not to allow an Austro-Serb or Austro-Russian rapprochement, so as not to lose a valuable third front in the Balkans against the Central Powers in case of war.

Austria was therefore the actual target of Entente diplomacy.

Results count more than motives. To a surprising degree, moreover, Entente statesmen knew what the effects of their policies would be and accepted them. But how was Britain responsible for this? It is easy to see why Russia, France, and Italy might want Austria weakened, but why should Britain, her old friend and natural ally, help undermine her position?

In fact, one can argue that Britain's policy (like Russia's and even, in certain respects, France's) was more anti-Austrian than anti-German. Although opposing German ambitions, the British took Germany seriously and were careful not to push her too far or trample her interests underfoot. They never took Austria seriously and were regularly ready to let her pay, or make her pay. Britain never encouraged France or Russia to provoke Germany; firmness and moderation were the watchwords. But from the mid-1890s on, she urged Russia to concentrate her power and attention on Europe, telling her that with time and patience she could become the arbiter of Europe – the worst possible threat to Austria. The British never liked Delcassé's anti-German stance over Morocco. But they worked to break up the long-standing Austro-Russian co-operation in Macedonia, valuable though they knew it to be for European peace, exploiting the Austro-Russian rift to promote a separate Anglo-Russian programme for the Balkans and Turkey. Macedonia became the birthplace of the Triple Entente; it was supposed to cement the Anglo-Russian entente at Austria's expense as the first Moroccan crisis had consolidated the Anglo-French accord at Germany's.

The British did not encourage France to try to recover Alsace-Lorraine; they did drop repeated hints to Russia about how co-operation in Asia would eventually help her in Turkey and the Straits. Britain welcomed the Franco-German agreement over Morocco in 1909 and showed little concern as the French first strained and then broke the Act of Algeciras so recently concluded. When Austria annexed Bosnia, legalising a situation long existing *de facto* and giving up her hold on the Sanjak of Novi-Pazar in the process, Britain helped promote an international crisis over the violation of a treaty thirty years old, whose relevant provision had never been intended by Britain herself to remain long in force. The British sometimes tried to calm French suspicions of Germany. During the

Bosnian Crisis and after, they impressed upon Russia that she had suffered a humiliating defeat at the hands of Austria backed by Germany – this regardless of the consequences for the balance of power and future Austro-Russian relations, and despite the fact that the British knew of the prior Austro-Russian bargain over Bosnia and considered Isvolski himself largely to blame for Russia's discomfiture.

While Britain in 1911 urged France to compensate Germany generously for her protectorate in Morocco, she simultaneously encouraged Russia to form a Balkan League, including Turkey, to stop Austria in south-eastern Europe. Grey rejected the idea of pulling Italy entirely out of the Triple Alliance, for fear of provoking Germany; but he welcomed Italy's co-operation with Russia and her concentration on the Adriatic, and he tried to quell anti-Italian press sentiment in Britain over Italy's aggression in the Tripolitan War. While Grey co-operated with Germany during the Balkan Wars, it was often at Austria's expense, and always with great care not to offend Russia. Although the outcome of these wars fatally tipped the Balkan balance against Austria, the frantic cries from Vienna for some consideration of Austria's position went unheeded as before. To Austria, the Foreign Office preached abnegation and restraint; among themselves, British leaders agreed that it would be better not to become entangled at all in Balkan questions and Austria's selfish intrigues, were it not that friendship for France and Russia required it. Meanwhile the British envoys at Sofia and Petersburg encouraged a Serbo-Bulgarian rapprochement under Russian sponsorship that would seal Austria's isolation and compel her to remain quiet. If a partition of Turkey became unavoidable, the British recognised that German interests would have to be taken into account. Austria, on the other hand, had good reason to fear that Britain would join with France, Germany, and Russia to cut her out.

On the eve of the war, the Foreign Office was aware of the fear prevalent in both Berlin and Vienna that Austria might collapse. Far from viewing this eventuality as a danger *per se*, Nicolson feared only that Russia and Germany might come together over the spoils, and urged preventing this by a close Anglo-Russian alliance. Grey feared rather what actually happened: a preventive war launched by Germany out of fear of Russia's growing strength and Austria's decline. His only answer to this was to work with the supposed German peace party under Bethmann, so as to conciliate Germany and get her to put still more restraining pressure on Austria. No thought of any action to help maintain Austria's independence and integrity was entertained. If Austria and Russia actually got into war, Grey hoped to keep Germany and France out of it – thus holding the ring for Russia, giving her the opportunity she had wanted ever since the Crimean War.

Finally, if one agrees with Fischer (as I do) that something can be learned of the general character and direction of a nation's policy before 1914 by seeing what it does and plans immediately upon the outbreak of war, then it is significant that Britain's contribution to the breakup of the Austrian Monarchy, the promises and concessions to Italy, Rumania, Serbia, and Russia which soon rendered it inevitable, began already on 5 August 1914, a week before Britain's declaration of war on Austria. Equally significant, while Britain always expected and even wanted a united Germany to survive World War I, to serve both as a balance against Russia and France and as a market for British goods, they considered Austria dispensable, reckoning freely from 1916 on breaking her up (even if Germany absorbed the German-speaking territories!) or on using a drastically reduced, federated, and Slav-dominated Austria in some kind of anti-German combination.

Of course there was no great anti-Austrian plot. The British did not think of Austria as their enemy; they tried not to think of her at all. They did not plan to isolate and destroy her; they simply did not concern themselves (as they never had earlier in the nineteenth century) with the question of whether the concessions and defeats forced upon Austria before the war, and the territorial sacrifices to be imposed on her during and after it, would leave her viable. Britain undermined Austria's position before the war – indeed, throughout the nineteenth century – and assisted in her destruction during it, in a fit of absence of mind, a state from which many British historians on this subject have not yet emerged. Austria was not Britain's concern, as Grey repeatedly told his ambassador at Vienna, Sir Fairfax Cartwright; Britain wished to be cordial to her without entangling herself. She was like China or Persia. The British had nothing against her, but she could do nothing for them, they in turn could not save her, and certainly no British interests would be sacrificed for her sake, including the only important British interest in the Balkans, keeping on good terms with Russia.

What makes Britain's responsibility for Austria's plight a heavy one, although less direct than Russia's or France's, is that Britain alone was in a position to manage the European Concert so as to control the Balkan situation. Russia was bound to be Austria's rival, Serbia and Rumania bound to have territorial aspirations at Austria's expense, Italy bound at least to watch Austria jealously. These problems were there and could not be solved or spirited away. But they could have been controlled. Russia was not bound to be Austria's enemy; throughout the nineteenth century she had always found it profitable to seek a *modus vivendi* with Austria whenever it was plain that an aggressive course would get her into trouble. The danger regularly arose when Russia got tacit or open Western support for a forward policy, as she did before 1914. Serbia would try all she could get away with, but would not commit suicide by fighting Austria alone; Rumania was entirely opportunistic, Italy not really vitally engaged in the Balkans. As for Austria, all through the century she had lived with international and internal problems that were insoluble but not fatal. There were so many dangers that her only hope was to outlive the threats and outlast her enemies; she always tried this course, and only abandoned it when it seemed too hopeless or humiliating, and violence appeared to be the only recourse. Right up to June 1914 all Austrian leaders, including those aggressively inclined toward Serbia and Italy, wanted an entente with Russia. Hence the situation was not inherently out of control, but only Britain could have exercised that control. France could not have checked Russia's diplomatic offensive, even had she wanted to; she was too dependent on Russian aid. Britain did not try, not so much because she feared losing Russia to Germany, or feared renewed trouble for India, as because she saw no reason to make the effort.

Instead, she expected Germany to do the whole job both of sustaining Austria and restraining her. It is strange that the

Germans have not made more of this. Most German charges against England were baseless or highly exaggerated, most German expectations and demands from Britain absurd or dangerous. But the old, long-standing German and Austrian efforts to get Britain to bear her European responsibilities by upholding Austria have a good deal to be said for them. Never mind that Germany had selfish reasons for wanting to involve Britain, that Germany herself helped greatly to create the Austrian problem, and that German support for Austria was anything but loyal and disinterested. The fact remains that German support for Austria and restraint of her and Russia helped prevent several likely general wars, and that Austria by her very existence and her policy was restraining Germany, preventing her from playing world policy with a free hand. Moreover, only the presence of the Habsburg Monarchy holding down the Danube basin kept Germany or Russia from achieving mastery over Europe. With Austria there and determined to remain an independent great power, it was very difficult for either of them to fight each other, or dominate the other, or combine for aggressive purposes. Let Austria go under, and a great war for the mastery of Europe became almost mathematically predictable. The Germans, William II in particular, had many irrational beliefs, including the apocalyptic vision of an inevitable fight to the death between Teutons and Slavs. But their fear of this contest, and the belief that Austria's impending dissolution must bring it on, were entirely rational.

The main trouble with leaving the task of supporting Austria to Germany alone was not that it was unfair or exceeded Germany's resources, but that it was counter-productive for peace. The more the Germans alone supported Austria, the more she became and was considered a German satellite, against her will; the more she and Germany, instead of restraining each other, became involved in each other's largely individual quarrels, the more Austria, despairing of finding help from Britain, France, or the Concert, would be prone to seek her salvation in violence, and the more Germany, fearful of Austria's demise or defection, would be tempted to push her into it – the scenario of 1914.

Only a commitment by Britain to use her influence with

France to help keep Austria in existence by maintaining a balance of power in the Balkans and restraining Austria, Russia, and the Balkan states alike could have prevented this. Such a policy had worked with Turkey for a long time, and she was far more vulnerable, weak, backward, despised, and dispensable than Austria. But the whole British tradition went against this. Despite many fine phrases, the British never understood what Austria's function really was in Europe, and how valuable she was to Britain. At best, Austria was for Britain a useful means to check France or Russia or to help Turkey; more often she was considered a menace to Turkey and a reactionary satellite of Russia or Germany, endangering the balance by her subservience and the peace by her reckless repressive policies. When France and Russia loomed as the chief dangers, Britain saw a united Italy and a united Germany under Prussia as the best answers. When Germany then became the chief danger, friendship with Russia and France was the solution. In both cases, Austria was forgotten or considered useless. As for the critical problem of east-central and south-eastern Europe, the British knew little and cared less, but supposed that Austria was an anachronism and that a liberal nationalist solution would be best all round if achieved by peaceful means. Even had they better understood what was at stake, they would not have changed their policy. For to support Austria, however cautiously, would be to abandon Britain's coveted freedom from commitments, to give up that policy of a free hand toward the Continent which accounted for Britain's greatness and which, only slightly modified, had worked brilliantly since 1900. By 1914, all the challenges to Britain were under control. The empire and the home islands had not been so secure in two generations, all without war, great expense, or binding alliances. To this day, the thought that Britain's pre-war successes in foreign policy might be connected with the final catastrophe, that in the struggle for peace, unlike her usual record in war, Britain this time won all the battles and lost the war, has not penetrated British historiography.

Yet it would be wrong to end on this note, as if Britain were especially to blame – as misleading as the current excessive concentration on Germany, and far more unfair. The basic point is that everyone saw the central threat to the European system in the decline of Austria, and no one would do anything about it. Russians, Serbs, Rumanians, Greeks, and Italians all exploited it: the French thought only of their security. Even Germany made the problem worse, by promoting Austria's survival not as a European independent great power, but as a German state and Germany's satellite, and by insisting against Austrian protests that war, if it came, must be fought as a great duel to the death between Germans and Slavs. The British, meanwhile, did not want Austria to die, but hoped that if she must, she would at least do it quietly. In 1914 Austria decided not to die quietly, and once this long-postponed decision to recover her position by violence was taken, there was no stopping short of a general holocaust.

The only reason for laying greater stress on Britain's role here is that objectively (although not psychologically) she had greater freedom to act otherwise and greater ability to change the outcome. The attitudes behind it all, in any case, were universal – the same short-sighted selfishness and lack of imagination, the same exclusive concentration on one's own interests at the expense of the community. Everyone wanted a payoff; no one wanted to pay. Everyone expected the system to work for him; no one would work for it. All were playing the same game – imperialism, world policy, *Realpolitik*, call it what you will – all save Austria, and she also would have played it had she been able. All believed, as many historians still do, that *sacro egoismo* is the only rational rule for high politics, that it even represents a higher realism and a higher morality, when it really is only a higher stupidity. And so the system was bent and twisted until it broke; its burdens were distributed not according to ability to bear them, but inability to resist. Inevitably the collapse came where all the weight was concentrated – at the weakest point. Two titles from Nietzsche and Nestroy sum the whole process up: 'Menschlich, allzu menschlich', and 'Gegen Torheit gibt es kein Mittel'. ('Against stupidity there is no medicine.')

5. World Policy, World Power and German War Aims

FRITZ FISCHER

The slogans which Wilhelm II proclaimed vociferously and which Bülow adopted without resistance, though in a somewhat smoother form, were world policy as the task, world power as the aim and naval construction as the instrument. The broad mass of the nation, especially its intellectual and economic upper strata, welcomed them on the whole very approvingly in the belief that it would be possible to secure for ever Germany's position as a World Power equal in rights and strength to England. Behind this belief was the conviction that the nation's unparalleled industrial advance, the industrialisation which was permanently dependent on the supply of raw materials from abroad, the development of overseas trade, and also the supplying and feeding of the growing population at home, could not be guaranteed unless it attained a position [of power] which was not limited to European frontiers. The intoxicating energy and speed of the boom caused them to overestimate the strength of the Empire's position in Europe. The uncertainties of the latter were fatally obscured by the deep-rooted Imperialist tension with England on the one hand and with France and Russia on the other.   (Herzfeld)

This judgement made by Hans Herzfeld in 1952 about Germany's position at the start of her Imperialist era proper, which was signalled by the appointment of Bülow and Tirpitz

From the *Historische Zeitschrift*, CXCIX (Oct. 1964).

to crucial offices in 1897, can be affirmed without any reservation in 1963. Its author, however, apparently no longer believes it to be right; otherwise one could not understand the premise of his criticism of my position, which he set out expressly by questioning the validity of my assertion that there was an 'active and conscious German striving for world power'. But it. appears entirely inconceivable that these aims of the German Empire at the start of the First World War should no longer have been in its political consciousness and should no longer have been seen as the object of German policy!

That this was not the case is shown – among many other statements from the period at the outbreak of the war – by the avowal of the editor of the *Preussische Jahrbücher*, a representative of the Wilhelmine era, the historian Hans Delbrück in his book *Bismarcks Erbe* (*The Bismarckian Inheritance*), which appeared in 1915:

> Bismarck's inheritance has been preserved . . . but it was only properly fulfilled the moment, as peace could no longer be preserved, we went to war, with as much confidence as he did, to defend first of all our very existence and thenceforward to be a World Power like ourselves among the other World Powers.

AUSGEKREIST

In 1896 the same Hans Delbrück, in complete agreement with the ideas of Gustav Schmoller, Otto Hintze, Erich Marcks and Max Weber – you need only think of Weber's Inaugural Lecture of 1894 (Fischer's error: the date is 1895 – Ed.) – formulated the 'German mission' in its classic form:

> In the next decades vast tracts of land in very different parts of the world will be distributed. The nation which goes away empty-handed will lose its place in the next generation from the ranks of those Great Powers which will coin the human spirit. Did we found the German Empire to see it disappear under our grandchildren?

For twelve years under Bülow, Germany believed she could

reach the objectives of 1897–8. But when the balance-sheet was drawn up at Bülow's departure (July 1909), it turned out that Germany was *ausgekreist*, had achieved none of her aims. In fact, even her European position itself seemed to be threatened, whereas under Bismarck her hegemony had been generally accepted.

Those World Powers already established, France, England, Russia and America, could block the impetuous pressure of a Germany aware of its very late appearance. To the same degree as they had acquired vast tracts of the earth since the 1860s and 1870s, they were also more successful at the turn of the century in getting what they wanted than the new competitor. In view of the possibilities for expansion, what else did the Entente of 1904 and the Russian-English understanding of 1907 signify than the exclusion of Germany from the major show-places of spheres of influence throughout the world, first in Egypt and Morocco and then in Persia, Afghanistan and Tibet; at the same time they also meant that Germany's rising industrial production met considerable handicaps in other areas, while the other Powers were successfully extending their influence, Japan in Korea and China, America in Cuba, Puerto Rico, the Philippines, Panama, Nicaragua and Mexico, England in South Africa and many other places round the world, France in Africa and south-east Asia, and Russia in East and Central Asia.

And what had Germany achieved in the twelve years of world policy? The lease of Kiaochow in 1897 for ninety-nine years, causing a great deal of friction with England, Russia and Japan; then in 1899, after England's withdrawal, two Samoan islands as sovereign possessions (an acquisition which went back to Bismarck's time), through their partition between Germany and America, which in fact left much ill-feeling in America, and which together with Britain's simultaneous withdrawal from the Caribbean helped prepare England's approach to America; then the purchase of some of Spain's legacy in the Pacific in 1899, the Palau Islands, the Carolines and the Mariana Islands – really a very paltry acquisition, though Bülow, announcing the completion of their purchase to the Kaiser, said that this gain '[will] prompt the people and the navy to follow Your Majesty further along the way leading to world power, greatness and eternal glory'. Similarly, when the Samoan islands, which have already been mentioned, were acquired, Bülow had justified it in a report lasting for several hours before the German Kolonialrat on the grounds of how it raised 'Germany's prestige in the world'.

These were the only German acquisitions overseas up to 1911, in fact to 1914 if we ignore the slight enlargement of the German Cameroons, even though the years 1897–8 had been the start for 'the struggle for world power and naval construction', marked by the passage of Tirpitz's two Navy Laws through the Reichstag in 1898 and 1900 by the use of all the means of modern mass persuasion.

WORLD POLICY AND 'INTERESTS'

Where and how did Germany try to gain influence and acquisitions in the subsequent seventeen years? Already since the 1880s in South Africa, from which Germany began to withdraw at the end of the 1890s after fierce friction with England (the Kruger Telegram of 1896); in the Congo and Central Africa in order to gain the territory of Katanga with its rich mineral deposits and to establish a connection with German East Africa or to make sure of part of the Portuguese colonies for herself; in Morocco and Egypt; in East Asia and the Pacific; in South America – Chile, Brazil, Argentina, Venezuela and Mexico.

Everywhere Germany's presence implied conflict, even though till the beginning of the century the fronts were by no means clear-cut. And for a long time also perhaps Anglo-French antagonism and the friction between England and Russia hid the tensions produced by Germany's rise and pretensions, which in fact finally caused the close rapprochement of those Powers.

Already in 1898 the attempt to acquire at least a part of the Philippines had failed. The near collision of the German overseas squadron and the American war fleet off Manila caused by this left resentment in the United States which was never to be forgotten. This reappeared through the Venezuelan affair, in which the Disconto-Gesellschaft, an active associate of the Great Venezuelan Railway Company, got the Empire to defend its investments by armed intervention. Although the blockade was carried out jointly with England and Italy, public opinion in the United States was excited primarily against Germany, and Theodore Roosevelt's use of the American fleet was celebrated as a victory of the President over the Kaiser. Around 1902 Wilhelm II tried to acquire a naval base in Mexico in Lower California, but met Japanese and American resistance. In President Diaz (1874–1910) the Kaiser had an admiring friend who looked to the German State as a model and who expected economic aid and help in military training – in Diaz's reception hall for foreign diplomats hung a portrait of Kaiser Wilhelm II. After Diaz's death as a result of the conflict in and over Mexico, Paul Hintze, the last German Ambassador there before the war, produced the idea, as did Arthur Zimmermann, who actually tried to put it into effect in 1917 as Secretary of State (the Zimmermann Telegram), of drawing Mexico on to the side of the Central Powers and of co-operating with Japan (Moltke was already thinking about this in August 1914) in a war against the United States, if she entered the war against Germany.

Or in the Far East where before and after the acquisition of Kiaochow and a sphere of influence in Shantung the China-Syndikat of the major German banks also tried to gain influence in central China by building railways, acquiring mining companies, building factories and founding trading settlements, once again in the fiercest rivalry with England, an action which led to political friction with England, Russia, America and Japan. Attempts were made to acquire further bases in Polynesia besides the South Seas possessions. These bases were above all intended as telegraph stations which would open up the Pacific area and be independent of the agencies of communication of the Great Powers.

Turkey, and the Balkan bridge to it, was the principal point of Germany's economic commitment and of her political prestige. According to Arthur von Gwinner, Director of the Deutsche Bank and initiator and supporter of the Baghdad Railway enterprise, here Krupp and Creusot, both backed by their 'respective governments and high finance', were fighting for a market for their war materials and for political influence.

In a classic manner Gwinner outlined the activity of Germany's foreign missions. They arranged foreign business transactions on behalf of German industry (most telegrams of the representatives of important German firms were communicated or passed to them by the Foreign Office), above all on behalf of the armaments industry, such as the supply of guns, rifles, munitions and warships, of electric and telegraphic equipment (AEG for high-power current and Siemens for weak current). All these transactions were always carried out in sharp competition with nations who in the long run had the greater capacity for playing off the dominance and monetary resources of their markets against the isolated Berlin one.

The outstanding rise of the German economy produced at the same time the shortage of capital. As Helfferich, Director of the Deutsche Bank and specialist in Balkan and Turkish questions, stressed to the Greek Prime Minister, Venizelos, on 27 January 1914, Germany felt on an equal footing with America in the modernity of her economy, even superior to America; moreover, as he said, 'German capitalist circles' differed from the French: 'In France state stock is preferred above all, while in Germany an additional industrial flavour is liked.' But German industrialisation had consumed vast investments, which were no longer available in the race for spheres of influence; this was directly contrary to France, which could employ enough investment-seeking capital politically, because she was less developed economically.

After glancing at the Central African policy of Chancellor Bethmann-Hollweg and his relations with England, this problem will have to be explored in a field crucial for the German economy and policy, the Balkans and Turkey during the years 1912–14. This examination is chiefly based on material previously unpublished, which is of decisive importance for an assessment of German policy immediately before the First World War, although it cannot be treated fully here.

THE DIFFICULT AND THE EASY WAY: MOROCCO, CENTRAL AFRICA AND ENGLAND

In the renewal of the discussions of German war aims in the

First World War the personality of the German Chancellor, Bethmann-Hollweg, and an assessment of his policy, have again come to the forefront of historical interest, especially by my critics. When a personality is singled out so sharply, it is necessary to look more closely at the turning-point which Bethmann-Hollweg's appointment signified in relation to Bülow's time, which began under the banner of 'world policy' and led Germany to isolation.

Against such an interpretation Bethmann-Hollweg himself could be cited as a witness, not only because he had been suggested to the Emperor as his successor by Bülow himself, but also because after Bethmann-Hollweg had been in office for half a year, he – obviously to answer objections to his conduct of foreign policy – ordered his Foreign Office staff to draw up a memorandum which demonstrates that since he had taken office there had been no departing from the hitherto accepted policy prescribed by his predecessor, *'especially not in the sense of a greater subservience to countries abroad'* (author's italics). In detail the Imperial Chancellor, among other things, wanted especially the following points pursued:

England: continuation of spinning the thread of understanding begun by my predecessor over several African questions, willingness for further understandings of this kind. Any modification of our Navy Law excluded.

This means that Bethmann-Hollweg considered his policy as a continuation of the dual policy of Bülow, especially in relation to England. On the one hand 'to try for an understanding' over colonial questions; but on the other hand to remain unyielding on the question of naval armament.

We have to consider briefly in this general setting (before turning to German policy in the Balkans and Turkey) Bethmann-Hollweg's and Kiderlen-Wächter's German policy in North and Central Africa, where also private economic interests went hand in hand with Imperial policy. Kiderlen-Wächter (for many years German Ambassador to Rumania, who had impressed the Kaiser by his reports, which were as sagacious as they were amusing) appears to have followed the harder line, but he could not have acted without the countenance of the Imperial Chancellor, Bethmann-Hollweg; Jagow, whose keynote was an anti-Slav one, later assumed a more flexible attitude to England, a mixture of patience and toughness – because of the ultimate aims of 'world policy'.

At the same time as the Bosnian crisis of 1908–9 and the *Daily Telegraph* affair, which blighted Bülow's last months as Imperial Chancellor, the Imperial government – entirely because of the Balkan danger – managed to reach a compromise with France over Morocco, where the Germans together with the pretender, Mulai Hafid, had been pursuing a policy which was risky and in the end condemned to failure. In the form of an interpretation of the Algeciras Act (February 1909), Germany acknowledged France's political position in the land of the Sherif and France in return acknowledged Germany's economic interests there. The most significant aspect of this treaty, which was both highly equivocal and is still in need of further interpretation, was the governmental support for co-operation between German and French interests in Africa. A project for a Franco-German plantation and settlement company in the border territory of the German Cameroons and French Congo, in the Ngoko-Sangha, put forward by the National Liberal Deputy, Dr Semmler from Hamburg, and the Editor-in-Chief of *Les Temps*, Tardieu, was pursued through the active good offices of the German Embassy in Paris, especially by the Counsellor of the Embassy, van der Lancken, with the occasional support of the Ministers Caillaux and Pichon, although under rising distrust and opposition from the French Parliament. Careful examination of the documents in fact shows that this project amounted to nothing more than an attempt at personal gain, at least on the part of the French company, which largely on that account did not have the support of the French Chamber, and because of which all the hopes of the Germans to gain a foothold in the French Congo came to nothing. A similar fate was suffered by the project for a German–French Central African railway, which should have gone through the South and North Cameroons and the French Congo to the Belgian Congo.

Certainly the idea of a continental bloc played a part in all this, as Bethmann-Hollweg at the same time tried for a *détente* with Russia (after the war crisis of 1909), shown by the evidence at Potsdam (November 1910) and in the Russo-German agreement of 19 August 1911, in which Germany expressed disinterest in Persia and Russia agreed to the extension of the Baghdad Railway (the construction had stagnated for some time), but which was a disappointment to both sides – as, for example, in the founding of a German bank in Teheran which failed through Russian opposition.

The disappointments in the form of the abortive Franco-German co-operation shown above and the lack of success in such indirect ways of acquiring economic spheres of interest led to the idea of 1911 of making political capital out of France's action in Morocco, which according to the German interpretation violated the Algeciras Act (and thus restored freedom of action to Germany), in obtaining a consolidated possession in Central Africa through a demand for compensation. (The compensation offers of France of 7 May and 20–21 June were thought too little.) By exaggerating the interest of Mannesmann Brothers and some unimportant Hamburg trading-posts on the west Moroccan coast, for the protection of which the Foreign Office allegedly sent the gunboat *Panther* to Agadir, and by stirring up, through the co-operation of the Foreign Office with the Pan-German League, public excitement at the same time, the Secretary of State, Kiderlen-Wächter, was fully conscious that Germany's goal of the French Congo in return for giving France a free hand in Morocco could only be reached by taking all risks, including the risk of war. In July 1911 his policy could be sure of the support of the overwhelming part of the German Press, but he did not receive the Kaiser's consent. In fact the *'Panther's* leap' had only been forced on the Kaiser by the repeated threat of resignation.

Furthermore, it can be left quite open whether the primary aim of Bethmann-Hollweg's and Kiderlen-Wächter's policy was not so much Central Africa as (repeating the first Morocco crisis) the breaking-up of France's military alliance with Russia and her Entente with England: the objective was no less than this – after all what would France have been without her Entente? She would have become a junior partner of Germany, a position which perhaps could have been eased through her membership in *Mitteleuropa*.

After hard negotiations, which were several times broken off, in the compromise reached at last, Germany was ceded strips of territory which gave her access to the Congo and Ubangi (4 November 1911). It was the result of both nations' backing down, France because she had not received the complete support by treaty from England (despite the Mansion House speech) and also because Russia was still not ready for war; Germany because the Kaiser especially shrank from the prospect of a war on three fronts for which Germany was as yet not ready militarily or economically.

Considering the nation's high expectations, the repercussion of this failure in Germany was of decisive importance for the future attitudes of the ruling classes, the military, navy, heavy industry and National Liberal bourgeoisie. Already during the negotiations of the summer and autumn of 1911, the mood of the Pan-German League, disappointed over the delays, had changed into outspoken hatred of England when she covered the French position. But also the excessive excitement and disappointment turned against its own government, not least against the person of the Kaiser himself. All this hate against England exploded in the Reichstag speech in November 1911, against which the Chancellor, Bethmann-Hollweg's – another instance of 'resistance'! – mollifying speech was unable to prevail, a speech he made because he did not want to break the thread with England, since she was the only country willing to try for an agreement with Germany.

The bitterness whipped up in the German people against the English continued and formed the background to the Supplementary Naval Law of May 1912 (practically a third Naval Law, which was to run until 1920). Under the determining influence of Tirpitz and the forces rallied behind him, this was submitted to the Reichstag on the day of Haldane's arrival, and supported, despite English wishes, by the Kaiser. The Reichstag passed it, although the nationalist parties there did not find it far-reaching enough. At the same time the War Ministry prepared to reinforce the army by nearly exhausting the limits of conscription (the first reinforcement since 1891), which led to the first increase in the army in 1912 (from 1 October 1912 an increase from 595,000 to 622,000 men). Under the impact of the excitement on both sides of the Channel, Bethmann-Hollweg, on the advice of Kühlmann, the Chargé d'Affaires in London, and with the help of Ballin and Cassel, tried through the Haldane mission (February 1912) to bring about a *détente* and reach an agreement between England and Germany, which was aimed at the same time at loosening England's ties with France and Russia. This attempt at a *détente* was of course distinctly limited by the barrier erected in the form of Tirpitz's Supplementary Naval Law.

Bethmann-Hollweg himself saw very clearly the contradiction between the attempted *détente* and the Supplementary Naval Law. Writing on 10 April 1912 to the former German Ambassador in Constantinople, Freiherr von Marschall, asking him to take on the post of Ambassador to London (after the Kaiser had decided to recall Metternich in June–July), he declared that 'the task of achieving a political agreement with England at the same time as passing the Supplementary Naval Law produced a bellicose atmosphere which made it tantamount to squaring the circle'. Because of this 'the talks now begun' (subsequent to the Haldane mission) would 'not lead to a settlement for the moment'. But because he considers the pivot of our policy now and in the future 'the state of our relations with England', he desired 'the deployment of our ablest people' in London, despite his regret at having to entrust, at the present time, 'our Near Eastern policy' to someone else.

Bethmann-Hollweg hoped through a neutrality formula, which would have neutralised England in case of 'warlike developments' on the Continent and in this way have paralysed the Entente, to obtain some relief for Germany on the Continent and at the same time achieve her colonial aims in Central Africa which had failed because of France. A settlement with England over the Afro-Turkish question would have allowed Germany to pursue the construction of the Baghdad Railway to Basra, in return for which England would have had her sphere of influence in Kuwait and on the Persian Gulf guaranteed. Beyond this, Germany – in return for renouncing prospecting rights along the Baghdad Railway beyond Baghdad – would have gained a half of each of the Portuguese colonies of Angola and Mozambique.

From the spring of 1914 the Congo question was again added as a subject for discussion to the negotiations between Germany and England over the Baghdad Railway and the Persian Gulf as well as the partition of the Portuguese colonies.

In his reports of 9 December 1912 and 11 March 1913 over the Congo negotiations with the British government, the German Ambassador in London, Metternich, had reported English territorial claims in the north-eastern Belgian Congo. These definitely affected German interests, since the Imperial Colonial Office and extensive economic circles desired at some future date to establish via the northern Congo a connection between the Cameroons and German East Africa (including Portuguese East Africa) and then to get hold of the valuable mines in Katanga for Germany alone or to exploit them together with England.

As a result on 20 April 1914 the Secretary of State at the Imperial Colonial Office, Solf, suggested to Jagow, Secretary of State at the Foreign Office, that they should take up the negotiations once more on the basis of these reports – in this way to include a third subject in discussions for a commercial entente. Accordingly England's claims, which were not clearly defined, should be limited to Upper Katanga, while Germany would make certain of securing for herself among other things the valuable territory to the west of Uganda. On 23 April 1914 Kühlmann answered Solf's proposals: as a result of soundings made to the British government England wanted to fix latitude 10° South as the limit of her claims in Katanga. Consequently, the important mineral area somewhat to the north of Elisabethville should be divided between England and Germany.

At about this time the Benguela Railway, Katanga's main link with the Atlantic, with the harbour of the same name in Portuguese West Africa (Angola), was already up to 60 per cent controlled by the Deutsche Bank in association with Belgian capital, after the original owners, the English firm of Williams and Company, had since 1908 got into increasing financial difficulties. Although the Deutsche Bank could not obtain an Imperial guarantee for it, it had taken on this commitment at the wish of the Chancellor, Bethmann-Hollweg, as a *quid pro quo* for receiving an Imperial guarantee of 3 per cent for the Baghdad Railway loan. It was Solf who got Bethmann-Hollweg to get the Deutsche Bank to invest in the enterprise.

This was part of a policy of *pénétration pacifique* (as practised by France in Morocco and by England in Egypt and elsewhere) which Germany practised in the Portuguese colonies, hoping ultimately to obtain them in part or in their entirety. Parallel to West Africa the Deutsche Bank also took over a great part of the Nyasaland Company's concessions in Portuguese East Africa.

While the neutrality agreement in a form satisfactory to Germany could not be obtained, especially because Germany was not prepared to make a cut in the Supplementary Naval Law (after all it was not Tirpitz's but Germany's fleet), the negotiations over colonial and Near-Eastern agreements which had already started in the summer of 1911 continued from February 1912 till July 1914 and seemed with their positive result – at least in the opinion of Bethmann-Hollweg and the Kaiser – to have produced a very intimate relationship between Germany and England. But it should be remembered that these territorial and economic agreements had no effect, as they were not ratified and, as was the case with the Portuguese partition plan, were clogged with many reservations.

Bethmann-Hollweg's effort to reach agreement with England, manifested in these months-long overseas negotiations between private interests and state organs, culminated in the co-operation between England and Germany during the two Balkan Wars and gained further depth during the London Conference of Ambassadors from November 1912 onwards. This co-operation enabled the localisation of these conflicts and prevented (at too early a date) complications between Austria-Hungary which could have extended the localised conflict into a general war.

If, as a result of the Anglo-German co-operation, the outbreak of the expected Austro-Serbian, and consequently an Austro-Russian and general war, was avoided, the Balkans and Turkey were none the less in another way theatres for economic-political quarrels among the conflicting Great Powers. In these quarrels in the year and a half before the outbreak of the First World War the German government (the Kaiser, Bethmann-Hollweg, Jagow, Zimmermann, Bergen, Wangenheim) and those leading men of the economy closely connected with them (Krupp, Gwinner, Helfferich) felt more and more strongly the limits of Germany's effective military-political range and economic-financial power. German imperialism had reached a dead-end.

BULGARIA: LOANS POLICY IN THE STRUGGLE FOR THE BALKANS

An example of this situation and the increasing difficulties of German policy was the arranging of the Bulgarian loan of 1913–14 of 500 million leva, which could only be carried out with the greatest difficulty on the Berlin market under the management of the Disconto-Gesellschaft. Despite pressure from the German Ambassador in Sofia, Michahelles, the intervention of Krupp, who was pushing the loan for his own interest, pressure from the Hamburg houses of M. M. Warburg and Schröder and Company, and from the Berliner Handels-gesellschaft under Fürstenberg, who had advocated a loan for Bulgaria because of the tobacco monopoly offered as security by Bulgaria (parallel with the tobacco monopoly offered as security for the Serbian loan), the negotiating of the loan seemed about to come to grief because of the shortage of money on the Berlin market and because of the resistance caused by this from the Deutsche Bank, which wanted and required the existing reserve of the capital market to negotiate a new Baghdad Railway loan, and also because of the resistance of the Disconto-Gesellschaft, which was preparing the market for the negotiating of a Rumanian loan. That the loan did not fail was due to the political events of May and June 1914, as well as the personal relationship of Krupp, Baron von Schröder and Max Warburg with the Foreign Office and Imperial government and the possibility of concluding a commercial treaty with Bulgaria, which made it appear desirable and necessary to enter into a politico-economic partnership with Bulgaria, which since the end of the Second Balkan War was trying to revise the effects of the Peace of Bucharest, especially to regain the northern part of the Dobrudja from Rumania, through acceding to the Triple Alliance.

In contrast with Germany after the Second Balkan War, Austria-Hungary was seeking close relations with Bulgaria to counterbalance the enlargement of Serbia as the nucleus of a

Slav empire, and at the same time, as Melchior, a member of
the Warburg banking house and representative in the negotiations for the loan, reported, to 'lock out' Germany from
Bulgaria and the eastern Balkans. Under these auspices the
conclusion of the negotiations with Bulgaria meant a necessary
settlement with Bulgaria after the desertion of Rumania, the
beginning of an attempt to block Austrian ambitions, and also
an attempt to frustrate the intentions of the Anglo-American
tobacco trust, which was also after a monopoly of Bulgarian
tobacco. The Bulgarian loan was at last settled through the
political intervention of the German Ambassador and with the
Disconto-Gesellschaft stepping into the breach left by the
Fürstenberg–Warburg–Schröder consortium, which was too
weak to affect it. The Disconto-Gesellschaft's change of
position was determined by the threat of the Rumanian loan
slipping into Franco-American-English hands.

Despite being repeatedly urged by the Under-Secretary of
State, Zimmermann, as well as by the Prussian Ministry of
Commerce, the Deutsche Bank held aloof from the new policy
towards Bulgaria, although it remained active in the German
interest in the Balkans. The representatives of Germany's
interest in Turkey feared that the German market would be
even more strained through the loan to Bulgaria than it had
already been through the economic crisis of 1913. But as the
Deutsche Bank as well as the Disconto-Gesellschaft and the
Dresdner Bank were forced to establish markets and commercial financing for those branches of industry connected with
them, it seemed doubly necessary through the crisis for the
Deutsche Bank to keep hold of the Turkish market, especially
the Asiatic Turkish one, and to prevent its falling into
Anglo-French hands. The Baghdad Railway – Gwinner stressed to Wilhelm II that it was not a commercial undertaking but
a political one, since it would reflect the position of the German
Empire, its prestige in the world, its financial power and
economic expansion – needed new sums for the construction of
the line to Baghdad and beyond in addition to the money
already invested for its rapid construction. The Berlin money
market had to be kept liquid for this.

Moreover, after the end of the Second Balkan War which
changed the Bulgarian–Turkish border, the Deutsche Bank

actively intervened in Germany's Balkan policy by the repurchase of the European Orient Railway shares from Austria. The Deutsche Bank in the 1890s had taken up these shares of the Hirsch–Rothschild railway construction going back to the eighties. But as the Bank's commitments in the Baghdad Railway began to grow, these had been transferred to Austria, and until 1912 the Bank had withdrawn from the lines in the Balkans outside Turkey. When the enlarged Serbia after the Second Balkan War wanted to nationalise those lines inside her own territory, the attempt was made with French help to internationalise all the lines.

With the support of the Imperial government the Deutsche Bank, in opposition to the Franco-Austrian co-operation, demanded from Austria the return of those shares sold to them, so that they could make good with these securities the danger to their influence on the Balkan lines, which were a bridge to their chief undertaking, the Baghdad Railway.

Austria, however, tried to come to an arrangement with France, in order to obtain the aid of the Paris money market to realise not only her own railway aims but also for Austria to build a community of interests between Albania, Serbia and Bulgaria, which would express itself, as the Austrian Ambassador, Szögyény, put it, in a 'community of tariff interests'. In this case Austria-Hungary, as later in the war, was trying to save at least part of the Balkans from its economically stronger German ally.

GREECE: DYNASTIC POLICY VERSUS FINANCIAL POWER

Unlike in Bulgaria, where political objectives could be developed with the help of a loans policy, Germany was unable to draw Greece into her Balkan bloc. Although the German Ambassador, Count Quadt, detected in Venizelos a leaning towards help from German capital, since he felt that they were too dependent on French capital, the German Foreign Office had to say resignedly that a loan for Greece as well could not be raised on the German money market. The German Ambassador in Athens, Count Quadt, actually believed firmly that the only proper course for Greece was 'to attempt a close union with Rumania and one with Turkey, which was showing new life to some extent in Asia at least. . . . . I believe that we should encourage Greece in this way of strengthening herself and eventually to give her the chance of keeping herself, as before, independent from France and the Triple Entente by granting her a loan.' But the Foreign Office adviser Rosenberg could only remark on this: 'Considering the burdens on the money market and the danger of fragmenting our financial strength, it does not seem right at the moment to influence our banks officially.' Consequently in December 1913 France gave Greece a loan to 500 million francs, in two instalments of 250 million, which Venizelos negotiated in Paris. In return for this loan France acquired a monopoly of arms supplies, the building of the link line from Larissa to the Orient Railway and the construction of the harbour at Salonica, which Greece had recently gained. On the order of his government the German Ambassador made futile protests to King Constantine at the exclusion of German industry from the Greek market, which that loan resulted in. As well as this, Germany failed to get the expected contract for building two dreadnoughts. To Germany's mortification the contract went to England instead.

In another sphere as well, tied very closely to the supply of arms, the Germans were outdone by the French. Although King George of Greece had promised, in 1908 at Corfu on Wilhelm II's insistence, to accept German military instructors into the country, the Venizelos government had then called in a French military mission under Major Eydoux; this was caused not least by Germany's attitude in the Crete question, which because of her consideration for a friendly Turkey was more reserved than that of the so-called protective Powers (*Schutzmächte*), which included Italy as well. The immediate effect was that Greece then ordered telegraphic equipment for the fleet, not from Siemens in Berlin as intended, but from Marconi in Italy; the Germans did not even get a share in this project with the Italians. It seemed that Wilhelm II's policy here, resting entirely on the dynastic connection, proved as barren as in Rumania. The same was the case after the murder of King George in May 1913, when William's brother-in-law, Constantine, took the throne, who was strongly influenced by his energetic Prussian-minded wife. His enthusiasm aroused by

Constantine's ability as a military leader in the First Balkan War, Wilhelm II sent him a congratulatory telegram; originally the Kaiser had actually wanted to award the 'Pour le mérite' to the Turkish commander, Muktar Pasha, as well as to Constantine, as he had done with Nogi and Stössel, the two opposing commanders in the Russo-Japanese War, since he believed it had made an excellent impression. The Kaiser further explicitly explained to Constantine the reason for his enthusiasm: the King, supported by his military glory, could now at last confront his Parliament. He also made him, as he had made King Charles of Rumania before, a Prussian Field-Marshal in December 1913 during a visit to Berlin, just at the time that Venizelos was taking up the 500 million franc loan from France.

On being given this honour, Constantine gave a speech to the German generals at Potsdam, where he appeared to denigrate the French military instructors in comparison with the Prussian General Staff school (represented by himself and the officers in his headquarters). This speech caused a political crisis in Athens and resentment in the Parisian Press. In the Reichstag Bethmann-Hollweg defended King Constantine's expressions against criticisms of the affair. He claimed that these remarks had above all destroyed the widely believed story that German arms and German military instructors had been beaten in the Balkan wars.

In the first half of 1914 Germany tried in vain to bring Greece and Turkey together over the islands question, which had led both Powers to the brink of war, and thus to draw Greece into a combination of Turkey, Bulgaria and the Triple Alliance. The Greek Prime Minister only went along with it ostensibly. In fact Greece was tied to France both financially and through the military mission. Because of this King Constantine had to reject Wilhelm II's urgent appeal to enter the war on Germany's side in August 1914.

RUMANIA: THE GREAT DISAPPOINTMENT

Wilhelm II's efforts over Greece were always clung to rather dubiously as a kind of private policy: many people feared that

new naval plans and ideas about naval bases in the Aegean, at
Valona, Mersina or Adana, took second place to his liking for
his summer seat, the Achilleion on Corfu, and for archaeology.
More promising were German efforts over Rumania, which
had belonged to the Triple Alliance formally since the 1880s
and had even renewed the alliance with Austria in 1912. In
Rumania as well Wilhelm II tried to use the dynastic-military
connection, through the visit of a delegation of officers to
Bucharest to celebrate King Charles's fiftieth anniversary as a
member of a Prussian dragoon regiment or through the mission
of Prince Eitel Friedrich. In contrast to the inscrutable but
purposeful policy of Ion Bratianu and Take Ionescu, these
gestures of a late monarchical style could achieve nothing. At
the same time, besides the financial–economic problems the
Greater Rumania movement had appeared, directed against
Hungary. It had gained strength since the Balkan wars.
Germany had been pressing the Hungarian Prime Minister,
Tisza, without any success for suitable reforms. Wilhelm II in a
public telegram of congratulation to Charles praised the
conclusion of the Peace of Bucharest in August 1913, in which
he played a part himself by advising Charles of Rumania to give
Kavalla to Greece despite Bulgaria's wishes, as a 'definitive'
solution of the Balkan problem. But relations were always
uncertain, especially after the Tsar's visit to Charles in
Constanta in June 1914, even though Wilhelm II became
suspicious over this gradually rather than immediately. In
Rumania also King Charles could not get his country to take
part in the war. Wilhelm II in July 1914, overestimating the
possibility, still believed he could influence him. In fact Charles
could hardly keep his country neutral after the set-back on the
Marne, the Austrian defeats in Galicia and the Russian
advance over the Carpathians. King Charles died at the end of
1914, possibly with the help of his pro-English sister-in-law
Maria von Coburg. The country was only kept neutral with
some difficulty till 1916 by the German successes of the spring
of 1915 and very frequent German financial interventions.

That Rumania did not join the First World War on
Germany's side was of great consequence, as the Germans
considered Rumania – as was the case with Turkey – an outpost
of their economic commitment in the Balkans and Near East.

From the 1880s the Disconto-Gesellschaft, and later the Deutsche Bank as well, had invested large amounts of capital first in railways, in the redemption (*Ablösung*) of the Strousberg railway enterprises, then in oil. The security for this was partly the receipts from the Orient Railway and partly toll receipts, mining rights and rights to use harbours, such as Constanta. In sharp competition with Anglo-Dutch and American companies, and less so with Russian ones, in the oil business, the Disconto-Gesellschaft and the Deutsche Bank (in competition with each other) set up a subsidiary banking and production investment system (Steaua Romana and Banca Generala). But the Disconto-Gesellschaft companies, because their bore-holes were less rich, were forced increasingly to join with the Anglo-American trusts. On the other hand, the Deutsche Bank through reinsuring itself with the Russians was able to form an independent pool, the primary aim of which was to set up an oil monopoly in Germany, having created a German bank-holding company as the exclusive supplier for the German market. The very keen rivalry between Salomonson (Disconto-Gesellschaft), who was backed by Deterding and Rockefeller (i.e. Shell and Esso), and Gwinner (Deutsche Bank), who was affiliated with producers in Baku, was not settled before the world war, but the Deutsche Bank had nearly gained a monopoly in oil because of the intimate relations of Gwinner and Helfferich with Wilhelm II.

At the same time since the 1890s Rumania had increasingly become the scene of very keen competition between Schneider-Creusot and Krupp, who were both trying to capture for themselves the supplying of arms to the Rumanian army. In all the years after 1890, and especially after 1905, the Kaiser acted as the energetic champion of Krupp's interests, and the danger, as it seemed in 1906, that a large order for howitzers and field-pieces might go from Krupp to Schneider-Creusot moved Wilhelm II to write such irritated marginal notes as 'blackguards!' He ordered Hammerstein, the German Military Attaché in Bucharest, to communicate this: 'they [the howitzers and field-pieces] must definitely be ordered from us in Germany, else I shall clear out of Rumania, throw her officers out of my army and break off relations!' The Foreign Office was used to bring this threat of serious consequences immediately home to the Rumanian government like an order through the German Ambassador.

The arms business again meant a serious commitment of international financial power to negotiating loans for Rumania, which at the height of the Balkan crisis attached itself more firmly to the French side. The Disconto-Gesellschaft (Salomonson) and Bleichröder tried to neutralise them through new loans, which were floated by a very serious straining of resources, as was the case with the two German loans to Rumania of the spring and late autumn of 1913. The French banking groups which had taken about a third part of the state loans of 1905, 1908 and 1910 for political motives refused to take any part in the loan of 150 million francs in the spring of 1913, which would have made it feasible for Rumania to rearm for the Second Balkan War. The loan of 250 million francs in the autumn went only to Germany, because the French felt their economic influence in Rumania was so secure that they overreached themselves and demanded from the Rumanian government in return for the loan the assurance that all the larger state orders during the next two years should go to France. The Prime Minister, Marghiloman, rejected this demand and turned to the Germans again, but they could only meet his request for financial aid with difficulty.

But the shipping orders promised to the Schichau shipyard went to the Italians. While France's 'treating Rumania indulgently as never before' marked imperceptibly her enlistment to the Triple Entente as well, the visit of the Tsar in June 1914 already mentioned gave the outward sign. Neither the intense activity of Krupp and the Rheinische Metallwarenfabrik which reinforced Krupp on the munitions side, and of Mauser-Rottweil and the Deutsche Bank, nor Wilhelm II's efforts with Charles and the Crown Prince, Ferdinand, and those of the Foreign Office with Rumanian politicians, especially with such conservatives as Carp, could stop Rumania from following her economic interests (the greater resources of the French money market) and her national aspirations (in Transylvania) and approaching the Entente.

THE BALKAN CRISIS, SERBIA AND BOTH BALKAN LEAGUES

After the Greeks, despite the pro-German inclinations of King Constantine, had come to depend heavily on France through the 500 million franc loan obtained by Venizelos in Paris in December 1913, a third Balkan League took definite shape because a certain rapprochement occurred between Greece and Rumania, the two chief gainers from the Second Balkan War and the two States most interested in preserving the *status quo* of the Peace of Bucharest of August 1913. This combination was strengthened, although there was no formal alliance, by the new Rumanian Foreign Minister, Take Ionescu, who had replaced the more conservative Majörescu, during a five-day visit to Athens, and who on the wish of the Turkish Minister of the Interior, Talaat Bey, intervened and mediated an agreement between Greece and Turkey, who had been close to war over the islands question, especially over Mytilene and Chios. It was made clear here that Rumania would not intervene in a Turkish–Greek naval war (such a war could only in fact have been carried out once both Greece and Turkey had received their two dreadnoughts, which were on order from England – a good example of how war and business are interrelated), but would intervene by an attack on Bulgaria if Bulgaria allowed Turkish troops to land in Dedeagach or if, as a result of a Turkish victory, Bulgaria accepted Kavalla for herself, which would have meant a breach of the Peace of Bucharest.

This combination becomes more interesting with the inclusion of Serbia into this group of two, which at the beginning had been praised in the newspapers on both sides as a coalition of the Greco-Latin civilisation against the Slavs. Serbo-Greek hostility was mainly due to the frontier demarcation of the newly-created State of Albania. Rumania contributed to reducing the tension, helped by the fact that the new state's ruler, the Prince of Wied, was nephew to the Rumanian Queen. Belief in a revived Balkan League was strengthened when Venizelos and Pašić (the moderate yet decidedly Greater Serbia-minded Premier of Serbia) visited St Petersburg, and had joint talks in Bucharest with Take Ionescu.

The settlement created by Rumania between Greece and Serbia led the three Powers to their frequently declared aim of bringing Turkey as well into their group of three, which an isolated Bulgaria would have had to join whether she liked it or not.

Of those countries mentioned above, Serbia for quite a long time had already been largely dependent on the French money market: as late as January 1914 she received a 250 million franc loan from France. Greece had just become dependent on the same. The Turks, whose financial administration, the Ottoman debt, was for the most part under Anglo-French control and which contained three times as much French investment as German, received a French loan of 500 millions in the spring of 1914. Although the Rumanians had received a French loan as late as October 1913, in her economic life the German banks, as has been shown, were in sharp competition in the oil interests with Anglo-Dutch-American capital.

Besides these financial connections it was very important that two of the above States were becoming increasingly opposed to Austria-Hungary through *irredenta* questions: Rumania because of Transylvania, and Serbia because of Bosnia and Hercegovina (and Croatia and Slovenia as well), which the Serbs had only allowed to be annexed in March 1909 under German pressure.

The difficulties of Germany's position in the Balkans were further added to by her diplomatic and economic activity in Serbia, Rumania and Bulgaria conflicting with that of her ally, Austria-Hungary. Already during the Bosnian crisis of 1908 when the Germans in their 'shining armour' had defended the Danubian Monarchy against Russia, they had taken over the economic position which Austria had previously held, thus causing strong complaints by Austria-Hungary. The import statistics of the Balkan States show very plainly how far the Germans had driven Austria out of this market.

In the years from 1901 to 1905 the German and Austrian shares of the total imports of Rumania were still almost equal with 27.1 and 28.5 per cent. But in 1913 the Austrian share had dropped to 23.4 per cent and the German had risen to 40.3 per cent. The example of Serbia is still more pronounced. While Austria-Hungary in 1884 held the leading position with 62.4

per cent of Serbia's total imports and Germany had only 14.9 per cent, by 1910 the proportions had nearly reversed themselves: the Austrian share had dropped to 19 per cent and the German had risen to 41.3 per cent.

The predominance of the Berlin trading company (Berliner Handelsgesellschaft) which had considered Serbia its own domain since the 1890s and had compelled Serbia to form a combined tobacco and salt tariff monopoly as security for its loans caused great alarm in Austro-Hungarian business circles, since their chief territorial market was the Balkans and it would have to remain so, given the needs and resources of the Dual Monarchy. To defend themselves from German pressure in Serbia, as was the case in Bulgaria, Austria-Hungary approached the French money market. French capital was to participate in the project for the 'internationalisation' of the new Serbian railways. An Austro-French company was planned by the two railway magnates, the French Vitali and the Austrian Adler, who were to raise the money, while an Austro-French-Serbian company intended to run the administration of the lines. At the same time this was meant to neutralise the Serbian demands for the nationalisation of the lines with material antidotes. In the face of these dangers mentioned above, the Imperial government's policy in the Balkans increasingly hesitated between seizing the Balkans as its own direct sphere of interest and conceding a predominant influence there to the Austro-Hungarian Monarchy. Austro-German relations were increasingly blighted by this.

This conflict of interests within the Triple Alliance was encouraged further at the beginning of 1913 and again at the beginning of 1914 when Serbia, which had already expanded considerably through the Balkan wars, seemed on the point of further expansion by aiming at union with Montenegro. If this happened, Austria wanted to respond by annexing the Lovčen and by handing over Montenegro's coastal strip with the harbour of Antivari to Albania (here Austria-Hungary was already marking out what was to be one of her principal war aims in 1914–18), to shut out the new Serbia from the Adriatic, which it had reached in 1913. For her part Italy, who had just renewed the Triple Alliance at the end of 1912, certainly did not want to allow such an increase in Austro-Hungarian power on the Adriatic. San Giuliano declared to the German Ambassador, Flotow, that if Austria-Hungary acted in this way Italy would have grounds for war. Only one compensation would cause Italy not to go to war: the cession of the Trentino.

Germany had already seen serious dangers in the difficulties which had arisen between the members of the Triple Alliance, Austria-Hungary and Italy, in their quasi-condominium over Albania (it seemed very reminiscent of the Schleswig-Holstein situation of 1864–6), and tried with all kinds of diplomatic influence to prevent Austria from acting on her own and to make her come to some understanding with Italy on this question for the sake of holding the Triple Alliance together. It was not only very important to Germany to keep Italy in the Triple Alliance because of the pressure on France, but also because of Wilhelm II's belief that the united fleets of Austria-Hungary and Italy together with his hopes for united fleets of Greece and Turkey would be equal to the Franco-Russian fleet (he does not seem to have thought of England as an opponent in the Mediterranean in the spring of 1914!). That the Kaiser and Tirpitz had new naval plans and ideas for naval stations in Asia Minor is known because of remarks of Wangenheim and of the Chancellor, who was afraid of such plans because of Anglo-German relations.

The dubious element in the Balkans in the period between the Second Balkan War and the World War, and in the new power relationships and their repercussions upon the Great Powers, lies in the fact that Germany also had plans for Balkan leagues, though with different combinations (the Kaiser was especially thinking of Greece and Turkey, while the Ambassador in Constantinople, Wangenheim, and following him the Foreign Office, were thinking of Turkey and Bulgaria), which could check the Rumanian–Russian alliance, which the Ambassador believed in existence. Serbia could also have been fitted into this combination. The Germans, as shown, were highly active economically in Serbia and believed that Serbia should be pulled into the Triple Alliance by the Austrians through trade treaties and a customs union.

Ostensibly German intentions seem identical with the plans of Ionescu Pašić and Venizelos. The last appeared to demonstrate by a visit to Berlin in December 1913 the new connection between Greece and Rumania as an approach to the Triple Alliance – possibly not without some cynicism. But in fact because French money and Russian diplomacy were very much at the bottom of them, these combinations were not only a threat to Austria-Hungary, especially in the case of Serbia and Rumania, but also in the last resort no less a threat to German policy in the Balkans and the East. Kaiser Wilhelm II built up all his combinations primarily on the monarchs, in Athens, Bucharest and then in Sofia. But these rulers did not have the same position in their States as the Prussian King, and he seriously underestimated these rulers' dependence on the attitudes of the Parliaments and their national aspirations. Consequently the Germans, by sticking to what were also foreign dynasties, were putting themselves against the strongest movements of the time. They continued with this approach in their aims during the First World War in setting up a chain of satellite monarchies – in Finland, Courland, Lithuania, Poland, etc.

These parallel but completely different plans for Balkan leagues, apart from the influence of the Entente, demonstrate also an active striving for independence for these nations and States, a striving for freedom from dependence on the Great Powers. Even the Turks were affected by this. During the war Wangenheim said that the 'Osmanisation of Turkey' (as he put it), which he noticed to be especially strong, had already been established before the war – the Young Turk revolution of 1908 was a product of it. The particular economic situation was still more important for Germany's acute situation in the autumn of 1913 and the spring of 1914 than the resistance from the currents of time, which were working against Germany. Above all, Germany could no longer meet the demands of those States for state loans nor attach them to her by economic penetration. Economic concessions were in fact given in return for loans. Instead, Germany saw the financially stronger rivals of the Entente overtake her, above all France and England and already behind them – often already mentioned explicitly in the documents – the United States.

THE CRISIS IN THE NEAR EAST: TURKEY MOVES TOWARDS THE TRIPLE ENTENTE

After the second Morocco crisis the German Foreign Office hoped to ease the strained relations with England through a 'global *entente*' which would have brought the Germans some consolidation in Central Africa through a simultaneous agreement with England and France, as the German Chargé d'Affaires in London, Kühlmann, was proposing, and which would have given her at the same time a free hand in the Balkans against Russia.

The Baghdad Railway question was bound up with others – the questions of the irrigation of Mesopotamia and of oil – which together with the agreement between the Anglo-Persian Oil Company and the Deutsche Bank–Shell group came up again in 1914 and formed the core of the London negotiations for agreement between Germany and England. Ballin and Wönckhaus were also demanding a solution of the questions of navigation and of the ports in the Shatt El-Arab. There was also the question over mining in Heraclea, where Hugo Stinnes saw German heavy industry's 'essential' interest.

The London negotiations showed that because of Germany's lack of capital, German interests in Turkey as well as in the Balkans were forced to come to terms with the other Imperial Powers. The coveted guarantee for the new Baghdad Railway loan could only be secured through a tariff increase, which in turn could only be obtained through the agreement of England and France in the Turkish financial administration, and this agreement would have to be bought by Germany through concessions to both Powers. This problem became even more serious, since Germany believed not only because of the economic crisis of 1913 that she was increasingly dependent on markets but also that in line with her economic development since 1880, she could not give up her claim to a position of world power, which she desired for herself and fully affirmed, but on the contrary must push towards further expansion.

Those European Powers who were rivals in Turkey had already discussed, in the 1880s and 1890s, plans for partitioning the Ottoman Empire. But not least through the German military missions and the Baghdad Railway, Turkey had become somewhat stronger; this, however, was followed by serious upheavals in the form of the Young Turk revolution, and in the Balkan and Libyan wars. When, in May 1913, before her temporary recovery in the Second Balkan War, Turkey's weakness was especially apparent, Wilhelm II believed that everything indicated that Russia, England and France intended a partition of Turkey. On a report about Russian troops gathering in north Persia the Kaiser wrote: 'Preparations for the partition of Turkey: it is apparently more imminent than was believed. In Palestine and Syria a life-and-death struggle between England and France has already broken out underhand. Therefore pay attention! Let us ensure that the partition shall not be carried out without us. I want Mesopotamia, Alexandretta, Mersina. The sensible Turks are already expecting this fate patiently.' In these reflections, as we know from Bethmann-Hollweg, the Kaiser was influenced by reports made personally to him from Professor Moritz, the Director of the Oriental Seminar in Berlin. The Kaiser worried the Imperial Chancellor by wanting ships sent to Alexandretta and Mersina to enforce German claims. According to one of the Kaiser's memoranda it was very important 'to have definite objectives in this event [the partition], instead of warning the Turks, which the present Turkish government does not deserve and would never be acted on anyway'.

The Kaiser (and in this he was entirely at one with his Chancellor, Bethmann-Hollweg) associated in his own mind these partition plans with co-operation with England, such as had been experienced for six months at the London Conference of Ambassadors, and with attempts to reach agreement with England on the basis of common interests (since 1911, in fact, the Baghdad Railway and colonial agreements had been negotiated). It was in this light that the Emperor commented on an article in the *Daily News* on the occasion of Lord Morley's visit to Berlin on 15 May 1913, which expressed the view that European peace would be safe if England and Germany worked together:

Splendid! This signifies introspection and conversion. I could not wish for a better . . . merciless judgement upon the policy of great adventures and Ententes of my uncle Edward

VII! In the long run a policy directed against Germans with Slavs and Gauls is absolutely unworkable for the Anglo-Saxons! We shall find one another in Asia Minor, either for the sake of Turkey (perhaps on the basis of the Cyprus Treaty, the *status quo* and defence of Turkish territory from Russo-Bulgarian aspirations) or at her expense!

The 'principal question' for the Kaiser was England's position 'with the French against the Germans or as a neutral'. How far the Kaiser was thinking in line with Houston Stewart Chamberlain's categories is shown by his remark about the London Conference of Ambassadors: 'Chapter 2 of the Barbarian migration is now closed. Chapter 3 now opens with the fight of the Germans against the Russo-French for existence. No conference can settle this because it is not a political but a racial question. . . . It is the question of to be or not to be for the German race in Europe.'

Also in the Liman von Sanders crisis England's position in a possible future war with Russia and France was the German Imperial government's chief consideration.

When, on 22 October 1913, the Russian Foreign Minister, Sazonov, was in Berlin, Wilhelm II believed it right that he should not tell him about the impending dispatch of General Liman von Sanders to Turkey. He believed this although the treaty concluded between the Imperial government and the Turkish government on 28 October 1913 contained the extraordinary innovation that Liman von Sanders should not only be the head of an enlarged military mission of German instructing officers but should also be the general commanding the First Army Corps in Constantinople. This arrangement caused a sensation and was felt in St Petersburg especially to be a provocation.

Because the three Entente Powers closed ranks against this arrangement, the Germans had to give way in the end, although this was cloaked by the appointment of Liman as a Turkish Marshal. The most interesting point in the Liman von Sanders crisis, however, was the belief of the Imperial government and especially of the Kaiser that they could play off England's special position on the Bosphorus (the English Admiral Limpus's position as commander of the Turkish fleet) against her Entente allies to isolate Russia (and France). So on 18 December 1913, when Zimmermann wrote to Wilhelm II, he received the Kaiser's full support in believing that 'His Majesty's gracious directives would be complied with, if we made a point of undermining as far as possible the understanding between Russia and England over this question and on the same grounds further play on the Dardanelles question and the English Admiral's command in the Bosphorus'.

It was because of their intention to detach the English from their allies and bring them towards the Germans that the Foreign Office held back over the Anglo-Turkish Dock Treaty of October 1913, which gave the English practically a monopoly of all Turkish shipbuilding, repairing, equipping and so on. The Foreign Office's position here seems to have been dictated entirely by political calculations, because German economic interests demanded loudly that the German government should intervene with the Turkish against this treaty. Krupp raised strong objections against this treaty several times. He did this first officially and then through his intimate friend, 'dear Diego' von Bergen, Referent in the Foreign Office, whose significant role in German policy from 1914 to 1918, especially in revolutionising Russia, I have shown in my *Griff nach der Weltmacht*. Wangenheim, Ambassador in Turkey, counselled his government that they should point out resolutely in London 'that we could not acknowledge any interpretation of the Dock Treaty which excluded us from any competition in Turkish shipbuilding'. And Günther, the second Director of the Anatolian Railway and thereby Helfferich's and Gwinner's representative in Constantinople, telegraphed angrily to Helfferich, who passed it on immediately to Zimmermann:

> By this [the Ismed Dock Treaty] our base in Turkey and maritime Constantinople is brought under English control and it will be said that the Baghdad Railway starts in an English arsenal and ends in an English net, the Persian Gulf. In our authoritative quarters they do not seem completely to grasp the consequence . . .

He gave urgent warning against allowing a *fait accompli*. As well as Krupp, the Deutsche Bank stood out against indulging the

English too much, since the question of its own existence was bound up with it, because a Baghdad Railway hedged in by the English would cause any loan negotiations in Germany to be illusory. In the same way Albert Ballin, Director of the Hamburg–America line, stood out against indulging the English, because it would injure German maritime interests in the Persian Gulf.

It is therefore all the more important that the Imperial Chancellor, Bethmann-Hollweg, decided himself out of political considerations not to upset England, but by accepting the Dock Treaty to provide a further element in building a German–English understanding, which would serve to isolate England and to break up the Triple Entente. Wilhelm II made this calculation quite on his own, as is shown by his marginal notes to reports from Pourtalès, for example that on 18 December 1913.

The Kaiser sketched out expressly the route which German policy should follow (20 December 1913). Wilhelm II wrote about a report from Wangenheim that England's relations with Russia were strained because of the Ismed Dock Treaty, which the Russians were taking worse than the Liman von Sanders episode:

> Marvellous! Consequently the Triple Entente has to submit to English interests! And it is important for Germany that we should not make her angry through a quarrel with us!

The Kaiser was impressed and took notice of the warning given by the *Daily Graphic* that England should not out of consideration for the Entente allow herself to be dragged into opposition to the German military mission, but on the contrary should try to maintain good relations with Berlin. He went on in fact to say that he believed:

> London's interests are more secured through co-operation with Berlin than through working with the Entente Powers! In German that means that the Entente does not correspond to English interests. Ergo it is no longer attractive.

Even England's final co-operation with France and Russia in

the Liman von Sanders question did not end German hope of England's breaking away from the Entente.

This very careful demeanour in Germany's relations with England was matched by an, at least initially, tough attitude to Russia, which only stopped when it came up against a common *démarche* of the three Entente Powers.

The Kaiser wrote a revealing marginal note (not printed in *Die Grosse Politik*!) to the report in which Zimmermann proposed that the German Ambassador should talk to Giers, Russian Ambassador in Constantinople, and should promise to keep German influence in Turkey in line with Russian wishes (the transfer of the First Army Corps to the provinces). In this note Wilhelm observed:

> As they [the instructions to Wangenheim] are herein drafted, no! They will have to be considerably altered! They look like a capitulation on our part to Russia! I am no longer in the mood to bargain with Russian wishes at the cost of my army and of Turkey. My officials forget that they have three million bayonets and a dozen ships of the line at their disposal!!!

Also in the marginal notes to Pourtalès's reports over the Russian position in the crises (where apparently the Kaiser was thinking about Russia's backing down in March 1909) can be found the hope of being able to bring the English out of the Entente:

> Once again Russia, as so often before, has tried one of her several attempts at bluff at our cost and through her allies. Naturally we will not allow ourselves nor the allies as well to be taken in by it! Turkey's prestige will increase as the result of any great Russian disgrace!

A similar conviction is shown by the Kaiser's marginal note to the assertion by the Russian newspaper *Retch* that the Entente would hold fast and united: 'Bluff! You have no idea at all! When the English have refused point-blank the union will come to an end!' Even after the settlement of the international conflict over Liman von Sanders, his role and activity remained a weight on German–Turkish relations and on Germany's whole Oriental policy. Conflicts arose over Liman, which give very revealing insights into the motives and impulses behind Germany's whole policy and at the same time into the apparently insoluble difficulties resulting from it.

Liman has been described as 'passionate and ambitious' (Pourtalès) and 'conceited and suspicious' (Gerhard von Mutius). His behaviour and interminable quarrels over protocol in claiming to have precedence at dinners over the Turkish Minister of War and Foreign Minister (on the Prussian pattern) put Enver Pasha out of sorts. Enver Pasha had just been appointed Minister of War at thirty-one and Germany was later to control Turkey through him. By this action Liman greatly endangered not only the activity of the military mission but Germany's whole policy. There was one event which was highly significant for the structure of the German Empire: without consulting or notifying the Imperial civil government (Ambassador, Foreign Office, Imperial Chancellor) Liman made a Bavarian lieutenant-colonel, Kübel, on 1 March 1914, Chief of the Railway Department in the Turkish General Staff. This led to a conflict which completely shook Germany's whole policy in Turkey.

During a journey of inspection of German and Turkish General Staff officers and representatives of the Anatolian Railway, this man clashed violently with the first Director of the line, Huguenin. In accordance with his instructions he demanded from him the extension of the railway network within half a year for military deployment. According to the estimates of the Deutsche Bank, the financial backer of the undertaking, these structural changes would have needed at least 100 million marks. But no security in Turkish assets or custom receipts was, nor could be, available, because everything, even the future receipts of graveyards – there were long negotiations over this, which in the end failed because of Turkish national feeling – and the wealth of the museum, had already been pledged to the German and French consortia. But the Deutsche Bank, to finance the speedy continuation of the railway, had already lent very great sums in the last loans to the limits of its resources, and to get security for a new loan had negotiated with the Great Powers for an increase in Turkish tariff rates from 3 per cent to 4 or 5 per cent, negotiations which had passed over the German government. In this conflict between the 'Anatolians' Helfferich and Gwinner and the banking groups and authorities dependent on them in Turkey, and the military mission, the Ambassador, Wangenheim, passionately sided with the Baghdad Railway and appealed to the Imperial Chancellor on 12 May 1914 to enforce the authority of policy over the short-sightedness and wilfulness of the military. The Ambassador said that the Baghdad Railway

> is the mainstay of our Oriental policy which H.M. the Kaiser began. A threat to the Baghdad could not only lead to an economic Panama but could also have incalculable effects for us politically. The military mission is not an end in itself, but only an expedient for our Baghdad Railway policy. [Jagow altered this in the report for the Kaiser to 'Eastern policy'.] Because of that it is indispensable that the activity of the military mission be subordinated to our political interests.

This event – the Near Eastern equivalent of Zabern – was so irritating and dangerous for the German Empire's whole policy that Bethmann-Hollweg tried to force the Kaiser to a decision by presenting a long immediate petition on 20 May 1914 – this was two months before the effecting of the German–Turkish alliance at the end of the July crisis. The Chancellor tried to make the Kaiser realise that Liman von Sanders did not seem to grasp:

> That his mission is not an end in itself, but only a means to an end. Germany's interest in the strengthening of the Turkish army stands and falls with our political influence at the Golden Horn. We are only interested in the success of the reform work if, and for as long as, Turkey remains on our side. If we fail to keep Turkish support, any increased battle-worthiness of their army would merely be a gain for our enemies. We have no reason to sharpen the Turkish sabre for France or Russia. . . .

These conflicts in question at the moment could 'cause

irreparable damage to our position in the Ottoman Empire'
and the Kaiser should therefore interpose his authority.

The Kaiser's marginal notes to this immediate petition of the
Chancellor reveal at a stroke the situation which the Empire
was in with its Oriental policy at the end of May 1914.
Referring to German influence in Turkey the Kaiser said:

> It is absolutely nothing compared with earlier! Turkey no
> longer intends to stick with us. She is trailing in the
> Russo-French wake, where money is thrown about, and is
> feeding us solely with words.

Wilhelm II was referring here to the large French loan to
Turkey, and brings out the outstanding significance of the lack
of German financial resources for German foreign policy:

> We cannot! [keep Turkey on our side] because we have no
> money! They are no longer on our side!

The Kaiser already saw the Turks in the Entente camp, who
were ready to give her not only money but also support in her
fight with Greece over the islands:

> While she amuses us with phrases and fine-sounding
> words and a few Turkish princes, she is joining Russia and
> the Triple Entente for anti-Greek aims. We are in fact
> sharpening Turkish weapons for them.

The 'dishonesty' and 'hollowness' of the Turks expressed itself
in that they 'even' wanted 'to buy cruisers immediately from us
now to use against Athens!' Through this Wilhelm II's policy
for a Greek–Turkish agreement was wrecked, and at a time
when German officers were trying 'to bring some order –
without money naturally [underlined by the Kaiser] – into this
ragged army'. Wilhelm II threatened:

> I will no longer stand for it. If the Turks want to make war
> on the Greeks over the islands, I will withdraw the officer
> mission!
> Turkey is beyond help, and of no further value! She may as

well go to pieces in the arms of the Triple Entente! Wilhelm
I.R. [Underlining by the Kaiser.]

It was not only French capital which the Germans could no
longer compete with and the Entente's policy which threatened
Germany's position in Turkey, but also the political situation
within the Ottoman Empire. The Kaiser said that the Young
Turk government would 'tell a pack of lies' to the Ambassador,
whereas Liman, 'with the army, has to deal with facts'. The
Young Turk government was approaching the Entente and
was 'lying, untrustworthy, empty, conceited and venal'.

Even if the Kaiser's lofty phrases put things too dramati-
cally, it none the less by and large corresponded to the state of
things and above all to the view of things held by the German
Imperial government. How greatly in fact Germany's economic and consequent political position in the East was
threatened in the spring of 1914 is shown, as already said, by
Germany's being unable to supply a sufficient state loan to
Turkey, which had to be issued on the Paris market with
enormous concessions to France to Germany's obvious disadvantage, such as railway concessions (as the Arghana–Bit-
lis–Van railway line) which came up against the Anatolian
Railway, and harbour concessions in Jaffa, Haifa, Tripoli (Asia
Minor) and Heraclea on the Black Sea which endangered
Hugo Stinnes's plans. The impossibility of Germany's furnish-
ing such a loan was shown by Jagow's attempted bluff to
obstruct the Franco-Turkish loan negotiations. Writing to
Wangenheim on 15 March 1914 Jagow reported a conversation
with the French Ambassador, Cambon. According to him he
had told Cambon that if the negotiations for the Franco-Turkish loan were not completed soon, he would be unable to resist
much longer the pressure from German financial circles for a
Turkish loan which he had held out against till then from
loyalty to France. Jago went on to say:

> This bluff does not seem to have failed to impress the
> French Ambassador because he told me that he wanted to
> communicate it to Paris. To be realistic I do not think it
> would be possible to meet Turkish financial needs in
> Germany.

This threat to Germany's political and economic position in Turkey can be seen above all, however, in the domestic German struggle between the two most important German exporters to Turkey, a struggle which probably ran parallel with the one above. On the one hand was Krupp in alliance with the Dresdner Bank (headed by Eugen Gutmann), which was the Deutsche Bank's keenest competitor, and on the other was the Deutsche Bank itself. Krupp and his ally the Rhenish metal and armaments factory (Rheinische Metall und Waffen-fabrik), whose board included Paasche, the Vice-President of the Reichstag, to stop themselves being driven from the Turkish market by Schneider-Creusot – look at the conditions about all arms to be supplied by France which was attached to the French loan to Greece! – wanted a 120 million franc loan for Germany to be negotiated on the Berlin market which would pay for their arms supplies to Turkey.

The Directors of the Deutsche Bank, Helfferich and Gwin-ner, fought this by addressing a string of forceful petitions to the Foreign Office which they definitely hoped the Kaiser would see. These Directors were already having to negotiate on the Berlin money market a badly needed loan of 250 million francs for the Deutsche Bank for the extension of the Baghdad Railway, and they therefore pointed out that from their long experience of the Berlin market it was impossible to raise two such loans for Turkey because of the difficulty over securities.

Since the 1860s there had been a tradition at the Berliner Platz of reserving the resources of the Berlin market for the floating of loans by one 'of the biggest banking groups. The Deutsche Bank was all the more dependent on the state of the market at the Berliner Platz being favourable to it, because not only was it facing competition from Krupp who hoped to force through loans for Turkey and Bulgaria with the Dresdner Bank on the one hand and the Berliner Handelsgesellschaft and Warburg on the other, but also the Foreign Office on political grounds was pushing forward for agreement with England, thereby endangering the security and the sale of Baghdad Railway securities.

Because of this, as Helfferich wrote to Zimmermann (by hand on 29 May 1914), there was a danger of the Deutsche

Bank's collapse with incalculable consequences for German economic life and for German policy.

> As things are going, everything is at stake over Baghdad. Not one of our Board of Directors can take the responsibility of going any further with the advances for the construction of the Baghdad Railway without the certain prospects of a Baghdad loan in the very near future. If the market is ruined for us by a Bulgarian or Turkish armaments loan we will have to shut up shop!

The bankers could not have expressed more clearly and openly the bankruptcy threatening this great company. Helfferich and Kankowski, the third Director of the Bank, threatened the Foreign Office with stopping the construction of the Railway, which would wreck German prestige in Turkey, unless the Empire supported and forced through an issue of the Baghdad Railway loan under monopoly conditions.

In fact the loan for Baghdad was floated by the Deutsche Bank alone. Krupp got his share for the industrial firms connected with him, which meant that the Dresdner Bank had to withdraw. But after the Baghdad Railway loan was negotiated, a way was found for issuing one for Bulgaria – on political grounds – though with some difficulty and, what is more, through the Disconto-Gesellschaft.

German Imperialism therefore was faced by a basic dilemma. If the armaments business could no longer find finance, German industry – an over-extended, heavy industry, dependent on exports – would lose its selling markets; but if investment facilities could not be found for the undertaking of the Baghdad Railway which would be under construction for many years, not only would German prestige suffer but also directly from this German political influence in Turkey and with it Germany's position in the East would be in danger.

The Kaiser's friend Gwinner wrote on 13 June 1914, two weeks before Sarajevo:

> We felt we had to undertake this sacrifice [i.e. of making large uncovered loans for continuing and accelerating the

construction] because everything depends on showing our strength to the Powers unfriendly to the Railway, and because a halt in the further construction, which would have been right from a purely financial and business point of view, would have been interpreted by our enemies as showing that German financial resources were inadequate to carry through this great enterprise and that Germany would therefore have to accept any conditions in the dispute over Turkish railway questions.

In June 1914, therefore, not only was Germany's bridge to the East, the Balkans, in danger, but also the object of German political and economic expansion in the East, Turkey itself, was in very great danger. Thus the moment had come, which Wilhelm II had already pointed out in 1907 as the critical point in relations with France, when he minuted a report over the threatening French rivalry in the East:

> Envy, nothing but envy; everyone is envious of us. But the French especially must be left in no doubt that they should not dare to rely on the Entente with Britain to amuse themselves by trying to supplant us in the East. These are vital interests which must be defended at all cost. If need be I will fight for them.

THE REVIVAL OF THE 'MITTELEUROPA' POLICY

The impasse which German imperialism had reached in 1913 was accurately expressed in Rathenau's resigned and blunt observation: 'The time of great gains has been missed for Germany.' But according to Rathenau they were all the more necessary for her because, as 'the most populous, richest and most industrialised country of Europe, with the most powerful army', Germany had a legitimate moral claim to an equal part of the earth as that of her neighbours. Rathenau saw 'a last possibility' of making up for Germany's lost opportunities in 'going after a central European customs union, which willingly or unwillingly, sooner or later, the States of Western Europe would join', i.e. Belgium and France and in the end England as well. 'The object should be to create an economic union which would equal, perhaps be superior to, the American.'

Behind these ideas was the thinking which had been formulated for the first time by the Tübingen political economist and former Austrian Minister of Commerce, Albert Schäffle: 'The British Empire and *Mitteleuropa*. . . . This European–German world ought to resist American–Russian exploitation in this way.' To this should be added Wilhelm II's statement a few months before the outbreak of the First World War in the spring of 1914, which, when taken with those of the spring of 1912, shows how strongly Germany was already conscious in her policy and economy of the world power of the United States. When disturbances had broken out again in Mexico in 1913–14 and it was thought that Germany ought to intervene there, together with England and France, the German Ambassador in Washington, Count Bernstorff, on being asked for his opinion, said that Wilson's policy had shown 'that Europe is not united and strong enough to resist American policy in the Western Hemisphere', and he forecast Europe's withdrawal from Mexico. The Kaiser minuted this with:

> England has left Europe magnificently in the lurch and discredited it. She ought to defend Europe's interests in Mexico together with the Continent and in this way smash the Monroe Doctrine.

In this situation of 1913–14 can be seen the consideration for England and wooing of her as well as the anti-American bias.

The *Mitteleuropa* concept makes it clear that Germany's striving for world power, which by 1912–13 seemed no longer to have any realisable objectives in the world – unless very restricted ones in a working association with England in Turkey and possibly in a partition of the Portuguese colonies – was moving demonstrably towards a European hegemony, at least in the economic sphere, a hegemony which, according to Rathenau, had been Germany's for a short time under Bismarck but which had not been sufficiently strengthened and which had been taken from her. For Germany the strengthening of her position in Europe had become a question of existence. According to him the power of civilised States (*Kulturstaaten*) depended on their economic power, and Germany's raw-material basis was too narrow. Germany was dependent on 'the charity of the world market', as long as it did not control sufficient sources of raw materials and safe markets. To ensure Germany's basis for life in the present and in the future, they needed *Mitteleuropa* and its complementary, Central Africa:

> It would be impossible in a generation to feed and employ a hundred million Germans from the product of a half a million square kilometres of our home ground and plot in Africa, and we do not want to depend on the charity of the world market. We need territory on the globe . . . in future partitions we must get hold of the necessary territory, until we are as satisfied as our neighbours.

Ideas like these came up in the Kaiser's talks with Rathenau, as for example one evening at Admiral Hollman's house, two days after Haldane's visit to Berlin, on 13 February 1912. Starting from his good relations with Alfred de Rothschild ('My highly respected friend') and the City of London, as well as his friendly relations with George V, the Kaiser developed his ideas to Rathenau. 'His plan is for a United States of Europe against America. . . . This would not displease the English. Five States (including France) would be able to do something.' It must remain open whether Rathenau had fired the Kaiser with his ideas or the other way round. What is certain is that Rathenau in the July of the same year, on 25 July 1912, while a guest of Bethmann-Hollweg on his estate at Hohenfinow – the two had had neighbouring estates since Rathenau had acquired Schloss Fürstenwalde and visited each other often – had put these ideas to the Chancellor and had met with Bethmann-Hollweg's basic agreement, as he expressly noted. Rathenau's report of it was:

> I developed my ideas: 1. Economics. Customs union with Austria, Switzerland, Italy, Belgium, the Netherlands, etc., with closer association at the same time. 2. Foreign Policy. The key to it: the German–French conflict, which lets all

nations grow fat. Key: England. Today disarmament is impossible. Start by increasing tension – although dangerous – also ruin England's position in the Mediterranean. Then alliance. Purpose: Central Africa, Asia Minor.

(A third topic of conversation was the reform of the franchise in Prussia and the general democratisation, which Bethmann-Hollweg showed great interest in as well as the then Under-Secretary in the Imperial Chancellery, Wahnschaffe.)

All the general points of German world policy appear in this conversation: *Mitteleuropa*, Central Africa and Asia Minor. The last two were the remainders of the, at that time virtually shattered, aspirations for world power outside Europe; the first point indicates a new solution in the form of a concentration on the extension of the European basis, a solution which came to be more and more the centre of Rathenau's political ideas. But above all, here, in July 1912, are the two principal aims in Europe and Africa which appeared two years later in 1914 in Bethmann-Hollweg's September programme: *Mitteleuropa* and Central Africa.

In this conversation there also figured a further fundamental idea of Rathenau: these aims could only be realised through an understanding with England, and better still through an alliance with England. As we have seen, an alliance with England did not really correspond fully with Bethmann-Hollweg's wishes, since he really wanted a small colonial agreement with her to keep her neutral, but not an alliance which would have robbed Germany of freedom of action. But Rathenau believed that they could get an alliance through further pressure on England, either through standing by the Supplementary Naval Law, or through diplomatic activity in the Mediterranean, possibly in Egypt, or Turkey, but more probably in Greece where the Kaiser had recently had high hopes. This policy was based on the assumption and aim that the English were ready to surrender the Entente with France and Russia and that this would make possible a complete reshuffle of the relations between the European Powers. Rathenau believed that this was not utopian but a possibility, since England would better be able to defend herself economically against America through a connection with Germany. Because of this he demanded publicly from England her making possible and acknowledging Germany's future position on the Continent in the sense of the *Mitteleuropa* plan (25 December 1913). On the first day of Christmas 1913 in the same article in which he demanded the creation of *Mitteleuropa*, he warned England: 'There is a serious, definite, particular concern growing up in the civilised States about helping us out of a problem which, if unsolved, must become a lasting danger to Europe.' With that he put England into the position of deciding over European peace: France did not come into the question because of her complete dependence on England. Indirectly, the island empire was loaded with responsibility for a possible outbreak of war. Here, in December 1913, the *Mitteleuropa* project was being offered in the sense of a peaceful partnership with England – but a year later, immediately after the outbreak of war when England had joined Germany's continental adversaries, it became an anti-English war aim.

Bethmann-Hollweg took up these ideas of Rathenau, together with the Central Africa and Baghdad Railway ideas of Kühlmann, the originator of the pamphlet *World Policy without War* (1914). They were the kernel of his concept of political war aims with which he opposed the stringent annexationist aims of the Pan-Germans. He did not consider indirect rule to be the only way, but in general he adhered to this programme till his fall and then passed it on to Kühlmann.

But it should be noted here that the German *Mitteleuropa* plans have absolutely nothing in common with the plans of the fifties and sixties of this century. In 1914 *Mitteleuropa* was seen essentially as a form of mastery and a confirmation of Germany's hegemony on the Continent and as a foundation for her as a World Power alongside the other World Powers, since the control of the main arteries of traffic in all directions and of the most industrialised part of the world, that is Europe, would made the German Empire equal to the powerful countries of America, Russia and the British Empire, in extent of territory, in size of population and resources.

These were not considerations made after the event, but ideas expressed at the time by the men who pursued this *Mitteleuropa* policy. There were many officials in the Prussian and Imperial higher bureaucracy who belonged to Schmoller's school. He had originated the doctrine of the 'three world empires', which the Germans should confront with *Mitteleuropa* as a fourth. Characteristic of his ideas was this observation made by him in 1890:

> Whoever is far-sighted enough to realise that the course of twentieth-century world history will be determined by the competition between the Russian, English and American and possibly Chinese world empires and by their aspirations to make all the other smaller States dependent on them, will also see in a *Mitteleuropa* customs union the seed of something which can save not only the political independence of those States from destruction but also Europe's superior, old culture itself.

Schmoller's lecture of January 1900 on 'The Economic Future of Germany and the Navy Bill' showed that this *Mitteleuropa* customs union had to be led by Germany. Schmoller said then:

> Just as Frederick the Great assembled the other German States to prevent Austrian annexionist aims, so the German Empire today must act as the focal point of a coalition of States, which can be of some weight among the world empires, and which can tip the scales in the great struggles among them, especially in the final, decisive fight between England and Russia. But that will only be possible with a stronger fleet than we have today.

He then continued:

> We should win over the small and middling States because they will see that we are not threatening them, that we are ready to guarantee their possessions and perhaps even their colonies, if they will make a peaceful economic alliance with us.

Mende's request for a definition of the words 'world power' seems naïve considering the crushing wealth of self-evidence, as does Engels's asking why only Germany 'grasped' at world power: the Germans believed that the others were already World Powers. (Mende and Engels are critics of Fischer – Ed.)

While Bethmann-Hollweg, Rathenau and their circle of friends were discussing *Mitteleuropa* plans on the plane of high policy in Hohenfinow and Berlin, other things were happening which merit attention in connection with this.

There had been private *Mitteleuropa* economic societies for a decade in Germany, Austria, Hungary and Belgium – discussions were in train in France as well – which were composed of political economists and Members of Parliament and which were encouraged by their respective governments. Their aim, which was discussed in several congresses, was to achieve the facilitating of monetary and commercial exchange and of passport and customs clearance matters. While the official announcement of its establishment in 1904 expressly rejected the pursuit of political aims, the chief founder and for many years the Chairman of the German Society, the Leipzig political economist Julius Wolf, had already pointed out at its founding what they ought to achieve by the consolidation of the economic base of the Triple Alliance. Although he declared officially that a customs union 'under today's conditions' would be utopian, he none the less saw the work of the society in aiming to prepare the way for a *Mitteleuropa* customs union, above all between Germany and Austria-Hungary, and he judged the work of the society as a service in 'preparation for great eventualities', as he put it. The members of the society were drawn from the crucial sectors of the German economy and from four of the parties which supported the Empire, the Conservatives, the Reich Party, the National Liberals and the Centre.

One of the most important representatives of business, the National Liberal Reichstag Deputy and Privy Councillor, Professor Doctor Paasche, who was later Vice-President of the Reichstag, resigned from the society in 1911 because he was dissatisfied with its cautious, temporising policy. In September 1913 he founded the German–Austro–Hungarian Economic Association which immediately separated itself from the other bilateral economic unions by announcing officially that its object was to remove the protective-tariff policy existing between the two countries. In April 1914, despite Article 11 of the Peace of Frankfurt which had given France perpetual tariff preference, Paasche demanded that they should at least provide customs-policy exceptions towards Austria-Hungary, if they were not allowed to carry a customs union 'for the present'. After the outbreak of war this society took the initiative sooner and more intensively than the *Mitteleuropa* economic societies in the question of an economic merger between Germany and Austria-Hungary.

THE ARMAMENTS RACE AND THE NATIONAL EUPHORIA IN GERMANY, 1911–14

The Balkan wars and the shock which they administered to Germany's position in Europe, as well as the previous defeat of her friend Turkey in North Africa by Italy, a member of the Triple Alliance, caused a general armaments race between Germany and the Entente Powers. In Germany as a result of the Bills of December 1912 the large increase in the army was accepted in the spring of 1913 (the Army Bill was moved in the Reichstag on 7 April 1913), but France answered this, even before it became law, by the introduction of three-year service, thereby largely nullifying its effect. (It is therefore really incomprehensible how Gerhard Ritter can call this increase in the army Bethmann-Hollweg's greatest feat of statesmanship!) This increase in the army was effected with the help of agitation from the National Defence League (*Wehrverein*) which General Keim founded in 1912 and which soon had more members than the Navy League in which Keim had agitated before. It was significant for his stand in this armaments policy that Bethmann-Hollweg, although warning of the perils of exaggerating the Slav danger in the Press and of overrating the slogan of the struggle of Slavs and Teutons (which, however, the Kaiser was continually mouthing), justified this Bill by the danger of 'Pan-Slavism' which had been increased by the changes in the Balkans. This was possibly done with an eye to the Social Democrats, who were anti-Tsarist, but in any case it was likely to cause Russia to increase her armaments. Moreover, this speech was quite in line with Bethmann-Hollweg's indulgent policy towards England. It corresponded with a remark of Moltke to Conrad on 10 February 1913: 'But the Slavs must attack first.'

France and Russia were rearming. As the Russians increased their army with French financial help, and as a result of this recovery in military strength after the humiliation of their defeat by Japan in 1904–5 and the humiliation of March 1909, Germany was faced by the pressure of a coalition which some years ahead would be superior to the Central Powers – they reckoned this would be the case in 1916 or 1917. Thus the army increase of 132,000 men approved by the Reichstag even before the Second Balkan War was of limited value for Germany's military strength because only 72,000 men could be conscripted by October 1913 (and so be deployable in the autumn of 1914).

That first upsurge of national emotion in Germany in July and August and again in November 1911 resulting from the diplomatic defeat in the so-called second Morocco crisis is excitement which must be judged to be an expression of isolation in foreign policy as much as a permanent claim to a position as a World Power. It was answered domestically in the Reichstag election of January 1912, in which the Social Democrats scored a great victory (34.8 per cent of the votes cast) and became the strongest party in the German Reichstag with 110 Deputies.

This victory for Social Democracy was at the same time a threat to the internal political structure of Prussia-Germany, where the outcome of financial reform had been provocatively the reverse of those simultaneous changes which had strengthened British domestic politics. This victory had given a strong domestic political impetus to the vote, producing co-operation between Social Democracy and the Liberal Left. Moreover, because of domestic developments in the southern German States, it was no longer a Social Democracy which could have been suppressed by force as a revolutionary party, such as the Kaiser had written about in his famous New Year Letter of 1906 under the 'lit Christmas tree' to Bülow:

First shoot the Socialists, behead them and make them harmless, if need be through a bloodbath. And then war abroad. But not before this has been done and not *a tempo*.

This was in the same letter in which he had connected their embarking on a possible war with an alliance with Turkey and the revolutionising of the Islamic world! The Conservatives and Pan-Germans in 1912 believed that there was a danger of creeping democratisation if the Chancellor, because of foreign policy dangers, gave way to the influence of Social Democracy in such fields as the Prussian franchise, or to the trade unions in social-political questions, which the majority of industrialists feared as greatly as the agricultural worker. In fact a controlling group of Ebert, Scheidemann, Noske, Heine and Frank had taken over the Social Democrats in this election, who appeared more acquiescent towards the Empire's military and foreign policy in the hope of political concessions and reforms at home. Bethmann-Hollweg had especially assumed office with the job of assimilating Social Democracy into the State. August 1914 showed the result of this development, although no serious political reforms had yet come about because of the resistance of the conservatives, above all of the Prussian Minister of the Interior, von Loebell, and Bethmann-Hollweg's own very cautious political position at home. Although Bethmann-Hollweg was on the whole liberal, he could only be called a conservative liberal who was on no account trying to change the Prussian–German government system fundamentally. It was exactly against the pliable, patient, expectant Social Democrats that the German Crown Prince directed his plan for a *coup d'état* in November 1913, which we will discuss below.

The growing nervousness and the accelerated nationalist upsurge in the winter of 1912–13 after the outbreak of the Second Balkan War are manifested in the army increases, in the domestic events connected with it, and in the change in the popular mood. Distrusting the Chancellor, Bethmann-Hollweg, and afraid that the army increase planned in the winter of 1912–13 would be too low, the National Liberals on 9 February 1913 held the meeting of their Central Committee in Berlin. In the main speech of Bassermann, their Chairman, there cropped up once again, as in the speeches of November 1911, disappointment over the outcome of the Morocco crisis: 'Other countries get territory; we get a new Army Bill.' Some days previously Tirpitz had told the Estimates Committee, with the approval of the Progressives and Centre (on 6–7

February 1913), that a German–English naval ratio of 10 to 16 was satisfactory for finding a basis for German agreement with England. But Bassermann made a stand against this: 'A Great Power should not tie itself down.' He declared that Germany could do too much conciliating England and not champion Austrian interests in the Balkans enough. With Bismarck and Bülow they had been able to accept that the government would demand what was necessary, but with Bethmann-Hollweg it was otherwise. Bassermann revealed that he had spoken to some high-ranking officers (Ludendorff) who were demanding that general conscription be used, and he produced some detailed demands himself (the formation of cavalry divisions in peacetime, improvement of the horse team, filling up the third battalions, etc.). The national revolution – such as the majority of the Reichstag, in 1914–17 and beyond to the end of the war, was to identify itself with – was raising its head. The parties could and had to demand more if the government itself was too weak: this was the sense of his speech.

In the debate Prince Schönaich-Carolath, who stood out for an agreement and community of interests with England, was isolated. Stresemann and an Africa specialist, Arning (post-war Headmaster of the Witzenhausen Colonial School), demanded that the National Liberal Party, which had supported the creation of the Empire, should also be a party for the expansion of the Empire. They discussed the question of a partition of Turkey – see the Kaiser's similar expressions – as well as the creation of a coloured army on the French pattern. Time and time again the debate referred back to the people's distrust of the Imperial government's lack of initiative in foreign affairs. In reporting the debate, those National Liberal newspapers edited by Arthur Dix, a pupil of Schmoller, said on 16 February 1913: 'Bismarck is not dead, Bismarck is alive, but not in the government, in the people.'

An extremely revealing letter from the same Bassermann to Schiffer of 5 June 1914 shows that the Conservatives were even more distrustful of the Chancellor, who had quite unjustly lavished honours on them. Indeed they despised him, as he said, on the grounds of both domestic and foreign policy. This shows the 'pressure', which my critics put forward so frequently, and which I in no way dispute, which Bethmann-

Hollweg was under and which limited his freedom of action so considerably. There can be no dispute about the Conservatives and National Liberals having been the strongest political forces in Germany before 1914.

A few weeks after this demonstration by the National Liberals, in April 1913, preliminary negotiations were held with party representatives. These were secret meetings; in them the Chancellor and the Secretary of State, Jagow, with representatives of the military departments, justified the Army Bill. To get them to vote in favour, Jagow spoke of the coming 'world war'. These words often turn up, as for example in the letter already cited from Bassermann to Schiffer of 5 June 1914, which contains the half-resigned observation that 'We are drifting towards world war.' This was three weeks before Sarajevo.

In these preliminary negotiations with the party leaders over the large increase in the army for 1913 it was already plain that if a war broke out with Russia over the conflict in the Balkans, it would be fought in the first phase by an offensive aimed at a decision in the West, since the representatives for the army only put forward as justification for the Bill a military plan about the deployment of troops in the West (the Schlieffen plan). Because of this, some of the Social Democratic negotiators, who really wanted to fight the Russians, not the Western democracies, dared to ask if this would mean the violation of Belgian neutrality. Bethmann-Hollweg answered evasively – in good faith. Twice before, in 1910 and 1912, the Imperial government had assured Belgium that in the case of conflict with France they would observe Belgian neutrality, and at the end of 1913 the Kaiser asked King Albert if Belgium would allow the Germans to march through.

A day after the speech by Bassermann, which we have quoted, to the National Liberal Central Committee, which in fact was made at the time of greatest tension in the Austro-Serbian conflict over a possible increase in the size of Serbia and her reaching the Adriatic, Moltke wrote that letter to Conrad which has often been cited and which according to Gerhard Ritter's ideas is to be taken as evidence of the German Chief of Staff's basic love of peace. Certainly Moltke (and this letter was certainly written only in agreement with Bethmann-Hollweg) warned Conrad (and therefore the Austrian government as well) of the undesirability of a preventive war against Serbia at that point in time, and this certainly led to disappointment in Austria, which had carried out a costly mobilisation. But this letter said nothing more than that a war of nations (which Moltke judged an Austro-Serb conflict would lead to!) would require the whole strength, both material and moral, of their peoples and that this would therefore have to be mobilised (10 February 1913):

> Politics and conduct of war are surely closely correlated. I still believe that a European war must come sooner or later and then it will be in the long run a struggle between Teutons and Slavs. It is the duty of all States who are the standard-bearers of Germanic spiritual culture to prepare themselves for it. But the Slavs must attack first. Those who can see this struggle coming will be clear that it needs the concentration of all forces, the use of all possibilities, but above all complete understanding by the people for the world-historic development.

A few days later the same Moltke, on 19 February 1913, told the Austro-Hungarian Military Attaché in Berlin: 'One should think very hard about beginning a world war'; and the Kaiser told the Austro-Hungarian Ambassador:

> It would be difficult to make the German people see the need for war: they will not understand the 'Durazzo' question [later 'Diakova', a small place on the Albanian–Montenegrin border, was often mentioned in the same sense! – Author]. Consequently we must not go over the edge for the sake of a few Albanian towns.

The Kaiser, whose influence is shown on every page of the official documents (it cannot be made light of simply because it was not very constitutional), had already, in November 1912, just after the outbreak of the First Balkan War, which German-English co-operation was still able to localise, ordered that his own people should be mobilised, through the use of propaganda, to be ready for the great war which could grow out

of an Austro-Serb conflict's becoming an Austro-Russian one.
'The everlasting stress on peace', Wilhelm telegraphed to
Kiderlen-Wächter from Rominten, 'at every opportunity –
aptly or inaptly – during the forty-three years of peace, has
produced a downright eunuchised outlook among the leading
statesmen and diplomats of Europe.' War between Turkey and
the Balkan States was coming, and it would therefore be
'better', the Kaiser continued, if 'it happens now – when it
would not suit Russia and France – because both of them are
not ready to take us on, than later when they would be ready.'
The people had to be informed 'before it happened', through
the 'activity of the Press', about the interests it would have to
fight for and in this way be made 'familiar with the idea of such
a war'.

And just that happened at the numerous celebrations held in
1913. In March at the centenary of the start of the 'War of
Liberation' the Chancellor read an appeal 'To the people'; in
June there were parades and speeches on the occasion of the
Kaiser's Silver Jubilee; there was the commemoration of
Lützow's death; there was the gathering of the German Princes
in the Hall of Liberty at Kelheim; and finally there was the
imposing mass demonstration at the unveiling of the memorial
to the Battle of the Nations in Leipzig, in October 1913, with
the Kaiser present – a demonstration which had a thoroughly
Pan-German character and in comparison with which the
meeting of the youth movement, at the Hoher Meissner, which
has so frequently been invoked with its vague and aimless
idealism, was politically ineffective, although this idealism
inspired these schoolboys and students half a year later to
volunteer for the war and to sacrifice and devote themselves to
it.

Some weeks later in November 1913 the German Crown
Prince demanded that a strong line should be taken against the
Social Democrats. This step showed how the ultra-
conservative and Pan-German circles which the Crown Prince
was intimately connected with had become worried by the
growth of Social Democracy. The Chancellor took this attempt
very seriously, as was shown by the thirty-or-so-page answer
which he drafted by hand to justify why he believed such action
was then unfeasible. In all this it should be remembered that

the Pan-Germans' indignation against the Kaiser because of his backing-down in 1905–6 and in 1911 went so far that they were toying with the idea of his deposition and the succession of the Crown Prince – a threat which must have been especially in the Kaiser's mind in July 1914, more so as the Kaiserin also was leaning towards the Crown Prince's views.

At the unveiling of the Battle of the Nations monument in Leipzig, Wilhelm II had met Conrad and had let himself be won over (on 18 October 1913) to his programme for action:

> I am with you there. The others [i.e. the other Powers] are not prepared, they will not do anything against it. Within a few days you must be in Belgrade. I was always a partisan of peace; but this has its limits. I have read much about war and know what it means. But finally a situation arises in which a Great Power can no longer just look on, but must draw the sword.

The strong anti-Serb attitude which he expressed then, he kept to during the following months as well. It must have been in this sense that, on 1 January 1914, the Kaiser, in his traditional speech to his commanding generals, let fall words which made it appear that he expected that a decision for war would be made in 1914. A statement with this meaning has come to us from two different places. The commanding general at Strassburg, General Deimling, at the official dinner for the Kaiser's birthday on 27 January 1914, announced that the war would come that year. On the same day the commanding general of the Rhine Army Corps at Koblenz, General Tülff von Tschepe und Weidenbach, at the traditional reception for officers said word for word: 'Gentlemen, I have to inform you that it will break out this year. Be ready for it. I have it from His Majesty's own lips.' Communications like those could not have taken place in both places without express instructions. In whatever way the pronouncement should be interpreted or whatever was its meaning – at least to increase their readiness for a war which was seen as unavoidable – it was a sign of the degree of anxiety which the Kaiser's thoughts had reached. He – almost using the same words as Moltke and Jagow – saw the approach of the struggle between Slavs and Teutons, in which he knew the

French would be on the side of the Slavs (see also his similar pronouncement made in November 1912), and the only undecided question was whether the Anglo-Saxons would support the French and the Slavs or the Teutons indirectly through neutrality.

One should take this frame of mind together with all the factors described in the preceding paragraphs of this inquiry, especially those we have just discussed: the German domestic situation; the widespread conviction that war was unavoidable and furthermore that a preventive war was necessary; the anxiety about being outstripped by the growing military strength of Russia and France; the tense nationality problem in and around Austria-Hungary and her obvious weakness; the crisis in German policies and economic advance in the Balkans and Turkey faced by financial competition from France; the emergence of the concept of *Mitteleuropa* as a counterpoise to America and Russia, which would have included France, Belgium, Holland, etc.; and finally, the hope, desired but always questionable, of being able to keep England neutral in the event of a great war breaking out on the Continent. In this light, Wilhelm II's forecast of 8 June 1914 becomes comprehensible: 'The third chapter in the Balkan War is coming soon, which we will all take part in. This is why the Russians and French are making colossal preparations for war.' And his order to the Imperial Chancellor 'to clarify relations with England'.

The latter was attempted by intensifying negotiations with England over the colonial and the Baghdad Railway questions (as has been shown) and finally, after the news had become certain of an Anglo-Russian understanding over a naval convention, the sending of Albert Ballin during the July crisis itself to London, where he may perhaps also have discussed co-operation with England against America. It was attempted ultimately by Bethmann-Hollweg's entire British policy during the July crisis, and even more finally by his offer to England on the night of 29–30 July, which already expressed their future war aims against Belgium as well as against France. If England would stay neutral, Germany would assure her 'that in case of a victorious war in Europe we would not aspire to any territorial increase at France's expense in Europe'. A corresponding promise over French colonies, which the English Ambassador inquired about, was not given. In the same way, 'provided that Belgium does not join against us', Germany would preserve Belgian integrity. Moltke repeated the same idea on 2 August, when the situation had already become very black, in an instruction to the Foreign Office, which showed very plainly still that originally only a continental war with France and Russia was being counted on:

> If England should make her neutrality in the German–Austrian–Russian–French war dependent on a German assurance 'that she would act leniently in the event of victory over France', this assurance can be given unconditionally in a very concrete form. There is no question of our destroying France, only beating her. English neutrality is so important to us that we can make this concession to her unconditionally.

Although Moltke spoke here in fact of a 'mere' defeat of France, this would have meant for all practical purposes – as has already been shown above – detaching France from her alliance with Russia and the Entente with England and making her politically and economically dependent on Germany, although this might have been made more acceptable through the *Mitteleuropa* programme. But this would have threatened England extremely since it would have ensured the basis for a German hegemony on the Continent. From 1912 the English had made it plain that they would not allow the overthrow of France. But Germany none the less had tried right up to the end to keep England neutral through concessions on secondary questions.

That English neutrality was still regarded as open on the same 2 August 1914 was brought out by one of the Kaiser's marginal comments to a newspaper report that the English fleet was protecting France's North Sea coast 'through the tying down of our fleets'.

> This is the help of one ally to another, instead of a position of neutrality. Since England is preventing my fleet's co-operating with my army against the enemy already at war

with me [this comment moreover is positive evidence of their thinking of co-operation between the army and fleet, which has often been disputed], this state of affairs cannot continue! England must show her true colours unconditionally! And at once, ONE WAY OR THE OTHER!

Only first the suspected and then clearly apparent opposition from England led not only to the hurried concluding of an alliance with the Turks, who in the middle of June had still been thought unfit to be allied with, but also to the programme of revolution, which was intended to cause revolts in Egypt and India as well as in the Dominion of South Africa, and to Moltke's demands to attempt to get Persia and Turkey, Sweden and Norway to go to war with Russia, and finally to the invitation to Japan 'to satisfy now her entire Far Eastern claims, preferably by war against the Russians while they were tied up in the war in Europe'. This extension of the war programme demonstrates the overestimation of Germany's domestic and foreign resources.

THE JULY CRISIS AND GERMAN WAR AIMS

Once the Imperial German government had taken the risk of continental war against France and Russia by not merely promising to support Austria-Hungary against Serbia and protect her from Russia during any warlike action but also by pushing its ally into it – contrary to Gerhard Ritter, I look upon the July crisis from the angle that it developed specifically from the entire intellectual, political and economic position of the Empire in Europe, not from a standpoint fixed by after-the-event apologies determined by war experience and the 'war-guilt question' – Bethmann-Hollweg believed that he could rely on a dependable tie with England. The Ministry of War and the General Staff had concluded their military preparations for the war, while the French and Russians still did not seem to have reached their full strength which would have been considered a threat to Germany, while economic developments were still undecided or retrograde.

It is with this whole situation in mind that the decisions taken by the Imperial German government in July 1914, eight days after the murder at Sarajevo, must be understood. Two representatives of German business, from heavy industry and banking, Krupp von Bohlen und Halbach and Karl Helfferich, who were both (with Arthur von Gwinner) close friends of the Kaiser and of the Chancellor as well – Krupp actually was closer to the Kaiser and the military – knew early on in the middle of July the decisions taken by the Kaiser and Chancellor on 5–6 July. They recognised their full magnitude and acted accordingly: they protracted outstanding armaments orders for abroad and 'no longer put back the shrinking gold resources into circulation'.. In the middle of July when Helfferich discussed in Berlin with the Krupp director and long-serving representative of Krupp's in the Balkans, Dr Mühlon, the supply of war material to Bulgaria and Turkey, Helfferich justified his momentary hesitation on the question of credit by his knowledge that 'Vienna . . . in eight days time would give an ultimatum to Serbia which would be very sharp and with quite a short time limit' and would demand 'immediate satisfaction' if Austria-Hungary were not to declare war on Serbia. Helfferich added 'that the Kaiser had expressed himself determinedly for this action. This time there was no hesitation.'

As Mühlon knew Helfferich's 'especially trusted relations with the leading men, who must know what is going on', he continental war of Austria-Hungary and Germany against von Bohlen und Halbach, who made this reply:

> He had been with the Kaiser himself this day. The Kaiser had also spoken to him about the discussion with the Austrians and the outcome, but he described the thing as being so secret that he would not once have dared to tell his Directors about it. . . . The situation is in fact very serious. The Kaiser has declared to him that he will declare war at once, if Russia mobilises. This time they would see that he would not fall back. The Kaiser's repeated stressing that in this case no one would be able to reproach him again with irresolution had an almost comic effect.

The Kaiser's repeated protestation that he would not fall back this time, which appeared 'almost comic' to Krupp, can only be understood if taken together with similar protestations from the side of the military, such as that of Moltke during the July crisis of 1911:

> If we again slink out of this affair with out tail between our legs, if we cannot pull ourselves together to present demands which we are prepared to enforce by the sword, then I despair of the future of the German Reich. Then I shall resign.

It also has to be taken together with the Pan-German threats to depose the Kaiser if he showed weakness again and to replace him with the Crown Prince, threats which must have reached the Kaiser's ears.

The Kaiser, the German military leaders and the Foreign Office insisted in the July crisis that Austria should immediately begin hostilities against Serbia. They agreed with the Austrian ultimatum to Serbia, which was so sharp that there was the greatest probability that it had to lead to war between the two countries. In this way they consciously risked a continental war of Austria-Hungary and Germany against Russia and France. What was crucial in the July crisis was that besides the Kaiser, the military and the Foreign Office, the formally responsible statesman, the Imperial Chancellor, Bethmann-Hollweg, also decided himself to take the tough line and to run that risk on 5–6 July. When the Kaiser threatened to show weakness again, Bethmann-Hollweg even disregarded him, as appears from the fact that Wilhelm's proposal for moderation ('Halt in Belgrade') was not passed on properly and in good time to Vienna. Similarly, the Chancellor rejected or delayed all English attempts at mediation or forwarded them to Vienna without stressing them enough. If Bethmann-Hollweg believed that in doing this he could 'localise' (contrary to all previous assumptions such as Moltke's) an Austro-Hungarian punitive war against Serbia, the minor Slav State, whose integrity the Tsarist Empire's prestige was tied to, and accepted that Russia 'is only bluffing', which the military and part of the Foreign Office professed to believe, although Bethmann-Hollweg's closest friends and advisers, the bankers, did not believe it, this is all secondary to the principal decision. That he none the less took it appears plainly from the notes in the diary of his private secretary, Kurt Riezler, which have not been published up to now but which show that Bethmann-Hollweg was certainly 'ready for war' in the July crisis.

To understand this decision, all the facts mentioned have to be valued as prerequisites for this political decision (*Willensbildung*), not least just those affecting the Empire's economic commitment in Austria-Hungary, the Balkans and Turkey, and the crisis which it had become involved in through it. To lay bare and to understand this development, especially its economic factors which led to the situation which developed after Sarajevo into the July crisis's origin, has been the purpose of this examination. And above all to answer the question why and how the Imperial government acted the way it did in the July crisis and why the country approved the decision and followed it enthusiastically. There can be no talk of any accidental 'stumbling into war'. Bethmann-Hollweg's actions at the beginning and at the height of the crisis were not ruled by destiny or a fateful tragedy, but were a conscious political decision. It appears that the interpretation put forward by a politician extremely favourable to the Empire and later in the war the chief apostle of the *Mitteleuropa* ideas in Austria, Baernreither, in his diary in an entry for December 1914, got to the heart of the matter, when he said:

> Seckendorff confirms what has been clear to me for a very long time. Germany was afraid that we would refuse to go along with them if war broke out over a question not directly concerning us. At Algeciras we were only second, later not even that. In the Morocco crisis we did not stand firmly by Germany. But war had to come, as things had developed, because of the mistakes of German and Austro-Hungarian diplomacy. So after the Sarajevo murder Germany seized the chance and grasped the opportunity which had arisen on the Austrian side. That is the history of the war.

Baernreither saw his interpretation of the July crisis confirmed through a talk with the Berlin East European historian and leader-writer for the *Kreuzzeitung*, the later German National Deputy, Otto Hoetzsch, in November 1915: according to Baernreither's entry, 'the German Kaiser sailed to Norway then [after 5 July 1914] certain that war would break out. All of it was organised very skilfully by Germany and the moment used very quickly with the sure intention of making a war which had become inevitable in the last years with the definite accompaniment of Austria.'

A week later Baernreither had this interpretation confirmed by Hoetzsch's Berlin colleague, the political scientist, Jastrow.

Arthur Gwinner, the Director of the Deutsche Bank, took the same line in a conversation at the end of August 1914 over the July crisis with the Under-Secretary of State at the Admiralty, Capelle, when he expressed very clearly the state of mind prepared to run the risk of war, especially in the Foreign Office, as well as bringing out the uncertainty about their Austrian ally: 'Lichnowsky [the German Ambassador in London] was not told that they wanted here [in the Wilhelmstrasse] to push it to the point of war.' When Capelle asked who had been doing the pushing, Gwinner answered: 'Herr von Stumm in the Foreign Office.' Because Capelle seemed to have doubts, he went on: 'Perhaps it was a whole group. They worked at it systematically, first of all to have Austria engaged in it firmly so that they could be sure of her. But the whole action in Serbia from the first was begun in such a way that the conflict was unavoidable.'

The historian, Karl Alexander von Müller, had the same idea. In the spring of 1915 he was asked together with Riezler to write an apology for July 1914 for the Chancellor. After examining the documents and consulting Riezler, who explained Bethmann-Hollweg's calculations during the July days, Müller turned down the request, but without omitting to note down the next night the pith of his conversation. Müller wrote:

> If they wanted again to risk a diplomatic trial of strength with the Dual Alliance, only a south-eastern question could be considered, that is one in which Austria had an interest as principal and in which Germany stood behind her.

Although the aims formulated immediately after the outbreak of the war were doubtless sharper in their form and more naked in their wants because of being made on the high tide of apparent military success, none the less in them appeared again the old aims of world policy and those worked for in the economic sphere in relation to Belgium and France. This is the one central significance of the September programme of Bethmann-Hollweg for the peace negotiations with France, which I analysed originally and which a great number of other people interested in it have done since. The secondary significance of it lies in that in this German programme aims and conditions for the realisation of these aims were expressed which German policy previously had amounted to, although the specific war situation had produced modifications. The description of German war aims should not begin from the verdict of 'boundless and extravagant demands' (Hölzle), but Germany's war aims policy has to be analysed as a product of German claims to world power, that is the claims to be or become one of the great World Powers. If in this process associations, which are unpleasant for a national view of German history, become clear, this has nothing to do with the historian's task.

6. Cabinet versus Economic Warfare in Germany: Policy and Strategy during the Early Months of the First World War

EGMONT ZECHLIN

Just after the second Morocco crisis had been settled by the Morocco–Congo treaty, the German Chancellor, Theobald von Bethmann-Hollweg, on 16 November 1911 wrote a confidential letter to Carl Weizsäcker, Premier of Württemberg, in which he defended his foreign policy against Pan-German and conservative charges of unpardonable softness. He acknowledged that some aspects of the Morocco agreement fell short of perfection, but expressly denied having pursued a military conflict for the attainment of limited colonial interests. His argument ran:

> Had I . . . allowed the war stage to be reached, we should not be somewhere in France, while the major part of our fleet

---

From the *Historische Zeitschrift*, CXCIX (Oct. 1964).

would lie at the bottom of the North Sea and Hamburg and Bremen would be blockaded or under bombardment. The German people might then well have asked me why? Why all this – for the fictitious sovereignty of the Sultan of Morocco, for a piece of the Sudan or the Congo, for the Mannesmann brothers? And they would have had every right to string me up from the next tree.

It is true that the Chancellor was ready, if necessary, 'to take the sword for the honour of the nation', as he noted down during these very days; but he was ready to act only 'in full awareness that any political act by a Great Power could pose the fateful challenge of war or peace'. Hence it was his 'duty so to conduct the affairs of state as to avoid a war that could be avoided, that did not involve Germany's honour'.

In March 1912, when the British threatened to strengthen their North Sea fleet, and Wilhelm II proposed to answer with a threat of war, Bethmann-Hollweg used the same argument to justify his request to be allowed to resign. He said 'that to provoke war when neither German honour nor German vital interests were at stake would be a crime against Germany's destiny, even if Germany could reasonably anticipate full victory. In November 1913 he conceded to the Pan-German critics of his Morocco policy that German foreign policy should be boldly conducted; 'but to begin rattling the sabre at every diplomatic crisis, even when Germany's honour, security and future are not under threat, is more than rash – it is criminal'.

Bethmann-Hollweg was mouthing no empty phrases to soothe his critics when he said he stood ready to wage war for Germany's 'honour' or 'vital interests'; nor was his aversion to sabre-rattling at the slightest sign of diplomatic trouble based on a kind of philosophical pacifism. As he put it himself, he was motivated by thoroughly practical considerations. Bethmann-Hollweg had a very clear picture of himself as the responsible head of a great European Power, and he knew that his role required a successful policy, based on national interest and implying an unlimited willingness to apply pressure tactics against other Great Powers, for the attainment of Germany's claims – if necessary to the brink of general war. Such a policy, of course, meant nothing more nor less than the resolve to stick out the crisis to the end, by accepting the risk of war. In his diary Kurt Riezler, kindred spirit and conversational partner to Bethmann-Hollweg, has testified to the Chancellor's willingness to use such pressure tactics in the second Morocco crisis; but following a discussion on 30 July 1911, he also noted down the limits to the risk of escalation that were set in the calculation: 'He does not aim at war as the only solution.'

The Chancellor, on the other hand, did not share the illusions of the conservatives. In the pre-war period they had repeatedly advocated preventive war, as a means of buttressing their domestic power; and on the eve of war, in July 1914, they fully expected that the impending passage at arms would strengthen the traditional patriarchal order. Bethmann-Hollweg, for his part, is on record as early as November 1911 as criticising his Pan-German and conservative opponents for 'thoughtlessly toying with war'. He told the Württemberg Premier, Weizsäcker, why. Among other things, it delayed almost indefinitely any hope for a sound domestic situation. Two years later he issued a stern warning to the Crown Prince, one of the severest critics of his foreign and domestic policies. In any future war undertaken without compelling reason the Hohenzollern crown as well as the future of Germany would be at stake. In July 1914, Riezler noted down the Chancellor's fears that 'any war, no matter how it may end, will mean the overturn of everything we know'. Bethmann-Hollweg was well aware of the instability and the unresolved stresses inherent in the Prusso-German constitutional system. Hence for domestic reasons alone he might have been expected to pursue a policy of peace at any price, to spare the German monarchy the extreme stress of modern mass war. The purported German pursuit of world power, often the subject of public discussion in pre-war Germany, likewise exerted no influence on the Chancellor's decisions during the July crisis, any more than did the clamour of the big trade associations.

In the spring of 1914, however, there were intimations of a trend that loomed as a direct threat to Germany's vital interests and future security.

As recently as November 1912 Moltke, the German Chief of Staff, had assessed the military balance of power in Europe in such a way as to justify the fullest confidence in Germany's ability to face whatever the future might have to offer; but when Russian rearmament began in the summer of 1913, and especially after details of the Russian army and navy programmes became known in the spring of 1914, estimates of the chances of military success had become increasingly pessimistic within the German General Staff. A crucial element in this respect was the view that even drastic increases in German military manpower could not in the long run redress the balance, since Germany would not be able to match Russia man for man. An added factor was that Austria, the only ally on whom Germany could rely, seemed to be growing perceptibly feebler in a military sense, on account of her unresolved nationality problems, thus endangering German plans for a two-front strategy which contemplated a powerful Austrian relief offensive in the East. There was more and more doubt, moreover, whether Italy and Rumania could still be considered dependable allies.

Chief Quartermaster Count Waldersee summed up this pessimistic prognosis in a memorandum which he transmitted to Moltke on 18 May 1914. Unless Germany were willing to have peace at any price, he concluded, it would be utterly irresponsible, before the judgement of history, to fail to do anything and everything possible to avert a crisis. Sharing the views of his deputy, the Chief of Staff confronted the Chancellor with this gloomy estimate of Germany's military and political prospects before the month was over. At the same time he unburdened himself to Jagow, the Foreign Minister. He said that he was depressed by the outlook for the future. Within two or three years Russia would have completed her arms programme. When that happened Germany, now still about evenly matched with her potential enemies, would no longer be able to stand up to their military superiority. Hence in Moltke's view there was nothing left but 'to wage a preventive war, in order to defeat the enemy, while we still have some chance to endure the struggle'. He advised Jagow to adjust German policy to the prospect of bringing about a war soon.

There can be no doubt that the judgement and advice of the Chief of Staff, the highest military authority in the land, left a deep impression upon the politicians and upon Wilhelm II. One visitor who had a long talk with the Kaiser about the overall situation found him deeply troubled. He thought that the great Russian arms and railway construction programmes meant that Russia was preparing for a war that might break out in 1916. He had actually considered whether it were not better to strike rather than wait. Bethmann-Hollweg's close associate Kurt Riezler has preserved remarks the Chancellor made about the July crisis, showing how deeply he was influenced by Russian developments in this likewise gloomy overall estimate of Germany's situation and thus presumably in his decisions at the time. Those developments betokened a shift in the balance of power. 'The future belongs to Russia', Riezler quotes the Chancellor on 7 July. 'She keeps growing and growing, bearing down on us like a nightmare.' Two weeks later he was even more outspoken. 'Within a matter of a few years we shall no longer be able to fend off Russia's growing claims and immense dynamism, especially if the present European constellation endures.' This was precisely Moltke's view, presented only a few weeks earlier to Jagow and possibly Bethmann-Hollweg himself.

Paris and London too were worried over the fact that a major increment in Russian power impended, indeed was already partly underway. It is all the more remarkable that there were voices, especially among British diplomats and generals – who could certainly not be credited with outspokenly pro-German sentiments – that judged Germany's situation in the face of this anticipated growth by one of the Entente partners in much the same way as Bethmann-Hollweg and Moltke. As early as March, for example, Sir Arthur Nicolson, the Permanent Under-Secretary in the Foreign Office, calculated 'that . . . Germany does fear the possibility, or even the probability that before long she will find herself in an isolated and critical position, unless she steers an entirely different course to that which she has hitherto followed'. George Buchanan, the British Ambassador in St Petersburg, related German expectations of a worsening of German political power in Europe directly to the irresistible growth of Russian military strength. Germany, he wrote to Nicolson on 18 March 1914, far from improving her military position by her most recent Defence Bill, would be far worse off in three years' time. 'Will she bring in another Army Bill? If she does, Russia will go one better; and in this race for armaments she can always outdistance Germany.' Buchanan summed up this military dilemma as bluntly as Moltke himself: 'Can Germany afford to wait till Russia becomes the dominant factor in Europe or will she strike while victory is still within her grasp?' The same thought occurred spontaneously also to Sir Henry Wilson, Chief of the Operations Division of the British General Staff, when he read a report on the Russian army programme: 'It is easy to understand now why Germany is anxious about the future and why she may think that it is a case of now or never.'

In the light of such an astonishing coincidence between these theoretical views and Berlin's concrete analysis of the situation, there seems to have been ample justice to German fears that the impending expansion of Russian power would bring incisive changes in Europe's still stable power structure, to Germany's disadvantage. It is particularly noteworthy that even in Britain resort to preventive war was viewed as a policy that might commend itself to Germany. This fact should pave the way for a rather less prejudiced view of Moltke's fateful counsel and Bethmann-Hollweg's grave decisions in the July crisis. It is true, nevertheless, that sympathetic appreciation of the German position stopped at the point where Russian military expansion impinged on the interests of the other countries concerned. In the last three months before the outbreak of war, the British Foreign Office, in the matter of its Russian policy, was sharply confronted with Britain's own security needs, compelling it to yield to the pressure for intensifying the Anglo-Russian Entente.

The German government, however, interpreted precisely this development as a second ominous indication that the balance of power had begun to shift inexorably and that Germany's position as a Great Power was growing more and more critical. During the month of May the German Foreign Ministry received unimpeachable documentary evidence, from within the Russian Embassy in London itself, that of late Russia, strongly supported by her French ally, was pressing Britain to elaborate the Entente treaty of 1907. The British Foreign Office, it was shown, had expressed willingness to meet these Russian importunities by agreeing to a bilateral naval convention on the model of the Anglo–French military agreement of 1912.

The German Foreign Ministry already had the full text of the exchanges between Grey and Cambon in 1912, confirming the talks that had been held by the British and French General Staffs and Admiralties. It must have been influenced in some measure by the apparent existence of far-reaching plans for military co-operation by the two countries in the event of war. It is true that both governments had expressly reserved the right to decide when and whether these military clauses were to come into effect; but Berlin is unlikely to have found this reassuring, for the two countries were pledged to consultation in the event that either should have substantial grounds for anticipating an unprovoked attack on the part of a third Power. It would almost certainly not always be possible to establish unequivocally which side was guilty and which innocent. The Wilhelmstrasse felt, moreover, that the combination of a military agreement with a pledge of consultation might well give rise to a moral obligation to provide assistance.

The intelligence from London confirmed that Grey had advised the Russian Foreign Minister in May 1914 that Britain had no objections to an agreement between the Russian and British Admiralties along the lines of the exchange between himself and Cambon. In Berlin this was bound to create fears that Germany would henceforth be confronted not only with even closer Anglo-French solidarity than had been experienced in the two Morocco crises, but with the crushing superiority, at the outset of any conflict, of a united three-Power bloc. These fears were undoubtedly enhanced by information from the same London source that Sazonov was strongly pressing for further strengthening and elaboration of the so-called Triple Entente, and even for its conversion, if possible, into a new Triple Alliance.

Grey had firmly rejected the idea of an alliance and was fond of describing the 1912 agreement with France as non-political and having purely technical military functions; but it was no secret to the German Foreign Ministry that Russia by no means viewed the projected naval convention in that light. Benckendorff, the Russian Ambassador in London, assured his Foreign Minister that once it was concluded

we shall, I believe, have attained our main goal, to put
something tangible in the place of the basically theoretical
and peaceful notions that have prevailed hitherto. . . . I
question whether there could be any stronger guarantee of
common military operations in wartime than the spirit of this
Entente, as it now stands revealed, reinforced by the existing
military agreements.

Sazonov himself was highly gratified at British willingness to
begin negotiating an agreement between Russia and Britain
without delay. In a 'top secret' letter of 28 May he told
Benckendorff – and thus almost immediately the German
government as well – that he not only welcomed the military
opportunities opened up by the projected convention, but also
attributed great importance to it in a general political sense.

We view such an agreement as a major step forward in
bringing Britain more closely into the Franco-Russian
alliance and an effective means for deepening appreciation of
common British and Russian interests. We are convinced
that it will exert a favourable influence on all matters
touching those common interests.

In Berlin these words were bound to be read as signalling an
immediately impending power shift.

It goes without saying that the German Foreign Ministry
tried at once to throw a spanner into the contemplated naval
convention. The secret intentions of the British and Russian
governments were publicised in the *Berliner Tageblatt* and the
Tag, in the hope of mobilising anti-alliance forces in Britain
against the Foreign Office. Grey himself was to be intimidated
by the threat of incisive counter-measures; but little was
achieved beyond a prompt Russian disavowal and a question in
the House of Commons, which Grey, in Jagow's view,
answered by somewhat tortuously denying the stories in the
German Press. Theodor Wolff of the *Berliner Tageblatt* was
further importuned by the German Foreign Ministry, which
wired him not to allow himself to be swerved; but the main
effort to dissuade the British government shifted to the
diplomatic sphere.

On 15 June Jagow called on the British Ambassador, Goschen, opening the discussion with an apparently plausible piece of dissembling in respect of the main object of his visit, the naval convention. He 'confessed' that Sir Edward Grey's statement in the House of Commons had greatly relieved him and 'that his mind was now completely at rest'. This tactical trick was intended to make his further remarks appear in London, not as an immediate massive threat that would commit Germany and incisively compromise Anglo-German relations, but as no more than a plain-spoken diplomatic warning.

'If the rumour had been true,' Jagow went on, 'he thought the consequences would have been most serious. Anglo-German relations would have, of course, lost that pleasant cordiality which he was glad to say characterised them at the present moment, but an even worse result would have been that there would at once have been a revival of the armament fever in Germany.' In view of Germany's geographical situation, facing France and giant Russia 'virtually alone', the German navy, if following the conclusion of an Anglo-Russian naval convention it would now have to take into account the British fleet as well, would understandably demand every sacrifice to meet such an emergency. Jagow admitted that probably none of the Entente Powers really wanted to attack Germany; but it must be borne in mind that more aggressive political parties might quite quickly gain the upper hand in both Russia and France. The following day, 16 June, choosing the same tactics, Bethmann-Hollweg put it more concretely. An Anglo-Russian naval convention, he said, would 'greatly encourage Russian and French chauvinism'.

This directive to Lichnowsky, the German Ambassador in London, drafted by the Chancellor himself, was intended to confront Grey even more emphatically with the estimate of the situation obtruding itself upon the German Foreign Ministry in May and June 1914, and to warn him equally emphatically against pursuing a policy that could only serve to strengthen the already 'bellicose tendencies of the Russian militarist party'. It was probably true that Russia did not immediately plan war against Germany, though we are very much constrained to take into account, in our political dispositions, that of all of Europe's Great Powers Russia is the most likely to be inclined to run the risk of a military adventure. . . . On the other hand, one can scarcely blame Russia for wanting to be much better armed, so that in any new eruption of a Balkan crisis she can cut a stronger figure than the last time round. Whether it will come to a European conflagration in such an event will depend exclusively on the attitude of Germany and Britain.

War could be avoided only if both countries jointly accepted the role of guarantors of peace in Europe. 'Otherwise the torch of war is likely to be lit by any inconsequential conflict of interest between Russia and Austria.'

The 'inconsequential conflict' that was here hypothetically postulated was actually triggered off unexpectedly by the assassination in Sarajevo – at least it was inconsequential at the outset. Barely two weeks earlier the Chancellor, feeling that the foreign situation represented a growing threat to Germany, tested the British Foreign Office for the last time. His purpose was to establish whether Britain was still prepared, possibly at the expense of Entente interests, to preserve enough freedom of action to provide a politically feasible basis for a possible Anglo-German solidarity of interests. In the event of an Austro-Russian conflict in the Balkans, he said, neither Germany nor England would be prevented – the one by the Triple Alliance, the other by her Entente obligations – from presenting a common front in that part of the world as guarantors of peace in Europe 'so long as we pursue this goal from the beginning under a common design'. Bethmann-Hollweg emphasised the passage just quoted, suggesting that he was indeed looking for enduring and effective co-operation with Britain. At the same time he suggested that an Anglo-Russian naval agreement would ineluctably prejudice any joint Anglo-German action to guarantee peace. This threat, by contrast, already points clearly to the decision the Germans were to take in the July crisis, namely to sabotage in so far as possible British mediation and thus destroy one of the most important elements conducive to the preservation of peace among the Great Powers.

Sir Edward Grey continued to deny that an Anglo-Russian naval convention was in preparation and changed his tune only on 9 July when he admitted in general terms that talks had taken place from time to time among British, French and Russian naval and military authorities. In a political sense the British Foreign Secretary's insincerity weighed less heavily in the balance than the fact that the time turned out to be too short for talks between Berlin and London to eventuate on the substance of Bethmann-Hollweg's directive of 16 June. The Wilhelmstrasse probably discounted as mere cynicism or political naïveté Grey's repeated assurances that Britain, despite military talks and agreements with her Entente partners, always retained freedom of political action in the event of a conflict. In any event, the German Foreign Office was convinced that this response left no door open to an Anglo-German understanding as a basis for long-term security.

Grey was doubtless quite sincere in insisting that Britain's freedom of action in the field of foreign affairs was not seriously curtailed, but his interpretation was also doubtless too narrow. Clinging to the literal text of the written agreements, he was underestimating the political substance and thus the crucial effect of both the actual military convention with France and the proposed naval agreement with Russia. He never fully appreciated the German concern that the growth of the Entente heralded a significant power shift in Germany's disfavour. Grey's artful foreign policy structure, seeking a compromise between isolationism and a policy of alliances in order to gain the advantages of both at the same time, was too unstable to vouchsafe an enduring political balance of power in Europe. The fact that the Russian Foreign Minister Sazonov was able, in June 1914, to exploit the British dilemma in the direction of persuading the British Foreign Office to adopt a more conciliatory attitude and to speed up negotiations on a naval pact is concrete evidence that the Ententes had only provisional character. A point had been reached at which Grey, in the interests of the security of the British Empire, could no longer close his mind to the political advantages of the alliance Russia was so generously offering. It must remain a moot point whether he was in any position, during the few remaining unquiet weeks before the outbreak of the war, to admit to himself the full gravity of the step he had taken, a step that heralded nothing less than the collapse of his whole foreign policy approach. Beyond doubt, however, it was no mere cynical gesture when he asked the Russian Ambassador on 8 July to see to it that the Russian government did everything in its power to reassure Germany and advise her that the naval talks held no threat to the Reich. This was part of a sincere endeavour to sustain German willingness to co-operate in the maintenance of peace, even at a critical juncture; but it does suggest that the main reason why Grey failed to comprehend Bethmann-Hollweg's concern was that he overestimated his own freedom of action in matters of foreign policy, under the impact of the rapidly rising Russian power potential and the increasing dynamism of Tsarist foreign policy.

It is true that German naval policy had from the beginning scarcely left the British Foreign Office any reasonable alternative to setting its sights for an entente. Hence any efforts aimed at a more or less close political alliance between Britain and Germany were bound to lack credibility in advance. Bethmann-Hollweg understandably viewed Tirpitz as the man chiefly responsible for the failure to reach an understanding with Britain, and thus for the quandary that ultimately, in July 1914, persuaded him that he must withdraw Germany's prior willingness to preserve the peace by a common effort, as had been done during the Balkan wars. The Chancellor did not believe that the way out of the political dilemma, in which Germany's *de facto* isolation seemed to be foreshadowed, lay in bilateral negotiations with Britain over local problems, even when such problems were of some importance. Actually, an acceptable agreement on the Baghdad Railway question had almost been reached and talks about the Portuguese colonies were proceeding satisfactorily; but on 6 June 1914 Bethmann-Hollweg told Ernst Bassermann, leader of the National Liberal Party, that relations with Britain had not improved of late. News about the Anglo-Russian naval convention was bound to revive painful memories in the Chancellor. As the price for British friendship, Germany would have had to forgo building a powerful navy of her own. 'It would be idle today,' he said, 'to consider whether we might have found this possible.'

In the face of a situation judged as growing more and more dangerous for Germany, Bethmann-Hollweg, as has already been said, also lacked the patience for the still feasible policy of settling conflicts of interest by direct negotiation. Yet after the news of the impending Anglo-Russian naval convention Germany seemed farther removed than ever from the readjustment of existing power groupings which she regarded as necessary. On the contrary, that very threat made such a readjustment more and more unlikely, especially with Russia growing stronger day by day. It was this conclusion that ultimately provided the impetus for the German decisions taken in the July crisis.

Ever since it had had knowledge of the Grey–Cambon exchange of 1912 and of the putative substance of the projected Anglo-French naval pact, the German Foreign Ministry had counted on Britain entering any war that might break out between Germany and the Franco-Russian Dual Alliance – though, understandably, it still hoped that in the end Britain might remain neutral. On 6 July, when by his assent he gave constitutional sanction to the 'blank cheque' to Austria, Bethmann-Hollweg had a long evening talk with Kurt Riezler on German foreign policy in which, significantly enough, he emphasised the grave implications of the looming agreement between Russia and Britain. 'Secret intelligence about the Anglo-Russian naval negotiations raises the serious prospect that in the event of war the British might try for a landing in Pomerania.' Within the frame of reference of Germany's political 'encirclement', which he felt to be more and more menacing, the Chancellor regarded the new naval agreement as 'the last link in the chain'. These developments weighed heavily in the balance for Bethmann-Hollweg, especially since Russia was growing stronger and stronger while Germany's only dependable ally, Austria, was growing weaker, almost certainly incapable of taking the field for the German cause, as he put it. 'The Entente is quite aware that we are as a result completely paralysed.'

Two quite separate but mutually reinforcing elements thus

influenced the German view of the situation: Anglo-Russian relations and the growing military strength of the Tsarist Empire; and to the Chancellor they signalled an intolerable threat to German power, the beginning of an existential crisis. It was at this precise juncture, when his fears had solidified into an utterly devastating impression, that the assassination in Sarajevo set off another Austro-Serbian conflict.

The assassination did indeed signal an immediate threat to the freedom of action of the Central Powers in south-east Europe, both in the political and economic spheres. The Greater Serbian and Pan-Slav nationalist movement not only laid claim to the Serbs, Croats and Slovenes within the Habsburg Empire but also served as an outpost of Russian Pan-Slavism, which used it as an ideological pretext for Russian expansionism. Serbia was the cornerstone of a political structure which Russian diplomacy was trying to put together, under Russian leadership but with French assistance. From the minutes of a Cabinet meeting that took place in St Petersburg on 21 February 1914, we learn that this policy was deemed to be essential against the possibility that it might become necessary to seize the Straits in the near future. As Foreign Minister Jagow put it on 18 July 1914, indirectly Germany too could not allow Russian dominance in the Balkans to become thoroughly stabilised.

It was in the face of this threatening shift in the balance of power against the Central Powers that Austria, on 5–6 July, got assurances of German backing for a war against Serbia. Certainly much more was envisaged than a mere punitive expedition in retaliation for the assassination, as shown by the aims enumerated in a handwritten letter by Emperor Franz-Joseph to the Kaiser. Serbia was to be isolated and reduced in size and eliminated as a fulcrum of Pan-Slav policy and as a political power factor in the Balkans; and before the day in point, 6 July, had drawn to a close, Bethmann-Hollweg had given his associate Kurt Riezler some notes showing that as far as the Chancellor's intimate circle was concerned Germany's 'blank cheque' was intended to be more than a response to Austria's chronic difficulties, rendered more acute by the assassination of 28 June. It was a reaction to the precarious developments within the European constellation which the

Chancellor had been watching with growing concern since May.

The Kaiser and Bethmann-Hollweg expressly stated that Germany's blank cheque would apply even if Russia intervened in the war against Serbia, i.e. if there were 'serious European complications'. In making these pledges the Chancellor was well aware that such a policy represented a naked challenge to Russia. Yet what he had written to Berchtold in February 1913 was truer than ever, in view of Russia's growing military strength and self-confidence. Because of its traditional ties to the Balkan states, Russia would find it virtually impossible to stand by idly if Austria commenced hostilities against Serbia. To do nothing would risk an immense loss in prestige. Bethmann-Hollweg was not engaging in empty dramatics when he confided to Riezler on 6 July that in his view any action against Serbia might well lead to a world war.

By taking advantage of the Austro-Serbian conflict, the German Foreign Ministry placed the Tsarist Empire in a serious predicament. Unless Austria was restrained, Russia would either have to capitulate or use its military might to counter the challenge by the Central Powers represented by the threatened subjugation of Serbia. Bethmann-Hollweg calculated that even if Russia shrank back and war was avoided, Germany might score a political success, in that the Entente might be disrupted. Riezler noted in his diary on 6 July 1914: 'Should there be no war – i.e. if the Tsar does not want war or a frightened France advises him to keep the peace – we would still stand a chance of manoeuvring the Entente apart over such an action.'

Indeed, the Foreign Ministry, at the Chancellor's behest, tried hard to move things in this direction. For one thing, Bethmann-Hollweg gave orders from Hohenfinow that for the ensuing weeks the German Press should as much as possible avoid any anti-French animus; and the German Embassy in Paris was instructed to promote a policy of non-intervention in the Serbian question in the French Press. By 16 July the Chancellor actually struck an optimistic note. 'We have reason to assume and certainly must hope,' he wrote Count Rödern, Secretary of State for Alsace-Lorraine in a private letter (actually drafted by Riezler), 'that France, currently weighed down with problems, will do all it can to keep Russia from intervening. If we succeed in keeping France itself quiet, let alone in getting the French to exhort St Petersburg to keep the peace, this would be bound to have an effect on the Franco-Russian alliance favourable to us.'

When Vienna's rejection of the Serbian reply note made it clear beyond any doubt that this design had not succeeded – in other words, that no wedge could be driven between the two allies by prevailing on France to restrain Russia – Bethmann-Hollweg unhesitatingly got set for the alternative solution to the crisis, war. Russia on its part showed from 26 July on that it was totally unwilling to tolerate any Austrian occupation of Serbian territory.

Austria in turn was resolved not to be deterred from invading Serbia, even in the face of Russian military pressure; and it was at this juncture that the German leadership insisted on maintaining its challenge to Russia, by consistently boycotting British mediation efforts and obstinately refusing to engage in any serious effort to restrain Austria from military action. Even the Kaiser was outmanoeuvred when he accepted the Serbian reply note in principle and concluded that there was no further reason for war. The Foreign Ministry then found pretexts for the assertion that the Tsarist Empire would have to accept full responsibility if a general war grew out of a conflict between Vienna and Belgrade that might have been originally localised.

The Chancellor unswervingly stuck to his design, even in the face of pressure from the military; until Russia took the expected and crucial step of ordering general mobilisation. It was that step, and that step alone, to which Bethmann-Hollweg looked for support, especially before German public opinion, for the theory of 'surprise attack'. This was to justify, at home and abroad, German mobilisation as a necessary response.

In February 1918 Bethmann-Hollweg had a confidential talk with Conrad Haussmann, a Reichstag Deputy of the Progressive People's Party. In the course of this discussion, speaking of German policy at the outbreak of the war, he admitted that Germany shared the blame to a considerable extent. When Haussmann challenged him directly, he went even further. 'Heavens, yes', he said, 'in a certain sense it was a preventive war.' In close correspondence with the motives we have tried to lay bare, he gave the reasons that had helped persuade him to risk a preventive strike. There was, first of all, the military judgement that two years thence Germany would have not been able to stand up to a war that was bound to come sooner or later. Less directly, he hinted at the conclusion that there was no longer any hope of realising a politically durable understanding with Britain. In the face of these developments in power politics, the Chancellor felt that even July 1914 could no longer be regarded as the best timing for a passage at arms, as the Foreign Ministry opportunistically kept insisting to Austria, in order to encourage that country to move against Serbia. It was merely the 'least unfavourable time'.

By getting Russia to declare general mobilisation, which meant taking the first and almost irrevocable step towards world war, Bethmann-Hollweg and his closest associates at the top succeeded in overcoming the internal conflicts within a badly divided Germany. It was Bethmann-Hollweg – with the help of three or four intimates in the Foreign Ministry – who set the course of German policy in the July crisis. He did so both in actual fact and in the constitutional sense. It is true that he needed the Kaiser's consent, but under the constitution he and not the Kaiser was responsible for German policy. Overcoming social and political counterforces, Bethmann-Hollweg did manage to influence, indeed to change the course of history in a unique way that will probably never be repeated. This was an event that is of outstanding interest to scholars and historians, amply justifying and even demanding that his plans and calculations, and the motives behind them, be fully described and analysed.

Thus he exploited the dynamism of a defensive war that seemed to have been forced upon Germany – 'for when that happens the whole nation will sense the danger and rise as one man'. He was convinced that only if this happened would there be a chance of victory. There is a curious contradiction here, however, since he was equally certain that 'war will destroy the world as we know it' – the very argument he had used against the critics of his foreign policy in the years before. In the light of this unresolved discrepancy between the unanswerable case for a preventive strike, fuelled by the hope that a nation united in struggle could achieve victory, and fear of cultural decadence and political revolution, Bethmann-Hollweg's option for war appears as the result of a classical conflict rather than of a hard-headed Imperialist calculation – a 'leap into the dark, into this gravest duty', as he himself characterised it in mid-July 1914.

Considered on its own, the decision identifies the Chancellor as a statesman whose views on Germany's destiny did not materially differ from the general national consensus. He opted for war as a means for preserving Germany's power and status as a Great Power, with rights equal to those of other Great Powers, thus falling in with the indisputable expectations of the 'Fatherland', which would have rejected as traitorous and dishonourable any failure to resort to this ultimate recourse. Bethmann-Hollweg was convinced that he was not responsible for the dilemma into which an ill-starred and aimless foreign policy had manoeuvred Germany in the summer of 1914; but he had no alternative to offer – except his fear that his successor would be even worse than his predecessor.

Two critical questions of fundamental importance may be directed to these ideas and this policy. First, how can this obsession with the maintenance of Germany's status as a Great Power and consequent freedom of action in the pursuit of isolated 'interests' be reconciled with the risks of a great European war that was likely to include Britain? And second, what persuaded the leading group centred on Bethmann-Hollweg that Germany could successfully wage war even against a Grand Coalition?

Both these questions will be examined in the following for the early months of the war, when the realities of world war invalidated the very premises and foundations of pre-war political notions and categories, which nevertheless continued to serve as the criteria for assessing the situation.

BETHMANN-HOLLWEG ON THE ORIGINS OF THE WAR

The moral issue of blame and responsibility for the outbreak of the war has profoundly preoccupied the European public as well as historians. Even when there is a disposition to picture German policy in terms of value standards that differ from those of the actors in the events, the question at issue may be usefully explored in an effort to gain a perspective of the historical problem concerned with the limitations of contemporary political outlook and to mark the frontiers beyond which freedom of action ceases. We are in a fortunate position in this respect, since the 'philosopher of Hohenfinow' (Bethmann-Hollweg) repeatedly and self-critically revealed the basic outlines of his policy, reproaching both himself and the Cabinets of Europe for the narrowness of their views on the political world order. This happened in the first instance in a long letter of 17 January 1918, addressed to Prince Max of Baden, whom Bethmann-Hollweg counselled on whether and in what circumstances he should accept a summons to the Chancellorship. At the time, January 1918, Germany seemed to have once more regained the military initiative by the peace negotiations at Brest-Litovsk; President Wilson was proclaiming new ideas for a democratic world order in his Fourteen Points; and mass strikes in Austria-Hungary (14 20 January) gave another hint of the revolutionary repercussions of the war.

Bethmann-Hollweg advised the Prince not to allow himself to be worn down in the struggle with the military powers, but to take over the affairs of state only at the moment of 'great crisis', when the situation at home and abroad had reached the acute stage.

Against this contingency – the stage just before defeat and revolution, when, the power of the Supreme Army Command (*Oberste Heeresleitung* – OHL) would have been weakened – Bethmann-Hollweg developed the basic outlines of his political *Weltanschauung*, intended as a testament for his successor.

The experience of the World War formed the point of departure for his reflection:

> Ever since I have been no more than a spectator, I am gripped day by day more deeply than before by the awesome grandeur of what we have undergone, by the sublime splendour of man's heroism and the sombre depth of his delusions, through which we are passing. This, the most stupendous revolution ever to shake the globe, cannot end, the nations cannot 'atone' before God and the world for all the horror they have done, unless mankind turns away

resolutely from the conditions that conjured up this war and
seeks to create something new in their place.

In the light of this ethically and politically radical view,
Bethmann-Hollweg deplored profoundly as untrue the excuse
put forward by Chancellor Michaelis, namely that the war had
been 'caused by a conjunction of unfortunate circumstances'.
The real causes were 'Imperialism, nationalism and economic
materialism, which in broad outline have governed the policies
of all the nations during the past generation', setting goals 'that
could be pursued by each nation only at the cost of a general
collision'.

In this letter to Prince Max of Baden, Bethmann-Hollweg
was still putting his main emphasis on 'a general disposition
towards war in the world . . . how else explain the senseless and
impassioned zeal which allowed countries like Italy, Rumania
and even America, not originally involved in the war, no rest
until they too had immersed themselves in the bloodbath?'
Charging himself and other pre-war politicians with having
accepted war rather than working for peace, the Chancellor
justified the peace policy of the Social Democratic Party (SPD):
'Many had more or less of an inkling of this development; but
basically only the Social Democrats openly pointed towards it,
and only they worked against the war with conviction. The
other parties fell more or less under the spell of Imperialism.'
He demanded that the consequences be drawn and that
'government should be in greater agreement with the true will
of the people'.

Political trends, as he saw it, would even so powerfully tend
in that direction, even at the cost of revolution.

So great is the force of this challenge, and so widely will the
ethical ideas on which it rests spread after this bloodbath,
that it is bound to prevail, even against the will of the
chauvinists and reactionaries who will survive, though their
future power will dwindle in the precise degree of their
present savage demeanour. I am utterly convinced that this
will happen, the more so since peace is unlikely to come until
the war-weary masses will force it in one way or another and

since these very masses will discern the full burdens and dimensions of the war only after peace has been concluded.

This may not reflect with complete authenticity what were the Chancellor's thoughts and ideas in 1914, but nevertheless it can be shown to bear a close relation to the issue of greatest relevance to our further presentation. In 1914 as in 1918 the Chancellor thought himself free of any passion for war, and he rejected the view that governments – more specifically the German government – were responsible for the hatred that developed among the nations of Europe. It was precisely these passions and these hatreds that destroyed all his political calculations, and he was gripped by the 'awesome grandeur' of shining heroism and the 'sombre depth of human delusions', even though or precisely because he had foreseen and feared the possibility of the war bringing about revolutinary change.

In his *Betrachtungen zum Weltkriege* Bethmann-Hollweg, as a contribution to a historical understanding of his policies, analysed the limitations of his political ideas more unambiguously than in the references to a general disposition towards war that are found in his letter to Prince Max of Baden. For himself and his critics he tried to answer the question why German policy had not been so conducted as to avoid a confrontation with the 'fateful question' in the first place. It seemed to him, he said, that 'there is a widespread overestimate of the degree of freedom of decision left to us in the last decade. Germany too was not immune to the dreams of power that dominated the world.' He felt that one must:

face the brutal fact that Cabinet policy was not determined by great humanitarian ideals and accept that statesmanship can and desires to do no more than allow the realisation of its aspirations to be dependent on the fortunes of war. . . . Politics had simply not yet won its way to the conviction that changing world conditions compelled the nations to revise their attitude to war. Ignoring the fact that in the existing power constellation any major shift among the Great Powers of Europe was bound to involve the whole world, those Powers had their eyes fixed only on the growth of their own

power. By common tradition, moreover, war was not only
the appropriate expression of national power but believed to
carry the power of moral regeneration. These ideas continued to proliferate despite the fact that total mobilisation of
whole nations and the sinister inventions of science had
turned what was once a chivalrous test of strength into
insensate butchery, bound in the long run to destroy all
moral feeling. Cabinets simply did not accept any collective
responsibility for all mankind.

Despite these admissions, which bear the stamp of the bitter
experiences of the World War, and represent a considerable
measure of public self-criticism and basically betoken a
political and moral deference to new forces, Bethmann-
Hollweg continued to justify his policies *in toto* in his memoirs.
'To take the view that Russia could not possibly have tolerated
frustration of her Balkan plans' and that this was foreseeable;
and that Germany 'therefore should not have supported
Austria in her aggressive actions against Serbia, would have
meant to accept self-emasculation for Germany'. To have
accepted the disintegration of Austria-Hungary would have
placed Germany in a state of dependency on Russia. The
Russians, he wrote, mindful of the absolute dominance
Nicholas I had exercised over a recalcitrant Germany, could
then have 'set the day at their pleasure when they might see fit
to expunge Germany from the circle of Great Powers'. Such a
'capitulation' had seemed to him impossible.
    The force with which this 'Great Power' concept had
manifested itself as a basic value and premise of the political
universe, independent of everyday political pragmatism, is
shown by the fact that precisely in the context of such searching
reflections there should have been a reaffirmation of a policy
based on self-interest for the preservation of Great-Power
status, together with a rejection of such essential limitations as
'self-emasculation' and 'capitulation'.
    On 23 July 1914, during the impassioned debate on the
German goal of enhancing Austria's status as a Great Power,
Prince Lichnowsky, taking a pragmatic oppositional stand,
had asked Jagow: 'What would you say if Britain or Russia
were to encourage the French to revitalise their badly depleted

prestige by engaging in a dynamic and dangerous foreign policy?' Once again this question documents the fact that there was no possible reconciliation between a formal approach based on the principle of all or nothing and the requirements of pragmatic politics. After the fact, Bethmann-Hollweg viewed this essential limitation in German political thinking as a basic fault, especially in his policy towards Britain: 'We considered only ways of dealing with immediate issues, ignoring the impending changes in the international power structure.' Germany was in peril and he lacked the necessary patience to unravel the larger issues.

IDEAS OF LIMITED WARFARE

From the limitations in political thinking, distilled from the German Chancellor's interpretation, important perspectives may be gained for the question: On the basis of what ideas and calculations could a war against a continental and even more a Grand Coalition seem acceptable, despite full insight into the ramifications of European power politics? Was there the firm expectation that the war would have to be fought to the bitter end, that is until there would be no further military resistance from the Russian giant and from Britain, protected by her navy and the seas?

Discussion of this crucial problem has left no trace, either in the diplomatic exchanges of the July crisis or in Bethmann-Hollweg's confidential talks with Riezler. Every ounce of attention and energy was preempted by the primary tactical task of steering the developing crisis in such a way that the war guilt should fall on Russia. Yet the decision in favour of this course of action was not an act of sheer desperation, despite what he felt to be an extremely grave emergency; and with all his agitation over the immensity of the risk of a European conflagration, Bethmann-Hollweg did tacitly assume that there was a chance of military success. Hence it may be taken for granted that he had a more or less clear idea where this chance lay.

The burden of our case, which we shall find confirmed in the ensuing account of German policy and strategy following the outbreak of war and the reactions to its military and political realities, is that Bethmann-Hollweg sought the military confrontation for the attainment of a defensive goal, the preservation of Germany's status as a Great Power. He was not after a struggle for world domination and was not, therefore, interested in fighting the war to the total military defeat of the enemy. True, Berlin did realise that a war among the Great Powers might seriously shake the balance of Europe, ultimately replacing it and its self-regulating power mechanism with the altogether different law-enforcement system of predominance by military victory; but it was hoped that successful advances by the German armies in the early phases of a war would serve to bring about an effective corrective to the pre-war shift of power, which was felt to be such a grave threat; and again that Germany's enemies, fearful of a war for predominance with its incalculable consequences to the tested balance of power structure, would shrink from pursuing any war to the bitter end. Such a war, limited in purpose and intensity, was accounted the ultimate permissible political weapon.

This rational approach to war exerted its influence particularly on the evaluation of Britain's possible role in a military confrontation. Even the last-minute offer of 29 July – or rather Bethmann-Hollweg's spontaneous reaction to the no longer expected and supposedly trustworthy news that Britain would remain neutral after all, for a price Germany would be glad to pay – must be seen from this point of view. Britain was to be reassured on the extent of German ambitions and persuaded that her entry into the war was unnecessary, since Germany was prepared to respect the main British concern, maintenance of the balance of Europe. This was to be achieved by preserving France's integrity as a Great Power, respecting Dutch neutrality, renouncing control over Belgium after completion of military passage through that country, and afterwards establishing an Anglo-German condominium over Europe.

The German Foreign Ministry had reason to anticipate that British neutrality would impose a severe strain on the Entente and possibly even call its continuance after the war into question – which would have meant an incisive shift of power in Germany's favour; but given British assurances of neutrality, Germany was basically prepared, on the very eve of the war, to forgo one of the most essential belligerent rights, the right of a free hand in concluding peace. Even though this would have been done only for the *quid pro quo* of British neutrality, it represented an unusually sweeping concession within the framework of traditional Great Power thinking; and it becomes understandable only in the light of a German intention not to use the war to achieve a position of predominance. The idea was that Britain would, however, accept changes in the *status quo* short of the achievement of such a position.

There was a basic error in this type of mechanistic thinking. A guarantee given by a Power, to the effect that it will voluntarily maintain a balance of power in the event it is victorious, represents a contradiction in itself. Only the self-regulating mechanism of a balance of power itself – or so it was generally felt – could offer a sufficient guarantee, certainly not avowals of self-imposed moderation, no matter how sincere, backed only by the word of a Cabinet. It is questionable whether the Germans and the British meant the same thing when they spoke of a balance of power; nor was there any reason for a tacit assumption that they could without difficulty reach agreement on a model of a balance of power that would satisfactorily meet the interests of both countries.

The Chancellor, following the brief interlude on 29 July, regretfully saw his expectations confirmed by Britain's entry into the war. He was not disconcerted, however, for he thought that the successful early border battles might offer the British impressive evidence of German power; and he hoped further that this shift in power would persuade Britain to acknowledge the German successes, pragmatically honouring them by assenting to limited corrections in the pre-war distribution of power. The basic criticism of the notion of a limited war in which Britain would remain neutral, as set forth above, can now be stated in more concrete terms as it is applied to a war that included Britain. It was quite unrealistic to expect that any power shift in favour of Germany and satisfying her need for security as a Great Power would have been, no matter what its nature, compatible with the British concept of a balance of power. Except possibly in the unlikely case of a political and military rapprochement between the two nations – which would indeed have had an almost revolutionary effect on the distribution of power in Europe, Bethmann-Hollweg would have been theoretically in a position to prevent the British Foreign Office from viewing any German-engineered change in the *status quo* on principle as heralding the danger of German predominance on the Continent.

What ultimately crushed Bethmann-Hollweg's hopes for a limited war was the realisation that Britain had always been predisposed to regard any such military confrontation as a war for predominance; and this brought to the fore his earlier pessimistic intimations that the war would bring on a complete upheaval of the existing order. Both the Chancellor and Kurt Riezler – according to his testimony of October 1915 – began to fear that 'Britain's tragic error was forcing us to strain our every resource, involving us in world-wide problems, compelling us to reach for world power against our will'. As long ago as 1948 Ludwig Dehio, a German historian, classes the great war between the two power blocs among the European struggles for predominance; and indeed, the British determination to force Germany to her knees did objectively turn the war into such a struggle on the Napoleonic model. In the final days of August and the first week of September 1914, this realisation crucially changed Bethmann-Hollweg's judgement of the war situation and of the likelihood that the war would secure German power in the peace settlement to come. The responsibility which he accepted with his decisions in the July crisis is defined by the fact that even then and before he was far from blind to the possible danger that the war might tend in such a direction. Still, what seems to have made it easier for him to accept that responsibility was the hope that the course of the war might remain subject to rational Cabinet control rather than governments being swept into a merciless war of annihilation by popular hatreds. Yet here lay the real risk of his policy in the July crisis, as he well knew.

Bethmann-Hollweg and those in the leadership who thought like him were free of what Dehio calls *hegemoniale Dämonisierung*, the demoniac drift towards a struggle for predominance, already latently effective in peacetime, but celebrating its triumph only in war. Throughout the war they were constrained to sober judgement and avoidance of self-deception by fear of the threat to the German leadership from defeat and a realisation that German power was severely limited by the general political situation, German dependence on the world market and Britain's ability to impose a blockade. Hence the Chancellor deeply deplored the brazen braggadocio of most German politicians, to say nothing of the great mass of the people, who from August 1914 onward indulged themselves in ecstatic dreams of vast German annexations that would indeed establish *Deutschland über Alles*. Yet Bethmann-Hollweg himself, to unite the people, had seen fit to make a plausible case for the myth of 'unprovoked enemy attack' in the July crisis, thus contributing his share in letting loose powerful aggressive impulses and lending a veneer of moral justification to any and all demands to be imposed on the 'ruthless' enemy. During the war he wanted to replace these dangerous illusions with hard-headed confidence in victory, by enlightening the people on the actual distribution of power and the prospects for the future as he saw them; but he no longer found himself able to accomplish this. Indeed, to buttress his own position at home, Bethmann-Hollweg repeatedly had to pay hostages to the people's unrealistic dreams of victory and to the hate-inspired annexationists. The German government was probably in a worse position than the Entente Cabinets to put into effect the German Chancellor's goal that belligerents must retain sufficient freedom of action to make pragmatic decisions at any time on the question of ending the war.

UNEXPECTED DECAY OF INTERNATIONAL LAW

In the narrower sense the war as an instrument of diplomacy seemed no more than an interlude rather than an incisively new element. When it was over, traditional Great-Power politics would be resumed, under circumstances more favourable to German ambitions. The Germans certainly expected that during and after the war the traditional European community of nations, governed by international law, would survive and continue its unrestrained jockeying for power. Such, at least, were the views held by the leading government officials, inured to orderly and legalistic thinking. They included the Chancellor himself and his deputy, the Minister of the Interior, Delbrück.

The formal declarations of war, the public admission that the invasion of Belgium represented a breach of international law for which restitution was pledged, must be viewed in this light. In the face of the military contingencies forced upon Germany by her central position and of the resultant violations of international law, they were efforts to keep the war from getting out of control, to keep it under the thumb of Cabinet policy. Behind all this there was also the notion that the situation was quite exceptional, arising only because Germany was threatened by a Grand Coalition. This notion clearly betokens the completely self-centred thinking that then prevailed in Germany. The Germans simply could not see themselves as a threat to other Powers.

The German political authorities were zealous in their observance of the Hague Convention, especially the protection of private property, and they resolutely set their face against precipitate action. In consequence they were particularly dismayed and disappointed by the quick decay of international law in the private sector. In choosing her economic weapons, Britain went far beyond prevailing notions of international law in her interference with private rights.

For example, all debts owed by British subjects to citizens of the Central Powers were declared null and void and their payment was treated as treason. Legal protection before British courts was revoked, even in the case of prize courts, an institution created specifically for wartime purposes. Even neutrals were no longer able to cash notes bearing a German endorsement. British joint-stock companies were forbidden to pay dividends to enemy aliens, and this applied even to neutral concerns in Britain. German enterprises were forced into liquidation and the yield was applied to obligations owed to British subjects. German patents were declared invalid, prompting the President of the Reichsbank, Havenstein, to remark that 'the theft of intellectual property is now officially sanctioned and promoted'. For a while there was even a regulation under which Britons were forbidden to have any business contacts with neutral companies in which Germans had an interest.

All these measures confronted Bethmann-Hollweg with a new situation. They shook the very foundations of his political views of a war that would be curbed and directed by reasoned Cabinet policy and traditional European public morality. In a broader sense they also pulled the rug out from under his efforts to limit and localise the confrontation. After the war, under the impact of its revolutionary momentum, he concluded that 'the World War has utterly destroyed what we once regarded as public morality'.

THE HAGUE CONVENTION AND THE EXAMPLE OF LONGWY–BRIEY

In this connection the treatment of the Longwy–Briey ore basin is highly instructive. Quite early on, this region entered into German annexationist planning against the day of peace; but Bethmann-Hollweg and his deputy rejected any intervention in its private ownership relations as a violation of the Hague Convention. When the Kaiser ordered the pits and smelters of Longwy–Briey seized, the Chancellor saw to it that the running of these works was suitably modified to bring it within the Hague Convention.

To this end the Chancellor, without consulting the Kaiser, made his own rules as he went along, putting them to the local officials – in this case the Governors of Metz and Lorraine – in the form of 'recommendations'. He promptly called to their attention that 'in the seizure of the French mines and steel-works decreed by His Majesty the inviolability of private property should be observed, as laid down under international law by the Hague Convention'. What Bethmann-Hollweg was doing was to exploit the military occupation of the ore basin, decreed by the Kaiser, for purposes of putting into effect his own ideas of politics and international law. There was no appeal from the Kaiser's order that Longwy and Briey were to be administered as a single unit; but following protests by the Reich Office of the Interior against the military character of this administration, the Lorraine bureaucracy co-operated in bringing it under the jurisdiction of that Office, which was an even more determined upholder of national and international law.

The German industrialist Thyssen had an interest in the

Longwy–Briey mines, as did other German steelmen; and to compensate for the loss of French plants, he wanted authority to exploit the Longwy–Briey pits during the war. To this end, he submitted three separate petitions, on 21 and 28 August and 5 September, capping the campaign with a personal visit to Headquarters some time between 9 and 12 September, made possible through the good offices of the Centrist Deputy, Erzberger. All these efforts were fruitless. Bethmann-Hollweg kept invoking the principle that private property was inviolable under international law in wartime. By manoeuvring official-dom in Prussia and Lorraine and taking advantage of factional-ism within the steel and coal industries, he succeeded in isolating and frustrating Thyssen completely.

The Governor of Metz held a meeting with representatives of the entire industry of the Lower Rhine, Lorraine and the Saar region, to which Bethmann-Hollweg dispatched his personal delegate, the envoy Stumm. Against Thyssen's protests, it was there decided 'that war-induced difficulties in importing foreign iron ore did not justify exploitation of the French pits on behalf of the German steel industry. The view was held that existing stockpiles and the German iron-ore mines in Lorraine and on the Lahn river were entirely sufficient to meet greatly reduced German needs during the war. The primary goal should be to put German pits back into operation.'

On the basis of the Chancellor's directives, the meeting worked out seizure methods that would not violate the rights of the French private owners. These measures amounted to no more than a kind of protective custody, to maintain the productive capacity of plant, by keeping the mines from becoming flooded, for example.

Bethmann-Hollweg instructed the Under-Secretary, Zim-mermann, to investigate the claims against the French government put forward by such as Thyssen and Kirdorf and to see whether they might be considered at the peace table. 'It goes without saying,' he said, 'that the form of indemnification envisaged by Messrs Thyssen and Kirdorf is out of the question. . . . If the Briey region should fall to Germany at the peace table, it would certainly be desirable that the French pits and property-owners were expropriated, but in that event the German government would assume legal ownership, with the right to dispose of the properties.' Before doing so, Bethmann-Hollweg proposed to transfer the properties from French to German government ownership. Petitions and visits and even the acceptance of suggestions did not imply that the government was susceptible to influence. Government officials had considerable power and independence, and conflicting views among the industrialists concerned offered further scope for manoeuvre. The government's financial interest in disposing of such properties should not be underestimated as a motive to the adoption of an independent policy.

This distinction between a wartime and a peacetime policy for the ore region of Longwy–Briey was more than merely a matter of sound administration, a tactical move on behalf of the government's financial interest as against that of private industry. This whole policy question and especially the Imperial seizure decree represented a major political event at the critical juncture from August to October 1914, touching the Chancellor's political strategy in an important point.

THE PROBLEM OF KEEPING THE WAR WITHIN DIPLOMATIC BOUNDS

The goal of this policy was to avoid prolonging the war by engaging in no more than the absolute minimum of military operations, since anything more than that was likely to institutionalise it and limit the scope for negotiation. The course of events was to be held at the diplomatic level of Cabinet policy, making possible the kind of pressure tactics that had proved successful in diplomatic crises. Military successes – rather than grand and final victory – were to lay the groundwork for what it was hoped would be a favourable issue to the great struggle. Prior to his departure for Headquarters the Chancellor, in his discussions with the Prussian Cabinet, avoided using the term 'victory' in a military sense, concluding with the hope that by the time of his return the German army and navy might have won peace on good terms. It was in line with such considerations that Bethmann-Hollweg laid down his policy in August 1914.

First, of course, came the deployment phase, together with a continuation of efforts initiated during the July crisis to gain diplomatic backing and the support of allies. Next it was necessary to await the great initial clash of the land armies, the resort to the 'fortunes of war'. These early battles would settle the basis for further political initiative – whether this was to be the defeat or outmanoeuvring of the army, possibly followed by massive invasion; or whether the army might fight through to operational freedom and security from disastrous collapse, thus regaining scope for political action.

Actually, such security seemed to have been provided by the German victories in the border battles in Lorraine, 20–22 August, and then the great initial successes of the German flanking wing, reaching their climax between 24 and 27 August. In the East, on the other hand, the disastrous consequences that followed when the initiative was lost were brought home to the whole nation; but fortunately for Germany, Hindenburg's clear-cut victory at Tannenberg on 30 August 1914 brought significant relief.

POLAND AND THE QUESTION OF INDUCEMENTS FOR ITALY

During the early months of the war relations with Russia and the closely associated Polish question were noted in only a general way on the German side, without receiving any methodical analysis. The problems of limiting and mastering the war in the West were very much to the fore. There was always a latent realisation that in one way or another Russian 'preponderance' represented a threat, but in these weeks the advocates of a German policy oriented towards the East remained in the background. During the ceaseless talks about the problems in the West, Jagow did repeatedly admonish that the East must not be neglected and that Russia would have to be pushed back and separated from Germany by several buffer States; but this stereotyped formula was about all, and nothing eventuated in practice. The whole Russian problem was simply postponed, with some general phrases, such as are to be found in the September Memorandum, for example.

Considerable signs of activity began to develop in this

political vacuum, however, once the military had given the impetus. The idea of encouraging an insurrection in Poland and, in a somewhat contradictory way, throughout the Russian minority regions, was considered in its political and military implications, but turned out to be quite at odds with strategic border security and with the Polish policy in Germany's eastern provinces envisaged by conservative Prussian interests. Various official agencies busied themselves with such problems, in a totally unco-ordinated way, for example the Polish and Ukrainian Section of the Deputy General Staff; certain Foreign Ministry specialists disposed to use revolution as a political weapon; the conservative citadels within the Ministries of the Interior of both Prussia and the Reich; and lastly some of the regional authorities in the eastern provinces. The idea of fomenting rebellion, however, was never able to develop any political momentum, because it was outweighed by military fears that such an effort might get out of control, and above all because Austria was disinclined to use such a double-edged sword.

The question of what would prove politically wise and feasible in practice had to wait until the Russian question once again asserted itself in political calculations. This took place in an effective way only when German political and military strategy was re-examined in November 1914 and underwent an eastward shift under the dual aspect of possibly seeking a military decision or a separate peace in the East.

Even before then, however, both the German government and the OHL were compelled to take a closer look at the Polish question, in the light of political and military actualities. For all three embattled powers that had once partitioned Poland the occupation of Polish territory by Germany and Austria posed immediate political problems that could not be left entirely to a future peace settlement. Directly after the outbreak of war Austria approached Germany with a clear-cut request that the reorganisation of Poland be tackled even before Russia had been decisively defeated. The aim was to prepare for the integration of Russian Poland with Galicia by establishing an Austrian administration in even those Polish areas occupied by German troops. Moltke and Bethmann-Hollweg were opposed to freezing a political solution to the Polish problem so early in the war. 'Let us kill the bear before we divide his pelt,' they said.

The German Ambassador in Vienna was directed to explain that Germany could not immediately accept the Austrian proposals, but would first have to examine the question thoroughly. The matter was put more plainly to Tschirschky personally. Germany wished to use delaying tactics, he was told, to avoid any premature conflict with Austria. Such Austrian pretensions, the Chancellor added, were bound to affect and even collide with German interests. The fate of Poland would have to be left to later agreement. Bethmann-Hollweg was emphasising, in other words, that he was not currently concerned with the Polish question.

This rebuff did not banish the political claims of Austria from the official exchanges, for Vienna continued to put them forward; but the German Chancellor did manage to keep open all of his options for solving the Polish problem at some future date.

As early as August 1914 the whole Polish question, which Austria had raised, became linked to the broader question of limiting the war. This was when the idea of compensatory territorial gains was extended to Austro-Italian relations. The Germans saw a possibility, first set down in an exchange between Wahnschaffe and Rechenberg, that the so-called 'Austrian solution' of the Polish question – excluding north Poland, however – might offer a way of providing Austria with satisfactory compensation for the cession of South Tyrol to Italy, which seemed essential to ensure Italian neutrality. Although this was the primary goal, Germany herself was nevertheless unwilling to be left empty-handed in this general territorial bargaining. The dialogue between Wahnschaffe and Rechenberg went into more and more detail, including serious discussion of possible exchanges of Silesian territory on either side of the Austro-German border. Here was the beginning of what later on, when the question of Italian entry into the war on the enemy side grew critical, was called the 'Silesian offer'. The Prussian Cabinet then authorised Bethmann-Hollweg to cede parts of Silesia, conquered as long ago as Frederick the Great, to Austria, if that were necessary as a last resort to persuade that country to meet the Italian demands.

Rechenberg, former Consul-General in Warsaw and Governor of East Africa, expanded this whole elaborate structure of territorial swops into a broader political concept in his correspondence with Wahnschaffe, who was Bethmann-Hollweg's Under-Secretary at the Reich Chancellery. Since Germany, although she bore the main burden of the war, stood to gain only meagre territorial increments in Polish and Austrian Silesia, compared with the vastly greater gains that would fall to Austria, Rechenberg, on 27 August, proposed that this discrepancy be made up for by economic advantages. While forging territorial gains in the East, he wrote, Germany would have to insist on compensatory trading privileges. In so far as possible, Germany, Austria and Poland should become a single trade area. This need not be done immediately, but should be tackled when existing commercial agreements ran out. The document in question was first presented at Supreme Headquarters on 3 September. Bethmann-Hollweg read it only on 11 September, although it had been sent to him a second time two days earlier.

Here, then, we find one of the sources of the *Mitteleuropa* notion, later to blend with other sources, as will be shown. It is noteworthy that this concept, relating more particularly to east-central Europe and the idea of territorial compensation, was not based on questions of economic structure. Rechenberg was thus moving in the direction of the traditional notion of a customs union, which had been mooted between Prussia and Austria ever since the middle of the nineteenth century.

THE MAIN PROBLEM: ENDING THE WAR IN THE WEST

The core of Germany's problem in limiting the war and keeping it under control was the strategy to be pursued against France and Britain. Bethmann-Hollweg and Jagow had realised fully from the early days of August 1914 on that Germany lacked the military means for vanquishing Britain. The Chancellor looked on the German navy even in wartime as no more than a means of applying diplomatic pressure against the peace negotiations to come. It had to be conserved to that end and its losses must be minimised. Bethmann-Hollweg never tired of making this clear to the German naval authorities. As early as 6 August 1914 he told the Chief of the Admiralty that it was 'absolutely necessary that we still have a large fleet by the time peace is concluded'. To his mind the only way of ending the war swiftly and in a way satisfactory to Germany lay in limiting it. To achieve this three things seemed to him necessary:

(1) Prompt strategic victory over the French armies in the field.
(2) French willingness to sign a separate peace after defeat, without fighting on to the bitter end.
(3) As a corollary, the Anglo-German confrontation must not be allowed to harden into a hopeless war situation by major combat action. A gentlemen's agreement between Britain and Germany on this point would be the prerequisite for what was hoped would be British realisation that their Empire stood to gain in power by virtue of German military successes. At the same time, this might form the beginning of a change in Anglo-German relations such as they were in the pre-war period.

AVOIDANCE OF A 'PEOPLE'S WAR' IN FRANCE

Bethmann-Hollweg's first premise also underlay the strategic concept of the German General Staff. Hopes that it would be met had reached their climax by 27 August 1914, and remained high until the strategic retreat after the Battle of the Marne, despite increasing doubts that the border battles would be sufficient. Following consolidation of the German front in September, hopes soared again with the decision to launch the offensive in Flanders on 18 October 1914; but when the attack on Ypres bogged down and was broken off a month later, the earlier hopes finally gave way to the reasoned view of a stalemate in the West.

Mindful of the complete military defeat of the French army in 1870 and the capture of Paris, Bethmann-Hollweg was thoroughly aware that even the greatest military successes were extremely doubtful political assets. If they were to be fully exploited, they had to be carefully buttressed in the political sphere.

The military successes in the West must not be imperilled by a people's war in France and the refusal of the French government to make peace. In the discussions among leading politicians during morning walks and rides, and in the political consultations in the improvised Headquarters offices, first in Koblenz and after 30 August in Luxemburg, there was frequent mention of the possibility that the French army be offered an alliance directly after its defeat and that France be spared, so that she 'would fight on our side'.

This was a notion of the Kaiser's, among others, which he discussed with Tirpitz, and which Tirpitz in turn discussed with Bethmann-Hollweg, Jagow and the Chief of the Admiralty, Pohl. Along similar lines, the carving-up of Belgium and the apportionment to France of Belgian industrial regions were discussed as possible ways of compensating France for the contemplated annexation by Germany of French industrial areas. In the brief time from 19 August to 27 August, when the military situation began to change, such considerations, however, never gave rise to a serious plan, let alone a possible offer of negotiations to the French government – even though Delbrück, the Minister of the Interior, as late as 20 October did discuss this solution with Bethmann-Hollweg, as a way of compensating France for the loss of Briey and Longwy and relieving the Belgian situation.

More significant were Bethmann-Hollweg's consistent efforts not to provoke the French people, especially the propertied classes, to continue resistance to Germany in the wake of further advances and the possible strategic defeat of the French army, which they might be motivated to do by an open German threat to private property, heralded by out-of-hand expropriations in Longwy–Briey. Such political motives are apparent in the drafts of a proclamation to the French people prepared by close associates of Bethmann-Hollweg.

These drafts were written at a relatively late date, around 6 September 1914, and they also display quite prominently, if not decisively, an element rather at odds with the policy described, namely a claim to north France as an operational base against Britain, against the eventuality that the French government might refuse a separate understanding with Germany despite a strategic defeat; but while this new element overlies the older motivations, the idea of sparing and respecting France remained intact.

The three drafts are by Riezler, the Chancellor's secretary, Mutius, his cousin, and Radowitz, and their common point of departure is the statement that Germany actually regarded the current confrontation with France as unnecessary and regretted having been forced into it by the Triple Alliance's coalition policy. Even at the last moment Germany would have been willing to respect the integrity of French territory, had Britain offered a guarantee of French neutrality. All three drafts studiously avoid any offensive locutions or victorious crowing; and in two of them (by Mutius and Radowitz) the valour of the French armies is singled out for praise and German victory described as a chivalrous issue achieved with neither hate nor passion. There was to be not the slightest reflection on French honour, lest that provoke irrational consequences. Similarly, care was taken to avoid provoking a conflict between government and people, although there was mention of the French government's ambiguous attitude in this 'unnecessary' war and of its ties and its dependence, especially on Britain.

Clearly, what was to be avoided was the kind of loss of legitimate authority capable of negotiating peace that had caused Bismarck such trouble when the French Imperial government fell in 1870 – in fact anything causing domestic chaos that might in turn lead to a revolutionary people's war. The French government, after all, had already left the capital and withdrawn to Bordeaux. The Germans were preaching their own maxim that the foremost duty of citizens was to maintain law and order. A guarantee was given that the exactions of war and occupation would be kept to a minimum and the urgent request was voiced that 'everyone should quietly pursue his occupation and resume his work' (Riezler). Radowitz went furthest in concretising the Kaiser's 'order' to officers and men, who were asked to ensure normal economic life, and he emphasised that private property would be inviolate; but as against these pledges all three drafts included a warning that all civilian resistance and every hostile act would be answered with the utmost severity. Another major limitation was that German troops 'would have to stay as long as your allies continue the war and keep your leaders from concluding a just peace with me' (Radowitz); or as Riezler put it in an enlightening formulation, 'in holding the northern part of your country under occupation, I await the moment when Britain will permit your government to make peace'.

Various possibilities of war and peace are discussed and proposed side by side in the several drafts. They display an uncertainty in political thinking that became more noticeable in the days between the original German advance and the failure of the offensive on the Marne, heralding a hesitant reorientation in ideas of limited war as a political instrument, now that the realities of war had begun to destroy the hopes entertained during the July crisis and the early weeks of August. This uncertainty is shown in Radowitz's contradictory formulation, already noted, to the effect that the Germans would continue to hold French territory as long as the Allies wished to continue the war and prevent the French government from concluding peace with Wilhelm II. The first condition could relate only to a general peace, the second, on the other hand, only to a prior separate peace. Riezler, however, seemed to count on the French government remaining largely paralysed because of its ties to Britain, despite any generous proclamations the Germans might issue on the occasion of victory. He thought that a state of latent war, at least, would continue.

THE BRITISH INTEREST IN PEACE TAKEN INTO ACCOUNT ON THE GERMAN SIDE

In the light of Britain's growing ties with Russia and France, Bethmann-Hollweg had feared British entry into the war; but he could never bring himself to believe that Britain had good reason for such a step, which he viewed as incompatible with British interest in maintaining a balance of power. He concluded that Sir Edward Grey, the British Foreign Secretary, had not foreseen the extent of British entanglement. The step had therefore been taken against Britain's own interest, and questions of honour and other imponderables had played an important part of it.

He hoped accordingly that superior political wisdom would soon prevail, influencing Britain in the direction of seeking a way out of the war as fast as possible. When Prince Lichnowsky, the German Ambassador in London, arrived back home, his report to the Chancellor on 8 August 1914, ran along similar lines.

Bethmann-Hollweg felt that the most important piece of supporting evidence was the fact that the German armoured cruiser *Goeben* had managed to break out of the Strait of Messina despite enemy naval superiority. To attribute this *coup* to a blunder on the part of the British admiral in command seemed so unlikely that Bethmann-Hollweg and the German Chief of the Admiralty were inclined to conclude that Britain was unwilling to strike any 'heavy blows' against Germany.

To encourage this supposed policy, the Chancellor urged that no military action be initiated against Britain, despite the existing state of war. He opposed the sallies by light fleet units ordered by the Kaiser and sought to prevent not only the commitment of the battle fleet proper, but for the time being even the use of German U-boats against British troop transports in the Channel. The response from the Chief of the Admiralty, Pohl, was that even if the conjecture concerning the *Goeben* were correct, Germany could not simply 'cease waging war'.

Yet this was precisely, what the Chancellor wanted. In a telephone conversation with Pohl, he tried again to enlist the admiral in his campaign to dissuade the Kaiser from the operational orders: 'My conscience leaves me no peace. Upon mature reflection I think it probable that Britain is holding back in order not to tip the balance in favour of prolonging the war. It would be extremely desirable if we followed suit, to afford an opportunity for Britain to bring about peace.' Pohl responded by citing the inexorable logic of war. The scheduled operations could not possibly be called off and such considerations must not be allowed to keep Germany from the vigorous pursuit of the war: 'It is Britain that has declared war on us and she must bear the consequences.' Pohl went on to point out that his influence and Bethmann-Hollweg's did not go beyond a certain point. Orders to limit hostilities could issue only from the Kaiser, and this could scarcely be achieved at this time. Despite his agitation, the Chancellor gave up. Matters would have to take their course, he said, since he himself could certainly not secure such orders from the Kaiser.

It was thus that Bethmann-Hollweg came face to face with the logic of war, with realities that could not be undone but 'must take their course'. Here were the sombre and incalculable forces that had thrown him into such turmoil when he had taken the seemingly unavoidable plunge into war in the July crisis, quite devoid of the exaltation that had then taken hold of the German people. Yet for a transitional period he still clung to his hopes and the concept based on them. He tried to 'freeze' the Anglo-German war and for the time being saw no need for contemplating effective new means in the war against a sea Power.

This attitude is betokened, for example, in his refusal to denounce British seizures of ships bound for Holland with cargoes of grain as flagrant violations of international law. Even more telling is the argument he used in a meeting with Tirpitz, Jagow and Pohl on 19 August, when Tirpitz proposed that as much territory as possible be occupied in the West, so that Germany might hold 'hostages' with which to exert political pressure on Britain. 'Even if we are successful in the West,' the Chancellor said, 'we shall presumably have to detach ourselves eastward at a later date, unless we were to abandon Austria. The occupation in France must be limited.' Tirpitz had his notes of this talk countersigned by Pohl and wished to use them to warn the Kaiser against Bethmann-Hollweg's 'misguided' policy towards Britain, but Admiral Müller, Chief of the Imperial Naval Cabinet, rejected such a private initiative as unconstitutional. Admiral Capelle, Under-Secretary in the Reich Naval Office, thought that direct representations to the Chancellor would be unwise, since Bethmann-Hollweg was likely to turn the issue into a jurisdictional dispute.

Tirpitz went back to the fray in another talk the next day. His immediate concern was the military and political defence of Tsingtao, threatened by a Japanese ultimatum. Jagow expressed doubts that Germany could vanquish Britain and said that the East and the Polish question must not be lost sight of and that a buffer State must be created to relieve the Russian pressure, while Bethmann-Hollweg considered whether a mutual assistance pact with France might be attainable. Tirpitz insisted that all such considerations must take second place. He was convinced that without *Lebensraum* overseas Germany would decline to the insignificant status of a land-locked nation. 'No matter how great our power on the Continent, without world stature our status as a World Power would be at an end. Commerce and industry, the essential sources of our economic power, would never recover.'

Close on the heels of the outbreak of war, Tirpitz was here giving an almost classic definition of the concept of world power (*Weltmacht*). The assertion of commerce and industry with their markets and raw-material sources, the maintenance or restoration of 'world stature' and the regeneration of 'World Power status', since an export-intensive Germany was dependent upon access to world markets – all these are used synonymously in Tirpitz's formulation. The war had destroyed Germany's world stature. As the Reichsbank President, Havenstein, had said and the Minister of the Interior, Delbrück, had foreseen even before the war, Germany had turned overnight into a closed mercantile State on the classic economic model.

A critical question is posed here: What was the feasible and possible course? Restoration of assured access to world markets or, alternatively, the creation of a great inland continental market? A particularly knotty point was whether the interior market should be built up only for the war period or for the time afterwards as well; and a particular point of dispute between Bethmann-Hollweg and Tirpitz was what was meant by 'assured' access to world markets and how it was to be achieved. In view of Germany's industrial structure, the ultimate basic decision was in favour of the world market. At the same time, however, the factual situation exerted its ineluctable influence in the direction of building up the home market for the war period. In these deliberations the statesmen were more inclined to think within a long-term context than the economic pragmatists, who were concerned with the immediate future of their enterprises.

THE DANGER OF BRITAIN TAKING A 'HARD' LINE
(27 AUGUST 1914)

A week later, military events in the West forced Bethmann-Hollweg to re-examine his policy towards Britain. His expectations that it might be possible to limit the commitment dwindled day by day. By 27 August 1914 it had become clear that Britain had involved herself on the Continent with great momentum through the unforeseen fighting power of her Expeditionary Force. By that day the conviction had spread beyond the General Staff at Headquarters that the successes of the third week of August had not decided the campaign in a manner that could be viewed as providing sufficient military and political guarantees of German power in the time to come. By means of a skilful strategic retreat, the enemy armies had avoided encirclement without suffering critical losses and demoralisation; and this meant that the Germans would have to fight further battles and possibly undertake a protracted siege of Paris and the time-consuming pacification of the country. This related most conspicuously to the British army, which had prevented the crucial envelopment of the northern flank.

That same day, again in discussion with Tirpitz, Bethmann-Hollweg, still reiterating the commonplace that 'the difficulties in concluding peace lie in Britain', stated for the first time that 'British obstinacy must not be underestimated' – on the contrary, 'it must be put very high'. Hence 'anything we can do to damage the British would be of the greatest importance'. Here is the essential point of a reorientation.

Tirpitz took advantage of the occasion to discuss a possible threat to Britain from the direction of the coast of northern France. He had already discussed this with the Quartermaster-General; and in a talk with Moltke, the Chief of the Admiralty, Pohl, had developed 'far-reaching perspectives' in this connection, looking towards exerting pressure on Britain. Bethmann-Hollweg allowed Tirpitz to outline the elements of his occupation plans, but as always in these days put him on the defensive by reiterating a request that the Suez Canal be blocked by ships. Tirpitz could not promise such a thing, since it was 'technically difficult', and his militant stance thus lost plausibility.

Yet the discussion was a significant sign of a change in course, based on the now evident fact that the British were resolved to fight to the limit; and henceforth opinion began to change in the direction of coming to grips with this new fact, although the older alternative continued to be a subject of discussion.

Political considerations concerned with the significance of the British policy of maintaining a balance of power, however, were not the only element entering into the controversy over the proper policy to be adopted towards Britain; nor was the idea of exerting political and strategic pressure by means of 'hostages' and occupied territory. Bethmann-Hollweg's initial hope that the Anglo-German war would 'swiftly roar past, like a thunder-storm' was not based purely on abstract political ideas; nor were German calculations upset by the striking power of the British Expeditionary Force alone.

GERMAN PRE-WAR CONCEPTS OF ECONOMIC WARFARE

Behind the whole dilemma stood a basic uncertainty on the crucial question as to who was the principal sufferer from the destruction of world-wide economic ties. Was it Germany, which had lost her world markets and international stature, but still had access to a great interior market as well as to the neutral nations of Europe? Or was it Britain, with all her sea-lanes intact, but shut out from her most important market, the European continent, having no sizeable domestic market of her own, and far more dependent on food imports?

Political considerations continued to be regarded as critical; but there was the added economic calculation that the war would end when economic interests required it. This aspect was emphasised especially by those who thought primarily in economic terms, which was expected to be the case in Britain. In Germany, on the other hand, the economic balance-sheet was not deemed to be a proper motivation for the German government to break off the war.

These basic considerations, especially the comparative economic capacity of Britain and Germany in wartime, were not discussed prior to the World War. The economic consequences of war were studied only in respect of the ability to stand up to it. The possibility that a war might have to be broken off because it 'did not pay' was disregarded. There was a discussion of the general problem, under the heading of 'economic mobilisation', fostered at the beginning of 1912 by the Minister of the Interior, Delbrück, who was impressed with the danger points in Europe, but it never went beyond the theoretical stage. There was a bitter jurisdictional quarrel until a decision of the Chancellor forced the Minister of Finance to make available funds from the general budget as of July 1915 for the purpose of at least compiling statistics on food grains.

In a way the fact of the war was taken for granted and political considerations of whether it could be ended or have been avoided were submerged in the overlapping technical and ministerial consultations on economic mobilisation. There were in fact certain preparations on the financial side – for example the provision of loan funds, to avoid a credit and economic squeeze when war broke out – but this work was entirely limited to technical contingencies inside Germany. There was a reassuring conviction that Germany's house was in order, allowing for a reliable assessment of economic and political contingencies in the event of war. Comparisons with the economic resources of possible enemies seemed uncalled for; and when such information was no longer obtainable during the war, scraps of intelligence were interpreted as symptoms of basic crisis that gave rise to soaring hopes.

These pre-war discussions nevertheless did lay the groundwork for certain general views on the economic consequences of a major European war. The basic conclusion was that the wars of the nineteenth century provided no reliable guide. It was necessary to go back to the Napoleonic period. The 'fearsome burdens' of that time, in the words of Delbrück, could be borne only by a country essentially based on agriculture, the people being fed by the products of their own soil. In the wars of unification in the later nineteenth century, on the other hand, no serious difficulties had been experienced, because the issue had been so swiftly settled, while there had still been no interruption in the supply of foods and raw materials. The structure of the economy, moreover, had been quite different then from what it was now. Both German industry and agriculture were now much more interdependent with the economies of other countries than had been the case in 1870. Delbrück concluded that there must be great and justified concern about the economic effects of a three-front war – he was already including Britain! – which would reduce Germany from a country reaching out on every side to the status of a closed economic region.

The essential elements of this view were the emphasis on the export-minded structure of the German economy, on the danger of a conflict with the Triple Entente, which had become obvious in 1911 and 1912, and particularly on a long-range blockade of the Channel and of the Mediterranean at Gibraltar, which would tend to isolate Germany from the world market.

Hence the focus shifted to the question of a 'reckoning', of forcible intervention into this complex network, with incalculable consequences. This was underlined in the memorandum which the Chief of Staff, Moltke, contributed to the consultations on economic mobilisation. The challenge was here met but imperfectly, note being taken only of possible regulation of the use of domestic output. Radical debarment from the world market was indeed foreseen, since the projection went far beyond the immediately plausible closure of the North Sea and the Mediterranean. There were no illusions that imports might come by way of the smaller neutral Powers, since the enemy controlling the sea would prevent this through political and economic pressures.

Yet there was a persistent expectation that a great neutral Power might not bow to such pressures, thus greatly easing the German dilemma, though the experts remained sceptical on this point. In this connection it was the American merchant marine that appeared as the gateway to the world market. The United States, it was thought, would not allow her markets to be foreclosed – on the contrary, she would seek to exploit her opportunities.

In a committee meeting on 21 November 1912, the German Foreign Ministry expressed itself in highly optimistic terms about this possibility; and the following day the argument was taken up by the Reich Office of the Interior, which was in charge of economic policy. The trouble was that the United States did not have enough bottoms of her own; and there was talk that she might recruit neutral merchantmen to sail under the American flag, which Britain would presumably be inclined to treat with greater respect than the flags of the smaller neutrals.

But the hopes which the experts staked on this American solution soon collapsed, when the representative of the Reich Naval Office indicated that Britain and France would certainly block the Channel at Dover and Calais and exercise priority options in the purchase of food imports from overseas, while the United States, presumably interested only in making money, would offer no objections. The assembled experts accepted this estimate of the situation, which turned out to be only too true later on.

Unfortunately, expert opinion does not seem to have had any effect on the formulation of national policy. Although Delbrück himself ended this particular analysis with an exclamation-mark, he reverted to the earlier hopes that there was a community of interest between Germany and America. They appeared in his concluding memorandum of 28 August 1913, which carried all the more weight, since by that time there were already contracts with companies in Rotterdam for shipments under the American flag of grain and feed, the only types of commodities ordinarily considered.

In August 1914 the predominant German view was that in the long run, at least, America would not allow herself to be pushed out of the German market and that her considerable economic and political power was bound to leave Germany with a certain freedom of action. This was not the central issue, however, but rather a symptom of how the question of who would be hardest hit was viewed. The Germans apparently thought that their country, with its large domestic market (including Austria), the Baltic Sea as a communication area, and a possible community of interest with a great overseas Power, was less vulnerable than the British Empire, which was far more dependent on uninterrupted world trade. Tirpitz expressed himself along such lines to Jagow and Bethmann-Hollweg on 19 August 1914, despite the forecasts of his own experts. On 11 September he noted that during the month of August Britain had lost 49 per cent of her trade and commerce – adding directly, however, that this was likely to strengthen British militancy. Lichnowsky gave a diametrically opposite interpretation of the situation. He told Capelle, Under-Secretary in the Reich Naval Office, that Britain was so deeply concerned with her trade with Germany that for this reason alone she would want to see the war ended within a reasonable time.

A representative statement of the German view of the economic changes brought about by the war was given by the Reichsbank President, Havenstein, to the Board of Directors of the Reichsbank on 25 September 1914. Havenstein concluded that the world economy had virtually collapsed. The major stock exchanges had ceased to function, there was a complete failure of the market and of quotations in foreign exchange and an equally complete cessation of international settlements. All countries had had to revert to a closed economy and all had been severely hit, being forced to seek new economic ties. The only saving grace was that Germany's chief economic enemy had been damaged at least as much as Germany herself in this world-wide process of financial disintegration, and especially by the credit squeeze, which only Germany, in contrast to other lands, and especially Britain, had been able to surmount smoothly and without a moratorium. Havenstein did not underestimate the resources of the modern world, but he did cite the complexities of modern economies in arriving at rather optimistic political and economic conclusions. In his view, organisational and financial problems had more importance in the modern world than such natural advantages as control of the seaways, which could not make up for the world-wide economic decay. Staking his hopes in the natural economic self-interest especially of America, Havenstein thought that Germany could expect much of her remaining international connections, despite the evidence of the early weeks of the war. 'The Baltic seaway is open,' he said, 'and it is to be hoped that we shall be able to arrange a reasonably regular and adequate substitute for imports and exports by the land route via Austria and such neutral countries as Switzerland, Italy and Holland, and thence further in American vessels.' Germany could count on the likelihood that the United States, which had a vital interest in the German and Austrian markets for cotton and copper, would vigorously seek somehow to open up a way to them.

There is much evidence to show that during the first month of the war Bethmann-Hollweg thought along similar lines. Apart from the political consequences they drew from it, those two antipodes, the ex-Ambassador, Lichnowsky, and the Minister of the Navy, Tirpitz, were agreed on this estimate of the situation, Lichnowsky being actually closer to the Chancellor's political views in holding that considerations of sheer economic expediency were bound to persuade Britain to break off the war. Bethmann-Hollweg held talks with both of them during August. Like Havenstein, moreover, he still counted on imports through the intermediary of neutral grain-traders as late as 29 August 1914, sending Delbrück suggestions to that end. These crossed the Minister's own proposals for the administrative regulation of such problems.

BETHMANN-HOLLWEG'S CHANGE OF COURSE

During the last days of August 1914 the strong fight put up by the British Expeditionary Force increased the Chancellor's fears that he would not be able to count on any British willingness to make peace, but that, on the contrary, the war would have to be fought to an end. Among his closest advisers faith was destroyed in the validity of calculations based on the assumption that British economic interest required a brief war; nor did similar calculations based on supposed American vital economic interest seem any more realistic.

A critical process of political and military reorientation now set in. The Chancellor feared, among other things, that his political opponents might turn out to have been right in insisting that British blockade-measures were not intended purely as methods of naval warfare, but stemmed from political motives of economic warfare. Between 27 August and 9 September 1914, it was decided to consider the possibility that Germany would have to face the most stubborn opposition in the economic sphere, far transcending the war as such. By 5

September Pohl was convinced that the Chancellor had changed course and even Tirpitz, who refused to believe in such a possibility, thought that a political 'breakthrough' was likely to take place at Headquarters, perhaps quite soon.

During these days the British government provided the Chancellor with several demonstrations of their resolve that seemed quite unmistakable. On 5 September they published the agreement that bound the Allies not to make a separate peace; and violating all the rules of diplomatic etiquette, they deliberately broke off the last personal ties with moderates within the German government by making public in a biased and insulting version the private talks between Bethmann-Hollweg and the British Ambassador in connection with the transmission of the declaration of war. In this account Goschen figures as a detached and embarrassed witness of a scene in which Bethmann-Hollweg completely lost his composure. Actually, the Ambassador himself was reduced to tears by the Chancellor's high-minded distress and had to ask leave to withdraw to the antechamber so as to regain his own composure before the Chancellery staff. This publication, which included the German neutrality proposal, took place on 31 August and became known at Headquarters on 4 September.

On that same day another piece of news transpired at Headquarters, causing further indignation and seriously troubling the Chancellor. Japan was said to be dispatching troops to the European theatre of war. Bethmann-Hollweg now gave up his protests against exacerbating the war against Britain by arbitrary German military action. He summoned the Chief of the Admiralty and questioned him on how the Trans-Siberian Railway might be bombed, the Suez Canal blocked and unrest fomented in India and Egypt.

Other realisations seemed to have strengthened his fears during these days that it was useless to count on British willingness to engage in talks. Three prominent German businessmen are known to have held views of the prospects of economic warfare at this time that differed widely from prevailing opinion. They were Gwinner, Director of the Deutsche Bank, Ballin, Director of the Hamburg–America Line, and Rathenau, Director of the Allgemeine Elektrizitäts-Gesellschaft (A.E.G.). They shared the view that in terms of economic policy time was on the side of the British and that the United States had a solidarity of interests with Britain.

On 22 August Gwinner told the Under-Secretary in the Reich Naval Office of his dissent from Lichnowsky's view that British interest in the German market would persuade that country to seek peace soon enough to affect the length of the war. Gwinner did agree with one element in the more optimistic estimate of the situation, namely that the structure of the British economy was even more sensitive and vulnerable than the German; but he pointed out that Britain had her back free and the cables at her disposal. She was methodically working for the destruction of German world trade and that would gradually give rise to a war boom.

This theme was varied by Ballin in a letter of 30 August to Admiral Müller, Chief of the Imperial Naval Cabinet, which Müller passed on to Tirpitz and Pohl on 2 September. The vast machinery of the world's economy had been brought to a standstill, he wrote. The network extending all over the civilised world had been cut and the contacts broken. Britain was now trying to start up the great engine again, without Germany. He hoped she would not succeed, despite the trump cards she held; but he conceded that the United States, by means of emergency legislation breaking hitherto untouchable taboos, was preparing to usurp Germany's place in world trade with a merchant navy bought up helter-skelter.

Lastly, Rathenau, in a letter of 7 September requested by the Chancellor, attacked the whole economic optimism of German public opinion as erroneous. Germans preferred looking at the map to looking at the globe, and this was why it was generally thought that Britain would fare worse than Germany in the course of the war – firstly, because she was a mercantile nation only moderately industrialised; secondly, because of the loss of her continental markets; and thirdly, because America would rebel against the European blockade. It was true that Britain would lose her continental markets, but in return only Britain and America would be left to supply world demand. They would divide these vast regions among themselves and thus grow more and more closely linked. After an initial crisis, the British economy would experience a vigorous boom, while Germany could expect the opposite. There was no real parallelism between German and British economic handicaps, and as soon as this was known Britain would be encouraged to prolong the war.

All three business leaders maintained good personal relations with the Chancellor. They were in correspondence with him or in personal contact at Headquarters; and it must be assumed that even before 11 September, when he read Rathenau's letter, Bethmann-Hollweg was aware of these pregnant economic analyses that emphasised Britain's interest in prolonging the war and that were so greatly at odds with German public opinion.

The crucial turning-point came on 4 September. On the day before, a letter of 28 August from Rathenau had been submitted to the Chancellor. Rathenau asked that timely thought be given to the future peace with France, which should be tackled only after a most serious effort concerned with Britain, but which should at the same time – and here was the crucial political element – be part and parcel of an approach by which Britain's carefully calculated end-game might be thwarted without risk to the German navy.

Rathenau outlined three steps: French-oriented economic warfare, the technical details of which he was preparing in collaboration with the Deputy Minister of War, under whom he was running the Military Raw-Materials Section; the counterpoise of a central European customs union centred on Austria, which he had proposed for the second time in a memorandum directly after the outbreak of war; and financial agreements with the major continental Powers concerning the capital market, which might result in the financial isolation of Britain and the United States – Britain being already isolated and committed to finance world trade, while America might thus be severely handicapped in building up a war industry.

On the basis of this letter the Chancellor had Mutius, on 4 September, ask Rathenau to make a more detailed presentation of his plans, in the hope that this might result in suggestions on how to control the problems arising from the protracted war that now threatened. The Chancellor emphasised that European disunity and internal enmity in the post-war period had to be taken into account – at least for a number of years.

A strategic defeat of the French army and the occupation of

north France, including the Channel coast and Paris, might offer scope for a more active policy. Such a calculation called for peace to be concluded with the French government as a basis. In the more probable case that France's allies would prevent her from concluding a 'just' peace, occupation without legal sanction would have to suffice. The only strategic security in such an event would be that the French armies would have lost their operational momentum, though without becoming fully neutralised, as would have been true in the case of an armistice.

RATHENAU'S CONCEPT AND GERMAN PRE-WAR ECONOMIC POLICY

For Bethmann-Hollweg the politically crucial point in Rathenau's very sketchy suggestions of 28 August was that the industrialist's views on a customs union – previously known to the Chancellor – were now strongly linked to an anti-British strategy. Rathenau was here influenced by his experiences in the War Ministry's Military Raw-Materials Section. His thinking was probably determined by the military situation in those days; for on 28 August the role of the British Expeditionary Force in severely shattering German strategic hopes became clear. It was surely no accident that Rathenau put the Chancellor's main strategic point at the heart of his alternative: the German navy must not be sacrificed. Presumably Rathenau knew by 28 August how much store the Chancellor set by the navy and an end to the war with Britain. His plans certainly met Bethmann-Hollweg's own thoughts half-way, for Rathenau was attacking aspects of German public opinion similar to those about which the Chancellor had recently become disillusioned.

Mutius (Gerhard von Mutius, close friend of Bethmann-Hollweg and Counsellor of the German Embassy at Constantinople), if no one else, must have pointed out, in his letter of September, the part in Rathenau's plan that had found the strongest response. We know Rathenau's first memorandum on a customs union with Austria – in continuation of his pre-war thinking – only from Delbrück's detailed criticism; but in Rathenau's letter requested by the Chancellor – and Mutius is bound to have commented on this request – the central European customs union as a weapon directed at Britain is at the very heart of the presentation.

Looking at Rathenau's concept, which actually goes back to pre-war times, one sees much in support of the view that he made the suddenly risen concern with the British threat of economic warfare the vehicle of his earlier plan, rejected both in peace and war by the executive bureaucracy in power. He was taking advantage of an opportunity to engage the Chancellor's interest. In so nimble and almost capricious a mind as Rathenau's, one factor was almost certainly his growing familiarity with the new situation. Founder and Head of the Military Raw-Materials Section, he became the creator of the German nitrate industry, which from the spring of 1915 on saved the country from disastrous munitions shortages. Here was a possible way of putting over after all an economic policy that had failed to draw interest in the pre-war period.

The first time that Rathenau brought his plan for a central European economic union to Bethmann-Hollweg's attention was during a visit to Hohenfinow, the Chancellor's country estate, on 25 July 1912. The actual occasion for the talk was the Chancellor's Russian visit in July 1912, which afforded him some reassurance for the state of current relations with that country and gave him reason to entertain hopes that a *modus vivendi* might be achieved, but which nevertheless conjured up sombre perspectives for the long run. Three days before Rathenau's visit, Bethmann-Hollweg had written to the Prussian representative in Karlsruhe. Russia's wealth in natural resources and brute manpower, he wrote, was nothing for Germany to be afraid of. At the same time, in the light of 'our softness engendered by our advanced civilisation', neither should it be underestimated. Yet during a talk in these days with Flowtow, later to be Ambassador in Rome, he had cast an eye over the grounds of his estate at Hohenfinow and wondered aloud whether there was any sense in reforestation, since the Russians were bound to arrive within a few years.

It was against such a background that Rathenau developed his concept of a customs union with Austria and the smaller countries of western Europe. He appreciated the dangers of a political offensive, but he was willing to stretch the situation a bit further, only to bring about a sudden turn when tension was at its highest, by concluding an alliance with the Western Powers. The key, to his mind, was settlement of the conflict between France and Germany, which 'redounded to the advantage of all the other nations'. Britain, in turn, was the key to that settlement. The goals must be Central Africa and Asia Minor. The inexorable logic of any Western reorientation, however, called for progress in the direction of parliamentary government. Bethmann-Hollweg expressed general agreement but ignored the relevant questions of foreign and economic policy. Concerned with the home front, he asked Rathenau to offer proposals for electoral reform in Prussia. Rathenau declined.

The discussion must be seen in the context of German concern with the Russian menace and the difficulties in the way of any Franco-German rapprochement following the Morocco crisis and the failure of the Haldane mission, which certainly provided possible arguments militating against Rathenau's ideas. Russia's industrial growth might make it advisable to maintain access to that huge market as well as to the West. Any incisive domestic reorientation opened up the whole question of the basic structure of the German Reich. The talk between Bethmann-Hollweg and Rathenau was a friendly affair among neighbouring estate-owners. It is fair to suggest that both men were brilliantly toying with ideas rather than considering them seriously.

It was Rathenau's lot during the ensuing period to have to listen again and again to almost stereotyped assertions of Germany's internationally oriented economic policy and agricultural protectionism, as against his ideas of a circumscribed central European economic realm. In 1912, 1913 and 1914, on the floor of the Reichstag, Germany's need for access to the huge markets available to the British and Russian Empires was sharply emphasised.

As late as 18 January 1914, a joint statement by the Chancellor, the Minister of the Interior (who had taken the initiative in the matter) and all other government agencies in the economic sphere, reiterated that there was no reason for basic changes in the tariff and trade policy pursued by Germany. The 1902 Tariff had stood up well and there was no reason for Germany to take the initiative in revising trade relations by serving notice of termination of the tariff treaties of 1906. Delbrück told the Reichstag that by and large the existing situation met all the needs of the German economy.

This continuation of traditional German tariff and trade policy conflicts with the view that there is a direct and inexorable line leading from Rathenau's pre-war *Mitteleuropa* notions – intended to secure a position of dominance for Germany – Bethmann-Hollweg's own policy in the July crisis and the reappearance, in the September Memorandum, of what is often taken to be the same *Mitteleuropa* project. There were many continuities in the transition from peace to war, the most important being that Germany's status as a Great Power was taken for granted, before and after; but German war aims were by no means identical with the goals of German pre-war *Weltpolitik*; nor is there any validity to the theory that the Germans wanted to advance to a new position of power through the war, their own borders having become too constricted in the light of the steadily growing pressure of economic growth and the accompanying hunger for prestige.

Quite apart from that, one would have to examine whether Germany's increasing participation in the internationalisation of industry and communications throughout the world – and especially in France – amounted to an invitation to 'direct political action', since this could only endanger the gains. The American Ambassador put such reflections to Gwinner in August. As reported by the German banker, the American said that in another twenty-five years, with things going the way they were, Germany would be completely invulnerable. Now she was staking everything on a single card. Gerard was unable to understand how the Kaiser could have reached such a decision. Commenting on this analysis to the Under-Secretary, Capelle, Gwinner, rather than using economic arguments, said he had been unable to make the American understand that technical considerations of mobilisation, deployment and similar elements put an unacceptable premium on delay in a political and military crisis. Gwinner was actually quite critical of Germany's policy at the outbreak of war and levelled charges of war-mongering. The sole motive that occurred to him was the restoration of 'Austrian prestige'.

Reflections on new economic approaches did exert some influence on policy, but there were no firm decisions, first because of the opposition of the experts and then because the military situation changed. These ideas stemmed primarily from the actual experience of economic warfare, which – it was projected – would extend into the post-war period; but in another way – for example, in Rechenberg's calculations – they grew out of the failure of German nationality policy, which made the old political instrument of territorial compensation appear shop-worn.

AMERICAN PEACE MEDIATION (5–20 SEPTEMBER 1914)

Before analysing the September Memorandum and going into its political and tactical history, it seems wise to consider a diplomatic initiative that was running separately, the first American effort to mediate peace, falling into the period from 4 September to 19 September and extraordinarily illuminating, and also affording us insight into the problem of the extent to which the Germans were really willing to make peace. At the same time it will give us some idea of the ideological world of the Allies and the United States.

Even before Britain had transmitted her declaration of war in Berlin, President Wilson had decided to offer the five major European Powers his good offices as mediator, with reference to the Hague Convention. This was done on 4 August 1914, in identical personal messages to the Heads of State of the belligerent nations. In deliberate violation of the principle of secret diplomacy, this step was made public a few days later in the *New York Times*, a practice to be followed on all subsequent occasions, probably for the purpose of exerting a certain moral pressure on the European Powers. On this occasion, the Powers unanimously rejected mediation as premature and suggested that it be tried at a more favourable juncture.

At a Washington dinner on 5 September, the former American diplomat Oscar Strauss asked the German Ambassador, Count Bernstorff, whether the Kaiser, in Bernstorff's view, was likely to be receptive to another mediation proposal by the President. Bernstorff admitted that he had no instructions on this point, but he did say that he thought Germany would accept mediation, if her enemies likewise displayed such willingness. Strauss reported this to the Secretary of State, Bryan, early the next morning, a Sunday. Bryan, with the President's approval and Bernstorff's permission, decided to pass on the conversation to Berlin and also to consult the British and French Ambassadors in Washington. The American Ambassador in Berlin, Gerard, was wired instructions on 7 September to report the talk to the German government and reiterate the President's willingness to address a mediation offer to the Allies as well, if the German reply were favourable. The goal was to convene a conference of the belligerent nations in Washington, at ambassadorial level. Bernstorff, subject to constant pressure from the American side, which he did not wish to evade, did from the beginning mention a stricture: the Germans would not be willing to accept an armistice with its attendant loss of momentum for the German armies. Both the British and German Ambassadors recommended that their Foreign Ministers not reject the American offer outright, with a view to public opinion in the United States.

Gerard now added proposals of his own to the mediation initiative, for which Bernstorff, in his remarks to Strauss, had given the original impetus – he was under the mistaken impression that it stemmed directly from Wilson. The American Ambassador was overwhelmed by Germany's military successes in the West and the East – the Battle of Tannenberg: 'Germany is walking through the French, English and Russian armies as if they were paper hoops.' He was deeply impressed by the way the German people had rallied in August and by the order and discipline they had displayed. He found it almost inconceivable that 1,200,000 volunteers should have enrolled in a few days – 'this of course in addition to the millions already on the army lists. . . . This will give you an idea of the spirit of the people.' Gerard already counted on the capture of Paris, the occupation of the Channel coast and the initiation of Zeppelin air raids on London. It was under the impress of such considerations that he spontaneously reiterated American willingness to mediate to Zimmermann, the Acting Under-Secretary in the German Foreign Ministry. He was sure that Germany would demand cession of all French colonies, if she were victorious in France. This conviction apparently went back to a talk Gerard had had with Gwinner, Director of the Deutsche Bank, in mid-August, when the American had mentioned the possibility of peace on the basis of the *status quo*. The banker demurred, pointing to the German successes in France. When the American pursued the point, Gwinner, with what was probably deliberate exaggeration, said on the spur of the moment that he was thinking of a war indemnity of 3 million dollars and cession of the French colonies.

Gwinner could scarcely have anticipated the effect on the American of his improvised reply, intended to apply solely to France. Gerard was under the impression that what the German told him represented official policy, which he was bound to find corroborated in the British White Paper that probably came to his notice in early September. Here he could read that Bethmann-Hollweg had specifically exempted the French colonies when, on 29 July, he had offered to respect the territorial integrity of France, if Britain would guarantee French neutrality. Gerard probably thought he would get a good reception by adding a proposal of his own in discharging his commission of informing the German government in writing of the content of the Strauss–Bernstorff conversation and reiterating the readiness of the American President to serve as a mediator. What he proposed to Zimmermann was that Germany, when Paris had been taken, might well make peace with France on the basis of a war indemnity and the acquisition of the French colonies; and that she could then accept American mediation to initiate peace negotiations with Britain and Russia.

It is not clear precisely what persuaded the American Ambassador to take this step, which went far beyond his instructions. Apparently he thought that the German march through the Allied 'paper hoops' and possible German annexation of the French colonies inevitably touched the very heart of American security interests, making it necessary for America to exert some influence on German ideas of what the peace should be like. Gwinner was a man strongly oriented towards Europe, and his casual remark to Gerard was almost certainly intended to apply only to the French colonies in Africa; but France also had islands and bases close to the Atlantic coast of America and

above all in the Pacific, where the French possessions represented a sizeable power factor.

Early on in the war, the United States was concerned not
only with the events in Europe but the possible involvement of
the Pacific area. An attempt to neutralise the Pacific having
failed, the American government faced the rising danger that
Japanese entry in the war might trigger off decisive power shifts
in Asia. The open-door policy and American interests in China
seemed in imminent danger from Japanese advances in the
Pacific, made on British sufferance, especially the attack on
Kiaochow. Culminating in the notorious Twenty-one Points,
the Japanese offensive did indeed open up more big holes in
Chinese sovereignty, marking the beginning of the crucial final
phase in the century of the Chinese Revolution; for when the
Great Powers, committed in Europe, failed to afford the
expected protection, the intellectual and nationalist movement
on 4 May 1919 was set off. Impressed by the display of superior
German power, Gerard, in contrast to his government in
Washington, associated Japanese expansionism with the
repercussions that might follow the destruction of the German
power base in the Pacific. The extraordinary spirit in Berlin
that wrung such admiration from Gerard persuaded him
that Germany would never forget the Japanese attack on
Kiaochow nor fail to revenge it. The key to this situation would
be a German attempt upon the French position in the Pacific,
and since that would affect United States interests, that
country must interpose in time.

Actually, while the German government fumed over Japanese behaviour in the Pacific area, it did not dream of such
sweeping maritime perspectives. It was Britain after all that
held dominion of the seas. If that were ever to be changed, the
issue would be settled in Europe. At best the Germans
anticipated that their power might be so enhanced at the end of
the war that Britain might guarantee them unimpeded access
to Africa.

Zimmermann did tell Gerard that success for the American
mediation effort would be more likely if the British could be
persuaded to influence the Japanese to change their policy. By
and large he rejected Gerard's special pleas at this first talk and
responded only cursorily to the American memorandum,

transmitted on 8 September, which contained the mediation proposal on the basis of Bernstorff's talks. For Zimmermann the crucial point was that the peace terms Gerard had in mind related only to France, providing no approach to peace with Germany's true enemies, Britain and Russia. Even when Gerard handed him the memorandum, he pointed out that a peace treaty along Gerard's lines – i.e. relating only to France and the French colonies – would in no way meet German security needs and that a 'day of reckoning' with Russia and Britain was inevitable. The German people would fail to comprehend any American mediation effort on the basis outlined by Gerard. From sheer self-preservation, the German government would not be able to take up the Ambassador's suggestion, well intentioned as it undoubtedly was. In the face of such massive opposition Gerard abandoned his private and unauthorised plan for a separate Franco-German peace. The Germans were clearly not prepared to accept his premises, namely that Russian mobilisation and the British blockade would continue. Henceforth he concentrated on Wilson's memorandum, which was to restore a direct line with Britain.

Bethmann-Hollweg ordered the American memorandum to be answered verbally on 12 September. He expressed appreciation for the offer but pointed out that a German victory over France would not solve Germany's security problem, since she would still be facing Russia and Britain. The Triple Alliance, moreover, had agreed by treaty not to make peace separately. The British Prime Minister, the London *Times* and British diplomats were all insisting that Britain would fight on doggedly and expected to win, the longer the war lasted. What America would have to do first was to persuade Germany's enemies to listen to peace proposals. Germany could accept only a peace that held out the prospect of being enduring. If Germany accepted the American mediation offer, her enemies were bound to interpret it as a sign of weakness, while the German people would simply not understand. In the face of the hardships they had suffered they wanted guarantees of security and tranquillity.

Gerard chose to interpret the note as 'an opening to mediation' and passed on its text to Washington with encouraging comments. By the time it got there on 16

September, the British reply was already six days old, the American Ambassador in London, Walter Hines Page, having transmitted an 'informal' reply from Sir Edward Grey, as well as some additional remarks, marked 'strictly confidential'. At the very beginning of his declaration, Grey described German war guilt and the violation of Belgian neutrality as 'grievous and irreparable. . . . No peace can be concluded that will permit the continuance or the recurrence of an armed brute power in Central Europe which violates treaties to make war and in making war assaults the continuity of civilization.' The crucial official demand was that 'any terms that England will agree to must provide for an end of militarist power and for reparations to make amends to Belgium'.

In his 'inviolably secret' supplement intended for Wilson, Grey thus defined his demands: The British people regard the German Emperor and the system of government that he stands for as they regarded Napoleon, a world pest and an enemy of civilisation, and hence there can be no permanent peace till he and his system are utterly overthrown. This certainly betokened a firm resolve to fight on, but Grey reinforced his rejection of the mediation offer by suggesting that the Allies would be agreed that any German peace proposal was bound to be nothing more than propaganda. Page read this as a threat of rejection of the United States as a mediator in any situation later on, if it involved offers on Germany's behalf which Britain considered inadequate. It is not surprising that, compared with this blunt language on the part of Grey, the State Department looked on Bethmann-Hollweg's reply as expressing acceptance. The reservoir of goodwill towards Britain that nevertheless continued to exist in Washington may be gauged from the fact that neither Wilson nor Bryan were deterred from their mediation efforts by the tone taken in the British reply.

Two days later, on 18 September, House and Bryan, encouraged by Bethmann-Hollweg's note, at the directive of President Wilson and with the approval of Bernstorff tried to lay the groundwork for a secret ambassadorial conference in New York, to include France, Britain and Germany. On that day, at a meeting in Bernstorff's New York apartment, of which supposedly only Bernstorff and the President knew, House managed to extract agreement for preliminary negotiations from the British Ambassador, Spring-Rice. House envisaged as a basis for these negotiations discussions on the restoration of Belgium and a general disarmament pact. He thought that this was indeed the minimum basis and he anticipated German agreement.

On 20 September House met Spring-Rice in New York. House said that Britain stood in danger of losing American sympathies. The United States was not prepared to accept the entire elimination of Germany; she wanted restoration of the balance of Europe rather than destruction. Invited to talk with Bernstoff, Spring-Rice let loose a tirade against his 'enemy' colleague. He said such a meeting was completely out of the question, since Britain was bound by treaty not to engage in separate peace negotiations. House vainly put forward once again his major argument. American policy, he said, sought to prevent 'that either Germany or Russia would gain a great preponderance'. In the long run, however, the British attitude prevailed, for given the choice between German and Russian predominance, House too thought Germany by far the greater evil. A German victory would mean 'the unspeakable tyranny of militarism for generations. . . . Fundamentally, the Germans are playing a role that is against their natural instincts and inclinations, and it shows how perverted men may become by habit and environment. Germany's success will ultimately mean trouble for us.' This was scarcely the mediating voice House adopted towards Wilson on 22 August 1914.

The words of Grey and House on the subject of peace mediation once more make plain the dilemma confronting Bethmann-Hollweg's policy. Faced with the choice between a compromise peace and war to the bitter end – the latter line being loudly proclaimed by Germany's enemies – he had no alternative but to accept the same course.

One question, however, must be asked with every emphasis in respect of German policy in the pre-war period and the early weeks of the war. How could matters have reached a point where a neutral mediator could speak of Germany in such fashion?

The British and the German attitudes in the mediation effort supplemented each other in a curious way. Grey during these weeks was afraid that Germany might assume continental dominance in the style of Napoleon; and his answer was war to the end, even to the elimination of the German political system and its representatives; and the German government, without having a true inkling of how radical this position was, got set for it by preparing for a 'continental blockade'.

Yet even if a readiness to conclude a compromise peace were assumed, the chances of success would have had to be assessed as very low. Even ignoring for the moment the call for the overthrow of the Kaiser, the unconditional British demand for the restoration of Belgium clearly provided no common basis for negotiation, even had the Germans forgone their claims for an indemnity and their minimum terms of changing Belgium's status as a nation and its use as a territorial hostage – let alone the much broader possibilities of German influence in Belgium, which Bethmann-Hollweg still thought negotiable.

Yet the demand for the elimination of militarism seems to have weighed even more heavily. Even when it was taken to mean sweeping disarmament – which was the way House viewed it – rather than to include the abolition of conscription, the General Staff, heavy weapons and the battle fleet (actually accomplished at Versailles), there can be not the slightest doubt that any intervention in the Prussian–German military system was thought totally unacceptable in Germany. By a remarkable coincidence 19 September, the day on which House was trying to lay the groundwork for talks between Bernstorff and Spring-Rice on disarmament questions, also saw Bethmann-Hollweg emphasise to his deputy, Delbrück, that if the Social Democratic Party really wanted a domestic reorientation, it would have to accept the Prussian conscription system, which it had pilloried as 'militarism'. He thought that this would be relatively easy, since surely the war had taught the Social Democrats the bitter lesson that any international disarmament and security system was beyond reach. Among the factors that militated against mediation was the great upsurge in nationalist sentiment that had swept the country in August.

It is a moot point whether during this brief period from 5 to 19 September mediation might have succeeded on some other basis. Zimmermann and Bethmann-Hollweg had said that any German government prepared to accept peace without demanding security guarantees from Britain and Russia as well would be swept out of office by aroused public opinion; and they had in mind that there was no hint of such guarantees in the American offer. Yet the dynamics of the embattled Entente probably precluded any compromise that would not have been considered unsatisfactory and unacceptable in advance and on principle, measured against the political concepts of the German government and the expectations of the German public. Thus the events surrounding the American mediation offer of September 1914 merely serve to highlight the incompatibility of the respective points of view, thus setting the scene for a war to the bitter end, which was precisely what the German Chancellor had wanted to avoid.

THE POLITICAL AND TACTICAL HISTORY OF THE SEPTEMBER MEMORANDUM

On 6 September 1914, proclamations to the French populace were being drafted in Germany, against the eventuality of the French armies being defeated in the field. On 8 September Riezler was working on the covering letter for a document entitled 'Preliminary Notes on an Approach to Peace', often described as the 'September Memorandum'.

Both efforts were part of a single event and they display parallels in thinking. The covering letter of 8 September must have been prepared after the text of the Memorandum itself was typed, hence the talks that led to the formulation of the Memorandum must have taken place between 6 and 8 September. There is a strong likelihood that the Memorandum was written at the same time as the proclamations, on 6 September.

Apparently a number of people were consulted, at the Chancellor's request. There is evidence that Tirpitz was asked for his views on war aims in the West and that he was familiarised with the thinking that went into the Memorandum. He too was pressing for a customs union with Austria, but he rejected as illusory the whole precautionary enterprise of a separate peace with France: 'The point is', he said, 'we shall never get Britain to agree to a peace in which we would compensate ourselves. The whole idea of a separate peace with France is impossible.' In a sense the request to Rathenau may also be considered as part of the preparatory work for the Memorandum, although his reply was not yet on hand when it was written. Apart from talking with his associates, Bethmann-Hollweg himself apparently made no written notes in preparation for the Memorandum. The men closest to him had already spent several days coming to grips with ideas of economic warfare, *Mitteleuropa* and how to exert pressure on Britain, and he seems first to have asked them to prepare an outline, before he began to concern himself thoroughly with all the relevant questions. He spent 11 September methodically examining the question of a customs union. He read Rathenau's letter of 7 September, studied Rechenberg's letter to Wahnschaffe of 27 August and the next day took note of Delbrück's refutation of Rathenau's plans. It was only then that he embarked on a real discussion with Delbrück, his deputy and the Minister chiefly concerned, in his letter of 16 September, which crossed Delbrück's letter of 13 September, and which Delbrück answered on 19 September.

This chronology is highly illuminating in assessing the Memorandum's background and significance. Since 8 September the attention given to this whole question had been lagging more and more, and there was a considerable loss of momentum. This is in marked contrast to the way in which news and opinion tumbled over each other between 4 and 6 September. The last remnants of this precipitate haste are seen in the technical and logical errors that dot the text of the September Memorandum.

This was the political situation that prevailed: After 27 August, Bethmann-Hollweg was constrained to review his policy in respect of Britain, as we have already seen. There was more and more bad news. On the military side there were the British Expeditionary Force and the Japanese landings, on the diplomatic front the barrier to a separate peace and Goschen's lack of discretion, and lastly in the economic sphere the danger that a boom in Britain might prolong the war. An added element of urgency was the anticipation of a great strategic success. Bethmann-Hollweg committed himself firmly to a policy of fighting Britain with every means available and of exploiting the military situation in France, preferably by efforts in the direction of a separate peace, but, if that were not possible, by occupation.

His change of policy was also useful to him on the domestic scene, for the maintenance of his position at Headquarters and the restoration of his political prestige, which had suffered by British entry into the war. He was under constant attack from his opponents, who kept probing for a crucial point at which they might discredit the Chancellor and undermine his standing with the Kaiser. Being in constant social contact with Bethmann-Hollweg, they were sensitive to the slightest nuances in his speech and went after him, hammer and tongs. Tirpitz actually visited him on 6 September, in an attempt to launch a new effort that might mark his downfall. Indeed, the September Memorandum may have started as a counter-manoeuvre. Tirpitz's plot was supported by the National Liberal Deputy, Paasche, leader of the Reichstag moderates, who announced a sweeping Supplementary Naval Bill, which the Chancellor opposed as 'premature'. Omission of the Social Democrats in this effort proved to be a political blunder of the first order by the Chancellor's enemies. Bethmann-Hollweg instantly went into action with the National Unity Front and made himself indispensable to the Kaiser for the maintenance of good relations with the Social Democratic Party. Tirpitz promptly realised the error. In a Prussian Cabinet meeting on 15 August 1914, Bethmann-Hollweg had actually succeeded in committing Tirpitz to a statement on co-operation with the Social Democrats by accepting some of Tirpitz's argumentation intended to counteract Conservative disquiet over the new situation.

Annexationist circles in Berlin were beginning their agitation at this time, and the Chancellor's reaction to this worrisome news affords further insight into the background and motivation of the September Memorandum. On 29 August the Under-Secretary, Zimmermann, had reported on a newspaper article by General Keim, President of the National Defence League (*Wehrverein*) and Council Member of the Pan-German League. From local observation and the opinion of propaganda experts, this was only one head of a hydra, to be followed by others that would grow back. To meet the threat,

Zimmermann inquired what exactly were 'the positive goals of German policy in West and East'. In his reply, sent to Press Chief Hamann the very same day, at the Chancellor's instruction, Riezler said that things were still in a state of flux with respect to the war-aims question. In Bethmann-Hollweg's view it was still too early to take decisions, since prompt peace with France was improbable and there was considerable uncertainty whether Germany would be able to dictate peace terms to Britain. This restraint was in sharp contrast to powerful sentiment for outright and totally unrealistic annexations that was rampant at Headquarters and in the ranks as well. Riezler said that the goal of the war was to secure Germany for an indefinite time to come both in the East and the West, by weakening her enemies. This formulation was taken over almost word for word in the opening sentence of the September Memorandum. Annexations, Riezler went on, would scarcely serve that end. They might indeed become a source of German weakness. As for weakening Germany's enemies, this might be done economically and financially, by trade pacts, etc. Riezler concluded on a note that shows that the debate within the Chancellor's circle had not yet crystallised. 'In the face of the difficulties posed, the different views and the confused situation,' he said, 'no wonder the people here are not yet sure what they will ultimately want.'

Tenor and content of this letter coincide with directives that Bethmann-Hollweg transmitted to the Foreign Ministry in Berlin two days later, on 31 August, as guidelines for the Press. He remarked that only the first chapter of the war had been concluded so far, that heavy, large-scale fighting still impended in France and, more importantly, that the course of the war with Britain was as yet quite uncertain. Giving his directive an optimistic tinge, he said that while there was justified confidence that the war would ultimately end victoriously, public opinion must display great patience and be prepared for severe and protracted hardships and even reverses. Hence any discussion of possible territorial gains, whether in Europe or the colonies, seemed quite out of place. 'The primary goal must be security against further war in the foreseeable future. The Press should be indoctrinated in that direction.'

This formulation about security against wars to come

henceforth became a stereotype in official communications and the Chancellor's speeches. It was sufficiently vague and ambiguous to serve as a tactical weapon without offering the gathering annexationist movement any needless provocation. In his letter of 29 August, Kurt Riezler had already spoken disparagingly of annexationist sentiment not only in the ranks but at Headquarters as well. Some of his diary entries also display this opposition to the military who seemed to compete in their annexationist demands with 'victory-drunk' public opinion. On 4 September he noted:

> If Europe fails to find some enduring form of commonalty on this occasion, it will mark the downfall of the Continent. Yet how is it to be accomplished? The soldiers with their blind faith in the steam-roller and their antiquated annexationist goals are doing hair-raising things in an economic sense. They first destroy cities and then try to impose indemnities.

On one occasion – 22 August – Bethmann-Hollweg had already dissociated himself from such plans of unrestrained greed by remarking wryly to Moltke: 'L'appétit vient en mangeant.' This military appetite was indeed taken up in the September Memorandum, which, however, managed to neutralise annexationism in a political sense at the same time.

On 5 September, with preparations for consultations on war aims (in which Rathenau and Tirpitz were included) still proceeding, along with work on a proclamation to the French people, Joffre's plan of attack for the following day was leaked to the General Staff by an indiscretion. It was the very plan that was put into effect to mark the beginning of the Battle of the Marne. The proclamation to the French people was forgotten – no further drafts were prepared, nor any final version. Estimates of the military situation grew increasingly pessimistic, and with them grew the need for codifying the changed policy course, as a preliminary outline of the peace to come. In meeting this domestic necessity Bethmann-Hollweg actually allowed his opponents to collaborate with his associates, as he told Delbrück. The covering letter includes the crucial qualification that these notes were to be considered 'preliminary', since the war was as yet far from decided and it looked as though Britain might succeed in holding her allies to a fight to the last.

ANALYSIS OF THE SEPTEMBER MEMORANDUM

The fact that there were differences of view in the war-aims debate at Headquarters is reflected in the differences between the covering letter and the September Memorandum itself. Taking the whole background into account, the letter emphasises reorganisation of economic conditions in central Europe, while the Memorandum, possibly bearing the stamp of Bethmann-Hollweg's influence to a lesser degree, mentions the establishment of a European economic union only as one among other goals in an overall armistice scheme that had to meet military requirements. Thus two rather different concepts appear side by side in the Memorandum, with no effort to conceal their rivalry.

Under 'General Goal of the War' we read: 'Security for the German Reich in East and West for the foreseeable future. To this end France must be weakened to the point where she cannot rise again as a major power, while Russia must be pushed away from the German border, her sway over the non-Russian peoples broken.' The weakening of France was to be accomplished financially by war indemnities and economically by the loss of mineral deposits; and she was to be made economically dependent on Germany through a bilateral trade pact. It is this Point 1 (together with Points 2 and 3, concerning Belgium and Luxembourg) that fails to square with Point 4, providing for a central European economic union that was to embrace western Europe as well and stabilise German predominance in central Europe in quite another way.

It was Delbrück who put his finger on the heart of this contradiction. 'One may well doubt,' he wrote, 'whether it be wise to bleed a country white when one wishes to incorporate it into one's own economic sphere. Annexation of the ore basin of Briey may well become unnecessary if France and Germany were to become a single economic area, to say nothing of other measures.'

On the premise that Britain was the main enemy, both possibilities discussed at Headquarters evidently got into the Memorandum side by side; and this dual approach seems to have survived in a later memorandum by Gwinner, undated but entering channels on 15 November. 'Further elaboration of peace terms,' he wrote, 'will depend on whether German policy proposes to exhaust France completely or work for reconciliation with the French.'

As against this clear-cut paradox in the goals formulated in the Memorandum, its immediate purpose – to lay the basis for a strategy against Britain by creating another Napoleonic 'continental blockade' – was expressed only covertly in the text. A trade pact with France was to 'eliminate British trade in France'. French Flanders with the ports of Dunkirk, Calais and Boulogne was to be separated from France and given to Belgium on condition that Germany would enjoy the right to occupy all ports of military importance. Thus the military did tip their hand. Indeed, as though to give *ex post facto* sanction to the change of course relating to the new estimate of Britain's attitude and justify falling in with Tirpitz's militant policy, the September Memorandum submitted to the arbitrament of the generals: 'It will be up to the appropriate authorities to evaluate the military value of this position vis-à-vis Britain.'

This view of the Memorandum as a first effort to assemble material on the use of all possible weapons in a fight to the end against Britain is confirmed in a letter that Lieutenant-General Graevenitz, the Württemberg military plenipotentiary at Headquarters, wrote to his Prime Minister, Weizsäcker, on 5 September 1914, at the very time, in other words, when Bethmann-Hollweg, under the impress of the strong line taken by the British, felt compelled to revise his British strategy. Summarising his talks with leading politicians and officers, Graevenitz reported to Stuttgart that 'the Chancellor, like everyone else, proceeds on the basis that Britain and Japan must be vanquished. Clear heads realise, however, that our current naval resources are not sufficient for that purpose and that we must yet build the greater part of our fleet, with French and Belgian funds.' In drawing the balance from his talks and adding his own conclusion, he suggested that Germany would have to familiarise herself with the idea of an intermediate peace, following the complete subjugation of France. It was precisely against such an eventuality that the September Memorandum was to provide a first basis for discussion. The starting-point was that such a preliminary peace with France must provide Germany with the means for further military and economic warfare against Britain. The main accent would lie in western Europe, especially the Channel coast, whence the war must be carried to Britain by means of an economic offensive, a counter-blockade on land, along Napoleonic lines.

FRANCE AS A WAR BASE

An important commentary by Rechenberg clearly shows that all this related primarily to the war as it then stood and the as yet unvanquished main enemy, Britain. This was further corroborated in Rathenau's argumentation of 7 September – the letter was actually read only on 11 September – in which his suggestions of 28 August were developed in detail.

The Chancellor's deputy, Delbrück, had assigned Rechenberg to work on the whole complex of the September Memorandum, as the best available man. Actually, apart from the overworked Ministerial Director, Müller, under whose jurisdiction the subject lay, there was no high-level official in any of the government departments concerned who was receptive to the *Mitteleuropa* idea. Only Schönebeck, one of Delbrück's advisers, had joined the ranks by October.

Between 13 and 18 September Rechenberg noted down key elements for his first general report on the September Memorandum to the officials concerned. The reason that they are preserved among the Chancellery files is that the Under-Secretary, Wahnschaffe, wanted them for information. Most prominent among these notes are technical details concerning customs and tariffs, etc. The life of the proposed customs union was put at ten years, with possible revision and extension at the end of that time. Rechenbereg discussed the voting ratio within the 'Delegation', the central customs union authority in charge of administration, control and review, which was to be 9:6:5 or possibly 9:7:6 for Germany, Austria and France – Germany, in other words, might have been outvoted by the other two

Powers. The proposed procedure was first to reach an agreement with Austria and then to impose the organisation on France and Belgium.

Crucial in the present context are the military clauses, which were no longer to be deferred until after the war. Point 17 provided for the razing of French fortifications in the north and east and a prohibition of their rebuilding. Germany was to have the right to occupy the Channel and western ports, possibly until the war with Britain was ended. The French army was to be demobilised and moved to the south. Point 18 applied similar treatment to Belgium. The remaining clauses dealt with other details, notably colonial questions.

Point 17 with its premise that ending the war with Britain remained a problem still to be solved formed the particular point of departure for Rathenau's proposals, embodied in his letter of 7 September. The effect of this letter did not reach beyond Bethmann-Hollweg at Headquarters. Its influence was exerted by way of the Chancellery in Berlin and the Under-Secretary, Wahnschaffe, to whom Rathenau sent a copy. Rechenberg in Berlin also took note of the Memorandum: and since Rechenberg had been entrusted with his current mission, Rathenau had been in constant touch with him. As he told Mutius with considerable satisfaction on 10 October, the day Antwerp fell to the Germans, he believed that something useful might eventuate. Rathenau once again explained his reasoning to the Chancellor's intimate. He did not think that peace would come soon; and since a German invasion of Britain was scarcely feasible, careful calculation justified the confident conclusion that Germany would retain a position of superior strength, even if the war were protracted. Bethmann-Hollweg read this letter too and thus accepted the collaboration between Rathenau and Rechenberg in Berlin.

Rathenau's letter of 7 September was based on two assumptions: contrary to the general expectation, he did not believe that the subjugation of France would cause Britain to seek peace but that the war would drag on; and secondly, again against expectation and as already mentioned, he felt that economic developments would favour Britain and America, because of the growth of the overseas markets. Accordingly, Rathenau's proposals were based on the idea of peace with

France along the lines of the Peace of Nikolsburg with Austria in 1866. Central Europe would be unified under German leadership, on the one hand in opposition to Britain and America, on the other hand politically and economically strengthened against Russia. The time was propitious, since the unexampled subjugation of France by the armies of Germany represented a conspicuous climax that would provide a suitable psychological background for such sweeping events. Britain's further treatment would be guided by the following considerations:

(1) Systematic demoralisation of enemy cities by means of overwhelming air power, on a far larger scale than heretofore. (In a technical sense this was still illusory and represented an overestimate of the new Zeppelin and aeroplane weapons systems – but it did foreshadow the air war of the future!)

(2) Utilisation of the western ports of France to breach the Atlantic blockade.

(3) Posing a threat to the British position in the Mediterranean, especially in Egypt, Suez and Gibraltar.

(4) Most important of all, the economic integration and emancipation of Central Europe. (The importance of a continental customs union was, of course, self-evident in this connection.)

Following military confrontation on the Continent, the war with Britain would continue in the form of protracted economic warfare; and it did not seem possible to offer any clear predictions on how this would run and end; but in well-informed leading circles it was generally held that Britain could not be forced to her knees by military means. In the perspective of such a long and indecisive struggle, the line between war aims and the means to attain them grew blurred. Even in Rathenau's plan, 'war measures' merge imperceptibly into the notion of *Mitteleuropa* as the 'final goal'. When Bethmann-Hollweg spoke of basically reorganising the economic situation in central Europe he certainly was not thinking solely of temporary measures intended only for the duration of the war.

It would be a mistake to view the September Memorandum

purely in terms of a strategic war-aims programme. In a permanent economic struggle with Britain, fluctuating for ever between war and armistice, it would be impossible, in retrospect, to distinguish sharply between intermediate and final goals, and indeed between war aims as such and the means chosen to attain them. Hence one should not underestimate the power shift in Europe that would have been inevitably associated with any central European economic organisation dependent on Germany. Such a thing would very likely have replaced the traditional balance of power with German predominance. Just how that position could have been secured by a European guarantee in the post-war period was an open problem; for the German government were aware that Germany lacked the power to force Britain to tolerate German preponderance in Europe. The struggle with Britain over German predominance in Europe thus almost inevitably grew into an Imperialist tug-of-war on a world-wide scale.

Yet there was no continuity at government level between the pre-war and wartime desire of the Germans to reshape the relations of power in Europe, centred on the *Mitteleuropa* idea, as Fritz Fischer maintains in *Weltmacht oder Niedergang*. Rathenau's *Mitteleuropa* plans may have been adapted to wartime contingencies straight from his pre-war concept, but at government level such plans were a direct response to the challenge posed by Britain's evident willingness to fight to the limit, forcing Germany to consider every resource at her disposal on the Continent to counter the threat. The moment it became clear beyond doubt that there would be a protracted economic struggle with Britain, *Mitteleuropa* took on the character of a carefully considered project, though still tentative and non-committal, because it was based on the anticipated subjugation of France. In the light of his fight against the annexationists, Bethmann-Hollweg may have welcomed the plan, if only because it seemed a likely means – or so Rathenau, at least, thought – for channelling German public opinion and its exaggerated expectations when peace did come.

In August Bethmann-Hollweg had aimed his hopes and efforts in the direction of limiting the war and keeping it under control; but he had not been able to rule out the possibility that it might unexpectedly expand into the economic sphere, thereby effecting a fundamental alteration in the existing field of force. Early in the month Rathenau had voiced fears to the Chancellor that the war might disastrously affect German markets outside Europe and that a search must therefore be made for possible substitutes on the Continent. It was against this background that Bethmann-Hollweg first engaged in talks with Delbrück on an economic programme that contemplated a central European customs union, the emphasis being placed on Austria, in keeping with Rathenau's memorandum; but no directives were issued at that time and the departmental consultations on economic policies to be pursued at the end of the war never got beyond the hypothetical stage. It was only the September Memorandum, with Bethmann-Hollweg's covering letter, that gave the departmental chiefs a basis for concrete discussion of a central European economic union, to their surprise.

These hesitant consultations on economic reorientation after the war were paralleled at Headquarters, first in Koblenz and then in Luxembourg, by preliminary discussions on economic guarantees for post-war Germany. It was on 21 August that the idea of a central European economic union first entered this debate. Riezler noted: 'In the evening a long discussion on Poland and the possibility of loosely integrating other countries with Germany – a central European system of differential tariffs, a Greater Germany with Belgium, Holland and Poland as immediate and Austria as a more distant protectorate.' Even before Rechenberg had presented his more limited eastern *Mitteleuropa* concept to the government, the Polish question had here already provided the impetus for a far-reaching examination of the idea of an interdependent central European economic system. True, it is not known to what extent Bethmann-Hollweg took part in these talks nor whether he thought the idea meaningful and feasible at this early date. The discussions among the politicians, at any rate, testify to uncertainty and irresolute improvisation rather than faith in victory and sweeping programmes of conquest. Quite evidently there was no consistent and practical picture of just how Germany's position could be made 'secure' after the war; and at this early stage of discussion the Chancellor did nothing to develop such a programme and a consensus around it.

Otherwise Delbrück, in his memorandum to the Chancellor of 3 September, could scarcely have challenged Rathenau's proposal so forthrightly. It did not contain a single new thought, Delbrück wrote. It was merely a one-sided presentation in a new guise of a problem that had ceaselessly preoccupied the statesmen of the two great empires for more than sixty years.

In these first controversial discussions the dominant element was not yet the aggressive turn against Britain with the idea of including western Europe and especially the Channel coast. This came to the fore – and drew Bethmann-Hollweg's attention – only after Rathenau's suggestion in his letter of 28 August. It was then that the realities of economic warfare with Britain required the Chancellor, too, to concern himself with plans for a central European economic union and envisage their realisation in the event of France's precipitate collapse. Even so, one may well question whether he shared Riezler's romantic faith in the durability of such a new order. He was certainly clear on one point – it could have been put into effect only by the harshest kind of coercion.

THE EXPERTS TAKE OVER

Seasoned in the ways of bureaucracy, the Chancellor managed to sidetrack discussion at Headquarters, where it was subject to many unconstitutional and semi-constitutional influences. Insisting that under established procedure the Minister of the Interior had jurisdiction in such matters, he succeeded in turning over the matter of the Memorandum on 9 September to officially detailed bureaucrats for preparation and processing. For reasons of secrecy and in order to avoid the politically irrelevant ballast of purely administrative contributions by lower-echelon officials, he instructed Delbrück to keep to the highest level of officialdom in the major departments. To avoid any political filibusters, Delbrück was also told to shun the vested interests.

Delbrück had a keen sense of jurisdictional privileges and never hesitated to invoke the Chancellor's basic directive of 9 September. He succeeded in outmanoeuvring even the Foreign

Ministry, allowing it participation in only the verbal consultations, represented usually by Johannes, Head of the Economic
Policy Section, occasionally by the Under-Secretary, Zimmermann, who had remained in Berlin. Delbrück secured
Bethmann-Hollweg's explicit agreement for this behaviour.

Having succeeded in keeping the policy-making function
from the hurly-burly of petty political intrigue by turning the
preparatory work over to professional civil servants, the
Chancellor now applied his own habits of thoroughness to the
task of carefully thinking through and analysing the main
issues. He was in constant touch with Delbrück, who fed him
the findings of the experts; for Bethmann-Hollweg was by no
means insensitive to the problems and solutions enumerated in
the Memorandum. On the contrary, he treated the total war
situation and the possible peace constellations as matters of the
greatest urgency and he was convinced that Germany lacked
the military leverage to vanquish Britain and to compel her at
the peace table to restore Germany's share in the world market.
Hence he felt that even new and unconventional solutions had
to be considered with great care and he saw such possibilities in
the proposals offered by Rechenberg and Rathenau. Yet he was
at pains to rule out any radical speculation and far-fetched
planning not based on an overall political concept. A remark in
a letter of 12 September 1914, from Riezler to Hamann,
however, does reflect the fact that the manifest change in the
military situation had given the government temporary relief
from the war-aims debate at Headquarters. 'There is less talk of
peace terms,' Riezler wrote, 'for the situation in the West is
quiescent at the moment, and in Galicia too things are far from
settled.'

THE DIALOGUE BETWEEN BETHMANN-HOLLWEG AND DELBRÜCK

It remains to outline in general tems the further course of the
discussions between the Chancellor and the executive departments, to illustrate the change that took place in the ensuing
months. Although the source material is available, the scope of
this essay dictates that we forgo the details of the various
estimates of the situation.

A first discussion is reflected in a written exchange between Bethmann-Hollweg and Delbrück in September. In his campaign against Rathenau's proposal of a customs union with Austria, Delbrück concentrated primarily on the economic aspects. His main argument was that complete abolition of agricultural tariffs would be unacceptable to German farming interests. The advantages accruing to German industry by virtue of its strong position, on the other hand, would seriously threaten the existence of Austrian industry. Under Rathenau's proposal Austria's expected opposition was to be overcome by means of a *coup*, camouflaged as a war measure. As a constitutional Minister and law-abiding administrator Delbrück sharply rejected such a course. He did, however, feel that it was worth considering a customs alliance with lower tariffs among its members and uniform tariffs for other nations. He was nevertheless unwilling to anticipate developments after the war, which was bound to bring about an essential overall shift in Germany's economic situation. This meant that economic relations with Austria would have to be re-examined in the light of overall economic relations rather than settled while the war was on. This did not mean that Delbrück refused on principle to envisage any improvement in the post-war economic situation. 'Unless we annex Luxemburg, Belgium and Holland – and I assume we will not, especially the two latter – we shall have to be intent upon building up their economic relations with us in an appropriate way.'

Bethmann-Hollweg's reply of 16 September was notably concise, in contrast to Delbrück's detailed exposition. He said that the question of an Austro-German customs rapprochement would have to be treated in the context of the central European economic union, discussed in his covering letter of 9 September. Further detailed examination would show whether a special status for the two allied Powers within such a union was desirable. The Chancellor was convinced, however, that the creation of *Mitteleuropa* as well as, more narrowly, settlement of Austro-German relations could not be realised 'on the basis of an understanding on common interests, but only in the event of Germany dictating the peace under force of political superiority'. This hard-headed judgement flew in the face of Rathenau's optimistic expectation that France could be won over to a 'voluntary peace' in the spirit of German peace policy in 1866.

On 13 September, in response to the programme for a central European customs union submitted to him on 9 September, Delbrück abandoned his long-winded manner of argumentation against Rathenau's proposal and mentioned the possible disadvantages of competition from Italian and French wines, Hungarian produce and French textiles in only cursory fashion. He had decided to give loyal allegiance to Bethmann-Hollweg, to get to know the Chancellor's arguments inside out. As a possible argument for such a radical upheaval he pointed out that Germany would be fighting for dominion of the world market rather than the home market. 'Only a Europe comprising a united customs area will be able to face the enormous productive potential of the transatlantic world with the requisite strength. We should thank God that the war gives us occasion and opportunity to abandon an economic system that is about to pass the apex of its success.'

Delbrück, however, did mention the domestic implications of a central European customs union. It could be brought into being only if the agrarian conservatives were outmanoeuvred by an anti-rightist liberal majority, and such a majority would not be able to dispense with the Social Democrats. Hence the process of coming to terms with the Social Democrats, which was already under way, must be continued side by side with the development of the *Mitteleuropa* concept, and there must be preparations for a new national policy, to be put into effect, of course, only after the war. Wahnschaffe and Delbrück, with Bethmann-Hollweg's approval, had already agreed on a compromise formula for the duration of the war: the groundwork was to be laid for a great post-war 'national regeneration'.

In his reply of 19 September the Chancellor admitted that 'so radical a reorientation' was bound to encounter economic and political difficulties. To bridge the possible disadvantages of total abolition of tariff barriers in central Europe, he proposed a transitional solution. Without dropping the basic scheme, tariffs which would at least be uniform were to be fixed for countries outside the union, for a list of the most important exports, together with low preferential tariffs for the countries within the union.

As far as the domestic aspects of the problem were concerned, the Chancellor also pleaded for taking advantage of an opportunity that might never recur, to root the Social Democrats firmly in a nationalist and monarchical spirit. The kind of reorientation contemplated, he said, meant that the Social Democratic leaders must realise that Germany – and Prussia in particular – would never surrender the firm foundations on which they had grown. There could be no loosening of stalwart German nationalism, of the system the Social Democrats had been so fond of decrying as 'militarism'. Let the Social Democrats pay less attention to 'international understanding' and more to the need for a strong system of military defence.

Bethmann-Hollweg, in other words, was not prepared to go so far as to concede a parliamentary system in any domestic reorientation with the Social Democrats. He appreciated the problems of Germany as an industrialised nation, but as the 'Squire of Hohenfinow' he was a conservative Prussian to the core. The domestic reforms he envisaged were not intended to contribute to weakening the conservative monarchist foundations of Germany and Prussia but to strengthening them by binding the Social Democrats to the principles that underlay the State. The Chancellor's *Mitteleuropa* plans did not include paying the price of a basic change of system. There was to be no domestic upheaval to go hand in hand with the new radical economic policy on the Continent.

Early in October, armed with a briefcase full of memoranda, Delbrück set out for Charleville and a further round of talks with the Chancellor on the issue of a customs union. The upshot of these talks shows clearly that virtually no political commitments had been made in previous discussion. The situation was still very far from having reached the stage of decision. Delbrück managed to convince Bethmann-Hollweg that the matter had not yet come to a head and that he must be given time to review all the technical details. At the same time, however, Delbrück clearly indicated that resistance to the plan, especially within the higher Prussian government echelons, could be overcome only if the Chancellor himself came out with a clear-cut programme and the unswerving will to put it into effect. What he was doing was to remove himself from the line of fire and to remind the Chancellor of his responsibility. Yet it was precisely such an official commitment that ran counter to Bethmann-Hollweg's inclinations; for the changed military situation and the failure of any French collapse to occur had undermined the very premise of the *Mitteleuropa* project covered in the September Memorandum; and the Chancellor was reluctant to enter into any premature commitment in respect of possible peace negotiations to come, in which Germany was now unlikely to be able to dictate harsh terms. As Delbrück put it in his memoirs, 'work on the project continued to the end of my term of office, but the Chancellor never did issue the policy declaration I wanted'. Interdepartmental committee meetings ran their course, but no longer under the whiplash of Headquarters.

'FROM THE MILDEST TO THE TOUGHEST': THE EXPERTS MEET

By mid-October the groundwork for a central European customs union had been developed within the Reich Office of the Interior to the point where discussion of the subject could be usefully continued. In a draft for a general position paper, Delbrück discussed the domestic political situation, especially the state of national minorities within Germany, and the Polish question, and in connection with the latter also the question of a customs union. In the matter of the Polish issue he inclined to the so-called 'Austrian solution' after the war and attacked the separatist policies of the generals in the field, who were working for the restoration of Poland, in concert with the Polish 'Young Turks'. In this connection Delbrück reverted to Rechenberg's idea of territorial compensation which, in the course of the customs union debate, became transformed into 'general political and economic concessions', the original concept dissolving into loosely connected sub-issues within a framework of traditional trade pacts.

On the basis of the work of his staff, Delbrück added a new argument to those he had previously used against a customs union with Austria, a project that had found few new friends beyond Rechenberg and Schönebeck. 'Austria,' he said, 'is so poorly consolidated in political and economic respects, its development potential so unreliable and obscure, that our own political and economic future would be endangered, were we to enter into closer ties with this decaying and disintegrating State.' After a polite disavowal of his ability to judge Austria, since he was not personally familiar with the country, Bethmann-Hollweg's deputy, in a later section of the letter, nevertheless identified himself with the view that the Dual Monarchy's economy was in poor shape and complained of its representatives' arrogance, which was totally inappropriate in view of the country's inefficiency and represented a severe strain on efforts at collaboration.

This was only three months after the July crisis, in which the restoration of Austria as a Great Power had been one of the main goals of German policy – a policy, by the way, that was still finding expression, at least in part, in Rechenberg's sympathies for an Austrian solution of the Polish issue. Basically, Delbrück's verdict meant that a cornerstone of that policy had been thoroughly undermined, lending further urgency to the need for a thoroughgoing overhaul of pre-war political alignments. Even in these early months of the war the problem of bringing about such a realignment became more and more like trying to square the circle, in view of Germany's military and economic dilemma.

Following the line of reasoning in his letter of 13 September, Delbrück presented an argument he described as crucial to the ultimate decision. If Germany had to anticipate that the war would impair her markets, if it were reasonable to assume that Britain would have to abandon her policy of free trade after the war and if it were likely that the British colonies would treat Germany even less favourably than heretofore, in respect of tariffs, then the disadvantages of integration with Austria would have to be accepted as a key to opening up the continental market. Such a decision was probably inescapable since Russia, no matter how she emerged from the war, was bound to become a most dangerous economic rival in the course of time, in view of her manpower and natural resources. The transatlantic world, moreover, possibly allied with Britain, might well turn out an even more potent rival; and against such opposition the countries of central Europe could scarcely prevail, either politically or economically, unless they were firmly united by economic and constitutional bonds.

It is readily seen that Delbrück was using arguments drawn from Rathenau's letter of 7 September. What the two had in common was the goal of a settlement and alliance with France, with which an arrangement over Belgium must be arrived at – the details cannot be elaborated here. Yet overall, as Rathenau summarised it in his diary, the opponents of his views had prevailed, in the wake of growing objections in the inter-departmental meetings during September and October.

Behind Delbrück's thinking about the various possibilities stood a defensive attitude to what was seen as an organised world of enemies that must be fought with its own weapons, if Germany wished to continue to cut any figure at all, in a political and economic sense. In such an embattled world the alternative that three great economic blocs might exist in harmony side by side by a policy of live and let live was not even considered. Such was the heritage not only of 'Imperialist' thinking but of the war-borne trend towards economic warfare. Throughout the discussions with the Chancellor, Delbrück refrained from voicing any decided opinions of his own, assuming instead the role of a purely non-political, technical and administrative adviser, which was made all the easier, since there was indeed much disagreement among the various departments. Another interpretation of his reticence, however, would be that it might have stemmed from his own conservative opposition.

Delbrück invited the departmental chiefs on 21 October to stimulate further work in the direction of elaborating a range of clear-cut proposals 'from the mildest to the toughest'. He passed on the different views to the Chancellor, on the assumption, he said, that they would be of interest to Bethmann-Hollweg in preparing for the difficult final decision. Delbrück was well aware of the immense burden of responsibility that ultimately weighed down on the Chancellor and no one else. He could not make the decision in Bethmann-Hollweg's place and he had no wish to do so.

NEW HOPES OF VICTORY IN OCTOBER 1914

During these October days Bethmann-Hollweg for the second time faced a major decision, since the military situation did not exclude the possibility that a decisive strategic success in the West might impend after all. Both another envelopment in the race to the sea and a great strategic breakthrough seemed possible. The capture of Antwerp was accounted a particularly impressive *coup* to remind the world of Germany's military power. Churchill was known to have been in that city until two days before its fall and to have called for resistance to the last. The fall of Antwerp thus became a powerful symbol.

On the basis of this estimate of the situation Bethmann-Hollweg asked Pohl, in a talk on 15 October, for an expression of opinion on the goals Germany should pursue in peace negotiations. Pohl enumerated the occupation of Antwerp, Bruges, Ostend and Dunkirk in the West, pushing back the Russians in the East and seizing Alexandretta and Mersina as naval bases in the South. Bethmann-Hollweg did at one point openly demur, admonishing the admiral not to 'talk too big', but as usual when it came to discussing war aims his rhetoric was conciliatory and Pohl thought that he assented. Tirpitz objected to Pohl's war aims on the ground that they contained nothing to indicate victory over Britain and was told in no uncertain terms that here too victory over France and Russia would be crucial. Once again, as in September, the thinking was based on a premise of German victory on the Continent, which was to lay the groundwork for a strategy against Britain.

On 19 October Bethmann-Hollweg invited Tirpitz too for a discussion of possible peace terms; and to that end he once again, on 22 October, asked Delbrück for detailed 'desiderata' against the event of peace negotiations. In style and outward form his directive was related to his covering letter for the September Memorandum. 'Even though there are no such signs so far,' he concluded, 'we must take the possibility into account that one of our enemies might suddenly collapse and we must not be taken by surprise in that event.'

This document supplanted Bethmann-Hollweg's prior directive of 9 September about background research which thus was in force for only six weeks and certainly did not, as

Fritz Fischer claims, form the foundation to the end of the war of German war-aims policy. In a technical sense, Bethmann-Hollweg was acting on the interdepartmental discussion about economic policy. The notion of a great central European economic area was not taken up. Instead, the Chancellor limited himself, in the question of future economic policy, to ordering that a substitute must be found, in the French and Russian markets, for the possible losses that might accrue to Germany in the world market for some years after the war. He mentioned the incorporation of the Briey ore region as one measure, precisely something that Delbrück, in his analysis of 13 September, had described as potentially unnecessary within the framework of a central European economic union. The Russian market was to be opened to German exports under a long-term trade pact that would lower the Russian tariffs of greatest concern to Germany. Bethmann-Hollweg instructed Delbrück to undertake a preliminary study of this question, taking into account the modalities that might arise from the possible establishment of a customs union with Austria. The accent had sharply shifted and a customs union with Austria was now secondary to a trade pact with Russia.

Interest in supranational organisation had been replaced in the directive by traditional forms of trade agreement, financial war indemnities and colonial agreements, territorial or in terms of economic policy. There were added proposals to secure 'freedom of enterprise abroad without prejudice to the right of national self-determination'. The most sanguine eventuality to be explored was victory over Britain, but it should be understood that this meant compromise on the part of the British after a German triumph on the Continent rather than the military defeat of Britain; for possible subjects for negotiation considered by the Chancellor were patent agreements, colonial tariff policy and certain measures to make it more difficult for Britain to move into the protectionist camp, which was bound to bring on conscription.

These ideas suggest that Germany hoped for a *status quo* with only minor changes. Only the severest British economic war measures were to be forestalled, together with too sweeping a revision of pre-war trade and military policy.

On 23 and 24 October Delbrück gave a major Press

interview on German economic policy. Over and above wartime needs, he described the revival of trade and industry as his main concern and expressed his expectation of co-operation with the neutral countries, since they, as producers, had an interest in markets. He tried to show, all in all, that Germany, owing to her gift for organisation and improvisation and her considerable degree of self-sufficiency, especially in the food sector, was able to face the prospect of economic warfare with confidence.

THE WAR STAGNATES: NOVEMBER 1914

On cursory assessment the political situation in October still seemed to leave a remnant of hope that the balance might tip in Germany's favour, in that one of her enemies might suffer sudden collapse; but during the ensuing weeks the forces shifted more and more. On 17 October, during preparations for the offensive in Flanders, Jagow expressed fears that the war would turn into a morass and slow down to a walk, from general exhaustion. This prediction came true in mid-November 1914. The war of position in the West became irrevocable. The Chief of Staff and the War Minister confirmed Tirpitz in believing that there was a complete stalemate in the West.

The inner leading circle – Bethmann-Hollweg, Falkenhayn, Zimmermann, Jagow and not least Tirpitz – now embarked on a round of talks and written exchanges that amounted to a major stock-taking and review of the political and military situation. Perhaps the most significant document for an understanding of the conclusions drawn from this critical situation was the 'Raisonnement', as Bethmann-Hollweg called his basic analysis of 19 November, which he transmitted to Zimmermann for reaction. It is here referred to only in respect of the main questions of concern: ending the war with Britain and the ideas relating to that end.

The issue to be settled – and this found dramatic expression in the leadership crisis at the turn of the year – was the shift of political and military emphasis to Russia, in order to get out of the blind alley into which Germany had blundered and regain the military initiative, by a combination of strategic success with efforts at a separate peace. Bethmann-Hollweg was extremely sceptical that his new effort would bring success but felt that he could not withstand Falkenhayn's unremitting pressure for a separate understanding with Russia because the war in the West had bogged down and despite every confidence the situation there had to be described as serious. At the very least, he remarked, all the possibilities in the East had to be considered with the greatest care, even though for the time being there were no signs whatever that Russia was prepared for negotiations. Hence he reviewed the alternative that seemed to him most likely:

> Should we fail to split Russia away from the Entente, we shall probably not be able to gain military mastery over any one of our enemies. We risk the danger that the war will take an unfavourable turn for us overall, through the intervention of Japan, the sheer manpower of continuing British reinforcements, and military reverses, which can never be wholly excluded in a war; but even in the absence of such an extremity, our only remaining chance would be for the war to come to a halt by virtue of general exhaustion, without a clear-cut military defeat on either side.

He then drew a conclusion that concisely summarised the ideas that have preoccupied us in the present account:

> In the event of peace we should have Belgium and northern France as bargaining counters, to the approximate extent that we now occupy those regions, while our enemies would be able to put up the greater part of Galicia and several of our colonies. Britain, in addition, would have the trump cards of an unvanquished fleet and unbroken dominion over world trade. Of itself this would not necessarily mean a situation unfavourable to our side, but we should not be able to impose more on Russia and France than we could now get from them, were either of them ready to conclude a separate peace.

Once again the impossibility of getting the better of Britain was the point of departure: 'Vis-à-vis Britain our power would be very slight. Even in the event of peace she would seek to play the role of protector of France, at least, maintaining political sway over that country in any future war with us.' He then outlined the limits of what might be attainable by peace: 'The results for us would be reduced in essence to a demonstration before the world that even the most powerful enemy coalition cannot bring us to our knees. While this might promote peace and further growth, the immediate effect would be that the German people would feel ill-rewarded for the immense hardships they have undergone.'

Following discussion of a number of fortunate contingencies and chances, Bethmann-Hollweg went a step further in his analysis. There could be no absolute confidence that Germany could win complete victory over France and Britain, he explained, even if Russia were split away from the Entente, for with competent leadership the military superiority of the Western Powers was very great and the German navy was probably not in a position to cut off Britain's food supply, not even for a limited period of time. Taking everything into account, the situation had to be described as serious, even with the greatest confidence on the German side. We note that all that was left of the grand plans was the traditional method of territorial bargaining in West and East.

Thus the Chancellor twice over-qualified and questioned the political concept of Tirpitz and Falkenhayn, his adversaries and rivals for the Chancellorship. Against the price that the situation in respect of Russia would remain essentially as it had been before the war, they wanted to create one in the West that would be more favourable to Germany, while at the same time eliminating the Triple Entente. Bethmann-Hollweg thought this beyond reach, with or without a separate Russian peace. In his view this was the direction in which the most hard-headed evaluation of Germany's military and political resources pointed.

In analysing the available options in the field of economic policy, we have seen that the basic view was one of a world without peace, a world in which the Powers were locked in struggle even without war. The November 'Raisonnement' contains a phrase that reflects perhaps for the first time an alternative view of the Chancellor, hinting at a first qualification of the militant spirit inherent in Imperialist thinking. It was to be openly expressed in Bethmann-Hollweg's letter to Prince Max of Baden, already mentioned at the beginning, and in his *Betrachtungen zum Weltkriege*.

'I AM NOT IN A POSITION TO ENLIGHTEN THESE GENTLEMEN ON THE MILITARY SITUATION'

Bethmann-Hollweg could imagine that the mere fact that Germany was able to maintain herself against the most powerful enemy coalition might promote peace and further growth; but a keynote also struck in his *Betrachtungen* suggests that a policy based so completely on imponderables would have implied, at least initially, the severest domestic political struggles. He was aware that he had very little freedom of choice if he tried to lead a Germany still under the spell of dreams of power along a road that offered no material securities and guarantees. Unfortunately this early insight was buried later on. Thus, as long as the situation permitted, he plotted his course along traditional lines of power politics, an approach to which he was personally and profoundly dedicated; not did he relinquish, in so far as possible, his hopes and ambitions for material guarantees of Germany's political integrity, even though political and military developments were constantly narrowing his scope for action. He had some room for manoeuvre left, of course, but he bitterly complained of his restrictions. In a crisis, he said, his domestic opponents would either have to see the true military situation for themselves or have to be briefed on it; but until that time came, he was enmeshed in a network of intrigue and attacks which charged him with being weak-kneed and which he refused to meet head-on.

A paradigm of this attitude is seen in his marginal note on a memorandum submitted by the German employers' associations in March 1915. Wahnschaffe's comment was that it would become necessary to open the eyes of men who spread such ideas about, to which Bethmann–Hollweg added: 'I am not in a position to enlighten these gentlemen on the military situation. They either accuse me of being weak-kneed or they grow anxious themselves. Neither course is welcome. Enlightenment can come only slowly, from the actual course of military events.'

The bitterness the Chancellor felt over the attitude embodied in this memorandum had been reflected some weeks earlier in a confidential talk he had with Theodor Wolff on 5 February 1915. 'We have been living a lie in both our foreign and domestic policy,' he said. 'Our people have been infected with a spirit of loud-mouthed braggadocio and irresponsible patter.' He had noted this insensate hatred of the enemy only on the home front, he added, much in contrast to the dead seriousness of the troops, which he had witnessed during a recent visit to the front. On this he staked his hopes, as he did later on in 1918, in his letter to Prince Max of Baden. 'It would be dreadful if this brash boastfulness and arrogance were to remain with us when peace comes. A horrifying thought – after the war there will be new men.'

There were immediate developments of which the Chancellor in March 1915 expected a salutary and enlightening effect. The situation grew progressively worse. More and more, during the winter of 1914–15, the preservation of occupied territory for bargaining purposes became a central point of policy, and ultimately this necessity restricted the possible scope of action in the East as well. At the height of the leadership crisis, when the Chancellor was fighting the Chief of Staff for the commitment of reserves in the East, Valentini, Chief of the Imperial Civil Cabinet, who worked closely with Bethmann-Hollweg, warned against endangering the territorial hostages in the West. Britain was the main enemy, he insisted, and a firm grip must be maintained on the occupied territories in the West, as a powerful means of exerting pressure on Britain.

By mid-March these territories seemed in danger. In a letter to Treutler, the Foreign Ministry representative at Headquarters, who had the job of maintaining liaison with the Supreme Command since the Chancellor had returned to Berlin, Bethmann-Hollweg drew a picture of the situation in the blackest colours, almost as though he were writing on the eve of Black Friday in 1918. He said that according to Press dispatches from Switzerland confidence in victory was sweeping France. There was a revival of economic life in the south of France and French military reserves were promising.

Bethmann-Hollweg saw greater danger that the enemy, even if he did not succeed in breaking through the German positions, might slowly push back the Germans more and more, by virtue of his superior manpower, artillery and ammunition:

> A German breakthrough, on the other hand, would exact tremendous casualties and merely bring us a few miles further on to an equally strong enemy position. At the present time we hold substantial territorial hostages. Our enemies still have enough money to ransom them at an acceptable price. It seems to me that our situation will grow worse with every month the war continues, quite apart from the additional billions we shall have to raise in that event. Hindenburg and his people concur in this judgement.

Without the triumphs of August and September to back them up, the German government once again, under much more acute pressure, were faced with the necessity of having to wait for the enemy to consider further German occupation of the territories in point as intolerable and on that account forgo fighting the war to the end, since the only alternative, a protracted and bloody war of position, might also be found intolerable. Meanwhile, the Germans had to watch idly as the world made economic arrangements that excluded Germany; and time was against her.

In the face of these developments, discussion of post-war economic policy was concluded for the time being. On 12 April 1915 Delbrück advised the Chancellor of the results of inter-departmental consultations on economic integration with Austria – as anticipated, no agreement had been reached. All the departments more or less rejected a complete customs union, since such close economic integration could not be carried into effect as a 'temporary measure' but was bound to lead to intimate political and military ties, which did not recommend themselves because of scepticism concerning Austria's capacity and durability. There were added problems in the apportionment of customs revenue, reconciliation of agricultural and industrial interests and finding a proper constitutional basis.

As for the second possibility, a looser kind of customs alliance, in which the member States would concede one another preferential tariffs, the main argument against this solution was that it might lead to 'economic isolation', since the principle of reciprocity on which it would be based was incompatible with the basis of existing trade treaties, the most-favoured-nation clause. Apart from the fact that recognition of such an arrangement by the enemy countries could be achieved only through a conclusive victory, its value was extremely dubious, considering the almost certain adverse effect on other markets of great importance.

The ministerial bureaucrats then came to grips with the basic question affecting the economic structure of Germany:

> Our commercial activities are organised in such a way today that unless the most serious interference with our entire economic life is to be risked, we must continue to have access to world markets, notably such major markets as Great Britain, the United States and Russia. It would be against our interests to limit ourself to certain circumscribed markets, even if these were to be expanded. Hence from the viewpoint of German economic policy a proposal to form a customs union with Austria and other central European countries cannot be recommended. A remaining third way would be to continue the kind of economic policy we have pursued heretofore, by concluding commercial treaties, preferably with tariff clauses.

Delbrück wished to envisage closer economic integration with Austria only if there were special political reasons that could not be ignored. He conceded that one such motive might be the imposition of closer political ties with Austria by forcing that country into a state of economic dependence on Germany, to counteract the possible freezing of wartime alignments even when peace returned.

Fritz Fischer views the continuity of the *Mitteleuropa* question as an essential link between peacetime and wartime. In my view this ignores the fact that both before and afterwards the conflict between an international and a regional marketing orientation continued to exert its effect undiminished within the official agencies and among the vested interests. The idea of a central European customs union was by no means the only solution, nor even the crucial one. That was one reason why it came to grief so quickly – trade pacts were far more amenable to compromise in the various directions. It is highly significant in this connection that the German Industrial War Board, in addition to the joint memorandum from the employers' associations, submitted a commercial treaty draft based on drastically lowered tariffs. Director Johannes of the Economic Policy Section of the Foreign Ministry rejected it:

> Such a standardisation would not be tolerated by other countries in the long run and sooner or later provide the occasion for a new break. There can be no doubt whatever that if the war situation were less favourable to us neither Russia nor France would dream of accepting such an agreement. Even Great Britain could not be coerced into accepting the kind of formulation proposed by the Industrial War Board.

Delbrück argued along similar lines, adding that any discrimination against British maritime commerce by means of special tariffs would redound to the disadvantage of the German merchant navy and thus gravely prejudice the revival of German overseas exports after the war. He also pointed out the devastating consequences for German agriculture. Even if the war situation at the time peace was concluded were to make it possible to impose such agreements on France, the terms were not desirable.

CONCLUSION

In conclusion, I append a few remarks that somewhat transcend the narrow limits of time and method within which this essay has been held.

Within the framework of the diverse and shifting estimates of the situation, consideration was given time and again to a multiplicity of plans and goals, each expressing some particular political possibility or concept. They were the subject of official and non-official discussions seldom ending in any decisions. They came in ranges 'from the mildest to the toughest', and they were all kept on the shelf, so to speak. The subjects discussed dealt with the most varied functions – tactical methods, hostages for bargaining purposes, forms of indemnity, ways of expanding German power after the war. There was a plethora of rival aims but never any well-thought-out plan of victory.

The question is how the government managed it that these various plans of action, placed at the disposal of the Cabinet as carefully prepared reserve policies, and then embalmed in some ministerial file, never reached a point of no return, never took on any dangerous political and propaganda momentum of their own.

There was no such danger so long as these papers rested in bureauracy's bosom, under the care of men of the intellectual rectitude of Delbrück and Solf, who had a sophisticated sense of self-criticism, and so long as the politically vulnerable Tirpitz avoided walking into one of the Chancellor's traps by committing himself to some plan laid down in writing, risking subsequent disavowal because sudden changes in the situation undermined the premises of the plan.

A man like Solf could ironically speak of 'the game of border-shifting'. Others, more mindful of aroused public opinion and annexationist propaganda, had to fall back on the compromise formula, '. . . in the event of a decisive German victory'. Yet one would have to search long among those responsible and in the know before finding anyone who really believed in such a possibility. It was simply a duty to display confidence in wartime.

A certain protection continued to be afforded by the flood of memoranda that made it easier to cover every contingency, even in the political infighting. Despite all the factors that facilitated control, Bethmann-Hollweg was not blind to the dangers of the war-aims issue. Secrecy, suppression of Press discussion and the exclusion of vested interests in the preparatory work, all were prophylactic measures. Bethmann-Hollweg knew and feared the constricting pressure of public opinion;

but since he knew the true situation he was confident of prevailing at the crucial moment, because of two weighty considerations. The time might come when out of the deep secrecy of diplomatic soundings a significant point of contact with the enemy might emerge, hinting at his willingness to negotiate. This might be thrown into the balance of the domestic political struggle over German leadership, placed before the two major political bodies, the Prussian Cabinet and the unofficial group of Reichstag leaders Bethmann-Hollweg had established. There the issue could be forged into a decisive and successful weapon to which the Kaiser could be won over.

It should be borne in mind how much political capital the Chancellor was able to make out of the wretched crumbs in sounding out Russia on a separate peace, an initiative that came entirely from the German side, without finding any echo, but that did admirable service in protecting his domestic policy and in the Polish question. As a last resort there was always publicity and the threat of a storm from the Left. Such eventualities, however, were quite remote at the outset of the war, expressed more as a latent threat in the struggle to preserve the National Unity Front and Social Democratic support, which were indispensable to the pursuit of the war.

In the end the whole question was never settled, right down to the Russian Revolution. Bethmann-Hollweg never had the slightest chance to make peace and was compelled to say so to the party leaders time and again; and so long as there were no discernible and feasible opportunities for peace, all the planning was consigned to the limbo of unreality; and one should guard against stultifying those responsible by suggesting they did not know it. The inner political leadership saw this limbo quite clearly, even though others were blind to it.

Despite the day-to-day struggle over the political truce on the home front, this tended to ease the severity of political conflict considerably for the Chancellor, even as it was probably responsible in part for the stridency of his opponents. Thus he was able to practise the art of 'dilatory compromise' (as a lawyer might put it) to the utmost, side-stepping the danger of losing his place to one of the deluded fanatics and concealing his view of the situation from observers abroad.

If there were any political limitations the Chancellor could not transcend, it was that he was unable to avoid or make up for the loss of German credibility in a world that had ceased to believe that the German government would be willing to compromise. For a long time his faith in Cabinet and secret diplomacy based on hard-headed compromise kept him from taking these limitations as seriously as they deserved. Here too the letter to Prince Max of Baden seems to reflect new insight.

Bethmann-Hollweg, furthermore, agreed with German public opinion and his domestic opponents on one point. He was not prepared to take a first, let alone a public step in offering a modified *status quo*. He could not bring himself to relinquish in advance the territorial hostages he wanted to use as bargaining counters, if not keep under German sway, at least in part. In retrospect, from the vantage pont of Versailles, this might have been Germany's only chance for achieving anything the Chancellor could have described as promoting peace. He thought that even much smaller steps would already signify sweeping admissions of weakness and hints of surrender, which he feared would merely bring on vociferous jubilation and even greater resolution on the part of the enemy.

It is a moot question how much scope he really had in this respect. We know too little about how firm was the Entente's resolution to fight the war to the end. Whatever the conclusions from further research, the question remains of how important German credibility might have been in world opinion – was it perhaps underestimated? Unfortunately, in the age of Imperialism – and perhaps in other ages as well – there was virtually no willingness to accept political risks without material guarantees.

APPENDIX

Holograph Letter from Bethmann-Hollweg to
Prince Max of Baden
(From the papers of Prince Max of Baden, Salem)

Hohenfinow, 17 January 1918

Most gracious Prince,

Your Highness has given me great pleasure with your handwritten letter of 20 December, such as has not come my way for a long time, and I must first of all ask your kind indulgence that my thanks are expressed so late. I have in the meantime found universal confirmation that the speech of Your Highness has made an impression that continues to deepen. The Kaiser, for one, was very much impressed by it. This was related to me by Herr von Valentini, whom I had the privilege of seeing before receiving Your Highness's letter. I am pleased also with the attitude of the Supreme Command, even though I continue to find its overall political stand obscure and displeasing.

In Your Highness's letter such a wealth of lofty political thoughts are touched upon that I fear my pen will be too feeble to respond to them all. Allow me to reiterate, however, that I gladly follow you in all that you now so handsomely describe as the basis of the 'unwritten law'; and if, in my letter, I mentioned that various methods may flow from that basis, I merely wished to suggest my uncertainty as to whether you find yourself able to approve the ultimate goal I believe I see coming, though I did not identify it at the time.

Ever since I have been no more than a spectator, I am gripped day by day more deeply than before by the awesome grandeur of what we have undergone, by the sublime splendour of man's heroism and the sombre depth of his delusions, through which we are passing. This, the most stupendous revolution ever to shake the globe, cannot end, the nations cannot 'atone' before God and the world for all the horror they have done, unless mankind turns away resolutely from the conditions that conjured up this war and seeks to create something new in their place. I too deeply regretted the phrase in [the reply to] the Papal Note about the coincidence of unfortunate circumstances that caused the war. Not only because it weakens our moral position, but above all because it is untrue.

Imperialism, nationalism and economic materialism, which in broad outline have governed the policies of all the nations during the past generation, set themselves goals that could be pursued by each nation only at the cost of a general collision. It is true that besides these general reasons there were special circumstances that militated in favour of war, including those in which Germany in 1870–1 entered the circle of Great

Powers, subsequently achieved world stature and became the object of vengeful envy on the part of the other Great Powers, largely though not entirely by her own fault. Both of these lines, however, the general and the special, are so closely interlinked that it is impossible to say on which side lay the more powerful driving force. For myself, I see the general constellation as the crucial element. How else explain the senseless and impassioned zeal which allowed countries like Italy, Rumania and even America, not originally involved in the war, no rest until they too had immersed themselves in the bloodbath? Surely this is the immediate, tangible expression of a general disposition towards war in the world.

Many had more or less an inkling of this development; but basically only the Social Democrats openly pointed towards it, and only they worked against the war with conviction. The other parties fell more or less under the spell of Imperialism. In France and Russia they deliberately set their course for war, but elsewhere too they ventured more and more on a slippery slope, allowing the idea of war to gain momentum, often consoling themselves with the thought that world war was unthinkable and could never come to pass.

Governments – in France and Russia, for example – followed the Imperialists, partly from conviction, partly from an unwillingness to offer resistance. Where they did not, they soon became too weak to change course, nor even wished to do so, as in Britain, which was not steering a direct course towards war, but also was certainly not thrown into fear and trembling by the idea of it, since in typical British arrogance and selfishness she thought it might promise immediate advantage to her rather than harm. Thus all efforts to reduce the danger of war by disarmament and courts of arbitration failed, as did the special effort to secure the peace by means of an Anglo-German understanding.

The nations are growing more and more aware of all this. At the same time the realisation is spreading that despite Imperialism and nationalism the great majority of people at bottom did not want war at all – or would not have wanted it, had they known its full horror, as it now stands revealed. It is taken for granted, therefore, that the governments alone were responsible for the war breaking out, against the will of the masses, for

Imperialism in all its forms attaining such power, for the fact
that Germany has drawn distrust and even hatred upon herself
throughout the world; and that it was the fault of the
governments that no peaceful way out was found in July 1914.
In whatever measure these beliefs and convictions may be
justified, they lead with inescapable logic to the conclusion that
there should be better government and that government should
be in greater agreement with the true will of the people. So great
is the force of this challenge, and so widely will the ethical ideas
on which it rests spread after this bloodbath, that it is bound to
prevail, even against the will of the chauvinists and reactionaries who will survive, though their future power will
dwindle in the precise degree of their present savage
demeanour. I am utterly convinced that this will happen, the
more so since peace is unlikely to come until the war-weary
masses will force it in one way or another and since these very
masses will discern the full burdens and dimensions of the war
only after peace has been concluded.

I know that the thoughts I am here voicing are neither new
nor original. In the course of the present cataclysm it has
always been my endeavour to isolate those general ideas that
will shape the future, so that I might form a correct estimate of
their inexorable consequences for Germany.

In this connection there also arises the question of Prussian
electoral law, mentioned by Your Highness. My own experience parallels yours. 'Poor Prussia!' I have often told myself,
asking whether the move to the general franchise may not
destroy our greatest and most tested values, whether the leap
we seek to make may not be too big and precipitate. Yet even
today I do not for a moment doubt the necessity and propriety
of the [Kaiser's] decision [promising introduction of the general
franchise in Prussia during the war]. Practically speaking,
there is no alternative. In realistic terms it would be impossible
to devise a form of popular vote that would avoid sweeping
democratisation unless it were based in some way on wealth
and privilege. Numberless inquiries have been conducted on
this subject, always with the same negative result; but this is
not really what determined me. The crucial consideration for
me was that the only kind of electoral law in keeping with the
just demand for a regime that would embody the popular will is

one that confers political rights with the same equality that
governs the hardships imposed by the war. This is no mere
theory but an ethical postulate stronger than any argument –
which may not be altogether unjustified – that the true popular
will can never be defined and that even the universal franchise
offers no guarantee that it will be carried out.

My view of the so-called parliamentary system is similar. It
is at bottom incompatible with our feudal constitution, for it
requires firmly organised majority parties, which we do not
have – or do not yet have. It provides Ministers who are not as
well qualified as under the bureaucratic system. Above all, it
harbours a host of political dangers which we can study in
detail in the Romance countries. Yet in the long run the
demand that even the members of the government should
embody the popular will as expressed in the legislature is a
necessary consequence of the war, for reasons already given,
and cannot be denied. Of course the forms must be adapted to
German contingencies, and it must not be overlooked that the
government too increasingly looks for firmer ties with the
legislature, for reasons of their own, at least during such critical
times as are likely to be with us long after the war. Count
Hertling's Chancellorship, for example, would long since have
reached its end, had he not been able to count on a parliamentary majority, which he was ultimately able to secure only
by including several parliamentarians in the government –
although one may well condemn the unseemly rivalry for these
posts that was displayed in the process.

I think that in judging the overall situation one should not be
deceived by the fact that even the major liberal parties have
acquiesced in the intrusions of the military into the political
sphere. As we know, the National Liberals have given blanket
approval in advance to all the military requests of the Supreme
Command, without even knowing in the least what they were.
Complete faith in the military qualifications of the Supreme
Command may be amply justified, but one is tempted to view
this policy as a symptom that our desire for popular democratic
government is coupled with a certain slavishness that seems
only the semblance of libertarian government while actually
longing for the absolutist leadership of a bureaucratic regime,
as was true of the Romans in the Augustan Age. Yet unlike the

Romans of that time we are not an ancient people exhausted from civil wars. On the contrary, those sections of our people who have, over the past generation, been our driving force, irksome and even dangerous at times, it is true – the Socialist masses, to speak bluntly – have infused a tremendous dynamism and youthful vigour into our nation. After the war these Germans will not rest content with empty political and economic liberties – they will demand real rights. These masses will simply run the National Liberal fossils into the ground, and topmost among the demands that can then be expected will be the repression of militarism, the more it now conducts itself as a dictatorial form of rule.

These remarks are not at all meant to suggest that the introduction in Germany of a fully formed democratic regime would constitute the ultimate wisdom, especially if it were established on some foreign model; but we should be able to discern the broad outline in which our direction is inscribed in letters of blood; and we should conduct ourselves in such a way as not to be engulfed by the flood.

I am wandering far afield, even though I can touch upon only a small segment of the thoughts and questions that obtrude when one tries to face reality; and even within that segment I see that I have only scratched the surface, only sketchily reviewed a few of many aspects. Perhaps I am exceeding the bounds of propriety in what I have to say and suggest. If so, my only excuse is that the stimulus came from Your Highness's letter.

Your Highness has had the great kindness to speak to me about the question of your Chancellorship, with a frankness for which I am most deeply obliged. Allow me to respond with the same frankness. I have welcomed it that this question has not become acute, since Your Highness is the heir to the throne of Baden. Perhaps it is not the general political attacks to which a Chancellor is exposed that are crucial; but judging from the way things have run throughout the war, came to a head last July and are once again pointing up towards a crisis, I cannot help feeling concern that sharp clashes between the two powers [i.e. the military and the political] will remain the order of the day; and I could wish that Your Highness were spared such conflicts. If it should come to another great crisis, however, in which Your Highness were to be summoned, the situation at home and abroad might be so acute that patriotism might demand that in despite of all conflict Your Highness accept. It goes without saying that I am absolutely convinced, knowing the political views Your Highness entertains, that the affairs of state would be in good hands.

And now I must ask Your Highness's gracious pardon for these importunities. If things were as they used to be and a face-to-face exchange were still possible, I might not have been tempted to impose upon your patience with these written remarks. They are indeed presumptuous in their inadequacy in dealing with great problems as yet probably beyond the power of the human mind. For this reason alone I ask that this letter be taken as a purely personal message. I was, after all, emboldened to write it only on account of the friendly and gracious sentiments Your Highness has always displayed towards me and I sincerely hope will continue to display.

With the greatest respect and gratitude, I remain Your Highness's obedient servant.

BETHMANN-HOLLWEG

7. Gerhard Ritter: A Patriotic Historian's Justification

KARL-HEINZ JANSSEN

Once during the last war Winston Churchill accused the Germans of having involved the world in wars of conquest and aggression five times in the past 125 years because of their hatred of the liberty enjoyed by their neighbours. He was not the only one to think this. In all the great post-war conferences over Germany, all the statesmen from both the East and the West agreed on one thing at least: the wars of 1870–1, 1914–18 and 1939–45 were caused by the Germans alone. Especially in the first years after the German Reich's unconditional surrender in May 1945, in the period of re-education, German as well as foreign historians and writers tried to find historical grounds for the crime of National Socialism. They maintained that there was continuity of political thought and military depravity, stretching from Martin Luther in the Reformation to Frederick the Great of Prussia and to Bismarck, the founder of the Empire, and from Kaiser Wilhelm II to Adolf Hitler, the war criminal.

Professor Gerhard Ritter of Freiburg protested at an early date against this ostensibly plausible but none the less only half-true, superficial and unwarranted interpretation of history. No one of the German historians who had remained in Germany had greater moral right or moral justification than Ritter. He had been freed by the Russians from the hands of the Gestapo in the April of 1945. Ritter, the doyen of German historians until his death in the summer of 1967, considered it

Specially written for this volume.

his political duty to undertake a sober and fundamental review of the traditional picture of German history, without showing any bias to either side. He did not see Germany's past as nothing but shadows: he also found positive and worthwhile aspects. He warned his fellow Germans against blind moral grounds, and in doing so he helped restore their self-confidence.

As early as 1948 when there was still a censorship imposed by the American military government, Ritter wrote that it was impossible 'to blame German diplomacy unilaterally and exclusively for the outbreak of the 1914 war and to explain its actions during the July crisis in terms of supposed plans for world conquest – this has been done so often and thoroughly by serious historical research, especially in England, America, Switzerland and Holland, that to repeat it would only be carrying coals to Newcastle'. But when his younger colleague, Fritz Fischer, began to repeat these accusations twelve years later, Gerhard Ritter was forced to react bitterly and indignantly. Twenty years' work, even his life's work, appeared in danger.

To Ritter's disgust the German Press took up and repeated, largely uncritically and even with approval, Fischer's sensational thesis that Germany was solely responsible for the First World War and that the German Reich was aiming at mastery of the world. Ritter looked on this extreme willingness to atone as amounting to political flagellation. He looked on Fischer's book, *Griff nach der Weltmacht*, as a deliberate attempt to obscure the German sense of history, which since the catastrophe of 1945 had taken the place of the earlier self-deification. He considered it a disaster, which caused him sadness and concern, when he thought of the younger generation.

These fears were not entirely unfounded. The young people who applauded Fischer and his assistants at the Congress of the German Historical Association in Berlin in 1964 were not so much interested in the guilt or innocence of their forefathers, as fascinated by the revolutionary element in Fischer's thesis. They were welcoming the rejection of an approach to history which stressed leading figures and pure Cabinet politics and its replacement with an analysis of the composition of the establishment, of social climate and hidden pressure groups, an analysis providing lessons for the present. These young disciples of Fischer believed like the conservative Ritter that Fischer was basically applying a Marxist approach to German history, although not admitting he was a Marxist, as this would have denied him any prospect of success in West Germany from the outset. Although Fischer did not dare to saddle Germany with the sole guilt for the First World War in the first edition of his book, his quotations and evidence were selected, and his exposition organised, in such a way that the reader could really reach no other conclusion. His magic word was 'continuity'.

Fritz Fischer made it rather easy for his most incisive critic, Gerhard Ritter, to cast doubts on his new historical picture. Ritter pointed out with some success how Fischer had made a series of wrong interpretations or reinterpretations of sources. Quite justifiably, he accused Fischer of totally ignoring the environment of the time and of not comparing the different kinds of foreign Imperialism, including that of the United States. He also noted a 'surprising lack of unbiased and genuine historical empathy'. Fischer had fallen into one of the pitfalls of his profession: he had applied contemporary categories, which were based on later experiences, to the past. In places his approach to history had become tendentious literature.

Ritter none the less did not fail to acknowledge the immense amount of research into sources done by his colleague and his service in researching the recent past. He also accepted tacitly Fischer's discovery of the disastrous inter-relation between economics and politics in Wilhelmine Germany. Fischer had had the tremendous advantage of being able to look at those sections of the German archives held in East Germany and closed to Ritter, which included the various war-aims pro-grammes drawn up by the German Ministers and their assistants. Ritter would have agreed with what a younger historian said of Fischer, that he had shifted a gigantic rock into the traditional path of German historical research, which had forced everyone to think about this historical problem com-pletely again.

When Fischer's work appeared Ritter had already published two volumes of his extremely self-critical examination of the problem of militarism in Germany. He and his pupils, even before Fischer, had been looking at the documents relating to the First World War and using them without regard for the person or country involved. He had not spared himself nor the interpretation of history he had so far accepted from scrutiny. In referring to the second volume of his work, *Staatskunst und Kriegshandwerk* (*The Sword and the Sceptre*), he said that he 'had not written the book without being cut to the core; what I describe here is the pre-war Germany of my own youth. All my life I have remembered this period as a sunny one, which seemed only to have been overcast by the outbreak of war in 1914. And now at the end of my life, using the eye of the researcher, I have been able to see much darker shadows than were seen by my own generation – let alone by my own academic teachers.'

Whatever can be said about the theses of Fritz Fischer and his pupils, Gerhard Ritter's arguments over the questions of war guilt and war aims are an indispensable complement. Unlike Fischer, Ritter had the advantage of living through the period and serving at the front in the First World War. He also had the necessary maturity and sovereignty of a great historian which allowed him to understand personalities and the actions of their time and to assess them justly and critically.

In 1960, that is a year before Fischer's *Griff nach der Weltmacht* appeared, Ritter had made the following assessment of Germany's role in the July crisis of 1914: 'Furthermore her political and military leaders were justified in saying that they had not wanted this catastrophe, and were simply overwhelmed by it; and we have no right to doubt the genuineness of their basic desire for peace. No one in a position of authority wanted to bring about a world war; in this sense the "war-guilt question" no longer exists.'

None of these statements can be maintained today. In fact the contrary must be maintained because of Fischer's research and that stimulated by his work, especially the studies of Egmont Zechlin, Karl Dietrich Erdmann, Fritz Stern and Andreas Hillgruber, and above all because of the knowledge we have of the diary kept at the time by the Imperial Chancellor Bethmann-Hollweg's private secretary, Kurt Riezler. Germany's political and military leaders did not want world war at any cost but they were consciously prepared to risk it. They were not overwhelmed by catastrophe: they made political events develop to the brink of catastrophe.

Two of Bethmann-Hollweg's self-critiques over his own guilt for the First World War were found by one of Ritter's pupils. On 5 February 1915 the Imperial Chancellor told the journalist Theodor Wolff, 'If you are speaking of guilt for this war, we must be honest enough to admit that we also have our own share in it. It would be an understatement to say that I am weighed down by this thought: it never leaves me; I live with it.' And six months after his fall from power he admitted on 24 February 1918 to the Reichstag Deputy, Conrad Haussmann, 'God, in one sense it was a preventive war. But if war was hanging over us, if it would happen two years later more dangerously and inevitably and if the military were saying that it was still possible for us to fight without being defeated but that this would not be the case in two years time. . . .'

Before Fischer put the chief or sole blame for the First World War on Germany, Ritter had been unable to clear the Imperial governments of all responsibility:

> There was a certain fatalism, a belief that a great war was inevitable, as well as a belief in strong national prestige and a desire to be accepted in the world, both of which could lead to political blindness. This was certainly not the case in Vienna and Berlin alone, but it was especially disastrous there because of the threat to the Central Powers' position. And in the judgement of history political blindness can also be construed as guilt.

Where Ritter spoke of 'disaster' and 'blindness', Fischer saw only 'intent' and 'premeditation'. The one interpreted German policy in the July crisis as defensive, the other as aggressive and even as a logical continuation of pre-1914 Imperial policy. Everything that Fischer brought forward as evidence, whether from Press, political or military sources, to prove that Germany was striving for world power, was rejected by Ritter and interpreted as manifestations of an exaggerated, new German nationalism, which showed itself to be illiberal, conservative and militarist. He thought that nothing could be more difficult than to determine precisely what educated and articulate German opinion understood by world policy and world power. Lastly, he thought that the striving for 'a German world policy' was only an expression of a desire for considerable political prestige.

Ritter readily acknowledged the threatening and aggressive tone of the chauvinist Pan-German League, but 'educated pre-war youth (to which I belonged myself) felt differently'. They followed such liberal scholars as Max Weber and Hans Delbrück and 'looked hopefully and with real enthusiasm towards a greater future even though they (like myself) wanted to have nothing to do with the restricted and exaggerated nationalism of the Pan-Germans'. Ritter wrote this as defence against Fischer's thesis, although two years before he had still thought that the unrestrained demands for political prestige put forward by the former general and Pan-German military writer, Bernhardi, and his excessive worship of war, could not be dismissed 'simply as the ideas of an extreme outsider'. He had also noticed a 'militarisation' of the German bourgeoisie which was bound necessarily to exert strong pressure on a weak Imperial government.

What especially annoyed Ritter was that Fischer had not taken seriously his analysis of the famous Schieffen Plan of 1905 and that he should repeat the allegation that Schlieffen, the Chief of the General Staff, had wanted to 'force' France 'out of the Entente' during the first Morocco crisis of 1905–6. In fact Ritter had been able to prove that Schlieffen had never pressed for war, although the opportunity for a defensive strike against France was extremely tempting after Russia's defeat by Japan. The leading figure in German policy at that time, Holstein, was also unable to bring about war because the Kaiser and his Chancellor, Bülow, wanted to maintain peace at almost any price.

The use of power does not necessarily mean the same thing as war and Ritter has shown here that Holstein in 1905 wanted to bark rather than bite, and to blackmail his enemies, in this case France, by brinkmanship. Holstein misjudged the factors of foreign policy, as Bethmann-Hollweg did in 1914, and was convinced that Germany with her temporary military superiority in Europe could risk a great war without actually having to engage in one. But at a critical moment the Kaiser and Bülow left him in the lurch, as they had not the nerve to maintain their position at the Algeciras Conference.

Holstein's policy of bluff and risk aimed at smashing the Entente (just being formed at that time) and at destroying the encirclement threatening Germany. France and Russia were to be forced into a continental alliance with the German Reich, which would finally force Britain to come to an agreement with Germany. In this way he set a precedent which was followed by the Foreign Office and Chancellors in the subsequent crises over Morocco and the Balkans (1909, 1911, 1912–13) and which increased the risk year by year. The intellectual material for this policy, in some ways very similar to the 'brinkmanship' practised by the American Secretary of State, John Foster Dulles, was provided by the same Kurt Riezler, who was both adviser and friend to Bethmann-Hollweg in the July crisis of 1914.

Riezler had realised that a war between the Great Powers in Europe would have disastrous consequences and would shake the European States to their foundations. War, which at that time was still considered by all governments to be the *ultima ratio* of policy, should be replaced by bluff as the 'chief requisite' of diplomacy. Consequently the risks should be calculated very precisely and above all mediation in an international crisis should not be allowed too early before tangible success had been achieved. Riezler did not deny the dangers. 'If a government because of its use of bluff should go further than it originally intended, or if its bluff should be called, then it would probably no longer be able to draw back, even if withdrawal were appropriate. Personal interests, the ambitions of those in power, or the outcry which could be expected from the nationalists, could bring about war, which would never have been justified by the interest involved.'

This is exactly what happened in the July crisis of 1914. On 30 July Bethmann-Hollweg had to admit that every State and nation, even Russia which was so maligned by German propaganda, wanted peace, but 'direction has been lost and the avalanche has begun to move'.

Gerhard Ritter did not accept this risk theory. It must be remembered that in his research he never came across Riezler's diary. In his third volume on the problem of militarism he referred to him in a short sceptical footnote. However, he went to great lengths to argue with two of Fischer's basic arguments, firstly, that Germany wanted a preventive war in 1914, and secondly, that she pressed Austria-Hungary to conduct a timely war of revenge against Serbia so that the balance of power in the Balkans and Near East should be changed to the advantage of the Central Powers.

Ritter knew very well what the German generals had said in favour of a preventive war, but it appeared to him to be far too vague and doubtful. He also did not accept as proof the pretty definite reports of journalists and diplomats in the summer of 1914, although he acknowledged as legitimate the increasing worry of Moltke, the German Chief of Staff, over the dangerous growth of Russian armaments. He was also fond of quoting a letter from the German Secretary of State, Jagow, in which he explained to the German Ambassador in London, Lichnowsky, that war was inevitable with Russia some day. Ritter interpreted Jagow's words 'I don't want a preventive war, but if war offers itself, we should not run away from it', as 'a depressed fatalism in the face of an apparently inevitable and growing danger, but at the same time a determination to meet it with everything in their power'. When Ritter wrote this he was not to know that a few weeks before the assassination at Sarajevo General Moltke had advised the Secretary of State, Jagow, to undertake a preventive war because Germany now had a good chance of seeing the conflict through to a successful conclusion before Russia's armaments programme was completed. This assessment of the position by Moltke made it somewhat easier for the German government to risk world war in July.

Ritter was also unprepared to accept Fischer's claim that Austria-Hungary was tagging behind German policy in 1914. It appeared after all as though he had turned the whole thing upside down. Ritter had his own theory. He believed that by giving a blank cheque to Austria-Hungary on 5 July – a free hand against Russia's Serbian ally – Germany was letting herself be led by Austria-Hungary. Looking at it from the 1960s he agreed with those critics like the German Ambassador in London, Lichnowsky, who thought at the time that an Austrian war with Serbia was absurd and stupid since it would complicate rather than simplify the problems of the Habsburg multinational empire. He none the less believed that, because of the pressure from nationalist street demonstrations, the

German government would have been branded as a traitor to everything German if it had left its Austrian brothers in the lurch. But this idea is hardly convincing, because what Great Power willingly allows itself to be led by another? Also Ritter was basically quite clear himself that the German statesmen had backed the Austrians out of considerations of pure political power, even at the time when the Russians unexpectedly mobilised. We know one reason for it from Riezler's diary: Bethmann-Hollweg wanted to use the Serbian crisis to break up the Entente, since the Franco–British–Russian bloc would hardly have survived if Russia had backed down once again in the face of German threats of war and sacrificed her vassal.

Ritter mentioned the other reason himself – the need of a Great Power for prestige and the fear of losing her last reliable ally. After the war Bethmann-Hollweg defended his policy by arguing that it would have been possible to back down even after Russia's general mobilisation and to sacrifice Austria-Hungary by referring the matter to the International Court at The Hague, but this would have amounted to 'the abdication of our world position without a fight'. Or as Ritter put it: 'Austria-Hungary could not afford to lose her position as a Great Power by accepting passively the activism of the Serbian nationalists, which had now gone as far as murdering the heir to the throne. And Germany could not afford to lose hers by refusing armed help because of her fear of Russia.'

Although Ritter doubted if it was worth running such an incredible risk to maintain the Danubian Monarchy, he basically had no objection to the decision of Germany's leaders to maintain her real or supposed world position in a world war: 'This drive for power and prestige was so accepted in Europe at that time that it is hardly worth discussing. After all England was not defending her own security from Germany in 1914 but maintaining her own moral and political prestige, her position as a World Power and her maritime supremacy.'

But the basic difference between Germany's attitude and that of the other Great Powers in the July crisis was that her policy was determined to a very great extent, far more than Russia's, by 'considerations of pure military technicalities'. In this respect Ritter was always outspoken. He castigated the disastrous naval policy of Grand Admiral Tirpitz which gave

Germany no military advantage but poisoned Anglo-German relations; similarly he castigated the acceptance of the Schlieffen Plan, which entailed a German deployment on one front in the West and a premeditated infringement of Belgium's and Luxemburg's neutrality. He castigated them both as a 'complete surrender of all political reasoning to military planning', since it subordinated the Empire's foreign policy to the pressures of mobilisation and produced the paradox of beginning a war over the Balkans by an attack on France. He condemned Germany's invasion of neutral Belgium as an 'act of force'. He was shocked by the General Staff's demand that France should dishonour herself by agreeing to hand over the forts of Toul and Verdun if she wanted to stay neutral. Nor did he suppress the fantastic figments of the imagination served up by the Army High Command as the basis for the declaration of war against France.

Yet these problems belong to the great complex relationship between politics and war, and in Ritter's eyes were also of secondary importance as far as the question of war guilt was concerned. He maintained that responsible statesmen always have a sphere of freedom of action in spite of everything. He was convinced that if relations between the Army High Command and the Imperial government had been better arranged the war would not have had such an unfortunate start for Germany and hardly such a disastrous end.

Gerhard Ritter could never quite free himself from the comfortable historical view adopted by so many European statesmen and politicians since Lloyd George, that the European nations had 'stumbled' into the First World War. This kind of generalising made the question of responsibility invalid and lifted it out of the emotional sphere, which Fischer's deliberately prejudiced interpretation has brought back again. Very much in the same way as when he discussed the question of war guilt, in discussing war aims Ritter found 'the statesmen more or less helplessly involved in the needs of war and the irresistible pressure from the unleashed emotions of so-called public opinion'.

Ritter's idea of German war aims is diametrically opposed to that of Fischer. According to Fischer Germany's war aims were innately expansionist, aggressive and Imperialist, reflecting the tendencies and forms of political, intellectual, economic and military pressure groups, who were now trying to reach their pre-war aims by force. On the other hand Ritter looked on German war aims similarly to her pre-war foreign policy as essentially defensive, even though not always free from blindness. Its aim was to obtain 'security in the face of a new struggle for existence', that Second Punic War which Germany's ruling élite believed inevitable throughout the whole course of the war, since Britain, 'their main enemy', could not be beaten at the first attempt. Ritter vigorously disputed the concept of a 'striving for world power', Fischer's *Imperium Germanicum* stretching from the Atlantic to the Urals and then from the Near East to Egypt and Central Africa.

If he had been able to prove that the First World War had been in fact a preventive war, Ritter's interpretation might have been more logical. If a power begins a war to forestall an attack threatening it, it will obviously do everything possible to stop a repetition of a similar danger. In our own recent history in the Arab–Israeli conflict, we have seen how a defensive war can turn quite unexpectedly into one of annexation. Annexations caused by fear do not necessarily come from a latent desire to achieve hegemony. If one adopts Ritter's approach and tries to put war aims in a universal framework and discovers similar manifestations in all the countries at war, it is not possible to explain away annexations in the sociological or structural methods employed by Fischer.

From Ritter's work on the question of war aims, six general tendencies and causes can be extracted inherent in the annexionist policies found in modern 'total' war:

(1) The danger myth. In Germany this came primarily from a fear of encirclement, in the other States from a fear of German hegemony.

(2) The moat concept. Despite technological advances in warfare which allowed space and distance to be covered at a much greater rate, the military, politicians and writers have overestimated the importance of buffer zones. This concept is still adhered to today.

(3) Emotions. One of the legacies of the French Revolution has been that sober considerations of *raison d'état* have

often been swept aside by an upsurge of nationalist and militant emotions. Neither the French, Germans, Russians nor Italians were aware that annexations and attempts to limit Powers' sovereignty would not ensure the peace they hoped for but would in fact sabotage it.

(4) The economic profit motive. Patriotic demands were usually accompanied by 'massive material interests'. A good example of this was the German demands for the ore of Lorraine, or French demands for the coal of the Saarland.

(5) The idealising of the power conflict. Everywhere intellectuals were employed in psychological warfare to provide a deeper meaning for the apparently senseless mass slaughter. In Germany numerous phrases were coined, 'idealism versus materialism', 'national unity against collective interests', 'patriotism against pacifism', 'heroism against the barter mentality', 'Western culture against Muscovite barbarism' and so on. Among the Western Powers the slogans ran on the lines of a 'crusade for democracy and liberty against autocracy and militarism'. Ritter felt that all this did not have much political danger but was a necessary stimulant during total war.

(6) The reparations principle. The search for a meaning for the war was supplemented by a search for a price. The people expect some compensation in return for their sacrifice in blood and property, a kind of reward which has been provided since time immemorial by the symbolic cession of booty, tribute or territory.

The shocking extent of German war aims and the strength and breadth of movements in favour of them in Germany has only become known since Fritz Fischer's book. There is no need to detail them here. Ritter, however, took away some of their sensationalism by continually comparing them with Allied war aims. His only purpose in doing this was to weaken his critics' arguments that Germany's unlimited war aims ruined all hope of a negotiated peace. According to Ritter the position was the same on the other side. When Germany explored the possibility of a separate peace with Russia in the autumn of 1914, Tsar

Nicholas was proposing to Paléologue a plan to break up Germany and Austria-Hungary. And when the Central Powers considered offering Russia in the spring of 1915 free access to the Dardanelles, the diplomats of Russia and the Entente were agreeing on a programme which ensured Russian possession of Constantinople and fortification of the Straits as well as the division of Turkey in Asia.

Ritter did not fail to point out the discrepancy between the seriousness of her position in the war and Germany's war aims, but he was able to prove that the French politicians also, at the end of the extremely bloody year of 1916, could think of nothing better than to plan to occupy or neutralise the whole left bank of the Rhine. The French Prime Minister, Aristide Briand, was following, even at that time, a policy which anticipated and actually went further than the Treaty of Versailles in its territorial conditions: Poland was to be enlarged in such a way that Berlin would have lost any military cover, while Denmark was to have all Schleswig and Holland East Friesland. He believed that these conditions were reasonable and modest.

Ritter accused Fischer's monumental work of being out of proportion not only because he had failed to adopt a comparative approach to the analysis of war aims. He also accused him of being unable to separate dreams and hopes from serious aims, and the tactically qualified ambiguities of the diplomats from the massive naked demands made by the Pan-Germans and the military.

Ritter's respect for Fischer's piece of work was not exactly increased when he was able to show up more than one methodological error and false or even falsifying interpretations of sources. The great historian and masterly biographer's passionate opposition was bound to be provoked by Fischer's attempt to put under the same roof such contradictory characters as the Chancellor, Bethmann-Hollweg, and General Ludendorff, the militarist *par excellence*.

Fischer justifiably replied that it was no good trying to analyse German war aims solely on the basis of the Chancellor's personality. He felt that the power of the military, of heavy industry and of agrarian pressure groups, of the Prussian nobility and the middle-class parties was more important than the futile moderating influence of Bethmann-Hollweg. But, as

in all his works, Ritter consciously made the responsible active
statesman the centre of his picture. For him the question of war
aims was only one aspect of the powerful struggle between
politicians and soldiers. He built his description of the first
three years of the war on the theme of the 'tragedy of
statesmanship', in this case the story of Bethmann-Hollweg's
tragic failure.

Seldom in recent German history has a statesman been
subject to such contradictory assessments as Bethmann-
Hollweg. He was a unique mixture of Prussian official and
highly trained intellectual with a Prussian Junker and West
German bourgeois ancestry. For decades the picture Germans
had of him was that painted by his enemies: weak-willed, an
official lacking great political gifts, a deplorable failure, a
despicable defeatist, in short a dreamer and philosopher. On
the other hand Fischer painted him as a Machiavellian in
sheep's clothing, a daring power-conscious politician, who
aimed cleverly and ruthlessly at world power despite all
opposition.

Neither of these extreme portraits does justice to what his
colleague Riezler called this 'peculiar man'. Gerhard Ritter too
found it difficult to unravel his puzzling personality. He
described him as an honourable statesman with a good
character, who 'tried desperately, but never despairingly, to
extricate his country from the snare of an overwhelming and
fateful war and to find a way out for his people from a hopeless
situation'. 'Painstaking and cautious, slow in making up his
mind and with no sure political instinct', he was neither a
fighter nor a man with an iron will, but was 'free from the
degeneracy of the demon of power'.

The apparent contradiction between Bethmann-Hollweg's
realistic and unrealistic war aims, his indecisive and uncertain
actions and finally his failure, were all explained by Ritter as a
product of the complicated constitutional set-up of the Wilhelmine Empire, that peculiar cross between a federal State and a
parliamentary democracy.

Unlike his enemies in the West, Bethmann-Hollweg never
ruled with the help of parliamentary majorities and so could
never feel that he represented the will of the people. The
moment when he first attempted it, he fell from power. His only

support was the confidence of a fickle ruler who was open to all influences. As Imperial Chancellor and Prime Minister of the largest federal State (Prussia), he was in the middle of a web of contradictory, often competing and mutually exclusive forces. He stood in between the higher ministerial bureaucracies of the larger federal States of the south and central Germany, which expected to be rewarded in the event of a successful end to the war, and a Council of Ministers from the Prussian State, who pursued other interests from those of the leaders of the Empire, above all in the Polish and other eastern questions. He also stood in between the parties in the Reichstag and the Prussian Diet, the great economic pressure groups, and last but not least the military, that force which at least while Germany was winning the war always found it easier than the politicians to obtain the sympathy and the confidence of the masses. Unlike in the Western democracies it was not in a subordinate position but held a position equal with that of the political power. Even the founder of the Empire, Prince Bismarck, found the constitutional set-up and the reality of the Empire so complicated that he was only able to conduct affairs through a balancing act. Bethmann-Hollweg also saw only one way to govern – 'a policy of working along the diagonals'. One cannot understand Bethmann-Hollweg's attitude to Germany's war aims without realising the nature of this makeshift policy. He himself once said of it that 'decisive measures, an open fight over internal questions would be possible and perhaps necessary if peace were secured and the external conflict brought to an end. During the war, however, it was in the national interest to follow the narrow and circumspect path between the emotions, conflicting interests and temptations.' Not without some measure of self-congratulation, he added that 'the diagonal is also a straight path and I believe I have kept to it'.

The government could not allow itself to be tied down by exaggerated war aims because of the Social Democrats, who were much the strongest party in the Empire and committed to fighting a defensive war. From the very first day of the war the Right opposed this collaboration with the Left, and because of the three-class franchise in the largest federal State of Prussia the Right was still the dominant force there. The Conservatives objected to Kaiser Wilhelm's including in his speech from the throne at the beginning of the war a phrase aimed at appeasing the Social Democrats: 'We are not being driven by any lust for conquest.'

The unity of the parties and the 'domestic peace', which was kept with some difficulty, already seemed to be breaking up after only a few months when the parties of the Right demanded a definite declaration in favour of an annexationist peace, while the Left pressed the Chancellor to renounce annexations in public. Bethmann-Hollweg, none the less, believed as always that he could paper over the cracks by patriotic speeches and ominous turns of phrase about 'real guarantees and securities'. Of necessity his observations to the representatives of the different parties and pressure groups were bound to be ambiguous.

None the less even Ritter has to admit that Bethmann-Hollweg did not have the sovereign will-power of a great statesman who, despite the requests and demands presented to him, has a clear, definite and attainable aim, an aim dictated by *raison d'état*. He revised this assessment, however, by adding that not even Bismarck, who has always been praised as a statesman of moderation, could resist the national emotions during the Franco-Prussian War. Unlike Bethmann-Hollweg who suppressed the war aims propaganda of the Pan-Germans, Bismarck artificially stimulated public demonstrations in favour of an annexationist peace, and thereby prolonged the war for several months. The annexation of Alsace-Lorraine poisoned relations between the two countries for decades. On the whole it only produces misconceptions if one tries to play off Bismarck against Bethmann-Hollweg. Of course, the founder of the Empire concluded a peace of reconciliation at Nikolsburg after the Austro-Prussian War of 1866, but it is often overlooked that Prussia at the same time annexed more States in north Germany, illegally deposing dynasties, acquiring the Guelphic Fund and ending the liberty of the old Imperial city of Frankfurt.

In the same way as Bismarck directed his war-aims policy from the start in 1870 to the annexation of France's eastern provinces, Bethmann-Hollweg is said to have committed himself during the very first weeks of the World War to a programme which envisaged the 'security of the German

Empire in the West and the East for the foreseeable future' on the basis of wide political, military and economic gains. This is the essence of the so-called September Memorandum, which Fischer discovered during his research in the East Berlin archives and which he maintained contained the war aims which the leaders of the German Empire were committed to until late in 1918.

Gerhard Ritter was quick to recognise the service performed by Fischer in discovering and editing this Memorandum, but in his own discussion of it there is some disquiet over this remarkable document. He tried to play down its importance, claiming that it was nothing more than a first, provisional and strictly secret draft, more a reflection than a decision. (Riezler's diary seems to support this impression, for although Riezler had drawn it up he had no word to say about it.) Ritter also believed that it was 'simply incorrect' to consider the September Memorandum as the basis of Bethmann-Hollweg's entire war-aims policy up to his dismissal. But this observation can again be disproved by Riezler's diary. The Chancellor struck to the essential points of the Memorandum until 1917, although naturally more or less firmly as the military situation changed. Up to this point therefore Fischer's interpretation is correct. But Bethmann-Hollweg was never ready to allow these aims to ruin any chance of a negotiated peace on the basis of the *status quo ante* 1914, if the enemy had been willing for such a peace.

Ritter in his justification did not go as far as Egmont Zechlin, who dismissed the Memorandum as a document produced almost by accident, a virtually unimportant list of the demands of the various government departments, and who considered the plan for a central European federation contained in it as a temporary expedient in the economic war against England. Ritter admitted that Bethmann-Hollweg like other important Germans had abandoned the idea of a purely defensive war because of the tidal wave of German victories in France – the fall of Paris seemed to be only a matter of days at this time – and instead wanted to transform basically the power relationships in central and western Europe and then in the East. Undoubtedly the Memorandum corresponded to the Chancellor's deepest convictions, and if there had been a quick total victory over France he would have looked on it as a sign of great moderation.

It is arguable if this would have been a moderate peace, since France would have been destroyed as a Great Power, her economy turned into a German dependency and put under heavy financial burdens for decades to come, as well as the loss of her richest deposits of iron ore and in certain circumstances the sacrifice of the Channel coast from Dunkirk to Boulogne, which would have been part of the German satellite of Belgium. But the Chancellor's demands were still a long way behind those of the Pan-Germans, who wanted to annex all north-eastern France from Belfort to Toul and up to the mouth of the Somme, to exploit the rest economically and eventually also to divide France into a republic in the north and a Bourbon monarchy in the south, making Toulon a German naval base, as well as expelling all the non-German inhabitants from the annexed lands. (The Kaiser also listened to these fantastic plans.) Consequently one had to take seriously Ritter's contention that Bethmann-Hollweg could only successfully oppose such massive militarist, and even criminal, plans, if he had a counter-programme of his own to offer. 'It would have been unthinkable at that time to meet this programme with a simple demand for the restoration of the *status quo* because of the inflamed desires of the nation for power and conquest.'

Ritter knew of course that it was hardly possible to explain Bethmann-Hollweg's war-aims policy merely as a product of defence against external and domestic enemies. Ritter believed he had found the real motive, which is both surprising and extraordinary: the Chancellor's guilt complex. As Bethmann-Hollweg felt he shared in the guilt for the global catastrophe – there is plenty of evidence for this – 'he had to try to find a "positive" war aim which would help him bury his own worry over the "catastrophe" and look to the future with some hope'. Ritter's own personal experience was also implied, when he added that 'The entire German intellectual world felt much the same desire at that time.'

In other words the Chancellor could justify the war he had risked to his own conscience and the nation if he could show that at the end of it there would be a generally improved situation for the Empire, that the war had not been waged for nothing. (In this remark Ritter unconsciously admitted that the First World War could not possibly have been a defensive enterprise at the very beginning, otherwise Bethmann-Hollweg could have been satisfied with defending Germany's frontiers and the maintenance of Germany's prestige, aims which he was quite prepared to espouse at a later date when the military situation was less favourable than in September 1914.)

What would have really made the war worth while was the creation of a great European common market under German hegemony. Ritter believed that this plan was the 'original and surprising aspect' of Bethmann-Hollweg's war-aims pro-gramme. He envisaged a central European economic union which besides Germany would also have included the five members of the present European Economic Community, as well as Austria-Hungary, Poland and Scandinavia. But the members would only have been superficially equal. Ritter was never explicit whether this project was intended to be voluntary or enforced, but consoled himself with the thought that European leadership would have been Germany's in any case if she had won. He drew from Riezler's diary the information that Bethmann-Hollweg, as well as his adviser Riezler, were entirely clear on one point: they considered the new 'central European empire of the German nation' to be the 'European trimmings of our will to power'.

Riezler of course only entrusted such thoughts to his own diary. Officially the Chancellor approved when the nation's expectations turned towards the 'idea of *Mitteleuropa*' in 1915 and 1916, stimulated especially by the book of the liberal Reichstag Deputy, Friedrich Naumann, and the victorious progress of German arms in the Balkans, which had opened up the land route Berlin–Vienna–Constantinople–Baghdad. The German educated middle class were fascinated by Naumann's Utopia of the formation of a central European association with a German–Austrian nucleus surrounded by Hungary, Rumania and the small Slav races, all profiting from the benefits of a large economic union, all united by a federal superstructure. Ritter even took some delight in remembering this: 'At long last appeared a quiet voice of reason and of goodwill, which showed us Germans a "positive" war aim – not merely defence of the country or the rape of foreign peoples, but

a fine tempting job of creating a German and European future.'
He also felt it a serious tragedy that the Habsburg Monarchy
had already decayed so much and that the Slavs considerably
distrusted the slogan *Mitteleuropa* as they thought it camouflaged German Imperialist designs. And one would say today
that they were justified.

The preparations made by Bethmann-Hollweg for annexing
Belgium, Poland and the Baltic States corresponded to his own
idea of Europe. Unlike the army he did not want crude
annexations but instead wanted to introduce indirect control of
their subject neighbours, which would help them to be
reconciled with the German Empire. Ritter, far from justifying
this policy in retrospect, thought it plausible that almost
everyone in Germany at that time wanted to secure the Belgian
point of entry into Germany as it was so dangerously near to the
Ruhr. Moreover, the German government had some justifiable
fear that Belgium after the suffering of the war would give up
her neutrality and become a dependant of England. Finally,
many Germans looked at this Belgian State, which was not yet
a hundred years old, as an artificial creation, whose disappear-
ance need cause no regret. Ritter none the less declared that the
Belgian question was 'the curse on the entire German war-aims
policy', as it robbed the war of its defensive character, had a
disastrous effect on the mood of the German working class and
was bound to prolong the war endlessly if Germany could not
defeat Britain in the field. In exoneration he cited a sentence of
the Chancellor's from November 1914: 'Belgium is a terrible
problem. We have to find the least bad solution.'

Bethmann-Hollweg failed to find a solution to that problem,
as he also failed to find one to Poland, which he originally
envisaged as a German buffer State and where his ideas
conflicted with various interests, Russian, Austrian, German,
Polish nationalist, Prussian particularist and brutal militarist
ones. 'One could call it a belated nemesis of history', Ritter
wrote, bearing in mind the partitions of Poland, which the
German military wanted to add to by a further fourth partition.

The Chancellor's actions over Belgium and Poland were so
unambiguous that Ritter could say very little to defend them;
but over the question of the Baltic States, that is the Russian
Baltic provinces, his action seemed remarkably contradictory.

Bethmann-Hollweg would have had no trouble at all in acting as an annexationist in these lands which used to belong to the Teutonic Order. They still had a considerable German population; public opinion, almost all the politically conscious members of the German Foreign Office, the Prussian Ministers, and above all the popular generals Hindenburg and Ludendorff, who were administering Lithuania and Courland, wanted to 'liberate' this area to protect East Prussia from further Russian invasion and at the same time to open up a new and fertile area for colonisation at the doors of the Empire.

When Bethmann-Hollweg hoped for a separate peace with Russia in September 1915 because of the successful German eastern offensive, he came out decidedly against annexing the Baltic States in a letter to the Chief of Staff, Falkenhayn. He pointed out that strategically they were too exposed, domestically it would not be desirable to acquire a revolutionary-minded Lithuanian population as well as the German ruling class of the area, and diplomatically it would create eternal bitterness between Russia and Germany because it would mean depriving Russia of her few ice-free ports. (Ritter especially blamed Fischer for interpreting this document as proof of Germany's 'striving for world power'!)

In the spring of 1916, because of the pressure of the nationalist journalists, the military and Austrian politicians, who wanted to divert Germany from Poland towards the north, the Chancellor himself decided to incorporate the greater part of Courland and Lithuania into the Empire. He even gave a public statement to the war-aims majority in the Reichstag that Germany could 'not restore voluntarily those peoples she had liberated, whether they were Poles, Lithuanians, Balts or Latvians, to the reactionary Russian regime'.

Ritter and his pupils have proved in great detail, using the example of the Baltic question, that Bethmann-Hollweg never thought for a minute that these demands for annexations would make it impossible to arrive at a general negotiated peace or to a separate peace with Russia. Naturally this was only known to a confidential circle – the Prussian Ministers, the main committee of the Reichstag and the representatives of the Greater German federal States. Bethmann-Hollweg came out with a typical remark of the autumn of 1916 when the Central Powers were preparing a peace initiative, that he was trying to conduct a policy for Germany guided by reason, not by the heart, and that it would be impossible for him to conduct policy solely in the interests of the Balts, since what mattered above all for him was what benefited Germany.

In the spring of 1917 after the Russian February Revolution when the German government was using the slogan of self-determination and when the Army High Command under Hindenburg and Ludendorff were demanding the annexation of Courland and Lithuania, the Chancellor produced a compromise formula – autonomy. It coincided with his old idea of self-governing buffer States, which would be associated with the Empire politically, militarily and economically. But the Chancellor also made it clear that 'if this [the conclusion of peace with Russia] can only be reached at the price of territorial conquests, then this should not prevent the conclusion of peace'.

At that time Bethmann-Hollweg's position had been gravely weakened through his struggle to reform the Prussian franchise and his continual conflict with the almost all-powerful army leaders who were strongly supported by German public opinion. In these circumstances he was forced to put his signature to a limitless war-aims programme drawn up by the generals at the main Army Headquarters at Bad Kreuznach on 23 April 1917, although his colleagues dismissed it as 'childish'. Bethmann-Hollweg put down on record that he had agreed to it on the pre-condition that 'we will be able to dictate peace'. This was in fact the position a year later at Brest-Litovsk, where the September Memorandum, or at least part of it, was realised, if only temporarily. At that time the Secretary of State was von Kühlmann, who followed and continued the peace and war-aims policy of the fallen Bethmann-Hollweg.

This had been preceded by the October Revolution and the complete collapse of the Russian army, whereas in April 1917 Bethmann-Hollweg could not hope for such a favourable end to the war in the East. He therefore added a comment preserved in the records, but which Fischer significantly ignored: 'I have signed the protocol as it would have been ridiculous to resign for the sake of such fantasies. Besides I will naturally not allow myself to be bound by the protocol. However and wherever peace should be possible, I shall follow it up.'

Since Fischer's research it has been popularly alleged that these limitless German war aims *a priori* prevented any chance of a negotiated peace. Ritter examined this allegation and did not find that the English, the French or the Russians (at least not before the October Revolution) were ready for a peace in which there should be no victors or vanquished. All the governments were scared of facing their populations without having won; all wanted to avoid showing signs of weakness in case the enemy raised its price. All put their hope in a war of attrition and all were most anxious to prevent their allies becoming suspicious by negotiating for a separate peace. The German statesmen were justified in having the same fears as well.

In the summer of 1915 Bethmann-Hollweg calculated what Germany might hope to get under the most favourable circumstances if she agreed at that time to an Allied invitation to a general peace negotiation. The result seemed disastrous. What it seemed she could obtain at best would be a strategic improvement of the eastern frontier, a small war indemnity from France (not even therefore the ore basin of Briey), and possibly the Belgian fort of Liège, although the integrity of Belgium would have to be restored. They could only make colonial gains in Africa by the exchange of Togoland and South-West Africa. Even at this favourable time in the war the German Empire would have lost its powerful political and military influence in Turkey and its economic interests in Anatolia and Mesopotamia, in the same way that Austria-Hungary would have had to give up her dominant position in the Balkans and certain Italian-speaking areas. The Central Powers had gone to war because of these interests and power bases, and these possible small gains would not compensate for their loss.

Bethmann-Hollweg argued that Germany would have gained a victory in having maintained herself, but as the Secretary of State, Jagow, put it, 'we would have to abandon our world policy for several years'. In other words she would have lost the war and been reduced to the position of a second-class Power. Taking the most pessimistic view of what

Germany could hope to gain, she might even have to give up parts of Alsace-Lorraine, to pay reparations to Belgium and lose all her colonies. None the less during the peace initiative of 1916 Bethmann-Hollweg was apparently ready for such a peace; the war-aims programme of the moment should not confuse one because it contained only the maximum demands, which would have been pared considerably at the conference table. By comparing the aims for conquest being pursued at that time in Paris, London, St Petersburg and Rome, Ritter found that Bethmann-Hollweg's demands amounted 'almost to a total renunciation'.

Germany's attempt at a negotiated peace was doomed from the outset. A Papal diplomat pointed out to a German colleague that peace could only be reached in one way: the Central Powers, at the peak of their military success, ought to make a general declaration agreeing to re-establish the *status quo* of France and Belgium as well as restoring Serbia's sovereignty. This kind of self-denying ordinance would make a very marked impression both on the neutrals and on the populations of Germany's enemies who were already tired of the war. But Ritter was able to show that the German statesmen could not even follow this poor chance, although it was presented at various times, as for instance during the Papal peace offensive in the summer of 1917 and again before the start of the German spring offensive of 1918. There were three main reasons why the German leaders could not take it up:

(1) Germany could not give up her 'pledges' in Belgium and north-east France, as long as no guarantee was given that the French would evacuate the areas of Upper Alsace which they had occupied or that the Allies would evacuate the conquered German colonies.

(2) As long as she did not want to risk losing her alliance with Austria-Hungary, Bulgaria and Turkey, Germany had to take care of their interests as well as her own and their lost territories had to be recovered. Germany had moreover made secret agreements to support her allies in gaining additional territory.

(3) Germany could not announce a unilateral self-denying ordinance without running the risk of the other side's

increasing its demands. There was also the other danger that any government making such a declaration would be attacked and brought down by extremist elements within Germany.

After the fall of Bethmann-Hollweg's government the course of Germany's war-aims programme was at last determined by the army, which had always been keen on annexations, and by the politicians who had associated themselves with the army's programme as well as various economic groups.

The most influential person in the Michaelis and Hertling Cabinets was the Secretary of State, von Kühlmann, and he was even less in a position than Bethmann-Hollweg to fight against Ludendorff's pressure. The army and those journalists instigated by it attacked him as soon as he made any attempt to act outside the war-aims programme which had been agreed on internally, as for instance at the start of the peace negotiations with Bolshevik Russia or during the Bucharest Peace Conference and in the summer of 1918.

Only on one occasion, owing to his tactical finesse, was he successful in defeating both the army and the Reichstag – during the Papal peace initiative of the summer of 1917. In agreement with the ruling élite he refused to make the renunciation of Belgium, which the Pope wanted, but he initiated a secret peace mission through the Spanish diplomat, Villalobar, and here he was ready to make even this renunciation if England in return acknowledged the integrity of the German Empire. The mission failed because of the jealousy of the Spanish Foreign Minister. Ritter doubted whether it would have been successful in any case, since Britain would never have acted without her allies' agreement and France would hardly have been able to guarantee Germany's possession of Alsace-Lorraine.

Besides, Ritter believed Kühlmann made a mistake in undertaking this diplomatic intrigue. Germany would have done better to have reacted immediately and positively to the Papal note. The moral success would have improved the German Empire's position. Kühlmann's tragedy was that he was trying to work with the diplomatic weapons of the nineteenth century in a modern, total, popular war of this century.

At the Brest-Litovsk peace conference Kühlmann played an equally dishonest game with the Bolsheviks. Both sides interpreted in their own sense the right of the population on the peripheries of Russia to self-determination, the one from the concept of the class struggle, the other imperialistically. But Kühlmann would have been prepared to accept the *status quo ante* if the Allies had accepted the Bolshevik invitation to the peace conference. The most recent work by Ritter's pupils has shown this beyond doubt.

Kühlmann was not to blame for the developments which led in February 1918 to the *Diktat* Peace of Brest-Litovsk. He had wanted neither the annexation of Livonia and Estonia nor the move into the Ukraine, but he had let things run their course after the Chancellor, Hertling, had let him down in his struggle with the army.

The Treaty of Brest-Litovsk has been generally used as confirmation of the war-aims thesis of the Fischer school. But Ritter, working from different premises, tried to minimise the significance of the peace treaty which was in fact ratified in the Reichstag by a large majority. With some justification he pointed out that this peace could only be a provisional solution and that it would immediately have been brought into question at a general peace conference. But the German conditions and especially their implementation of the Peace in the summer of 1918 cannot simply be explained away in terms of defensive and economic necessity, as Ritter tried to do in defending his hero, Kühlmann. What Ludendorff and some of the economic leaders were pursuing in Russia at the time was Imperialism pure and simple.

Ritter was really shaken to discover that in the Allied countries as well, where the militarists could not get their way as in Germany, the few voices of reason had been stifled by the wave of bellicose feeling so that the suicidal European civil war had to be fought through to the bitter end, to the surrender of one of the parties.

Germany could certainly have had peace in the summer of 1917, provided that she had merely given up those areas annexed in 1871, Alsace-Lorraine, besides Belgium. But, as

Ritter once said, 'The German people at all levels of society were never ready to renounce Alsace-Lorraine before final and irrevocable defeat since they had become for the Germans, as for the French (perhaps even more for the Germans!), a national "emblem", the heirloom and symbol of their proudest period of recent history.'

To the end of his life Ritter never fully recovered from the loss of 'German Alsace'. But he also realised the crime against European peace which the German Empire had committed in its first hours of existence, when fully conscious of its power it crossed its set frontiers. This alone should have made Ritter, who was aware of the confused situation in Wilhelmine Germany, of the excessive nationalist feeling, the chauvinist dreams of power and the fatalistic blindness, find a different explanatory expression from that which he used, 'the belated nemesis of history'.

8. Social Darwinism as a Factor in the 'New Imperialism'

H. W. KOCH

In spite of general recognition, particularly because of the massive documentation in the works of Fritz Fischer and Imanuel Geiss, their critics have frequently been sceptical over their methodology and conclusions. Thus the *Journal of Modern History* noted in Geiss's work a preconceived thesis which is noticeable both in his arrangement and selection of documents. 'Can we be certain,' asked the reviewer of *The Times Literary Supplement*, 'that Bethmann-Hollweg and his colleagues were so different from other European statesmen in their almost unconscious assumption of the Darwinian necessity and empirical morality of war?' He explicitly warned against an interpretation of Germany's attitude during the July crisis which was made in isolation from the general 'European fever'. Professor Butterfield, too, warned against confusing the existence of military plans with the foreign policy of a particular country and of considering plans which emerged after the outbreak of war as historical sources for pre-war policy. Particularly in this connection, Butterfield argued, great care should be taken with the conclusions drawn from the material submitted by Fritz Fischer; and he urged caution against overestimating Pan-German propaganda before comparative studies on the Pan-Slav agitation or militaristic agitators in Great Britain and France were available.

Fritz Fischer and his pupils frequently speak of a specifically

From *Zeitschrift für Politik* (Hochschule für Politische Wissenschaften, Munich), XVII (1970).

German Imperialism, of a specifically German brand of Darwinian thought, which inevitably produces the impression that the German brands of Imperialism and Social Darwinism are fundamentally different from similar manifestations in Great Britain and the United States. Undoubtedly the diaries of Kurt Riezler, his book *Grundzüge der Weltpolitik in der Gengenwart*, the writings of Bernhardi or the memorandum of the Pan-German agitator General Gebsattel to Crown Prince Wilhelm are all evidence for the existence of Imperialist and Social Darwinian modes of thought. However, the question arises whether Social Darwinism in particular represents a specifically German mode of thought. Unfortunately, historical research in Europe (if one excludes the tentative beginnings in an article by Hans-Günther Zmarzlik and some of the early writings of Jacques Barzun) has produced no significant comparative study over the role of Social Darwinism in the political thought of the European Great Powers. There exists no analogous essay to that of Richard Hofstadter's *Social Darwinism in American Thought*. As long as the scholar lacks a work of this kind and high quality, and as long as the abundantly available source material has not been touched, let alone fully exploited, it is a little too early to agree with generalisations based on nothing more than the opinions of Riezler and other prominent German politicians. We simply lack an additional dimension which would enable us to recognise and judge the influential intellectual 'unspoken assumptions' – or prejudices – with which many politicians approached problems at the turn of the century.

Every analysis of intellectual movements, such as those represented by the influence of Darwinian ideas, is inevitably bound to run the inherent risk of artificially isolating an intellectual movement. After all one must not forget that the stock of Darwinian ideas was inextricably interwoven with other intellectual movements. One may also object that few read Darwin or Spencer; but with equal justification one could ask how many National Socialists had actually read *Mein Kampf*, how many Socialists *Das Kapital*? These questions can be countered with the same reply which Georg Lukács has given in connection with the influence of the works of Nietzsche. One need not have read any of these authors in order to be ideologically influenced by them. Secondary works, periodicals and newspapers frequently manage to simplify the essential core of an elaborate thesis, and at a popular level spread the content of many ideologies. This process of popularisation of systems of ideas can at a particular point in time become socially and therefore by implication politically significant.

The object of this essay is precisely to outline this process of the popularisation of the ideas of Charles Darwin, their effect in breadth as well as in depth, those ideas which in the last quarter of the nineteenth and during the pre-war period of the twentieth century apparently justified the urge towards Imperialism and which caused the mass psychosis, whose hysteria we find best illustrated by the outbreak of war in 1914 which was greeted by the masses with relief in the capitals of Europe.

Not without justification has the nineteenth century, in so far as we limit ourselves to central and western Europe as well as the United States, been called an age of liberalism, a liberalism which was a reaction to the centralising tendencies of absolutism, and whose principles we find expressed by Locke or in the American Declaration of Independence. The principles of liberalism represented the essence of all those ideals whose realisation was hoped and worked for in central and western Europe during the nineteenth century in order to spread them finally across the entire globe for the benefit of mankind. These principles included, of course, personal liberty, liberty of political expression, the pursuit of happiness and the sanctity of private property. At the same time it was recognised how important it was to control political institutions and the executive through a well-informed public opinion. Generally speaking, liberal politicians proceeded from the premise that personal and political liberties were part and parcel of natural law, the core of which in turn was based on the assumption that the ultimate objective of all human striving lay in the full satisfaction and realisation of the positive capacities of man.

However, already at an earlier stage, but particularly in reaction to the French Revolution, a tendency emerged, though initially in no way attempting to touch the foundations of the liberal creed, under the impact of growing industrialisation and developing technology, for the natural sciences to move towards empiricism, away from the *a priori* assumptions of natural law theories. The liberal movement, however different it may have been in character, influence and political tactics in the various regions of central and western Europe, brought on to the political stage a commercial and industrial middle class whose liberal ideology changed – initially almost imperceptibly – as it gained economic and political power. During much of the nineteenth century this class was the spearhead and pathfinder of liberal reforms, and the growth of trade and industry made its growing hold upon political power and the spread of liberal principles seemingly inevitable. But the Industrial Revolution in Europe had not only created a new middle class, but also a growing urban proletariat, which in time began to formulate its own political and social demands. Vis-à-vis this new working class, liberals now began to defend the political and social *status quo* and consequently were bound to appear as conservatives and reactionaries.

Political positions changed; liberalism transformed itself from a middle-class reform movement to a bastion of defence of the existing political, economic and social order. Under the circumstances it was hardly an asset that 'liberalism' lacked a systematically developed and formulated theory. As an effective political movement it frequently combined basically different elements, co-operating for specific ends and purposes; it was devoid of a clearly defined and common ideological basis. In Great Britain, for instance, Nonconformists managed to work hand in hand with Jeremy Bentham, well known for his radical atheism.

In view of the growing complexity of social problems, themselves an inevitable consequence of the Industrial Revolution, 'liberalism', the political expression of a commercial and industrial middle class, ought to have become the movement of the entire national community for promoting the interests of all classes – a necessity which, for instance, Max Weber and Friedrich Naumann realised – if 'liberalism' was to remain a politically active force. The individualism of its early period ought to have fused with the social realities of an expanding modern industrial society. To continue as an important political force, 'liberalism' ought to have acted both as the protector of individual rights as well as the protector of those threatened by unrestrained individualism.

The failure to achieve a transformation of this kind is one of the root causes of the decay of the politically organised 'liberal' movement in Europe. This is not to say that liberal principles themselves decayed, but simply that the cause of social reform came to rest in the hands of political movements which hardly described themselves as 'liberal'.

A modern industrial society which demanded social reforms in the name of the happiness of the greatest number found itself confronted by the archaic nature of the liberal concept of the State, according to which the latter should exercise only a 'night-watchman' function, to protect private property. The rest could be regulated by private contract. It is here that one meets the dilemma of nineteenth-century liberalism: should it jettison its economic philosophy of *laissez-faire* by subjecting the economic and social affairs to state control, or should it accept the risks inherent in the consequences of an unregulated industrialism, such as the threat to the social and political *status quo*? To resolve this dilemma would have required a fundamental revision of liberal premises.

At this point of confrontation with an apparently insoluble dilemma began the path leading way from natural law theories towards the natural sciences, supported and substantiated by the measurable scientific experiment. Of course, all did not come as suddenly as it might appear. One need only think of Ricardo or Malthus in the early nineteenth century, let alone the scientists of preceding centuries. What is new, however, is the impact of this change of direction, both in breadth as well as in depth.

The first important example that comes to mind is Herbert Spencer's social philosophy. Although derived from the ethical and political ideals of Utilitarianism and as yet not made logically dependent on the natural sciences, particularly on biology and biological evolution, the centre of Spencer's philosophy was occupied by a new concept of organic development. He postulated that nature progresses on a constant straight line, from energy to life, from life to intellectual activity, from that to the formation of society and from thence towards civilisation. Nature progresses from simple forms of society to more complex, more differentiated and more integrated civilisations. He argues that human society provided a good example for the observation of those criteria which differentiated lower from higher stages of development, the obsolete from the useful new, the able from the unable, and by implication, therefore, good from evil.

Logically Spencer's argument should lead to the conclusion that State and society were becoming more and more complex as well as integrated. But Spencer – and this highlights the liberal dilemma and paradox – 'liberal' that he was, endeavoured to prove that a society of growing complexity was actually upholding a State which in practice through the growing reductions of its functions would simplify itself to the extent that in the end there would be no rational reason any more for its continued existence. To meet this paradox Spencer maintained that the origins of the State lay in a society organised primarily for war. A growing industrial society was making wars superfluous and the centralising functions of the State as well. As long as industry and society were left to themselves, the evolutionary process would assure the survival of the ablest, and all legislation would become obsolete the moment when this process had brought about the perfect integration of the individual and society. Consequently, Spencer was a fanatical opponent of all forms of state interference in industrial and social problems. The net result of his philosophy implied the giving up of the principle of the happiness of the greatest possible number in favour of the principle of selection through the survival of the ablest.

Spencer, in the context of this essay, represents a random example to demonstrate how liberal principles were virtually appended to the progress of the natural sciences. Spencer's influence, however, seen from a European perspective, should not be exaggerated. The situation which Spencer believed he saw in the British Isles was described on the European mainland at different levels, to take Comte, his pupils and Positivism as simply one example. What it is important to realise, though, is that older natural rights theories as well as religious revelation were pushed aside by the march of progress. In an age of industry and the ascendancy of the natural sciences they lost any influence or general relevance.

The merit (a term which used in the context does not include qualitative value) of having underpinned the 'liberal' principle of *laissez-faire* in all spheres of life with the natural sciences and of giving it not only a local but a global impact belongs to Charles Darwin. He developed his evolutionary theories for the first time in *The Origin of Species*, in which he attempted to contradict the traditional belief of the separate creation of all species of plants and animals. In his second main work, *The Descent of Man and Selection in Relation to Sex*, he went a step further and submitted all the evidence he had collected to prove that man, like all living creatures, had developed through a process of natural selection from simpler, more primitive forms. While Spencer had developed his ideas without any direct logical dependence on the natural sciences, Darwin created the important link between the natural sciences on the one hand and social and political sciences on the other. He had hit upon a simple principle of movement and development which helped the better understanding of the entire history of mankind. Like Marxism, whose founder and early representatives frequently expressed their affinity with the thought of Darwin, Darwin's hypothesis was revolutionary because it destroyed the foundation of all ideas hitherto accepted about the nature of man and human life, and caused fundamental re-thinking of much that had so far been taken for granted and as self-evident. Much as Marx believed he had found the key to social change in the class struggle, Darwin believed he had found it in natural selection through struggle and the survival of the fittest. The coincidence that Darwin's theory came at a moment when rapid progress was being made in the other natural sciences and at the same time as new States were emerging in central and southern Europe, or successfully asserting their existence, as in the United States, can be assumed to have greatly assisted the rapid spread of his teachings. Moreover, in order to gauge Darwin's influence relatively accurately we must not ignore the general spread of literacy. True enough, Darwin had his precursors like Lamarck; even Leibniz had occupied himself with evolutionary theories. But their discussions never moved beyond the relatively small circle of scientists or those interested in science. The immense spread of periodicals beginning about a century and a half ago, written for the specialist as well as for the layman, supplemented during the last quarter of the nineteenth century by the quick growth of newspapers, particularly in Anglo-Saxon countries, increased the reader's forum. Scientific articles and their hypotheses found their own vulgarised 'version' for the 'wider public' in the daily papers. In other words, there was now not only a new scientific theory, but also a popular Press and an educated or semi-educated public to absorb it.

To begin with, Darwin had not the slightest intention of applying his biological revelation to a field other than biology. But – and he realised that himself – his theory responded to the call of the *Zeitgeist*: it supplied a perfect principle of causality, a principle which many of his contemporaries elevated to a creed in the natural sciences, a creed which was quickly torn from its biological context and applied to a social and political environment. The theory of evolution, the concept of the selection of the fittest through the struggle for existence, revolutionised therefore not only biology but a society whose character became pronouncedly industrial. This variation of Darwinism has generally become familiar under the term 'Social Darwinism'. The impact of the vulgarisation of Darwin's ideas and their popularity, and their application in many areas of political, economic and social life, resulted to a certain degree in the progressive eclipse of liberal principles, especially in the field of international relations.

Two variations of Social Darwinism dominated; the first had a dynamic, the second a static nature. Social Darwinism was dynamic in the sense that in international relations it served as a motive power as well as justification for expansionist policies; in practice this meant territorial aggrandisement, acquisition or further expansion of colonies and naturally the kind of armaments necessary to secure new gains. The alternative was considered to be stagnation and decay – a belief in change through territorial, economic and military expansion.

The static variety applied (mainly in parts of western Europe and the United States) to the field of domestic politics, especially social policy in the debate over which, in the words of Richard Hofstadter:

Social Darwinism was seized upon as a welcome addition, perhaps the most powerful of all, to the store of ideas to which solid and conservative men appealed when they wished to reconcile their fellows to some of the hardships of life and to prevail upon them not to support hasty and ill-considered reforms. . . . It was those who wished to defend the political *status quo*, above all the *laissez-faire* conservatives, who were the first to pick up the instruments of social argument that were forged out of Darwinian concepts.

In order to analyse as well as illustrate Social Darwinism, we should first of all examine its impact upon international relations. This requires a minor digression, a sketch of international relations in Europe during the nineteenth century. The Congress system of European diplomacy after the fall of Napoleon I has been described very accurately by F. E. Hinsley as a coalition of States, organised for the purpose of defence of commonly accepted values and agreements. This meant no unilateral change of existing treaties or of the territorial *status quo* without the consent of the other signatory Powers. The basis of this system was the defence of the principle of monarchic legitimacy and the existing social order by governments which, under the impact of the French Revolution, had combined against the majority of elements contained in their social structures making for change.

But because of continuing and fresh conflicts of interest among the European Great Powers, the Congress system was short-lived. But this did not mean that the Powers abandoned a platform with planks of commonly accepted agreements. In place of the Congress system was put the so-called 'Concert of the European Powers', which could be upheld as long as monarchic legitimacy and the social *status quo* were to be defended and while on the other hand the physical strength and the economic growth rate of the Powers remained relatively stagnant.

On various occasions the Concert seemed near to disintegration, for instance when there was an attempt to extend it to the Ottoman Empire, over the Italian question in 1859 and 1864 and over the German question in 1866 and 1870. But – to stay with Hinsley's argument – a closer look shows that the visible events had been preceded by a slower but remarkable change in the relative distribution of power, which had made the political premises of 1815 obsolete in so far as they concerned Italy and Germany. The real distribution of economic power was no longer in accord with that of 1815. The real significance of this process lies in the fact that these changes took place within the existing framework of power and of the power structure. Consequently, in spite of change the principles of the Concert of the European Powers survived even though they were suspended on occasions.

Between 1871 and 1890 the territorial *status quo* was still generally accepted, but from 1890 onwards until 1914 it slowly decayed and for the first time since the *ancien régime* the Powers of Europe were compelled to rely upon a balance of power among themselves and the means generally associated with this – alliances and armaments.

The reasons for the decay of the European Concert are as manifold as they are debatable. Firstly, the Concert had developed within a European framework, but it was now increasingly subjected to pressures originating from areas outside Europe, pressures which the European Concert simply was not strong enough to cope with. The problems of the Straits and of the Egyptian question are but two illustrations. Secondly, one notices the awareness of the growth of a power vacuum outside Europe, which increasingly touched upon the older traditional interests of the European Powers. International stability depended no longer simply on the distribution of power in Europe, but on the distribution of power in a global sense.

Thirdly, the growth of the democratic universal franchise, the entire process of democratisation, brought the emotion of the masses as a logical consequence into the spectrum of all those factors upon whose correct assessment a stable European policy was based. The growth of democracy brought forth the age of mass politics and its emotionally rather than rationally formulated appeals to the masses, and thus unintentionally and unconsciously produced a new concept of the State with a vastly greater range of functions. In 1815 the respective governments were confronted by their respective societies. Although the conflicts between society and State had not been fully resolved, in 1914, temporarily at least, behind every government in western and central Europe stood the solid, though class-conscious, phalanx of a national community. The criteria of power were no longer the degree of political stability, maturity and geographical advantages, but they were of an industrial, economic and organisational nature.

Every State (irrespective of whether it was orientated along the rational or the romantic concept of the nation) had acquired a specific identity, had become a specific organism, subject to the natural laws of life and death, growth and decay. And Social Darwinism provided a plausible theory, which apparently confirmed all these assumptions scientifically. Suddenly there existed a consciousness of and a differentiation between satisfied and unsatisfied, between old and young nations – everything apparently supported by proofs produced by the natural sciences, by the adaptation of Darwin's theories.

The renewed discussion over the 'responsibility' for the outbreak of the First World War has placed particular emphasis upon the German representatives of Social Darwinism. Less well known are their Western colleagues. In Great Britain none other than Walter Bagehot adopted the Social Darwinian gospel. 'Conquest,' he wrote, 'is the premium given by nature to those national characters which their national customs have made most fit to win in war, and in most material respects those winning characters are really the best characters. The characters which do win in war are the characters which we should wish to win in war.' One has to bear in mind that Bagehot was a highly sophisticated political theorist. The forms in which these arguments were reproduced in the daily Press, and in popular and service journals, are considerably cruder.

The *leitmotif* of liberalism in the nineteenth century had been the belief in continuous human progress, a progress apparently verified by the advances of the natural sciences which finally produced the concept of human progress through the struggle for existence and the selection of the fittest through it. When this concept was applied to a social and political environment, to individuals and to nations, it was bound to deepen the existing cleavages between the peoples, particularly in an age of strong economic competition, in an age in which social unrest –

it was assumed – had to be directed into 'harmless channels', an age of new and young nations filled by a sense of mission, whose specific nature had not been closely defined and was therefore not fully articulated. The search for purpose and a sense of national existence led into many directions. Nietzsche finally condemned the Christian religion; he drew the ultimate logical consequence from the principle of the survival of the fittest, namely that existing moral categories and values stood in the way of this kind of selection. His alternative was a race of supermen, produced and selected through the right of the stronger.

On a broader, more popular level a general interest in evolutionary theories was naturally generated which at that level turned into a vulgar propagation of brutal strength and the worship of martial qualities. Charles Pearson in his book *National Life from the Standpoint of Science* wrote: 'The path of progress is strewn with the wrecks of nations; traces are everywhere to be seen of the hecatombs of inferior races, and of victims who found not the narrow way to perfection. Yet these dead people are, in very truth, the stepping stones on which mankind has arisen to the higher intellectual and deeper emotional life of today.'

The elder Moltke made his own logical conclusion when he equated the Darwinian portrait of nature with the battlefield, expressing the spirit of the times with the words that 'war is an element of the order of the world established by God, without which the world would stagnate and lose itself in materialism'.

Here perhaps we can see the expression of and the connection of Social Darwinism with cultural pessimism, which, quite contrary to the thesis put forward by Fritz Stern, was a much more far-reaching phenomenon than a purely German one. It can be recognised in most nations in the throes of industrialisation at a particular point in time. One should think, for instance, of Thomas Hardy's *Far from the Madding Crowd* or the brothers Henry and Brooks Adams, especially the latter's book *The Law of Civilisation and Decay*. The growth of an industrial society, the dislocations in the traditional social structure caused the change categorised by David Riesmann from the 'inner-' and 'tradition-directed' man to the 'outer-directed' man, a type whose system of values is no longer determined by religion or tradition but by an environment in which he has no roots, where his values are determined by his 'peer-groups': all these disturbances were bound to cause deep psychological dislocations from the perspective in which everything new was also abnormal. Because of the Industrial Revolution an old and proud middle class found itself displaced or in the process of being displaced by a class of *nouveaux riches*. Representatives of that older class, like Henry Adams, looked back to a supposedly Golden Age. They considered war inevitable; only an act of God could cleanse the world from the abominations and excesses of the selfish materialism of the new Industrial Age. This view emerges clearly from the changes in attitude noticeable in the range of Adams's works from his *History of the United States 1801–1817* to *The Education of Henry Adams*. He had hoped by using the methodologies of the natural and the still infant social sciences to come nearer to historical truth. He had at first added Social Darwinism to a universe determined by Newton; the sum proved false through the discovery of a radioactive substance and the Second Law of Thermodynamics. 'There is a universal tendency to the dissipation of mechanical energy any restoration of which is impossible . . . within a finite time . . . the earth must . . . be unfit for the habitation of man.'

On the one hand evolution led from protozoa to man; on the other hand, however, entropy led from heat to cold. Adams's final conclusion therefore was that the solar system would be reduced to chaos through the cooling of the sun and end in death by heat emitted and spent by the sun. The march of liberal progress through the natural sciences here found its antithesis as well.

The growing modernity of industrial society appeared to Henry Adams as sufficient evidence for the waste of energy, as in the examples of the motor-car and the aeroplane. By comparison with the eternity of Christian universalism as symbolised by the cathedrals of Mont-Saint-Michel and Chartres, with the age in which all bent their knees before the 'one God', man was confronted by a multiplicity of ties on the one hand, depersonalisation on the other; in fact man was standing in the antechamber of chaos. Adams was not sure whether man would step through the last door. Still, in a letter in 1905 he expressed his opinion that if we maintain the rate of progress which we set in 1600, then we will hardly need another century and a half until our entire intellectual foundations are turned upside down. In that case, he argued, law as theory as well as an *a priori* principle would make way for brute strength. Morality would become the police and explosive materials would attain global effectiveness in their destructive power. Disintegration would overwhelm integration.

Ample evidence for similar expressions can be found in the published materials in central and western Europe of the period. The well-known articles of the *Saturday Review* between 1896/97 have been often – too often – quoted. This journal was not by any means the only one which poisoned the international climate with its Social Darwinism. Shortly before the First World War the well-known monthly, *Nineteenth Century*, published an article entitled 'God's Test by War'. It is worth quoting at some length:

> Amidst the chaos of domestic politics and the wave-like surge of contending social desires the biological law of competition still rules the destinies of nations as of individual men. And as the ethical essence of competition is sacrifice, as each generation of plants or of animals perishes in the one case, or toils and dares in the other, that its offspring may survive, so with nations the future of the next generation is determined by the self-sacrifice of that which precedes it.

This sacrificial impulse, the author says, 'is the root source of all human morality and finds its crown in patriotism'. And he goes on to ask:

> What of England? Is the heart that once was hers still strong to dare and to resolve and to endure? How shall we know? By the test. That which God has given for the trial of peoples, the test of war.

Of course, says the author, one has to be prepared, and the implication of this is:

> that victory is the result of efficiency, and efficiency is the

result of spiritual quality. Thus then efficiency in war, or rather efficiency for war is God's test of a nation's soul. By that test it stands, or by that test it falls. This is the ethical content of competition. This is the determining factor of human history. This is the justification of war.

Victory in war is the method by which, in the economy of God's providence, the sound nation supersedes the unsound, because in our time victory is the direct offspring of a higher efficiency, and the higher efficiency is the logical outcome of the higher morale.

Hence it follows that if the dream of short-sighted and superficial sentimentalists could be fulfilled – if war could be rendered impossible on earth – the machinery by which national corruption is punished and national virtue rewarded would be ungeared. The higher would cease to supersede the lower, and the course of human evolution would suffer arrest.

And coming back to victory the author emphasises that:

victory is the crown of moral quality, and therefore while nations wage war upon one another the survival of the fittest means the survival of the physically best.

The real court, the only court in which nations' issues can and will be tried is the court of God, which is war. This Twentieth Century will see that trial, and in the issue which may be long in balance, whichever people shall win it the greater soul of righteousness will be the victor.

The shadow of conflict and of displacement greater than any which mankind has known since Attila and his Huns were stayed at Châlons is visibly impending over the world. Almost can the ear of imagination hear the gathering of the legions for the fiery trial of people, a sound vast as the trumpet of the Lord of Hosts. . . .

A prophecy indeed: One may say that this is at best an illustration of the use of Darwinian concepts by a crackpot. But this is contradicted by any careful scrutiny of the newspapers and periodicals of the period, especially between 1890 and 1914. They offer more than ample examples of Social Darwinian currents of thought in Germany, Britain and the Empire, the United States and France.

Particularly in France agitation with Social Darwinian undertones was consciously supported and partly even guided by the government and the army. As a result of the aftermath of the Dreyfus affair not only French public confidence in the army but also morale within the army had been seriously shaken. While in 1897 the number of officer cadets at Saint-Cyr was 1,920 by 1911 the figure had declined to 871. After the fall of the Combes Cabinet reaction set in, aiming at restoring both confidence and morale. The publicity offensive conducted with Social Darwinian arguments opened up old sores and became once again the propaganda of revanchism. That Germany's foreign policy was added grist to the mill of French foreign policy requires no further elaboration.

But journalists and writers were not the only ones who spread the poison contained in Social Darwinism. Statesmen, like Lord Salisbury, Joseph Chamberlain, Bethmann-Hollweg, Delcassé and Theodore Roosevelt, did so in the same measure. Of the so-called 'case studies' there are many in which Social Darwinian agitation occupied the centre of the public stage, from the Spanish–American War to the Boer War. 'We are a conquering race,' maintained Senator Albert J. Beveridge. 'We must obey our blood and occupy new markets and, if necessary, new lands.' That in the course of the 'pacification' of the Philippines orders like that of General Jake Smith were issued – 'I wish you to kill and burn; the more you burn and kill the better it will please me' – seems no more than a logical corollary.

An important example of European significance is represented by the Anglo-German naval rivalry. Whatever reasons there were for and against, the acrimonious public debate which accompanied it was marked by an excess of extreme Social Darwinian argumentation. A nation expands or it decays, the indicators of expansion being the number and value of actual colonial possessions. To protect them and itself a nation required a strong navy, even if only conceived as a 'risk fleet'. Those lessons had been driven home well enough by the most influential naval writer of the period, Captain Thayer

Mahan. In view of the psychological climate the build-up of strong naval forces not only in Germany but in the United States and Japan appears not natural but logical. The literary advocates of navalism made themselves heard with their consensus aptly summarised in the opinion 'that lasting good is only evolved in this world through strife and bloodshed. While injustice and unrighteousness exist in the world, the sword, the rifled breech-loader and the torpedo boat become part of the world's evolutionary machinery, consecrated like any other part of it.' The German arguments were not one iota better.

Purely within the context of Anglo-German relations and their occasional difficulties, even the naval rivalry would probably have been responsible for some ups and downs in the relations between the two countries, but they alone could hardly have caused the systematic deterioration of feeling and sentiments at all levels of both respective societies. The responsibility for this seems to lie primarily with the psychological climate in which the differences between the two countries grew. In such an atmosphere that amorphous body called 'public opinion', whether in the form of Navy League or the *Flottenverein*, could be mobilised at an instant's notice and relied upon to support any crazy armaments scheme, for in the end everything turned on the question of survival of the fittest. Social Darwinism largely eliminated rational public discussion on a broader level and replaced it by emotional outbursts which – on both sides – saw in any of the opponent's suggestions or arguments a mere stratagem and further confirmation that the slightest concession would be a step towards defeat in the struggle for existence.

Even here history is not without its own irony. At about the same time as the first ironclads sank the Turkish fleet off Sinop, a Bavarian artillery sergeant had fired the first underwater shot and members of the Russian court were treated to a performance of a Mozart quartet in an underwater diving-boat off Kronstadt. The weapon of the future was experiencing its birth-pangs and outdating – even before they were built – all those products of steel and sweat in which Anglo-Saxon and Teuton sailed forth for battle in 'the struggle for existence', called upon 'to fear God and dread nought'. Both nations survived, but in the shadow of super-Powers in whose armoury battleships are mere scrap-metal. Ironically, what has survived is the underwater boat.

While the dynamic variation of Social Darwinism was characterised by the doctrine of progress through the elimination of unfit nations, the second variation, static in nature, was marked by the elimination of unfit individuals. For the first time a prominent British review spoke up in favour of a nationally directed policy of euthanasia as a means of 'racial' selection.

That is not to say that because of this the nineteenth century loses its claim to have been 'the Age of Reform'; it merely qualifies this claim. Moreover, it must not be forgotten that social reform varied in its intensity from country to country, from continent to continent. From this point of view the United States was the most backward nation, the German Empire the most progressive. But in Germany the entire social question had been subordinated to the interest of the State and its stability, while social reform in western Europe was based on different foundations. There, in the classic home of liberalism, the liberal reform movement had carried the banner of reform as far as the middle class which it represented allowed. From then it passed into the hands of the Socialists.

In an age of the growing emancipation of the masses and the expansion of the suffrage, in an age of improving living standards, rudimentary political wisdom forbade the propagation of the concept of the elimination of unfit individuals. This would hardly have been conducive to the settling of the unruly spirits of the working classes. Hence the rise of racialist theories represented a welcome element to supplement Social Darwinism and to provide a common denominator for the otherwise strictly segregated class structure of a nation. It was a common denominator which helped to integrate all classes in the age of the 'New Imperialism'; even the lowest social strata now had a yardstick with which to measure those below their own miserable existence.

Racialism was not dissimilar to the role played by slavery in the southern states of the United States. Less than 10 per cent of their population were plantation-owners with more than fifty slaves, 6 per cent held up to fifty slaves, 8 per cent had only one or two slaves. That is to say, if slavery was really the cause of the American Civil War, 76 per cent of all Southerners fought for an institution in which they had no material share – except its symbolism.

Much the same is the case with racially influenced Social Darwinism. The racial theories which were rampant in Europe and the United States were in reality antidotes to potential social revolution. 'Race' became a symbol, elevated to the equivalent of 'nation'. As long as the masses, even for a limited time, could be made to forget the injustices and the exploitation of the society within which they lived, there was more chance of reducing dangerous stresses arising within the nation. Nationalism, perverted into race hatred, pushed the class struggle into the background for a short time.

The so-called 'scientific elaboration' of racial theory had preceded Darwin. Gobineau had laid its foundations in his essay on *The Inequalities of the Human Races*, an essay which inspired the history of the Aryans and laid the basis for comparison and classification of political institutions. Influenced by the results of the comparative method in philology and mythology, it was suddenly believed that signs of unity had been found in the primitive institutions of the Aryans, especially their most famous branches, the Greeks, Romans and Teutons. This product of doubtful scholarship was quickly taken up by the popular media of communication and injected into the mental fabric of the nations. There the famous branches were soon narrowed down to a respective nation, namely to the one which one was a member of.

For the British the burden of Empire presupposed the existence of a divine power which had selected them for a divine mission through the evolutionary process, through the survival of the fittest. Or as Cecil Rhodes put it, 'I contend that we are the first race in the world and the more of the world we inhabit the better it is for the human race.' As the word spread in the Anglo-Saxon world of the superiority of the race and its world mission, Germans quickly noted the change from previously held theories of the 'common Teuton stock' to the more selective Anglo-Saxon base and replied to it with Germany's mission to bring *Kultur* to the world in general and to the 'uncivilised Slavs' in particular. 'We are the salt of the earth,' said Kaiser Wilhlem II. With each nation discovering its own mission, its own specific racial superiority, if not hatred at least dislike and suspicion of the foreigner and his evil designs began to prevail over more serious domestic issues. In Europe national exuberance, already on the verge of excess, gathered further force.

Furthermore, the nations of Europe, especially Germany, Austria and France, experienced the process of industrialisation which was much more genuinely a 'revolution' than that which had taken place in Great Britain. In central Europe, the German Empire and Austria-Hungary, this process displaced large parts of the population from their place on the 'status ladder', especially artisans, small traders and farmers, and reduced them to proletarian status and dependence. A new industrial middle class stepped into their place, marked by the slogan current in all Western languages, the 'money power of capitalism'. Money power, capital interest, etc., had ever since the beginning of Christian religious instruction, intuitively rather than reasonably, been associated with one race – the Jews. The association of capital and Jewry, existing in some cases, but mainly based on a series of unproven assumptions, resulted in a further association, that of Jewry and the age of industrial modernity. The smoking stacks of factory chimneys, money power, the preference for 'community' before 'society' provided a fresh impulse to a tendency latent throughout European society – anti-Semitism. Anti-Semitism in particular, racism in general, came together with the popular desire of the age of the natural sciences to discover the elements of nature in human life, a discovery which, so it was thought, would provide the chance of cultivating them in the interest of the race of European–Aryan civilisation. In an age of growing depersonalisation, the disintegration of traditional ties, race became the last bulwark in the defence of national individuality.

Social Darwinism and, closely connected with it, racism, the reaction of many levels of the population to the materialism of an industrial age, created that psychological climate in which political decisions were made, 'national interests' interpreted. They provided some of the 'unspoken assumptions' of the era. In the popular reaction to the outbreak of the First World War, as well as in the fatalism of some of the leading statesmen, was expressed the often never admitted conviction that war was inevitable: it was the Lord's sword which was sweeping away evil, furthering good, to discard the rotten to make way for the healthy, to replace, as Germans believed, 'materialist civilisation' with the '*Kultur* of the spirit'.

Typical examples of men who represented the *Zeitgeist* have already been mentioned, but none of them went as far as to carry these 'principles' to their logical conclusion. This role was preserved for a man who was only one among thousands on Munich's Odeonsplatz in August 1914 listening to the proclamation of war and who subsequently volunteered for military service. However, the years in which his *Weltanschauung* was shaped were those of the turn of the century and the first decade and a half of the twentieth century. His 'ideology' was hardened by the years of front-line experience and that of the short-lived Soviet Republic in Bavaria. To dismiss Hitler's ideological tenets as 'the product of the doss-house' is an inadmissible simplification of complex events – quite apart from the fact that Hitler was never in the economic circumstances which would have compelled him to seek refuge in a 'doss-house', except for a very specific purpose.

It is a simplification which totally ignores the intellectual currents of the turn of the century, those currents, coming second- or third-hand, which influenced the young Hitler. In *Mein Kampf* he remarks that at an early stage he had learnt to look at history from a specific point of view. 'To study history and to learn from it means to look for those driving forces and to find them, which represent the causes of the results, which before our own eyes are historical events.' As it has been correctly remarked, the emphasis of this sentence lies on the principle of causality, a sentence which amounts almost to a creed in the natural sciences. It outlines clearly how Hitler approached problems: from his point of view clear, cool, emotionally detached, or 'ice-cold' as he would have called it. From this perspective he observed the world, as it appeared to him in Vienna. The existing social realities were unimportant when compared with the question of their origins and the circumstances which had brought them about. The search for a causal principle pushed social reality into the background; his 'scientific method' preserved him from becoming 'sentimental'.

Every reform impulse was bound to fail, unless the root of all evil had been discovered, until the roots of national society had been freed from poisonous weeds. The logical conclusion therefore was to eliminate all those forces which polluted nation and race, the extermination of that which in his judgement was destructive to life or unworthy of living. As Marx and Lenin postulated an economic determinism, so Hitler postulated a biological determinism.

Any assessment of Hitler's views has to bear in mind that he looked at realities as the product of certain laws. He considered his task to find these laws; once they were found, they formed a *Weltanschauung* whose precepts would direct action. The essentially self-taught Hitler believed he was acting methodologically like a natural scientist.

The 'laws' which Hitler believed he had discovered derived directly from a rampant Social Darwinism and racism; their radicalisation in his anti-Semitism came from the economic and social upheaval of central Europe and the specific conditions of the Habsburg Empire, the hothouse of most of the ideas which were to dominate central Europe during the following decades. Freud, Wittgenstein and Mahler are only three examples of many; even only a first reading of Karl Kraus's *The Last Days of Mankind* makes it apparent how in that environment that kind of *Angst* psychosis could originate which was instrumental in giving Hitler – for lack of a better term – the courage to pursue his principles to their criminal logical end and to take the step from theory to practice.

Hitler's so-called 'scientific method' had shown him the 'Jew' as the solvent of any national order, as the prime element of decomposition of a society in the throes of industrialisation. 'Rootless Jewry' was for him the destroyer of racial and national (that race and nation could be mutually exclusive he did not realise at this early stage) individuality, the agents of materialist industrial depersonalisation. In other words, like many of his contemporaries in the Western world, he analysed political and social problems with the aid of medical–biological categories, and the inevitable consequence of the discovery of an allegedly harmful germ is the attempt to exterminate it.

The Social Darwinian component of his thought is best expressed in his concept of 'living-space', or in the brutal words formulated before his SS Guard at Christmas 1940: 'Bird, you eat or you die.' From his point of view the war which broke out in 1939 was neither necessary nor useful. In view of the Russo-German pact Poland could not defend herself anyway, hence the 'dictates of reason' commanded Poland to accept the German demands, particularly since neither Britain nor France could assist their ally. That Poland did not give in, that Britain and France continued the war, was in Hitler's view contrary to all reason. Consequently an explanation was required which consisted in turning the 'un-understandable' into a 'conspiracy of world Jewry' and from there to proceed to the final step – genocide. References to such a possibility are contained in Reichstag speeches of 1939, and to the actual execution in his speech of 8 November 1942.

Hitler adhered to these lunatic principles to the last minute of his life. In his political testament, the largest part of which consists in blaming 'world Jewry' for having caused the war, he placed great emphasis upon drawing a clear distinction between the 'humane' means he had deployed to solve the 'Jewish problem' and those means used by the Allied air forces to annihilate 'innocent women and children'.

To a man locked away in his Headquarters in East Prussia or in the bunker of the Reich Chancellery in Berlin, a man who had never entered Auschwitz or Treblinka, the technically 'perfect' system of mass murder in the gas chambers was bound to appear more 'humane' than the death of parts of Germany's civilian population by napalm and phosphor.

It would be absurd to attempt to deny that Hitler was a demon and a phenomenon, but his *Weltanschauung* is explicable (this must not be confused with 'excusable') in terms of the intellectual environment of the turn of the century; as a political and 'ideological' phenomenon he is explicable in terms of the specifically German and Austro-German conditions which first helped to shape him and under a specific set of circumstances made him acceptable to the German people as their leader. No doubt, Hitler in many respects represents the German intellectual and political tradition, magnified and distorted to a perverted degree – but he represents no less ideas and systems of ideas once popular and even respectable in Europe as a whole.

However thin and tenuous it may be, the connection exists between the liberal belief in progress, the march of science and Auschwitz.

9. War Guilt 1914 Reconsidered: A Balance of New Research

KARL DIETRICH ERDMANN

OUTLINE OF THE CONTROVERSY

The controversy on the origin of the First World War has not yet come to an end. In its first phase between the two wars it centred on the war-guilt clause of the Treaty of Versailles, as it was formulated in Article 231 and interpreted in the Covering Letter of 16 June 1919. The thesis of this note was that Germany had deliberately unleashed a general war, that the motive of her action was to establish her rule over a subjugated Europe, and that this war was 'the greatest crime against humanity and the freedom of peoples that any nation, calling itself civilised, has ever consciously committed'.

International research during the inter-war period resulted in a far more balanced evaluation of the origin of the war. As far as German historical writing is concerned the war-guilt clause was so closely linked with the question of reparations that an apologetic approach was almost inevitable. But what was the position of historical research outside Germany? Let us turn to some outstanding historians who at the same time belong to the most severe critics of German and Austrian policy. I am thinking of the Englishman, G. P. Gooch, the Frenchman, P.

Lecture given by Professor Dr K. D. Erdmann to the History Teachers' Association of New South Wales in 1977.

Renouvin, and the Italian, L. Albertini. Here we read: 'The war was the child of the European anarchy, of the outworn system of sovereign states. The Old World had degenerated into a powder-magazine, in which the dropping of a lighted match was almost certain to produce a gigantic conflagration.' It is a

> mistake to attribute exceptional depravity to any of the Governments which, in the words of Mr Lloyd George, stumbled and staggered into war. Blind to danger and deaf to advice as were the rulers of the three despotic empires, not one of them desired to set the world alight. Yet, though they may be acquitted of the crime of deliberately starting the avalanche, they must jointly bear the reproach of having chosen the path which led to the abyss.

> In the general appreciation of the events most French historians have abandoned the idea of a unilateral responsibility of the Central Powers; they admit that Russian politics to say the least had been imprudent.

> To attribute the responsibility for making war in July 1914 to the Central Powers is not to deliver judgement on the conditions which drove Austria to war with Serbia and led Germany to support Austria. To state that Austria and Germany acted as . . . has been shown . . . is not to assert that from their own point of view they had not good reasons for seeking to change a state of affairs injurious directly to Austria and indirectly to Germany. The same holds good in respect of France and Russia. These two powers manifested no great fear of the tempest that was being unloosed. Nay, they seemed almost ready to welcome it in certain conditions, hoping perhaps that its end might turn out to their advantage. The fact is that the question of the war is an entirely different one from that of the rights and wrongs of the war.

Drawing the balance of the inter-war research, French and German historians came to the joint statement that 'the documents do not permit to attribute, in the year 1914, to any one government or nation, the will to cause a European war'. With particular regard to Germany, it carries on:

> German politics in 1914 did not aim at unleashing a European war. They were mainly determined by treaty obligations towards Austria-Hungary. To counteract the threatening dissolution of this state, assurances were given to the government in Vienna which were as good as a blank cheque. The German government was led by the conviction that a localization of the conflict with Serbia, now, as in 1908/09, would be possible; nevertheless they were prepared if necessary to take the risk of a European War.

These views on the origin of the First World War did not remain unchallenged.

The perspective shifted in consequence of the Second World War. This is particularly true for German historiography. The complete breakdown of Germany inevitably led to a reassessment of German history. Historians found themselves confronted with the question of continuity: Was National Socialism a break in German history or was it the logical and necessary outcome? That implies the question whether the Second World War, which unequivocally was unleashed by Germany, was a direct sequence to the First World War in motivation and aims. Ludwig Dehio was the first to discuss the problem of continuity and discontinuity of the hegemonial wars in Europe. Friedrich Meinecke gave a critical evaluation of the development of thought in Germany, and Gerhard Ritter presented a thorough analysis of the roots and implications of militarism in Germany. Fritz Fischer published his challenging books on German war aims and war policy. They provoked a heated controversy which in the meantime has calmed down but had not yet come to an end. The main protagonists in the intellectual arena of the debate on the origins of the First World War and Germany's war aims were Fritz Fischer, Gerhard Ritter and Egmont Zechlin.

This surge of new historical research on the First World War, motivated by the question of continuity, received a new impetus from the fact that historians now gained free access to an overwhelming mass of documentary materials, especially in the archives of the German Foreign Office. Bethmann's own private papers were destroyed during the Second World War. My own contribution to this debate was a study on Bethmann-Hollweg and a critical edition of the diaries of Kurt Riezler. Riezler was Bethmann's closest collaborator before and during the war, as long as Bethmann was Chancellor. He acted as a sort of secretary for public relations. The particular value of the diaries is that they were written under the direct impression of conversations with Bethmann and give the most intimate testimony we possess of the thoughts and motives of the German Chancellor.

The controversy of Fischer, Ritter and Zechlin centred on two main problems:

(1) What were the aims of Germany in the pre-war years? Was she intending war?
(2) What were the expectations and motives guiding her attitude in the July crisis, and in connection with this: What were the German war aims during the war?

These were the main positions in the controversy:
A. At least since 1912 Germany under the chancellorship of Bethmann-Hollweg aimed at bringing a continental war about against France and Russia. This war was intended to give Germany a hegemonial position in Europe as a basis for her strive to world power. The war aims, as they were formulated during the war, had already guided German policy in the pre-war years. This is the view of Fritz Fischer. The pivot in the German calculations of the chances of success is, for him, the assumption that Bethmann-Hollweg reckoned with British neutrality in the case of a great continental war.

B. The counter-thesis of Gerhard Ritter is as follows: Germany's attitude in the July crisis of 1914 was fundamentally defensive. Germany had no aims reaching beyond the preservation of the actual territorial *status quo*. Her purpose after the murder of Sarajevo was to back Austria, her only ally, who was threatened by decomposition in the struggle against Serbian nationalism. Too late the German Chancellor realised that the conflict between Austria and Serbia could not be localised, and that it would turn into a general war. In consequence of the Russian general mobilisation, the German government lost its freedom of decision and became dependent upon the mobilisation timetable of the General Staff. The latter had bound themselves to the Schlieffen Plan, which meant launching an offensive against France with the great mass of the German Forces as early as possible and before the Russian mobilisation was completed. This led, according to Ritter, to the grotesque situation that a war to stand by Austria-Hungary on the Balkans started with an invasion of neutral Belgium. The decisive factor for the fateful inflexibility and failure of German policy in the July crisis was, according to Ritter, the Schlieffen Plan.

C. A third thesis is represented by Egmont Zechlin. He shares Ritter's view that the motivation of Germany's behaviour was basically defensive, but he differs from Ritter in stressing the preventive character of German action in the July crisis. And whereas Fischer, as well as Ritter, believes that the policy of the German government was based on the assumption of the neutrality of Great Britain, Zechlin maintains that, on the contrary, Bethmann-Hollweg was convinced that in the case of war, Great Britain would side with the Entente powers.

These three interpretations of the origins of the war have to be tested by going into the details of some of the main problems under discussion. Whereas during the inter-war period, the international discussion on the origins of the war of 1914 was not focused on Germany and Austria alone; after the second war, the particular 'German problem' and the question of continuity of German history preoccupied historical research in the Federal Republic to such an extent that the international background of German development before the first war seems to have been rather neglected. This point has repeatedly been raised by L. C. F. Turner, Canberra, among others, who himself has set an example of how the interpretation of Austria's and Germany's planning for war should be placed into the broader context of military and political developments in Europe.

The preoccupation of historical research in Germany with the question of continuity has the consequence that some authors tend to make certain domestic factors primarily responsible for the war. Such factors are:

(1) Economic imperialism of industry and capital in their drive to gain foreign markets and opportunities for investment.
(2) Social imperialism in the leading classes who were seeking an outlet for existing social tensions in an expansionist policy.
(3) Social Darwinism as an element of national mentality which acknowledged and practised ruthless struggle for survival as a law of nature.
(4) Structural conditions of political decision-making, in particular with respect to the relationship between General Staff and Government.

But whatever the importance of socio-economic, socio-psychological and structural factors may be, the British historian James Joll, in a recent report on the war-guilt controversy, is certainly right in reminding us that 'the true stuff of history is individual men and individual choices' and that 'our curiosity is not satisfied by the statement of broad historical laws unless they can be precisely observed in concrete instances'. This is a clear argument for the fact that not only circumstances and general tendencies, but also individual men make history. One of the central figures in German policy before the war and in the July crisis 1914, when the fatal decisions were taken, was the Chancellor Bethmann-Hollweg. According to the imperial constitution it was he who was responsible for the policy of Germany, and he lived up to this responsibility. Today, as we shall see, we can grasp more clearly than before the motives which guided his actions.

CONTINENTAL OR WORLD POLICY? THE QUESTION OF A
PREVENTIVE WAR

The century between the revolutionary wars and the First World War was for Europe, as a whole, the longest period of peace ever experienced in the course of modern history. It is true that there were several short and violent conflicts during this period of peace. But the wars for national unity in Germany and Italy towards the middle of the century, and several wars on the fringe of, or outside Europe, such as the war of Greek Independence, the Crimean War, the Russo-Turkish War, the Boer War, and the Russo-Japanese War, remained restricted to few powers and did not spread into a general conflagration.

The political pattern of Europe was a system of states with five leading powers. This pentarchy had developed during the eighteenth century and was restored after the breakdown of the Napoleonic empire. Later, when Germany was unified under the leadership of Prussia, this system was modified, but not suspended. On the contrary, the German national state was for a period of twenty years under the chancellorship of Bismarck, one of its strong pillars. The Empire was saturated and regarded the balance of power within this system as a guarantee of peace and of its own security. The changing alliances of the Bismarck period were calculated on the permanence of its existence.

The feeling of occupying an adequate position in the European system decreased, however, with the transition from the 'Bismarckian Continental' to the 'Wilhelminian World' policy. With no other of the imperialist powers did the national basis for colonial and economic expansion seem so insecure as with Germany, who stood under the growing pressure of her two continental neighbours in East and West. Any energetic move in world politics in North Africa, in Turkey, in the building of the navy, or wherever it might be, provoked reactions on the French, British or Russian side. This made Germany conscious of her own limited geographical and political field of action. Riezler saw this as a 'dilemma between continental considerations and world political interests'. Was there a way out of this dilemma?

This question leads to the concept of *Mitteleuropa* (Central Europe). What was its meaning, and how is it evaluated in the context of the discussion in the origins of the First World War? *Mitteleuropa* appeared in the political discussion during the pre-war period in several variations and pointed either to a preferential system of customs, or to a customs and economic union, or maybe to an indirect rule of Germany over her neighbours within a more or less limited geographical sphere. It was possible that the concept of *Mitteleuropa* could assume a militant hegemonial accent, but it could also be seen as a way to peaceful agreements leading to an economic geographical structure of such extent and resources that its weight could compare with other empires.

Did this concept influence the policy of Bethmann-Hollweg? He was confronted with these ideas one year before the war by his friend Walther Rathenau, one of the leading figures in German industry. Fischer maintains that these ideas that Rathenau formulated in a memorandum in 1913 became decisive for Bethmann-Hollweg. Egmont Zechlin, in a critical comment to Fischer, pointed out the fact that, on the contrary, in January 1914, the Chancellor, in agreement with all the departments concerned, came to the conclusion that there was no reason for Germany to give up her most successful trade policy in favour of an economic concept of Central Europe. And actually the Secretary of the Interior, von Delbrück, rejected the idea of a closed Central European economic area. Of course, Bethmann-Hollweg was in favour of economic expansion. But expansion obviously meant for Bethmann-Hollweg an increase in trade and economic influence and perhaps the acquisition of colonies. There is no indication, however, that before the outbreak of the war he thought of expansion in continental territorial terms.

It is well known and was always accepted in German historical writing, that quite apart from the various possible forms of Central Europe, a number of political writers advocated territorial annexation at the cost of Germany's neighbours. Both Theodor Schiemann, who had written books on Eastern European history and was a friend of the Emperor, and Paul Rohrbach were of the opinion that the Empire of the Tsar was in decay and would soon break apart, and that then the Baltic countries should fall to Germany. But there were also counter-voices. The eminent historian of Eastern Europe, Otto Hoetzsch, who was a political commentator of the leading conservative paper, the *Kreuzzeitung*, was of the opinion that Russia was an organic phenomenon in history and on the way to a great future. And it is exactly this evaluation of Russia which became decisive for the leading political élite before the war. Bethmann-Hollweg and the General Staff were convinced that the strength of Russia would rapidly increase in the course of the coming years.

Today we are able to realise perhaps even more clearly than at the time, to what extent the balance of military power in the immediate pre-war years was shifting to the disadvantage of Germany. We owe to Norman Stone a valuable study of the war in Russia. It includes precise information on pre-war plans to increase the numerical strength of the Russian army, its equipment with artillery and the construction of strategic railways. With the 'great programme', which was deliberated throughout 1913 and became law in June 1914, 'the Russian army ostensibly became a European super-power, in conformity with the economic growth that Russia had experienced since 1906. The annual recruit contingent was raised to 585,000, for three-year service, such that the peacetime army alone would reach almost two million men – three times as large as Germany's. Infantry divisions would rise to $122\frac{1}{2}$ (from $114\frac{1}{2}$), to Germany's 96, and there would be 8,358 field guns to Germany's 6,004'; on the eve of the war 'German generals felt very weak when they contemplated the forces of other generals. The army had fewer battalions than the French army (1,191 to 1,210), and in 1914 fewer guns than the Russian army (6,004 to 6,700), to the 1,876 battalions of which it was also, of course, inferior.'

We know from the Riezler diaries that the vision of the constantly growing power and greatness of Russia oppressed Bethmann-Hollweg like a nightmare. If it was true that for the coming years a continual shifting in the power relations to the disadvantage of Germany had to be reckoned with, and if we take into account that according to the general conviction of the time in all countries, war was regarded as a legitimate means of policy, then it was not far to the idea that the possibility of a preventive war should be included in the calculations. Or, to speak with Norman Stone, 'it was not surprising that the German military urged for war before it was too late'. There were nationalist propagandists, like the chairman of the Pan-German League Class, or the General von Bernhardi who desired war or even demanded it. It is not easy to evaluate their influence on the attitude of the Germans towards war, as there were other political writers who warned against a war. And if Bernhardi published a book under the title *Germany and the Next War* (1912), Hans Plehn, who as representative of a German news agency lived in London in close contact with the German Ambassador, wrote a book with the characteristic title *German World Policy and No War* (1913). And in 1914, on the eve of the war, Kurt Riezler published his *Outlines of Present World Policy*. Here he expounds his conviction that the tendency of national expansion, which he observed as a determining factor in this age of imperialism, was counteracted at the same time by cosmopolitan tendencies such as the interdependency of economies. These tendencies called for peaceful arrangements between states. From a national point of view – which was his own – the high level of techniques in armament production no longer made wars profitable. In which direction did the compass of German foreign policy point; to war or to peace?

It is uncontested that during the last years before the war, Bethmann-Hollweg tried to improve relations between Germany and England, to obtain, under the nightmare threat of the Franco-Russian Alliance, England's promise of neutrality in the case of a continental war and to loosen the ring of the Entente. What exactly made him strive for a detente with England and for her promise of neutrality? This is a crucial point in the debate on the origins of the First World War. And the answer to this question, as to the sense and purpose of Bethmann-Hollweg's England policy, is the real dividing line between the antagonistic interpretations.

Fritz Fischer in his book *Griff nach der Weltmacht* is right in pointing out the fundamental importance of the British War Minister Haldane's mission to Berlin in February 1912. The result of his analysis, however, does not stand up to documentary evidence. It is necessary to go into the details of this question to get the later policy of Bethmann-Hollweg during the July crisis into the right perspective. Fischer maintains that in 1912 England had offered 'neutrality in the case of an unprovoked attack on Germany', and that Bethmann-Hollweg had persistently rejected the offer. According to Fischer, he would not have been content with less than a British offer of neutrality, which would have been effective in the case of Germany being entangled in any war with the continental powers. Bethmann-Hollweg, so Fischer says, wanted a 'free hand on the continent', and in 1912 and 1914 he was less concerned with the preservation of peace than with keeping England out of a future war.

Fortunately we possess the editions of the British, French and German documents. They show clearly that the British government, contrary to Fischer's assumption, never made any offer of neutrality, and explicitly not even in the case of Germany not being the aggressor. The British government as a result of repeated discussions in the Cabinet never went beyond the offer of a mutual assurance of peaceful intentions. The final proposal reads: 'The two powers being mutually desirous of securing peace and friendship between them, England declares that she will neither make nor join in any unprovoked attack upon Germany and pursue no aggressive policy towards her'. What did this formula mean?

Sir Edward Grey tried to convince the German Ambassador Count Metternich, that it implied neutrality in case of an unprovoked attack upon Germany. Sir Eyre Crowe, on the contrary, commenting on Haldane's report of his Berlin visit, where the latter had proposed a quite similar formula of goodwill, pointed out, that 'an assurance that neither party harbours any hostile designs . . . is no more than what every state is bound to profess to its neighbours. It is nothing justifying any counter concessions on either side.'

Bethmann-Hollweg wanted to obtain a more precise formula and include a mutual engagement of neutrality in the agreement, if possible, an unequivocal absolute neutrality. As it became clear, however, right at the beginning of his conversations with Haldane, that the British government would not be willing to subscribe to such a far-reaching commitment, Bethmann-Hollweg and Haldane, according to the diary of the latter, 'sat down at a table with pencils and paper and went on a voyage of discovery'. The result was the 'sketch of a conceivable formula' which included a mutual engagement of neutrality 'if either of the high contracting parties becomes entangled in a war in which it cannot be said to be the aggressor'. The British Cabinet, however, on the advice of Sir A. Nicolson, rejected such an engagement of conditioned neutrality. For 'who can say', Nicolson wrote, 'who is in reality the aggressor? A

Country, and history furnishes many examples, may be forced by the political action of her adversary to assume the role of an apparent aggressor'. Bethmann-Hollweg, on the other hand, took the sketched formula as starting-point for his persistent but unsuccessful endeavours to obtain, if not an engagement of absolute and unequivocal neutrality, at least the assurance that Britain would remain neutral, if in a continental war Germany was not the aggressor. Although, like Nicolson, he saw that 'it was very difficult to define what was meant by aggression or unprovoked attack' he submitted to London with the approval of the Emperor the following proposal:

> If either of the high contracting parties becomes entangled in a war with one or more powers, in which it cannot be said to be the aggressor, the other of the high contracting parties will at least observe towards the powers so entangled, a benevolent neutrality, and use its utmost endeavour for the localization of the conflict. If either of the high contracting parties is forced to go to war by obvious provocation from a third party they bind themselves to enter into an exchange of views concerning the attitude in such a conflict.

In vain the German Ambassador also tried to persuade the British government to add to their proposed goodwill declaration of non-aggressive intentions, the promise 'to observe at least a benevolent neutrality should war be forced upon Germany'; and this promise was not to be binding unless the British wishes were met with regard to a reduction of the German naval programme. The British government for obvious reasons did not agree. They did not want to bind their hands in a future war in which the Entente powers might be entangled. Therefore they refused to enter any explicit engagement of neutrality, even if Germany were not the aggressor. Bethmann-Hollweg could not refuse what was never granted him.

The above quoted documents show clearly that it is not possible to construct on the evidence of the Haldane mission and the following negotiations a German Chancellor striving for a 'free hand against France' in a 'continental war provoked by Germany'. Wolfgang Mommsen comes to a similar conclusion: 'It is obvious', he says,

that the government of Bethmann-Hollweg did not at any time until May/June 1914 seriously contemplate the idea of attaining any of its objectives by war . . . [Bethmann-Hollweg] stuck to a peaceful policy all the more so as he was convinced that the existing political order would not survive it. Fritz Fischer has argued again and again that Bethmann-Hollweg's repeated attempts to negotiate a neutrality agreement with Great Britain were part and parcel of a policy of expansion by means of war. Britain should be made to stand aside in order to allow Germany safely to crush France and Russia; this, he maintains, was the core of German calculations. This is, however, not borne out by the sources.

What was the attitude of the government and the General Staff towards a preventive war? There had been a temptation to start a preventive war against France in 1905, when Russia was paralysed by a war with Japan and by a revolution. But however much Schlieffen, the Head of the General Staff, may have been tempted to profit by the favour of the hour, defeat the French army and deliver Germany once and for all from the nightmare of a war on two fronts, it was characteristic for German politics that the Emperor and the government resisted any such ideas. In the last years before the outbreak of the World War, the Chief of the General Staff, von Moltke, came to the conviction that as war in any case seemed inevitable, it was better to have it soon and as long as Germany still had a chance of winning.

In this context John Röhl, Fritz Fischer and Adolf Gasser regard a conference of the Emperor with his high ranking military advisers on 8 December 1912 as a key event. The conference took place after the first Balkan War, which had brought Europe to the verge of a general conflict. Under the impression of information given by the German Ambassador in London, Lichnowsky, that England would back France should a continental war break out, the Emperor discussed the situation with Moltke, Tirpitz and the chiefs of the Staff of the

Admiralty and of the Navy Cabinet. He regarded it as necessary that Austria should take an energetic stand against the Serbs. In the case of Russian help for Serbia he reckoned with the inevitability of war. At that time he was prepared to take the same risk which Germany actually took two years later. Moltke declared: 'I regard a war as inevitable and the earlier the better'. Tirpitz contradicted: The fleet, he said, was not yet ready. What was the outcome of this conference? Was it the starting point for a premeditated war, as Fischer and others would have it?

According to Admiral von Mueller, the Chief of the Navy Cabinet, to whom we owe the only private report on this conference: 'The result was virtually nil'. It was characteristic that the man who was responsible for German policy, the Chancellor, had not even taken part. It is therefore misleading to call this conference a war council. On the contrary, the German government together with England exercised a moderating influence on Austria and at that time helped to avoid a world war. Was this only a postponement to gain time?

There is no proof to be found that the Fischer school is right in maintaining that from then on, Germany systematically prepared for the provocation of a war. This extreme thesis has been widely rejected, even by those historians who otherwise are inclined to acknowledge the positive and challenging effect of Fischer's first book. Others like Hajo Holborn, Golo Mann, Hans Rothfels, Wolfgang Mommsen and Karl-Heinz Janssen are of the opinion that it is impossible to draw a direct line from the Kaiser's conference of 1912 to the July crisis of 1914. This opinion is shared by L. C. F. Turner in review articles of books by J. A. Moses and John Roehl. As a specialist on military history, he closely examined the correspondence between Moltke and Conrad von Hoetzendorf, the Austrian Chief of Staff, and comes to the conclusion, that 'there is no hint in these letters and recorded conversations of any binding mandate that Germany should go to war in July 1914; in fact the documents demonstrate the contrary'. Commenting on a conversation of Moltke with Conrad von Hoetzendorf at Carlsbad, on 12 May 1914, he states that 'Moltke's attitude was gloomy, but his remarks were not those of a chief of staff who anticipated that a major war would break out within three months'.

Egmont Zechlin, in a forthcoming book, deals in detail with the 'war council' and its interpretation by Roehl and Fischer. He states that in the report on the *Kriegsrat*, not a word is mentioned about the alleged motive for a hegemonial war; nothing allows the interpretation that William II, let alone Bethmann-Hollweg, had decided to unleash a preventive war and gain the hegemony for Germany over the continent, and that they were only awaiting the appropriate moment for the start. Fischer and his school lay emphasis on a remark of the Kaiser in those days, that even Bethmann-Hollweg had got 'accustomed to the idea of war'. Zechlin's counter-argument is: the realisation of the danger of war is not identical with the will to have a war. In view of the international tensions and a permanent situation of conflict, it was a widespread conviction that the danger of a world war was imminent. Indeed, Bethmann-Hollweg reluctantly got accustomed to the idea that his policy, the cornerstone of which was an understanding with England, would not lead to the desired restraint on the continent; that war might become inevitable and that one day he might have to take the risk.

For the moment, a general conflagration was avoided, although the Balkan wars might easily have set the whole of Europe on fire. In view of the growing danger, Germany took certain preparatory measures. John Röhl is right in pointing out that the Kaiser's conference did not remain without any consequences. The German press was used to make the people familiar with the idea that the Balkan conflicts which threatened the position of Austria might also lead to a situation in which Germany could feel induced to draw the sword. Other steps followed: like the increase of gold reserves by the Reichsbank and the buying of grain on foreign markets, but it is generally accepted that these steps lacked system and co-ordination, and that Germany was economically and financially inadequately prepared when war broke out in 1914.

In 1913, Germany made a belated effort to increase the strength of the army which had been neglected by the building of the navy; measures were taken to adjust the strength of the German army to the numerically highly superior forces of the potential enemies. But are steps of this kind, such as were taken on all sides, the proof of a will deliberately to launch a war of conquest? The Kaiser called for alliances with Bulgaria, Turkey, and if possible, with Japan. On the very day of his conference with the military leaders he wrote: 'Any power that is to be had is good enough to help us. For us it is a question of life or death'. This, as Zechlin writes, certainly sounds more like a cry of despair than the decision to fight for hegemony. The Kaiser liked very strong words, which stood in contrast to his timid nature. In the words of Gordon A. Craig in his recent book on Germany: 'The ebullient ruler, who gave the age its name, certainly never wanted a war at all'. And to quote what Karl-Heinz Janssen said in an evaluation of the Kaiser's conference: Bethmann-Hollweg 'did not let himself be shaken in his efforts to come to an understanding with England, with whom at that time Germany was cooperating in the Balkan crisis. A few days later he wrote to a friend: "We must not fall into the nervous politics of a puppet, otherwise the patience of the others might give way". In this, I cannot read the resolution to lead to war. Fischer, however, maintains the contrary.'

But what about the General Staff? Did Moltke plan a war? Discussions, of recent years, on the origins of the First World War have brought two remarks of Moltke to light; in which he takes a clear stand in favour of a preventive war. One was mentioned above, that was during the Kaiser's conference, when he said, 'I regard a war as inevitable and the earlier the better'. The other was during a private conversation with the Secretary of State, Jagow. In his unpublished diaries we find the following passage which was first made known by Egmont Zechlin. A few weeks before the murder in Sarajevo, Moltke invited Jagow to accompany him in his car from Potsdam to Berlin. 'On the way,' so we read,

Moltke explained his view on the military situation. He was heavily depressed by the outlook into the future. In two or three years Russia would have finished with her armaments (expansion). He expected that the superiority of our enemies would then be so considerable that he could not see how we should be able to stand against them. At present we should still be a match for them. There was no choice for us, according to his view, but to start a preventive war, as long as we still had some chance of holding our ground. The Chief of the General Staff gave me to understand that it would be advisable to direct our policy towards having an early war . . . I replied that I was not willing to evoke a preventive war. And I reminded him of Bismarck's word, that you could not look into the cards of Providence.

What was the reason for the Chief of the General Staff, in contrast to the government, advocating a preventive war? There is not the slightest proof for the thesis of the Fischer-school, that Moltke was moved by a will of conquest. His feelings were anxiety and worry. He was depressed by the conviction that a war was inevitable and that by waiting, the situation could only get worse.

What consequences did this conviction of his have for his own actions? Were his words on preventive war the expression of a determined will or of a fatalistic attitude? Was there a joint and coherent planning of the German and Austrian staff for a war which they were to fight together? Since 1905, the German General Staff was fixed on the Schlieffen Plan. What did this mean for the corresponding planning of the operations in Eastern and South Eastern Europe? L. C. F. Turner points to a very lucid analysis of the situation by the French General Staff. In 1912, so Turner writes,

Poincaré asked the Minister of War for a report on the probable consequences of military intervention by Austria in the Balkans. On 2nd September, the French General Staff gave their considered opinion that such an intervention would put Germany and Austria 'at the mercy of the Entente'. The General Staff based their view on the argument that Austria would have to employ at least seven of her sixteen army corps in the Balkans, that this would fatally weaken her forces deployed against Russia in Galicia, and that because of the relative weakness of the German forces in East Prussia, the Russians would be able to mount '*une offensive tres dangereuse dans la direction de Berlin*'. If the Germans strengthened their forces on the Eastern front, the French army, with British support, would enjoy a substantial superiority in Lorraine; moreover Austrian action in the Balkans might well lead to a rupture with Italy. The French

General Staff doubted whether Germany would permit Austria to indulge in a Balkan adventure but, if she did, a general war would result in which 'the Triple Entente would have the best chances of success and might gain a victory which would cause the map of Europe to be redrawn'.

The German staff was of course fully aware of the danger which resulted from the application of the Schlieffen Plan to a war by the Central Powers on three fronts against Serbia, Russia and France. It stands to reason that close co-operation between Germany and Austria would have been a pre-condition, if there had been a concrete plan to launch a preventive war in the near future. But there was nothing of the kind; nothing more took place than an exchange of opinions between Moltke and Conrad von Hoetzendorf. There was no precise joint staff planning. This total deficiency resulted already in 1914 in a disastrous defeat of the Austrian army in Galicia. Gerhard Ritter went into the details of this lack of co-operation. Could it be explained as blind lack of foresight or was it just inability to co-operate? All we can say is, that there was no premeditated planning. Moltke reacted more than he acted. Before even the first shot was fired, his will seemed to be paralysed by the feeling that it was impossible to bring the war to a good end.

JULY CRISIS, 1914

What was the attitude of the German General Staff in the month between the assassination of the Archduke Prince Ferdinand on 28 June and Austria's declaration of war on Serbia on 28 July? If the thesis of a premeditated war were correct, you would expect to find the German General Staff involved in systematic preparations. Nothing of the like can be observed. It is well known that at the time all top leaders were on vacation. When, on 5 July, the decision was taken to give Austria the so-called blank cheque, neither the Chief of the General Staff nor his representatives were consulted or were present, at the council which the Kaiser had summoned in Potsdam on 5 July. You may argue, of course, and this is the fashion with some historians, that the absence of the military top leaders was a sinister Machiavellian intrigue to deceive the world as to the real intentions of Germany. Could it not be possible that the various departments of the General Staff were on the alert and all the time received their directions from their senior officers even though these were not on the spot?

An answer to this question is given in an article by the Canadian historian Ulrich Trumpener, which I regard as an outstanding contribution to the research on the July crisis. He enters into the details of what the Intelligence Service of the General Staff were actually doing in July 1914. This Service was responsible for obtaining news on mobilisation and all other war preparations, particularly of Russia and France. If, during the so-called 'War Council' on 8 December 1912, the alarm clock had been set for war a year and a half later, then certainly the murder of the Archduke would have given the signal. The Chief of Intelligence himself was on leave and did not return to Berlin until 25 July, two days after the Austrian ultimatum to Serbia, the same day that Moltke returned to Berlin. During these weeks there were no significant changes in 'the sleepy routine of the General Staff'. Trumpener comes to the conclusion that even a few days after Austria's ultimatum to Serbia, and despite the tense situation it created in the Balkans, 'the leading men of the Great General Staff were as yet unconvinced that a clash with Russia and her French ally must necessarily ensue'. Anyway, the Intelligence apparatus was at last set going and then acted well. In the days to follow, the General Staff were well and promptly informed on all mobilisation preparations going on in Russia, first as part mobilisation against Austria and then as general mobilisation against Germany. The news coming from agents in Russia 'convinced Moltke and his advisers on 28 July that they faced a full-fledged implementation of Russia's contingency plans for war with both Austria-Hungary and Germany. . . . The army authorities in Berlin had considerably more, and better, information on the scope and tempo of Russia's 'premobilization' measures than is reflected in the various collections of diplomatic documents and other civilian government records.' It is well known, and need not be repeated here, what efforts Moltke now made to ensure that the general mobilisation in Austria and Germany did not come too late.

Trumpener points to another fact which shows that up to July the General Staff did not realise that war was so near. In the month leading to the July crisis they were 'busily negotiating with the civilian authorities to obtain funds for a major upgrading of the countries' strategic railroad system'. Part of the construction could have been started by 1915. In short, on the eve of Sarajevo, the military and civilian authorities of the Reich were working on a long term project for the enhancement of Germany's military capabilities vis-à-vis France and Russia – a project which was obviously superfluous if these two countries were to be attacked in any case in 1915, or the following year at the latest'. Trumpener summarises the results of his research as follows:

There is . . . no concrete evidence to support recent allegations that Moltke and his advisers at the Great General Staff were in fact determined – since the winter of 1912/13 – to attack France and Russia by 1915 at the latest, and that Germany's political leaders, on the eve of Sarajevo, were in agreement with the army's intentions and prepared to act accordingly . . . Whatever may have prompted the Kaiser and his Chancellor in early July to encourage Austrian militancy vis-à-vis Serbia, it seems clear that neither they, nor the army authorities in Berlin, believed at that time that Austrian action against Serbia would necessarily lead to a military showdown with the Entente powers . . . It is furthermore clear that the army's preparations for a great war in the weeks following the Potsdam meetings of July 5–6 were much less thorough than has often been claimed.

All this, however, does not mean that the German government, and, in particular, Bethmann-Hollweg, were not aware of the great risk they took when they gave the blank cheque to Austria. As evidence of Bethmann-Hollweg's attitude in the July crisis, the Riezler diaries are of outstanding importance. On the evening of 6 July, after Bethmann-Hollweg had just given the Austrians the assurance of Germany's full support against Serbia, he had a conversation with his friend and secretary Kurt Riezler on the terrace of his estate, Hohenfinow, near Berlin. The notes Riezler took on the following day show that there is no doubt Bethmann-Hollweg realised that the action against Serbia would be regarded by Russia justly or unjustly as a provocation, and that it might mean general war. This was, in the words of Hermann Kantorowicz, a *'dolus eventualis'*. Through the Reizler diaries, it has now become evident that it was not the gradual development of the crisis that made Bethmann-Hollweg realise the danger of a general European war. On the contrary, from the very first step he took on 6 July, he was aware of this risk. This is a considerable correction of former views which I had also shared, before I succeeded in getting the Riezler diaries. Under the impact of Riezler's testimony, Ritter acknowledged (in the 2nd edition of Vol. 2 of his *Staatskunst und Kriegshandwerk*) that from the beginning it had not seemed very convincing to assume that Bethmann-Hollweg had set strong hopes on a localisation of the war. And he comes to the conclusion: 'Bethmann-Hollweg gave the blank cheque in the full knowledge that this meant the risk, not only of a local but of a continental war'.

But Ritter does not accept another highly important piece of evidence which results from the Riezler diaries; that is the fact that Bethmann-Hollweg did not reckon with British neutrality in a continental conflict. Ritter and Fischer share the view, that Bethmann-Hollweg's alleged conviction of British neutrality was the very basis of his policy, although in the views of Ritter and Fischer respectively, the ends and purposes of this policy look very different. If Bethmann-Hollweg did not reckon with British neutrality, then in the eyes of Ritter, his policy was that of an irresponsible gambler and adventurer; whereas for Fischer, Bethmann-Hollweg's depending on British neutrality was the very pre-condition for the continental war he wanted.

There is, however, ample documentary evidence that neither the German Foreign Office, nor the army, nor the navy, reckoned with the neutrality of England. Bethmann-Hollweg's fears of Britain joining the war against Germany were confirmed by information that the German government received from a member of the Russian Embassy in London about negotiations which were going on between London and St Petersburg about a naval agreement, similar to that which already existed between England and France. The assassination at Sarajevo occurred in a moment of crisis in the relationship between Britain and Germany. Bethmann-Hollweg's evaluation of British policy of course did not stop his efforts to seek as good a relationship as possible with Great Britain. For, if there were any possibility at all left of localising the Austro-Serbian conflict, then, as in 1912, it could be only with the help of London. But could a European war not be avoided then, so Bethmann-Hollweg was convinced, England would be on the other side. The importance of this statement cannot be overrated. It breaks the cornerstone of Fischer's construction. The German Chancellor had no illusions as to where England would stand. When he took the risk of a war against three of the great powers he was fully conscious of the uncertainty of the outcome.

So why did he, to use the words of Riezler, take this 'leap in the dark'? It was certainly not for reasons of economic imperialism. There was of course plenty of competition between Germany and other commercial and industrial nations in the world, and Fischer maintains in his two books that economic imperialism, and the drive for economic expansion, belong to the essential causes of the war. But German industry and trade were constantly growing stronger in peace and had no advantage to gain from a war. So far we have only one thorough analysis of one particular economic foreign relationship, namely of that between Germany and France. The author Poidevin, comes, in his brilliant study, to the final conclusion that there was competition as well as co-operation between Germany and France on the economic field, and that the genuine causes for the war between Germany and France are not to be found here.

But what about social imperialism as a driving force behind Bethmann-Hollweg's policy? It is true you can find dozens of contemporary testimonies which show that there were many persons, and certain groups who looked for an outlet for social tensions in expansionist policy, or even in war. As far as Bethmann-Hollweg was concerned, however, we know from Riezler that the contrary applies. Bethmann-Hollweg, conservative by nature, was convinced that a war, whether it ended in victory or in defeat, would cause a revolution of all existing order. That war, as other conservatives held, would strengthen the patriarchal elements of society, was to his thinking, an illusion. Bethmann-Hollweg himself was afraid of its inevitable social consequences. In Riezler's diaries there is no trace to be found of a social imperialistic motivation for Bethmann-Hollweg when he took the fatal step.

Neither was the wish for territorial gains a motive of Bethmann-Hollweg's policy before and during the July crisis. In his private talks with Riezler, there is no hint which points in this direction, in contrast to the extensive reflections on war aims in the diaries of later date, once the war had started. The formulation of territorial war aims is a product of the war, but not its cause. Pierre Renouvin has shown the casual relationship of war and war aims for France in a convincing piece of research. His opinion is that in Germany, as in France, the war aims developed and were formulated after the war had started, and not before. In a Franco-German meeting at Dijon in 1965, Renouvin agreed to the present writer's formula, that the 'war aims' were rather the product than the cause of the war and that this was valid for France and Germany alike.

As motive for the attitude of Bethmann-Hollweg during the July crisis, we find in Riezler's diaries, instead of expansionist programmes and the *Griff nach der Weltmacht*, a deep concern about the status of the Austro-Hungarian multinational empire. The coherence of this state was challenged by Serbian nationalism, backed by Russia and Russian Pan-Slavism. Germany's own position in the system of the great powers of Europe, on the other hand, was highly dependent on what was happening to Austria-Hungary, her only weighty ally.

For Bethmann-Hollweg there was more at stake than keeping Serbian nationalism at bay. In this respect the Riezler diaries lead beyond the thesis of Ritter. The policy of Bethmann-Hollweg was a deliberate challenge to the Entente powers: he reckoned with the possibility that a quick and energetic action against Serbia, keeping the conflict localised, might have the effect of disrupting the Entente. His motive had nothing to do with *Nibelungentreue* to Austria, as it was called at the time. On the contrary, in Riezler's diaries, we meet with the idea that one day it might be possible to come to an understanding with Russia at the cost of Austria's Balkan aspirations.

The challenge of the Entente by Germany and Austria

opened two possibilities for Bethmann-Hollweg, so we read in Riezler's diaries; either a political regrouping of the powers, and that meant Germany's deliverance from the nightmare of coalitions, or war. An often quoted passage in the diaries from 1914, written under the fresh impression of a conversation with the Chancellor, runs: 'If the war comes from the East so that we fight for Austria-Hungary and not Austria-Hungary for us, we have the chance of winning. If war does not come, if the Tsar is not willing or if a nervous France plays for peace, we still have the chance of manoeuvring the Entente apart'. Historians, who under no circumstances want to give up the thesis that Germany was bent on war, maintain that this passage shows a preference for the violent solution. This, however, cannot be upheld in the context of other diary notes from those days. To give a few examples: 'A quick *fait accompli* and then friendliness towards the Entente, then it will be possible to get over the shock'. In a conversation with Bethmann-Hollweg the question was discussed whether there was a chance of changing the European constellation. It would be possible, Riezler writes, 'if Russia, not fully supported by the Western powers in the Serbian question, came to the conclusion that she were bound to come to an understanding with us'. And in another note on a conversation with the Chancellor: 'If the Serbian affair were to pass off well without Russia mobilizing, that means without war, it might be possible to come to an understanding with a Russia disappointed by the Western powers'. These texts speak for themselves. The preference was unequivocally for a political solution. But the calculation proved to be erroneous. The conflict could not be localised.

The conception of Bethmann-Hollweg's policy in the July crisis, such as it emerges from the Riezler diaries, fits neither into the pattern of a Germany pushed into a war against her will, nor of a Germany wilfully pushing into war. Egmont Zechlin found a very adequate term for this attitude. He called it *'praeventive Abwehr'* (preventive defence). This seems to me to be more to the point than 'preventive war', although Bethmann-Hollweg himself, some time later, called the First World War 'in a certain sense' a preventive war. Fischer shares the opinion that preventive war is not the right term, because on the side of the Entente there was objectively no intention of attacking Germany. In my view the term *praeventive Abwehr* fits better than preventive war, because Germany, though taking the risk of war, had hope of disrupting the Entente without a war.

The policy of the German government during the July crisis corresponds to a theory of calculated war risk developed by Kurt Riezler before the war. In the modern world, so this theory goes, war no longer pays. But the states are not willing to do without arms. They use them in critical situations as a threat without really intending to apply them. The steering and managing of a crisis can only be successful if handled with rational calculation and high political ability. It is counteracted by the dynamics of nationalistic mass emotions and the mechanism of pre-determined mobilisation procedures. Because the development of the July crisis could not be kept under control and got out of hand, the decision of the German government to take the risk of war turned out to be a decision for war.

THE PRICE OF PEACE

The problem of war guilt reaches a new dimension if, assuming that not one of the governments really desired war, you put the question the other way round: did they truly want peace? To this question, for all countries concerned, the answer is, 'no'. For, however inclined some states were to intervene in favour of peace, not one of them was prepared to take the decisive steps. That would have meant withdrawing from existing alliances and engagements and giving up certain political aims. And these aims were not arbitrary constructions, they were deeply rooted in the history and individuality of the states. In the Austro-Serbian conflict the national and the supranational conceptions of state clashed. No more than the Serbs would give way, could Austria be expected to refrain from suppressing Serbian nationalism. Germany could not afford to lose her last ally. She supported Austria in the first phase of the crisis, cherishing the hope that with quick and energetic steps the necessary action could remain localised to Serbia. And in the second phase of the crisis, when a European war threatened to develop out of the Austro-Serbian conflict, Germany could try to hold Austria back, but she did not declare that the *casus foederis* was not given, because that could have meant fighting alone in a future war on two fronts. The Russian government, for internal and external reasons, was dependent on success in the Balkans. It was paralysed by the fear of an alternative between war or revolution. For France the alliance with Russia was just as vital as the alliance with Austria was for Germany. It was owing to this alliance with Russia that after years of isolation France was gradually regaining a position of power in Europe. And for this reason she supported Russia with her pledge of loyalty. England had relatively the greatest freedom of action in the crisis. But for the eventuality of war, her position was determined by the naval rivalry with Germany as the potential European hegemonial power.

It was these comprehensible and deeply rooted interests which guided the responsible statesmen in the crisis. Not one of them wanted a world war. Every one of them in the course of the crisis sooner or later saw the danger of a general war. One or the other took certain precautions which show their desire to avoid it: Hence William II's and Bethmann-Hollweg's belated efforts to hold Austria back (proposal: halt in Belgrade; direct negotiations between Vienna and St Petersburg), Grey's intervention (proposal: ambassadors' conference), Poincaré's warning that Russia should not provoke Germany. But no-one was willing to pay the price for peace. Though desiring peace, the firm will was lacking. Russia could have had peace if she had refrained from supporting Serbia; Austria could have had it if she had agreed to the German or British proposals of settlement; Germany could have had it, had she with reference to the defensive character of the *Zweibund*, made the *casus foederis* dependent on Austria's acceptance of these proposals; France could have had it correspondingly, had she made the *casus foederis* dependent on Russia not ordering general mobilisation sooner than Germany did; England finally could have had it, had she at an early date made perfectly clear what attitude she would adopt in the case of war. Had it been neutrality, then France would have acted in the above sense towards Russia; had it been assistance for her allies in the Entente, Germany would have reacted, as above indicated towards Austria, because in that case, a localisation of the war would have been hopeless from the beginning. That Grey did not give a clear answer to the question: Neutrality, or war on the side of England's allies, must be understood as a consequence of the uncertain internal situation of the country. Grey had first to win Cabinet and Parliament over to the idea of a possible war on the side of France. But it was also the lack of transparency in the policy of Grey himself, which left open the question of how far England was bound in consequence of the Entente with France, and how far she still had a free hand.

Peace could have been preserved in 1914, had Berchtold, Sazonov, Bethmann-Hollweg, Poincaré, Grey, or one of the governments concerned, so sincerely wanted it that they were willing to sacrifice certain political ideas, traditions and conceptions, which were not their own personal ones, but those of their peoples and their time.

Is this guilt? You need not indulge in historic fatalism to realise how the time was moving towards war, and how little space was left to the individual statesman for liberty of decision. Was it lack of ability on the part of those who were in office? There was certainly no statesman of outstanding capacity among them. We have the famous words of Lloyd George, the later British war Prime Minister, in which he placed all responsible protagonists on the same level:

> Amongst the rulers and statesmen who alone could give the final word which caused great armies to spring from the ground and march to and across frontiers, one can see now clearly that not one of them wanted war; certainly not on this scale . . . Had there been a Bismarck in Germany, a Palmerston or a Disraeli in Britain, a Roosevelt in America, or a Clemenceau in authority in Paris, the catastrophe might, and I believe would, have been averted; but there was no one of that quality visible on the bridge in any great State. Von Bethmann-Hollweg, Poincaré, Viviani, Berchtold, Sazonov and Grey were all able, experienced, conscientious and respectable mariners, but distinctly lacking in the force, vision, imagination and resource which alone could have saved the situation. They were all handy men in a well-behaved sea, but helpless in a typhoon. . . .

They 'desired peace but had not the resolution and boldness to do the simple things that could alone ensure it'. These words, directed after the war against French hegemonial policy, were to establish a moral equilibrium in Europe and may miss the extent of activity and consciousness of those responsible, but they are to the point, as far as folly and blindness are concerned. In the belief of doing the right thing for their country, they did not realise what they were doing and where the path was leading them. The difficulty in judging the men responsible for the foreign policy of the time is, that it is so easy to say here is a mark, and here is another, where this or that person should have acted differently. But if we look exactly, and if we judge the persons not from the position of our own retrospective wisdom, we know where history led, but from their own situation and the political values of their time, then it seems comprehensible that they acted as they did. The relationship of this general entanglement in the situation and the undeniable liberty and responsibility left to the protagonists does not permit a verdict by simple legal or moral categories. The way to an adequate estimation of the war-guilt problem seems to have been shown by the British historian Gooch, when he summarised the result of the post-war phase of research on the origins of the war of 1914. Since then, the violent renewal of the controversy after the Second World War, and particularly the Riezler diaries, permit a more exact evaluation of the character and degree of Germany's responsibility than was possible before the new sources were brought to light. But it seems to me that the wisdom of Gooch is still valid when he recalled Hegel's words that a 'tragedy is the conflict not of right with wrong, but of right with right'.

10. July 1914. Reply to a Polemic

EGMONT ZECHLIN

In a document, 'July 1914' (*roro aktuell* 1983), directed against Zechlin, Hillgruber and Erdmann, Fischer refers, in this polemic against Zechlin among others, to an article in the *FAZ* (*Frankfurter Allgemeine Zeitung* of 8 July 1982) in which the latter had stated the fundamental points of his research into the July crisis. We are reproducing it here in its original form (I) as the basis for the consequent anti-critique (II).

I

When the German government, with the so-called 'blank-cheque authority' of 5/6 July 1914, gave Austria-Hungary full power and a free hand to take action against Serbia, the intention was not only to support and maintain the federal Habsburg Empire, but also to counteract an incipient shift of power within the European states system. The problems which were coming to a head during that period of some weeks and which had deep-seated causes, were as follows:

(1) Upheavals in south-east Europe. After Russia, in the eighties, under the ideological banner of the Pan-Slav movement, had brought about a threat of war, the victories in 1912 of the Balkan States over European Turkey offered her the chance of reopening the power-struggle with the Habsburg monarchy

---

Translated by Brian J. Follett.

over the claims to supremacy in this area. In spring 1914, Russian diplomats with the support of the French were negotiating the formation of a new federation of the Balkan states under the protectorate of the Tsar. For this purpose, the Quai d'Orsay and the Foreign Office were estimating a military force of about a million bayonets which would have an enormous influence on the European balance of power and which would be capable of paralysing the forces of Austria-Hungary to such an extent that Germany could no longer rely on the support of her alliance partner.

(2) From information secretly received by the German government from the Russian embassy in London, it appeared that the Triple Entente was about to engage in a more closely linked scheme of alliance. The prime factor in this was to be a naval agreement between Russia and England which, similar to the one between France and England in 1912, also implied a political commitment for the island kingdom – 'a last link in the chain', commented Bethmann-Hollweg on the eve of the 'blank-cheque authority'. London was even more unable to avoid the demands of her French and Russian partners when, in return, Russia appended a new comprehensive agreement concerning central Asia, in which they pledged themselves to non-involvement in Persia and thereby also to maintain the 'security of India'.

Thus, following the spate of imperialist offensives at the turn of the century, there came a concentrated development through which the Triple Entente, by a limitation of their spheres of interest in their colonial and world policies, released enough military forces to be able to turn their attention more to the conflicts and crises in Europe. With these moves to restrict the growing dynamism of the emergent German Reich, Germany herself was in danger of being confronted by concentric pressure such as had worried Bismarck, as the *cauchemar des coalitions* – a nightmare which had pursued him to the very end of his days. At the very least it threatened to limit her freedom of movement and of action as a great power and also within world politics.

(3) The German General Staff and also the government, in future had to reckon with military inferiority. Whilst the sword of Damocles, in the form of dissection by the various national

movements, hovered above the Kaiser's army, Russia, having completed by about 1916 both the huge reform of her army and also the strategic railway network in Poland, had at her disposal a massive army, a mighty Russian steamroller, which seemed to be capable of reaching the gates of Berlin if war ever engaged the main German forces in a campaign in France. Thus Bethmann-Hollweg also based the decision for the 'blank-cheque authority' on 'Russia's increasing claims and immense explosive potential', which in a few years time would have been irresistible, 'especially if Europe remained in its present form'. 'The future belongs to Russia which is growing and growing and imposes itself upon us as an ever-increasing nightmare.' In July 1912 he had gained the impression, while on a journey there, of 'wealth of resources and of a sturdy people', and, while later gazing at his own parkland on his estate Hohenfinow in Mark Brandenburg, he reflected on 'whether there was any purpose planting new trees; for, in a few years, the Russians would be there'. Even after the war Bethmann-Hollweg was still trying to justify his policy in the July crisis by saying that, even with the sacrificing of Austria-Hungary, 'Moscow's bloodless triumph would have heralded an epoch of extreme Russian oppression' and Germany would only have survived this 'as a submissive vassal at the beck and call of its Eastern master'.

(4) The critical change in the situational appraisal in the weeks and months before the assassination at Sarajevo caused the German leaders to use the localised Austro-Serbian conflict as a preventive factor against the increasingly dangerous external-political threat. This primarily and intentionally defensive objective, of securing and strengthening the international position of the Reich and its freedom of movement within world politics, was the main preoccupation of German policy in July 1914.

To challenge this theory there are no indications at all, neither in pre-war history nor even in the July crisis, which could be produced to show that the German government – even after the so-called Council of War of December 1912 – in any way in accord with the aims of 'imperialist conquest of the national ruling class', had been planning an expansionist war with conquests in the east and in the west with the intention of gaining the hegemony in Europe and thereby the basis of a policy of world supremacy far beyond that of a mere claim to international recognition. It is far more possible that here certain plans for the event of war are being identified as an apparent intention to instigate such a war and, subordinated to actual government policy, are the day-dreams of some political, social and economic groups directed at a 'greater Germany' and at 'war objectives' which, in fact, were only the product of the war situation itself and only in the end grew into a mutual striving for hegemony.

Nevertheless, the Chancellor made no secret of the fact 'that any action against Serbia can lead to a world war'. Even Wilhelm II reacted to Emperor Franz Josef's call to him to keep faith with the alliance, first of all by saying that 'a serious European complication had to be reckoned with'. The general public had also gained this impression when they heard the news of the murder of the Archduke, the successor to the throne. Bethmann-Hollweg himself had already in February 1913 warned the Austro-Hungarian Foreign Minister that Russia, 'in objective terms, could not simply sit by and watch any military action of Austria against Serbia without loss of prestige'. Just as this turned out to be true in historical retrospect for the July crisis, so too, did the Chancellor's warning that any supporters of a more peaceful policy would be 'simply brushed to one side' by the Pan-Slav movement. Even if he was taking a risk with his so-called 'leap into the darkness', Wilhelm II had already, at the time of Franz Josef's appeal, advised them 'not to waste this present opportunity which was so favourable for us'. In his opinion, St Petersburg would ponder for a long time before issuing any call to arms, because they were 'not yet ready for war' and the Tsar would not be able to side with the murderers of Sarajevo. In addition, immediately after the assassination, there was a feeling among the general public in Europe that the Austrians were to a certain extent justified in taking reprisal action against Serbia.

However, in order to prevent the involvement of any other powers, it was agreed among the diplomats of the alliance to make 'one swift blow' and present the world with a *fait accompli*. If then England and France, under pressure from the threat of war, would sue for peace in St Petersburg, Berlin could expect to have a chance to 'manoeuvre the Entente apart'. 'If the Serbian affair could be concluded successfully without Russia mobilising', thus went the train of thought, then a satisfied Austria-Hungary could come to an understanding with a Russia which had felt herself let down by her Entente partners. For this purpose thoughts were already turning to certain Russian diplomats, like the Ambassador in Constantinople, M. N. Giers, who had already offered their services in secret to the Foreign Ministry as opponents of the Entente. If there are signs that, on the day of the issuing of the ultimatum in Belgrade, Bethmann-Hollweg believed in the success of the 'localising' policy, he nevertheless still bore in mind the possible course of developments in the event of its failure: 'If war were to come, it would come through a Russian mobilisation *ab iratio*, so, apart from some notional negotiations there would be then nothing more to negotiate, because we must then immediately strike, in order to have any chance of winning!'

The idea, however, of 'settling everything by diplomatic success', was just as much a miscalculation as that of 'changing or loosening the current compositional structure of Europe' by means of and in the course of the crisis. There would have been a risk, in any case, with a march on Serbia, of inciting the Pan-Slav movement in Russia to the point of blood-letting and putting the Tsar's government in an extremely difficult situation. But now, too, the element of surprise had been lost. In Vienna more than two weeks went by in discussions with the reluctant Hungarian President and in close examination of the background to the assassination, in order to formulate the ultimatum according to proper international law. When at last, in the late afternoon of 23 July, it was handed over in Belgrade, Poincaré was just leaving after a visit to St Petersburg where he had agreed with the Russian allies to defend the 'sovereignty and integrity of Serbia'. This was in accordance with the supplementary clause of 1899 to the Franco-Russian alliance stating mutual commitment to the maintenance of the balance of power in Europe and the inclusion of the Balkan states in the strategic concept of the French General Staff after the first Balkan war of 1912. And that Russia was in earnest, is shown by the reaction of the cabinet council in St Petersburg to the ultimatum to Serbia (23 July). Already on the following day it was decided that there should be a partial mobilisation against Austria and, because Germany would also have to be contended with in the event of war, a meeting on 25 July presided over by the Tsar called for a 'war preparation period' involving the whole Empire.

On this day, still therefore unaware of the simultaneous developments in St Petersburg, the Foreign Ministry pressed its alliance partner in Vienna to make haste with the preparations, which had been going on for some time there, for the declaration of war and for the campaign in Serbia, and in the late afternoon the official emissary in Belgrade, acting on instructions, found the Serbia reply to the ultimatum to be unacceptable and forthwith broke off diplomatic relations. Again, on the following day, 26 July, Moltke informed his wife that the war against Serbia would 'remain localised' as long as Russia undertook no enemy action against Austria. How could he otherwise have allowed the Austrians and their main forces, at the cost of protecting the borders with Russia, to march on Serbia, with the result that the military units later, with great difficulty and delay, had to be repositioned for the battle against the Tsarist state. That Berlin was still thinking in terms of diplomatic negotiations is reflected in the routine affairs of Department 111B of the General Staff which was responsible for secret intelligence and the spy network. It was not until now that the intelligence officers under the various general commands were instructed to send out 'field-contacts' and agents 'and still without undue haste', in order to find out whether war preparations were taking place in Russia and France. When, in the late evening of 26 July the announcement of the Russian war preparation period was received, the 'field-agents' were informed over the Königsberg transmitter that 'the tense situation would possibly require all their efforts for a period of some weeks'.

Furthermore, the attitude of the German government to the English efforts at negotiation can be explained by that same consistent attitude which they had displayed in the course of the events of 5/6 July.

Grey's suggestion of a negotiation between Austria and Russia brought about by the four other great powers was immediately accepted. This followed the pattern of German calculations for negotiations to take place after the march into Serbia. 'A rapid *fait accompli* and then friendly with the Entente and then the shock can be withstood.' But it was just because of this that the French and Russian diplomats refused to accept this course of action. Similarly, the Central Powers declined such a solution to the Austro-Serbian conflict by touchline negotiations of any ambassadorial conference, because then the Viennese cabinet could have their hands tied and the southern Slav question could be shelved.

However, the political offensive had become a boomerang in the meantime. Just as they had estimated that the Tsarist state would sacrifice their Serbian 'brothers' and their positions in the Balkans, now the German government was confronted with the choice of either allowing a war to develop or abandoning a partner who would only, in any case, be at their disposal in a Balkan conflict and who had earlier even threatened that, if German help in the alliance was not forthcoming, it could 'just as well belong to the other group'. This time the Viennese cabinet had been encouraged by no less than the Kaiser and the Kanzler of the German Empire to exploit this propitious hour for 'action', and rapidly too. If, at this moment, the German leaders had relinquished their own freedom of action – and how well this was understood in Vienna – so, too, would any submission now in the face of Russian military pressure threaten them with a diplomatic and power-political defeat and even possibly a national loss of prestige, which could be ill afforded by a Chancellor who already, since the Morocco crisis, had been exposed to the Pan-German campaign for haste. Finally, only that would remain which was expressed as all the dangers for the security and future of the German Empire embodied in the decision of 5/6 July.

This explains why the 'blank-cheque authority' was not withdrawn in those hours during which the risk threshold was being crossed. It seemed more acceptable to consider ideas put forward repeatedly by the militarists and also often discussed, ideas which had already been recommended by the elder Moltke with special regard to Russian rearmament. After the failure of the attempt to avoid pressure from the coalition by prising apart the Triple Entente, and when the Central Powers were being confronted instead by a Russia prepared for war, it was to be expected that this, now more than ever before, should be the case, especially when in the years to follow and in circumstances much less favourable to Germany, there would be crises and tests of strength for the alliance groups to face. Already in the weeks before Sarajevo, the younger Moltke had relied upon the Secretary of State at the Foreign Ministry to focus their policy on rapid moves towards a war; for in two to three years, as a result of Russian rearmament, the supremacy of the enemy would be so great that he could see no way for 'us to become master of the situation'. Jagow refused at the time to accept the need to cause a war and reminded them of Bismarck's words, that it was impossible to predict Providence. However, in the event of a defensive war, as Moltke also considered it to be, he did not wish to condemn it 'in principle and *a limine*'. Then again, immediately before the ultimatum to Serbia, he replied to the warnings of the Ambassador Prince Lichnowsky by saying that he wanted no preventive war, 'but if a battle should come, then we should not gripe'.

Thus German policy may be seen as a kind of double strategy. In any event it was even now still believed that the Tsar, according to all the psychological estimates of his love for peace, would rather come to terms with any march against Serbia than risk war with all its unpredictable political and social consequences. However, the more it seemed to be moving towards a call to arms, the more the Foreign Ministry, with due consideration for the Social Democrats, adopted a tactic of labelling Russia with the odium of the aggressor. But in the end, as Bethmann-Hollweg admitted in a meeting of the Prussian State Ministry on 30 July, 'all direction had been lost and the stone had begun to roll'. When he now refused 'to be drawn into a huge world-wide conflagration' by Vienna, it was too late to prevent escalation into a war. His grounds for now demanding the acceptance of the 'stop-in-Belgrade' formula are characteristic of the whole conflict situation. According to this, Austria's political prestige and the military honour of her army would be preserved and her position in the Balkans, compared to Russia, would again be strengthened by the 'humiliation of Serbia'. This was the very thing that St Petersburg would never allow. But, for the Chancellor of the

German Empire, all this was a Fate lying over Europe at the time, 'greater than any human power'.

None of the countries had 'wanted' this year, yet none of them felt cowed either by the risk or by the war itself. On 19 July it had been decided in the Austro-Hungarian cabinet – without even informing their German allies – to 'cut Serbia down to size' by transfer of its border territory to Bulgaria, Greece and Albania and to regard the rest of it as a sort of vassal state of the Habsburg Empire. This confirms what the Tsar wrote to the King of England, that Vienna was intent only on 'destroying' Serbia. In St Petersburg the war faction surrounding the Grand-Duke Nicolaj Nicolajewitsch seized the opportunity to 'settle the scores' with Austria. Paris, no less than Berlin, had no desire to lose an alliance partner and also the Foreign Office was more prepared to run the risk of war than to gamble with the Triple Entente. The action taken by the Central Powers led to a feeling of solidarity, in apprehension of an increase in the power of the German Empire and its possible policy of hegemony, as had been discussed in no uncertain terms in the exchange of correspondence between the Entente countries. Of crucial importance here was that a regional conflict situation, which was linked with aspects vital to the security and also to the political interests of the great powers, was becoming the object of a power struggle between two polarised alliance groups which had even been pre-programmed to produce a chain reaction. And those responsible failed to withdraw from this devil's punch-bowl.

Even if, nowadays, it is possible to gain greater insight into the ambitions, intentions and decisions of those countries, including also the German leadership, there still remains the question of with what aims and on what basis the German Empire, in view of the prevailing European power structure, could consider a war with the grand coalition to be endurable. In a confidential discussion with his predecessor, Reichskanzler Bülow, immediately before his departure for the HQ in Koblenz on 13 August, the Chancellor expressed his expectations in the following way: 'There will be a violent but short, very short storm. I estimate a duration of the war of three or, at the most, four months and I have based my policies on this. And then, despite the war and, in fact, because of the war, I am hoping to arrive at a really friendly, trusting and loyal relationship with England, and through England, with France as well'. Even in view of the great successes of the German armies in France and the general air of conceited self-confidence prevailing in German public opinion, Bethmann-Hollweg was staking all on the presumption that the common-sense of the opponent's men of state would see to it that the war would not be drawn out further than the necessary extent of military operations and that the peace could be arranged between cabinets at a normal diplomatic level. That these expectations also were a huge miscalculation was certainly brought home to him a few weeks later.

II

Fritz Fischer's critique covers the following points:

(1) I isolate repeatedly the July crisis from the interwoven circumstances before and after.
(2) I take up repeatedly the 'categorising of Fate', making the 'power of fate' responsible for the outbreak of war to thus exonerate German policy.
(3) It was my repeated intention with the interpretation of the First World War as a 'defensive preventive war' to put the 'blame' on the other side.
(4) I distort, in my interpretation, Fischer's portrayal of German motives and objectives as an expansionist war with conquests in east and west.
(5) In addition there are further comments by Fischer which, likewise, are dealt with by me in the following reply but which are directed mainly in similar fashion at Karl Dietrich Erdmann and Andreas Hillgruber.

To (1): The paragraph in the *FAZ* concerned the July crisis which had its origin in the fatal 'blank-cheque authority' of the German government of 5/6 July 1914. The 'before and after' has been dealt with in detail by me in earlier publications (recently in my book, *Krieg and Kriegsrisiko*, 1979).

To (2): Here Fischer's critique revolves around the title of my *FAZ* essay: 'Nobody could withdraw from the devil's punch-bowl'. The editor took this title from a line of thought which can be seen above at the end of the penultimate paragraph: that, in fact, 'those responsible had failed' to withdraw from the pre-programmed chain reaction of the alliance groups. If I am now to be accused of that dark fatalism as is seen in the case of Bethmann-Hollweg, then my conception of history could be reproached as merely being a 'personalistic' perusal which even Fischer considers to be an antiquated method. How am I then otherwise to make the German leaders responsible for a whole line of miscalculations: for expecting to compel the powers to negotiate by a sudden swift coup against Serbia, for speculating that the Central Powers would be provided either with a diplomatic success if the ultimatum were accepted or with a legal permit for a military intervention if it were refused (the Serbian government, as is well known, avoided the issue by use of clever wording), for hoping that the Tsar would show his peace-loving nature and that France would hold back, and finally for contemplation of a time-limited cabinet war.

To (3): I have never presented the idea of the preventive war more simply, analysing it, moreover, in its historical sequences from the militarist angle and in its different connotations, above all drawing attention to the fact that it was only after the failure of the policy of localisation and dislocation of the Triple Entente and, above all, in view of the escalation of mobilisation by the Russians, that it became acute for the political leaders. This is taken particularly from Moltke's memo of 28/29 July where he mentions the fatal consequences of the military preparations of the probable opponents as they increased from day to day. According to Duden Encyclopaedia the concept of 'defensive' has a dual rendering; 'defending, holding off' and 'concerned with securing or security'. Now that does not mean that there would have been reasons for attacking the Triple Entente. But after the ever-increasing number of crises in the previous few years, a trial of strength and somehow a collision between the alliance groups had to be reckoned with. A crisis situation could more especially be expected when the Russian cabinet, on 21 February 1914, made the decision to take possession of the Turkish Straits within about three years, something which, according to the participants, would also mean war on the western borders. Therefore the results of my research support the fact that Berlin, being in a defensive situation, intended, with the deployment of the whole strength and weight of the German Empire, to bring about a loosening and reallocation of the whole power structure within the western states system. According to Bethmann-Hollweg this was a 'leap into the dark', but with the intention of avoiding, if at all possible, any future warlike collision of the alliance groups. With this train of thought the 'blame' is in no way being 'put on the other side'. In fact, nowadays there is a chance, seeing things in temporal retrospect, to put right the apologetic historical record which had provoked the apportioning of blame at Versailles, stating that the cause of the outbreak of war in 1914, in all objective considerations, was the mere interest in gain of the opponents and the motives and intentions of the main figures.

To (4): Already in his book, *Krieg der Illusionan*, Fritz Fischer has attributed to German policy the intention in the July crisis of making the European powers 'submit'. That this was not only a 'word', is shown much more clearly now that, in support of this, he cites the so-called 'September programme'. This 'provisional sketch' which the Chancellor commissioned on 6 September 1914 was, according to my investigations, more a storage tank of somewhat contradictory impressions from economists, bureaucrats and militarists. For what was now clearly becoming an extended war with the Empire, it was meant to create a counter-blockade, a 'modern kind of Continental blockade' with its origin in France. This memo contained a proposal by Walter Rathenau, then director of the raw materials department of the War Ministry and by Kurt Riezler, for a central European economic system with a loose federation of both defensive and offensive alliances 'round about us', in other words of vassal states. It is arguable now whether he meant 'conquests' or 'submission' (whereby in any case the second presupposes the first): Fischer, who published this 'September programme' again in his 'polemic' in connection with the July crisis, here allocates, to decisions made by the German leaders in July 1914, war objectives which only arose later from the actual war situation. That is not only methodologically out of order but in this case also misleading. For there is absolutely no proof that the German government unleashed a war for the sake of such vast objectives nor even that it ran the risk of such a war. A context for this September memo can be seen in the Pan-German political journals of the pre-war years. But this again was not the politics of the government itself. Neither can the decisions – or rather misdecisions – of the German leaders be deduced from the structural or more particularly the social conditions of Wilhelmine Germany. In fact, as far as the First World War is concerned – as indeed at any time in the course of human co-existence – it is a question of a massive complex web of social, political, economic and military factors each in themselves needing to be weighed separately. The outbreak of war in 1914, however, is an extreme and striking example of the serious consequences of international disputes and inter-relationships with their associated diplomatic activities and counter-activities within a system of states. In this particular case it was, for both alliance groups, a matter of their 'security and balance' and also of their potential power-position in any consequent European crisis together with its automatically associated trial of strength. The action against Serbia belongs in just this category. 'In order to construct a dyke across the rising tide-water of the Pan-Slav movement and to ensure peace for our countries' thus ran the words of advice of Kaiser Franz Joseph in his handwritten letter to Wilhelm II, when he recommended that this pivot-point of Pan-Slav politics should be 'eradicated as a power factor in the Balkans' and, instead of a Balkan confederation under Russian patronage, a new one should be formed under the patronage of the league of three. This was the risk that, indeed, in the words of the German Chancellor, 'could lead to a world war'.

To (5): Fischer still insists on his theory that the German leaders had planned and instigated the hegemonial war trusting that England would remain neutral and the fight would only be against Russia and France. He even quotes Gerhard Ritter who was absolutely 'flabbergasted' when he read my sentence about the enmity of England, in the event of a war, being 'probable if not even certain'.

According to Ritter's theory it would be wrong to believe that

Bethmann-Hollweg would have been prepared to take upon himself the risk of a war against three great powers. But the fact remains that the British government had repeatedly declared their intention to enter the war in the event of a German attack on France. Therefore, the possibility of the enmity of England in the event of a European war is actually an indication that the German government had in fact not wished for the Great War that it became, but had seriously been counting on being able to localise the Austro-Serbian conflict.

Finally, a word on the 'state secret surrounding the Riezler diaries'. The criticisms levelled at the editing of these will be dealt with by the editor himself, Karl Dietrich Erdmann. In addition, however, there will be quoted here another scene which took place in the Reichskanzlei in February 1915. It was then that the Munich historian Karl Alexander von Müller, while on a hospital train which he was accompanying to Belgium, received a telegraph to go to Berlin. There he was severely criticised by Kurt Riezler for allowing the *Süddeutsche Monatshefte*, of which he was the chief editor, to publish 'some extremely hasty and over-weening war objectives' which were causing the Chancellor some difficulties with his policies. What was of even greater importance was what the Chancellor's right-hand man – who, in fact, in the course of a few weeks, had been promoted to Under Secretary Legationsrat and also official spokesman – had to say about the intentions of German policy in the July crisis. Müller, as an historian well versed in how to handle source information, wrote all this down on that same night in the sleeper while on his way back to Munich. From this corroborative account from early in 1915, the conversational jottings of Riezler from the time of the July crisis, which have come to light in the edition of Riezler's diaries, can be emphatically confirmed. For instance, the following sentence is to be found in Müller: 'The tactical thinking was in fact similar to that three years before at Agadir, during the Morocco incident, when a critical situation, brought about with aston- ishing rapidity, was intended to produce the diplomatic defeat of one of the opponents and thereby the loosening or the disintegration of the enemy alliance. . . .' All this offers an insight not only into the political intentions of the July crisis, but also into the continuation of a strategy, with which it was hoped to counter the 'ring formation', but which, in exerting pressure, according to one of Bülow's speeches in 1906, would produce a counter-pressure, and both together could lead to explosions. In fact, this policy of Germany's, which was adhered to particularly by Holstein and later also by Kiderlen-Wächter, had more the effect of stirring up the mistrust of the neighbouring powers against the objectives of this new super power, and thereby drawing them even closer together. However, just before his death in 1909, Holstein bequeathed the advice that 'before the ring of great powers closed in on us, we should try with all our might and determination not to be cowed by anything at all and break this ring apart'.

These were the tactics also used by the German leaders in the July crisis, but without any flexibility and without any concept of crisis-strategy to prepare them to take the bitter decision within an ever-narrowing field of manoeuvre and, along with the other European powers, to take it in time to prevent the spread of the fire threatening in the Balkans.

Notes on Contributors

KARL DIETRICH ERDMANN, Professor Emeritus at the University of Kiel. Among his many works are his edition of the Riezler Diaries.

FRITZ FISCHER, Professor Emeritus of Modern History at the University of Hamburg. Author of *Griff nach der Weltmacht* and *Krieg der Illusionen*.

IMANUEL GEISS, Professor of Modern History at the University of Bremen. Author of *Der polnische Grenzstreifen 1914–1918* and editor of *Julikrise und Kriegsausruch*.

KARL-HEINZ JANSSEN, Political Editor of *Die Zeit*. Author of *Macht und Verblendung, Kriegszielpolitik der deutschen Bundesstaaten 1914–1918* and numerous other works.

JAMES JOLL, Professor Emeritus at the London School of Economics and Political Science. Among his many works are *The Second International, Intellectuals in Politics* and *Europe Since 1870*.

HANNSJOACHIM W. KOCH, Senior Lecturer in History at the University of York, visiting Professor of the Free University of Berlin. His works include *The Hitler Youth: Origins and Development 1922–1945, Der Sozialdarwinismus: Seine Genese und Einfluss auf das imperialistische Denken, Der Deutsche Bürgerkrieg 1918–1924, A History of Prussia* and *German Constitutional History in the 19th and 20th Century*.

JOACHIM REMAK, Professor of History at the University of California, Santa Barbara. Author of *Sarajevo, The Origins of World War I* and *The First World War: Causes, Conduct, Consequences*.

PAUL W. SCHROEDER, Professor of History at the University of Illinois. A specialist in international relations whose works include *The Axis Alliance and Japanese-American Relations 1941*.

EGMONT ZECHLIN, Professor Emeritus of Modern History at the University of Hamburg. Author of many works including *Die deutsche Politik und die Juden im Ersten Weltkrieg* and *Kriegsausbruch 1914 und Kriegszielproblem in der internationalen Politik*.

Bibliography

The literature concerning the outbreak of the First World War as well as that on German war aims has become so vast that it is virtually impossible even to list a representative cross-section. Readers are referred to the bibliographies contained in the works of Albertini, Langer, Taylor and Schmitt.

Albertini, Luigi, *The Origins of the War of 1914*, 3 vols (Oxford, 1952–7).

Aleksić-Pejković, L., 'La Serbie et les rapports entre les puissances de l'Entente 1908–1913', *Balkan Studies* (1965).

Andrew, Ch., 'German World Policy and the Reshaping of the Dual Alliance', *Journal of Contemporary History* (1966).

——, *Théophile Delcassé and the Making of the Entente Cordiale* (London, 1968).

Barnes, Harry Elmer, *The Genesis of the World War: An Introduction to the Problem of War Guilt* (New York, 1927).

Barraclough, G., *From Agadir to Armageddon, Anatomy of a Crisis* (London, 1982).

Basler, Werner, *Deutschlands Annexionspolitik in Polen und im Baltikum 1914–1918* (Berlin, 1962).

Baumgart, W., *Deutsche Ostpolitik 1918* (Munich, 1966).

Beloff, M., *Imperial Sunset* (New York, 1970).

Berghahn, V. R., 'Zu den Zielen des deutschen Flottenbaus unter Wilhelm II', *Historische Zeitschrift* (1970).

——, *Der Tirpitz-Plan* (Düsseldorf, 1971).

——, *Germany and Approach of War in 1914* (London, 1973).

Bestuszhev, Igor W., *Bórba v Rossii po voprosam vnésnei politiki 1906–1916* (Moscow, 1961).

——, 'Russian Foreign Policy February–June 1914', *Journal of Contemporary History* (1966).

Bihl, W., 'Zu den österreichisch-ungarischen Kriegszielen 1914', *Jahrbücher für die Geschichte Osteuropas* (1968).

Birke, Ernst, 'Die französische Osteuropapolitik 1914–1918', *Zeitschrift für Ostforschung* (1954).

Birnbaum, K. E., *Peace Moves and U-Boat Warfare: A Study of Imperial Germany's Policy towards the United States April 18, 1916–January 9, 1917* (Stockholm, 1958).

Bourne, K., *Britain and the Balance of Power in North America, 1815–1908* (Berkeley, 1967).

Bovykin, V. Y., *Istorii vosniknoveniya pervoi mirovoi voiny; otnospheniya Rossii i Frantsii v 1912–1914* (Moscow, 1961).

Bradley, F. N., 'Quelques aspects de la politique étrangère de Russie avant 1914 à travers les archives françaises', *Etudes slaves et est-européennes* (1967).

Bridge, F. R., *From Sadowa to Sarajevo* (London, 1972).

Burchardt, Lothar, *Friedenswirtschaft und Kriegsvorsorge. Deutschlands wirtschaftliche Rüstungsbestrebungen vor 1914* (Boppard, 1968).

Butterfield, Herbert, 'Sir Edward Grey in July 1914', *Historical Studies V, Papers Read to the Sixth Irish Conference of Historians*, ed. J. L. McCracken (London, 1965).

Calleo, D., *The German Problem Reconsidered. Germany and the World Order 1870 to the Present* (Cambridge, 1978).

Carlgren, W. M., *Neutralität oder Allianz. Deutschlands Beziehungen zu Schweden in den Anfangsjahren des Ersten Weltkrieges* (Stockholm, 1962).

Carsten, F. L., *British and German Radical Movements in the First World War* (London, 1982).

Conze, Werner, *Polnische Nation und deutsche Politik im Ersten Weltkrieg* (Cologne–Graz, 1958).

Cooper, M. B., 'British Policy in the Balkans, 1908–9', *Historical Journal* (1965).

Craig, G., 'The World War One Alliance of the Central Powers in retrospect', *Journal of Modern History* (1965).

Dakin, D., 'British Sources concerning the Greek Struggle in Macedonia, 1901–1909', *Balkan Studies* (1961).

Dallin, Alexander *et al.*, *Russian Diplomacy and Eastern Europe 1914–1917* (New York, 1963).

Dedijer, Vladimir, *The Road to Sarajevo* (New York, 1966).

Dehio, Ludwig, *Deutschland und die Weltpolitik im 20. Jahrhundert*, 2nd ed. (Frankfurt, 1961).

Deutsch-französische Vereinbarung über strittige Fragan europäischer Geschichte (Braunschweig, 1958).

Droz, Jacques, 'Die politischen Kräfte in Frankreich während des Ersten Weltkrieges', *Geschichte in Wissenschaft und Unterricht* (1966).

Engel-Janosi, Friedrich, *Österreich und der Vatikan 1846–1918*, 2 vols (Graz–Vienna, 1958–60).

Erdmann, K. D., 'Zur Beurteilung Bethmann-Hollwegs', *Geschichte, Wissenschaft und Unterricht* (1964).

——, 'Problèmes politiques de la première guerre mondiale', in *XIIe Congrès International des Sciences Historiques* (Vienna, 1965).

——, 'Discussion sur le buts de guerre de Bethmann-Hollweg pendant la première guerre mondiale', *Historiens et géographes, Bulletin de la sociéte des professeurs d'histoire et de geographie* (1968).

——, (ed.), 'Kurt Riezler – Tagebücher, Aufsätze, Dokumente' (Göttingen, 1972).

——, 'Deutschland im Ersten Weltkrieg. Methodische Fragen zur Auswertung der Schriften und Tagebücher Kurt Riezlers', in *Jahrbuch der Akademie der Wissenschaften in Göttingen* (Göttingen, 1973).

——, 'Zur Echteit der Tagebücher Kurt Riezlers. Eine Antikritik', *Historische Zeitschrift* (1983).

Fay, Sidney Bradshaw, *The Origins of the World War*, 2 vols (New York, 1928).

Feldmann, Gerald D., *Army, Industry and Labor in Germany 1914–1918* (Princeton, N.J., 1966).

——, (ed.), *German Imperialism 1914–1918* (New York, 1972).

Fellner, Fritz, *Der Dreibund. Europäische Diplomatie vor dem Ersten Weltkrieg* (Munich, 1960).

——, 'Zur Kontroverse über Fritz Fischers Buch *Griff nach der Weltmacht*', *Mitteilungen des Instituts für österreichische Geschichtsforschung* (1964).

Fischer, Fritz, 'Deutsche Kriegsziele. Revolutionierung und Separatfrieden im Osten 1914 bis 1918', *Historische Zeitschrift* (1959).

——, 'Kontinuität des Irrtums. Zum Problem der deutschen Kriegszielpolitik im ersten Weltkrieg', *Historische Zeitschrift* (1960).

——, *Griff nach der Weltmacht. Die Kriegszielpolitik des kaiserlichen Deutschlands 1914–18* (Düsseldorf, 1961), 2nd ed., 1962; 3rd ed., 1964; special ed., 1967. (English translation: *Germany's Aims in the First World War*, London, 1966.)

——, 'Weltpolitik, Weltmachtstreben und deutsche Kriegsziele', *Historische Zeitschrift* (1964).

——, *Weltmacht oder Niedergang. Deutschland im Ersten Weltkrieg* (Frankfurt, 1965) (Hamburger Studien zur neueren Geschichte, Bd. I).

——, 'Vom Zaun gebrochen – nicht hineingeschlittert. Deutschlands Schuld am Ausbruch des Ersten Weltkriegs', *Die Zeit* (1965).

——, *Krieg der Illusionen* (Düsseldorf, 1969).

——, *Juli 1914: Wir sind nicht hineingeschlittert. Das Staatsgeheimnis um die Riezler-Tagebücher. Eine Streitschrift* (Hamburg, 1983).

Galantar, Joszef, 'Stefan Tisza und der Erste Weltkrieg', *Österreich in Geschichte und Literatur* (1964).

——, 'Die Kriegszielpolitik der Tisza-Regierung 1913–1917', *Nouvelles études historiques* (Budapest, 1965).

Gasser, A., 'Der deutsche Hegemonialkrieg von 1914' in Geiss, I. and Wendt, B. J. (eds), *Deutschland in der Weltpolitik des 19. und 20. Jahrhunderts* (Hamburg, 1975).

Gatzke, Hans Wilhelm, *Germany's Drive to the West: A Study of Germany's Western War Aims during the First World War* (Baltimore, 1950).

Geiss, Imanuel, *Der polnische Grenzstreifen 1914–1918. Ein Beitrag zur deutschen Kriegszielpolitik im Ersten Weltkrieg* (Lübeck–Hamburg, 1960) (Eberings Historische Studien, Heft 398).

——, 'Zur Beurteilung der deutschen Reichspolitik im Ersten Weltkrieg. Kritische Bemerkungen zur Interpretation des Riezler-Tagebuchs', in H. Pogge von Strandmann and Imanuel Geiss, *Die Erforderlichkeil des Unmöglichen. Deutschland am Vorabend des Ersten Weltkrieges* (Frankfurt, 1965) (Hamburger Studien zur neueren Geschichte, Bd. 2).

—— (ed.), *Julikrise und Kriegsausbruch 1914. Eine Dokumentensammlung*, 2 vols (Hanover, 1963–4).

—— (ed.), *Juli 1914. Die europäische Krise und der Ausbruch des Ersten Weltkrieges* (Munich, 1965).

Gottlieb, Wolfram William, *Studies in Secret Diplomacy during the First World War* (London, 1957).

Grenville, J. A. S., *Lord Salisbury and Foreign Policy* (London, 1964).

Groh, Dieter, 'The "Unpatriotic Socialists" and the State', *Journal of Contemporary History* (1966).

Guinn, Paul, *British Strategy and Politics 1914 to 1918* (Oxford, 1965).

Gutschke, Willibald, 'Erst Europa, dann die Welt', *Zeitschrift für Geschichtswissenschaft* (1964).

——, 'Bethmann Hollweg und die Politik der "Neuorientierung". Zur innenpolitischen Strategie und Taktik der deutschen Reichsregierung während des Ersten Weltkriegs', *Zeitschrift für Geschichtswissenschaft* (1965).

Hallgarten, Georg Wolfgang Felix, *Imperialismus vor 1914. Die soziologischen Grundlagen der Aussenpolitik europäischer Grossmächte vor dem Ersten Weltkrieg*, 2 vols, 2nd ed. (Munich, 1963).

Hanak, H., 'The Government, the Foreign Office and Austria-Hungary, 1914–1918', *Slavonic and East European Review* (1969).

Hantsch, Hugo, *Leopold Graf Berchtold. Grandseigneur und Staatsmann*, 2 vols. (Graz–Vienna, 1963).

——, 'Harcourt and Solf: The Search for an Anglo-German Understanding through Africa 1912–1914', *European Studies Review* (1971).

——, 'The Debate on the July Crisis Continues: Professor Fischer's second volume and its aftermath', *European Studies Review* (1974).

Hatton, P. H. S., 'Britain and Germany in 1914', *Past and Present* (1967).

Helmreich, E. C., *The Diplomacy of the Balkan Wars 1912–1913* (Cambridge, Mass., 1938).

Herzfeld, Hans, 'Die deutsche Kriegszielpolitik im Ersten Weltkrieg', *Vierteljahrshefte für Zeitgeschichte* (1963).

——, 'Zur deutschen Politik im Ersten Weltkrieg. Kontinuität oder permanente Krise?', *Historische Zeitschrift* (1960).

Hillgruber, Andreas, 'Riezlers Theorie des kalkulierten Risikos und Bethmann Hollwegs politisches Kalkül in der Julikrise 1914', *Historische Zeitschrift* (1966).

——, *Deutschlands Rolle in der Vorgeschichte der beiden Weltkriege* (Göttingen, 1967).

Hölzle, Erwin, 'Das Experiment des Friedens im Ersten Weltkrieg', *Geschichte in Wissenschaft und Unterricht* (1962).

——, *Der Geheimnisverrat und der Kriegsausbruch 1914* (Göttingen, 1973).

——, *Die Selbstentmachtung Europas* (Göttingen, 1975).

——, *Quellen zur Entstehung des Ersten Weltkrieges. Internationale Dokumente 1901–1914* (Darmstadt, 1978).

Hubatsch, Walther, 'Ursachen und Anlass des Weltkrieges 1914', in *1914–1939–1945. Schicksalsjahre deutscher Geschichte* (Boppard, 1964).

——, *Die Ära Tirpitz. Studien zur deutschen Marine-politik 1890–1918* (Göttingen, 1955).

Jablonowski, Horst, 'Die Stellungnahme der russischen Parteien zur Aussenpolitik der Regierung von der russisch-englischen Verständigung bis zum Ersten Weltkrieg', *Forschungen zur osteuropäischen Geschichte* (1957).

Jaeckel, H., *Die Nordwestgrenze in der Verteidigung Indiens 1900–1908 und der Weg Englands zum russischen-britischen Abkommen von 1907* (Cologne, 1958).

Janssen, Karl-Heinz, *Macht und Verblendung. Kriegszielpolitik der deutschen Bundesstaaten 1914–1918* (Göttingen, 1962).

——, *Der Kanzler und der General. Die Führungskrise um Bethmann Hollweg und Falkenhayn (1914–1916)* (Göttingen, 1967).

Jarausch, K. H., 'The Illusion of Limited War: Chancellor Bethmann-Hollweg's Calculated Risk, July 1914', *Central European History* (1969).

——, *The Enigmatic Chancellor: Bethmann-Hollweg and the Hubris of Imperial Germany* (New Haven, 1973).

Joll, J., 'The Unspoken Assumptions', Inaugural professorial lecture delivered at the London School of Economics (April 1968).

——, 'War Guilt 1914: A Continuing Controversy' in Kluke, P. and Alter, P. (eds), *Aspects of Anglo-German Relations through the Centuries. Addresses and Papers given at the opening of the German Historical Institute London* (London, 1978).

Kann, R. A., 'Erzherzog Franz Ferdinand und Graf Berchtold als Aussenminister, 1912–1914', *Mitteilungen des österreichischen Staatsarchivs* (1969).

Kantorowicz, Hermann, *Gutachten zur Kriegsschuldfrage 1914*, from the papers edited by Imanuel Geiss (Frankfurt, 1963).

Kazemzadeh, F., *Russia and Great Britain in Persia, 1864–1914* (New Haven, 1968).

Kehr, E., *Der Primat der Innenpolitik*, ed. H. U. Wehler (Berlin, 1965).

Kennedy, P. M., 'The Development of German Naval Operations Plans against England, 1896–1914', *English Historical Review* (Oxford, 1974).

Koch, H. W., 'The Anglo-German Alliance Negotiations: Missed Opportunity or Myth', *History* (1969).

——, *Der Sozialdarwinismus. Seine Genese und Einfluss auf das imperialistische Denken* (Munich, 1973).

Krieger, L. and Stern, F. (eds), *The Responsibility of Power, Historical Essays in Honour of Hajo Holborn* (Garden City, 1967).

Krumreich, G., *Aufrüstung und Innenpolitik in Frankreich vor dem Ersten Weltkrieg, Die Ein Einführung der dreijährigen Dienstpflicht 1913–1914* (Wiesbaden, 1980).

Lafore, Laurence, *The Long Fuse: An Interpretation of the Origins of World War I* (London, 1966).

Langer, W. L., *The Diplomacy of Imperialism 1890–1901* (New York, 1951, reprinted 1956).

Lee, Dwight Erwin (ed.), *The Outbreak of the First World War, Who Was Responsible?* (Boston, 1958).

Link, Arthur S., *Wilson: The Struggle for Neutrality 1914–1915* (Princeton, N.J., 1960).

Lynar, Ernst W., Graf von (ed.), *Deutsche Kriegsziele 1914–1918* (Darmstadt, 1964).

Mamatey, Victor S., *The United States and East Central Europe 1914–1918* (Princeton, N.J., 1956).

Mann, Golo, *The History of Germany since 1789* (New York, 1968).

Marder, A. J., *The Anatomy of British Sea Power: A History of British Naval Politics in the Pre-Dreadnought Era 1880–1905* (London, 1964).

——, *From the Dreadnought to Scapa Flow*, vols. I–IV (London, 1961–70).

Markert, Werner, 'Die deutsch-russischen Beziehungen am Vorabend des Ersten Weltkriegs', *Osteuropa und die abendländische Welt* (Göttingen, 1966).

May, Ernest R., *The World War and American Isolation 1914–1917* (Cambridge, 1959).

Meyer, H. C., *Mitteleuropa in German Thought and Action* (The Hague, 1956).

Mommsen, W. J., 'The Debate on German War Aims', *Journal of Contemporary History* (1966).

——, 'Der italienische Kriegseintritt und die Krise der Politik Bethmann Hollwegs im Frühjahr 1915', *Quellen und Forschungen aus italienischen Archiven und Bibliotheken* (1968).

——, 'Domestic Factors in German Policy before 1914', *Central European History* (1973).

Monticone, Alberto, 'La missione a Roma del principe von Bülow 1914–15', *Quellen und Forschungen aus italienischen Archiven und Bibliotheken* (1968).

——, 'Salandra e Sonnino verso la decisione dell'intervento', *Rivista di studi politici internazionali* (1957).

Moses, J. A., *The Politics of Illusion: The Fischer Controversy in German Historiography* (Melbourne, 1975).

Neck, Rudolf, *Arbeiterschaft und Staat im Ersten Weltkrieg 1914–1918*, I (Vienna, 1964).

——, *Österreich-Ungarn in der Weltpolitik 1900–1918* (Berlin, 1965).

Nelson, H. I., *Land and Power* (London, 1963).

Nish, I., *The Anglo-Japanese Alliance* (London, 1966).

Papst, Klaus, *Eupen-Malmedy in der belgischen Regierungs- und Parteienpolitik 1914 bis 1940* (Aachen, 1964).

Petzold, Joachim, 'Zu den Kriegszielen der deutschen Monopolkapitalisten im Ersten Weltkrieg', *Zeitschrift für Geschichtswissenschaft* (1960).

Pikart, Eberhard, 'Der deutsche Reichstag und der Ausbruch des Ersten Weltkrieges', *Der Staat* (1966).

Poidevin, R., *Les relations économiques et financières entre la France et l'Allemagne de 1898 à 1914* (Paris, 1969).

Poletika, N. P., *Vosnikovenie pervoi mirovoi voiny (Yulskii krisis, 1914)* (Moscow, 1964).

——, *Politik im Krieg. Studien zur Politik der deutschen herrschenden Klassen im Ersten Weltkrieg 1914–1918* (Berlin, 1964).

Rathmann, Lothar, *Stossrichtung Nahost 1914–1918. Zur Expansionspolitik des deutschen Imperialismus im Ersten Weltkrieg* (Berlin, 1963).

Rauch, Georg von, 'Neue sowjetische Literatur zur Vorgeschichte des Ersten Weltkrieges', *Jahrbücher für die Geschichte Osteuropas* (1964).

Remak, Joachim, *Sarajevo* (New York, 1959).

——, *The Origins of World War I* (New York, 1967).

——, *The First World War: Causes, Conduct, Consequences* (New York, 1971).

Renouvin, P., *Les origines immédiates de la guerre*, 2nd ed. (Paris, 1927).

——, *La première guerre mondiale* (Paris, 1965).

——, 'Les buts de guerre du gouvernement français', *Revue historique* (1966).

Rich, N., *Friedrich von Holstein*, 2 vols (Cambridge, 1965).

Ritter, G., *The Schlieffen Plan* (London, 1958).

——, *The Sword and the Sceptre*, 4 vols (London, 1971/74).

——, *Der Erste Weltkrieg. Studien zum deutschen Geschichtsbild* (Bonn, 1964) (Schriftenreihe der Bundeszentrale für politische Bildung, Heft 65).

——, 'Die politische Rolle Bethmann Hollwegs während des Ersten Weltkrieges', *Rapports*, IV: *Méthodologie et Histoire contemporaine*, edited for the Comité International des Sciences Historiques (Vienna, 1965).

Rochat, Giorgio, 'L'esercito italiano nell'estate 1914', *Nuova Rivista Storica* (1961).

Rohlfes, Joachim, 'Französische und deutsche Historiker über die Kriegsziele', *Geschichte in Wissenschaft und Unterricht* (1966).

Röhl, J. C. G., 'Admiral v. Müller and the approach of war 1911–1914', *Historical Journal* (1969).

——, *Delusion or Design? The Testimony of two German Diplomats* (London, 1973).

——, 'An der Schwelle zum Weltkrieg: ein Dokumentation über den "Kriegsrat" vom 8. Dezember 1912', *Militärgeschichtliche Mitteilungen* (1977).

——, *From Bismarck to Hitler. The Problem of Continuity in German History* (London, 1970).

Rolo, P. J. V., *Entente Cordiale* (London, 1969).

Rosen, Edgar R., 'Italiens Kriegseintritt im Jahre 1915 als innenpolitisches Problem der Giolitti-Ära', *Historiche Zeitschrift* (1959).

Rothwell, V. H., *British War Aims and Peace Diplomacy, 1914–1918* (Oxford, 1971).

Roy Bridge, F., 'Tarde venientibus ossa: Austro-Hungarian Colonial Aspirations in Asia Minor 1913–14', *Middle Eastern Studies* (1970).

——, 'The British Declaration of War on Austria-Hungary in 1914', *Slavonic and East European Review* (1969).

Scherer, A. and Grunewald, J., *L'Allemagne et les problèmes de la paix pendant la première guerre mondiale* (Paris, 1966).

Schieder, Wolfgang, 'Italien und Deutschland 1914–15', *Quellen und Forschungen aus italienischen Archiven und Bibliotheken* (1968).

——, (ed.), *Erster Weltkrieg. Ursache, Enstehung und Kriegsziele* (Cologne, 1969).

Schlörer, Alfred, *Krieg–Staat–Monopol 1914–1918. Die Zusammenhänge von imperialistischer Kriegswirtschaft, Militarisierung der Volkswirtschaft und staatsmonopolistischem Kapitalismus in Deutschland während des Ersten Weltkrieges* (Berlin, 1965).

Schmitt, Bernadotte E., *The Coming of the War 1914*, 2 vols (New York–London, 1930).

——, *The Origins of the First World War* (London, 1958).

Schottelius, H. and Deist, W., (eds), *Marine und Marinepolitik im kaiserlichen Deutschland 1871–1914* (Düsseldorf, 1972).

Schüddekopf, Otto-Ernst, 'Politik und Kriegsführung. Die Kriegszielpolitik der Mittelmächte während des Ersten Weltkriegs', *Neue Politische Literatur* (1965).

Schwabe, Klaus, 'Zur politischen Haltung der deutschen Professoren im Ersten Weltkrieg', *Historische Zeitschrift* (1961).

Smith, Jay C., *The Russian Struggle for Power 1914–1917: A Study of Russian Foreign Policy during the First World War* (New York, 1956).

Sösemann, B., 'Die Tagebücher Kurt Riezlers. Untersuchungen zu ihrer Echtheit und Edition', *Historische Zeitschrift* (1983).

Steglich, W., *Bündnissicherung oder Verständigungsfrieden. Untersuchung zu dem*

394   THE ORIGINS OF THE FIRST WORLD WAR

Friedensangebot der Mittelmächte vom 12. Dezember 1916 (Göttingen, 1958).
——, *Die Friedenspolitik der Mittelmächte 1917–18* (Wiesbaden, 1964).
Steinberg, J., *Yesterday's Deterrent: Tirpitz and the Birth of the German Battle Fleet* (London, 1965).
——, 'The Copenhagen Complex', *Journal of Contemporary History* (1966).
——, 'Germany and the Russo-Japanese War', *American Historical Review*, (1970).
Stern, Fritz, *Bethmann Hollweg und der Krieg. Die Grenzen der Verantwortung* (Tübingen, 1968).
Steiner, Z. S., *The Foreign Office and Foreign Policy 1898–1914* (Cambridge, 1969).
——, *Britain and the Origin of the First World War* (London, 1977).
Stevenson, D., *French War Aims against Germany 1914–1919* (Oxford, 1982).
Stieve, F. (ed.), *Diplomatischer Schriftwechsel Isvolskis 1911–1914*, 6 vols (Berlin, 1925).
Stone, Norman, 'Army and Society in the Habsburg Monarchy 1900–1914', *Past and Present*, (1966).
——, 'Moltke-Conrad: Relations between the Austro-Hungarian and German General Staffs, 1909–1914' *Historical Journal* (1966).
——, 'Hungary and the Crisis of 1914', *Journal of Contemporary History* (1966).
——, *The Eastern Front 1914–1917* (Cambridge, 1975).
Sheehan, J. S., 'Germany, 1890–1918: A Survey of Recent Research', *Central European History* (1968).
Taylor, A. J. P., *The Struggle for Mastery in Europe, 1848–1918* (Oxford, 1954).
——, 'The War Aims of the Allies in the First World War', in *Essays Presented to Sir Lewis Namier* (London–New York, 1956).
——, *Politics in Wartime* (London, 1964).
——, *War by Time-Table; How the First World War Began* (London, 1969).
Ternovsky, R. N., *Sovietskaya istoriografiya Rossiiskovo Imperialisma* (Moscow, 1964).
Thayer, John A., *Italy and the Great War: Politics and Culture, 1870–1915* (Madison, 1964).
Turner, L. C. F., *Origins of the First World War* (London, 1970).
——, 'The Russian Mobilisation in 1914', *Journal of Contemporary History* (1968).
Trumpener, U., 'War premeditated? German intelligence operations in July 1914', *Central European History* (1976).
Übersberger, Hans, *Österreich zwischen Russland und Serbien. Zur südslawischen Frage und der Entstehung des Ersten Weltkrieges* (Cologne–Graz, 1955).
Valiani, Leo, *La dissoluzione dell'Austria-Ungheria* (Milan, 1966).
——, 'Le origini della guerra del 1914 e dell'intervento italiana nelle richerche e nelle pubblicazioni dell'ultimo ventennio', *Rivista Storica Italiana* (1966).
——, *Il partito socialista italiano nel periodo della neutralità 1914–1915* (Milan, 1963).
Vietsch, E. v., *Bethmann-Hollweg. Staatsmann zwischen Macht und Ethos* (Boppard, 1969).

Vigezzi, Brunello, *L'Italia di fronte alla prima guerra mondiale*, vol. I: *L'Italia neutrale* (Milan–Naples, 1966).

Wegerer, Alfred von, *Der Ausbruch des Weltkrieges*, 2 vols (Hamburg, 1939; 2nd ed., 1943).

Wernecke, Klaus, *Der Wille zur Weltgattung* (Düsseldorf, 1970).

Willequet, J., *Le Congo belge et la Weltpolitik (1894–1914)* (Brussels, 1962).

Williamson Jr., S. R., *The Politics of the Grand Strategy* (Cambridge, Mass., 1969).

Würthle, F., *Die Spur führt nach Belgrad: Die Hintergründe des Dramas von Sarajevo 1914* (Vienna, 1975).

Zechlin, E., 'Friedenbestrebungen und Revolutionsversuche. Deutsche Bemühungen zur Ausschaltung Russlands im Ersten Weltkrieg', *Aus Politik und Zeitgeschehen* (1961).

——, 'Das "schlesische Angebot" und die italienische Kriegsgefahr', *Geschichte in Wissenschaft und Unterricht* (1963).

——, 'Deutschland zwischen Kabinettskrieg und Wirtschaftskrieg. Politik und Kriegsführung in den ersten Monaten des Weltkrieges 1914', *Historische Zeitschrift* (1964).

——, 'Die Illusion vom begrenzten Krieg', *Die Zeit* (1965).

——, 'Probleme des Kriegskalküls und der Kriegsbeendigung im Ersten Weltkrieg', *Geschichte in Wissenschaft und Unterricht* (1965).

——, 'Bethmann Hollweg, Kriegsrisiko und S.P.D.', *Der Monat* (1966).

——, 'Motive und Taktik der Reichsleitung 1914. Ein Nachtrag', *Der Monat* (1966).

——, 'Die türkischen Meerengen-Brennpunkt der Weltgeschichte', *Geschichte Wissenschaft und Unterricht* (Kiel, 1966).

——, *Die Deutsche Politik und die Juden im Ersten Weltkrieg* (Göttingen, 1970).

——, *Kriegsausbruch 1914 und Kriegszielproblemin der internationalen Politik* (Göttingen, 1972).

——, *Krieg und Kriegsrisiko. Zur deutschen Politik im Ersten Weltkrieg* (Düsseldorf, 1979).

Zmarzlik, Hans-Günther, *Bethmann Hollweg als Reichskanzler 1909–1914* (Düsseldorf, 1957).

Index